American Sports
From the Age of Folk Games
to the Age of Spectators

Benjamin G. Rader

University of Nebraska—Lincoln

PRENTICE-HALL, INC., ENGLEWOOD CLIFFS, NEW JERSEY 07632

Library of Congress Cataloging in Publication Data

RADER, BENJAMIN G.
    American sports.

    Includes index.
    1. Sports—United States—History.
I. Title.
GV583.R3   796'.0973   82-3660
ISBN 0-13-031369-6   AACR2

To Barbara Koch Rader

©1983 by Prentice-Hall, Inc., Englewood Cliffs, N.J. 07632

Printed in the United States of America

10   9   8   7   6   5   4

Prentice-Hall International, Inc. *London*
Prentice-Hall of Australia Pty. Limited, *Sydney*
Prentice-Hall Canada, Inc., *Toronto*
Prentice-Hall of India Private Limited, *New Delhi*
Prentice-Hall of Japan, Inc., *Tokyo*
Prentice-Hall of Southeast Asia Pte. Ltd., *Singapore*
Whitehall Books Limited, *Wellington, New Zealand*

87 - 3667

Contents

PART III: THE AGE OF THE SPECTATOR (1920
TO THE PRESENT)   **171**

Preface

The main purpose of this book is to explain how and why the informal games of colonial Americans evolved into modern, spectator-centered sports. On one level, this task has required an examination of the fundamental changes in the organization, rules, management, finances, and ethos of the games. On another level, it has entailed an examination of the social, cultural, and economic circumstances that have shaped American sport history.

American Sports presents one way (certainly not the only way) of generalizing about the transformation of American folk games into modern sports. As the title suggests, the central theme, stated in its simplest form, is that American sports passed from an era of folk games to a player-centered era and finally to a spectator-centered era. I have entitled these eras or stages The Age of Folk Games (1607–1850), the Age of the Player (1850–1920), and the Age of the Spectator (1920 to the present). Such a division should not be viewed in hard and fast terms. Baseball, for instance, became a spectator-oriented sport long before 1920 while tennis did not become a full-fledged spectator sport until the 1970s. Nonetheless, the use of eras or stages permits us to understand more fully the principal transitions in American sport history and offers more comprehensible explanations of why sport changed over time.

A few concluding observations are in order. First, the reader ought to be warned that I have focused only upon human physical contests which in due time enjoyed large audiences, were governed by carefully defined rules enforced by a bureaucracy, and involved high degrees of athletic specialization. Thus I have largely ignored such leisure activities as hunting and hiking and mental games such as bridge and chess. Horse racing and auto racing furnished a more formidable problem. When these activities impinged upon the main course of American sport history, I have attempted to give them proper attention. However, since they involved contests in which mechanical devices (i.e., the auto) or nonhumans (i.e., horses) furnished most of the power required for success, I have not treated them as major sports. In short, I felt constrained to restrict my coverage to those sports and activities that elucidated the theme of the evolution of folk games into spectator-centered sports. Finally, the reader ought to be warned that vast gaps exist in our knowledge of the history of American sport. Until these are filled by painstaking research, the historian must rely upon the limited evidence available. Despite this handicap, much of the enjoyment in writing this book has stemmed from the problems of reducing to some sort of logical and coherent form the history of American sports.

Acknowledgments

In writing a book of this scope I have acquired many large and unpayable debts. The several hundred students in my experimental History of Sport classes have been a continuing source of inspiration. They have corrected me on facts and interpretations more often than I would like to remember. William J. Baker, Jack W. Berryman, Olwyn Blouet, Esther Cope, Mary Doak, Bruce Dunning, Allen Guttmann, Jon Hamilton, Stephen H. Hardy, Maxine Isenberg, Harry Jebsen, Jr., Guy M. Lewis, Peter Maslowski, Donald Mrozek, Russell Nye, Dov Ospovat (deceased), Donald Parente, Val Pinchbeck, Jr., Anne E. Rader, Stephen L. Rader, Joseph Svoboda, and Vernon Volpe all—sometimes unwittingly—made helpful suggestions or provided me with additional sources that I otherwise would not have consulted. The footnotes in this book, I hope, adequately reflect my extensive debts to others who have researched various areas of American sports. Without their work this book could not have been written.

I owe debts for assistance of other sorts. Humberto Ramirez photographer and sometime tennis opponent, kindly made the photographic files of the *Lincoln* (Ne.) *Star* and *Lincoln Journal* accessible to me. On several occasions personnel with these newspapers generously provided me with data otherwise difficult to locate. The University of Nebraska Research Council awarded me two grants-in-aid for microfilming (1977–1979) and a summer senior research fellowship (1977). An internal leave-of-absence in the Spring Semester of 1977 and a Faculty Development Fellowship in the Spring Semester of 1979 greatly facilitated the research and writing of this book. I owe an additional debt to James A. Rawley, Chairperson of the Department of History, and Max D. Larsen, Dean of the College of Arts and Sciences, for help in obtaining typing assistance and copying funds.

For a marvelous job in typing the final draft of the manuscript, I am indebted to Karen Williams, Linda Kirk, and Sandra Pershing. My colleagues in the Department of History—though several of them had genuine reservations about sport history as a legitimate field of inquiry—invariably supported my work.

I am indebted to several persons for critical reviews. At one stage or another, T. S. Breen, Joan M. Chandler, Frederick C. Luebke, Michael O'Brien, Glenn Potter, Harold Seymour, John C. Schneider, and anonymous persons reviewed and offered useful observations on parts of the manuscript. I benefitted immensely from critical readings of the entire manuscript by Melvin Adelman, C. Robert Barnett, Steven A. Riess, Leverett T. Smith, Jr., and Ronald A. Smith. I owe a special debt to Michael T. Isenberg, who not only read all the manuscript with a perceptive eye but served as an invaluable source of information and ideas on numerous questions of fact and interpretation. The generous help of these people saved me from many errors. Of course, for the errors and mistaken interpretations that remain, I alone am responsible. I owe the largest debt of all to my wife, Barbara, who spent many hours listening to my fumbling efforts to conceptualize the history of American sports, typed parts of the manuscript at various stages, and offered valuable suggestions at many points in the development of the book. Furthermore, she unfailingly sustained me when my spirits ebbed.

Part One

The Age of Folk Games, 1607-1850

Life in the British colonies in North America was quite different than what we know today. Unlike people today, the colonists paid little attention to precise measurements of time. The daylight hours and the rhythms of the seasons rather than the clock regulated their daily lives. Almost all of their communication involved direct, face-to-face encounters. For the power to produce goods, they relied almost solely on animals or humans. As late as 1790, some 90 percent of the population lived on farms. Their politics and social arrangements were based on traditions and social deference. The common people ordinarily deferred in matters of judgment to their "natural" superiors. Black slavery existed in all of the colonies, though it was far more pronounced in the South. Ties of kinship were exceedingly important. The father ruled the family with a firm hand. Religious beliefs profoundly influenced many colonists, both in their outward behavior and their inner sense of self. The church, state, family, and social hierarchy reinforced social stability.

From the time of the American Revolution (1775–1783) to 1850 the citizens of the new nation began to experience profound changes in their way of life. The election of Andrew Jackson in 1828 symbolized the precipitous erosion of social deference. Instead of being subjects of the king or the state, all (white) men were now "citizens." The age of the "common man" had arrived. The steamboat, the canal, and eventually the railroad and the telegraph sped up the pace of transportation and impersonal communication. Steam gradually replaced animal, human, and water power. Most of the people became exceedingly time-conscious. Foreign visitors in the 1830s reported that Americans were always in a "terrible hurry," "pitchforking" down huge quantities of food at "breakneck" speed in order to get back to their work. Soaring material aspirations induced astonishing geographic mobility, fractured kinship ties, and encouraged extreme forms of individualism. Americans could no longer depend upon class deference, an established church, nor the small, close-knit community to insure social order. They frequently turned to the individual conscience hoping to mold an internal set of values that would guide the individual safely through the bewildering changes that were transforming American society.

Americans prior to 1850 rarely engaged in physical contests that can be properly labeled sports. Their folk games were far less formal than modern sports. The rules of their games were relatively simple, unwritten, legitimated by custom, and sometimes revised to fit the circumstances of the moment. The rules prevalent in one locality often differed sharply from those in another, and the significance of the game usually extended only to the immediate region. No bureaucracies or referees supervised contests, and few players trained for their performances in a systematic fashion. With the emergence of a "sporting fraternity" in the early nineteenth century, some of the folk games began to take on a more formal character. For financial gain the fraternity offered urban dwellers "blood sports," prize fighting, horse racing, pedestrianism (footracing), and billiards. While the sporting fraternity operated outside the mainstream of American culture, it encouraged a higher degree of athletic specialization, professionalism, and a stricter distinction between playing and spectating roles. Thus the direct antecedents of modern spectator-centered sports can be found before 1850.

1

The Folk Games
of Colonial America

Before dawn on Christmas Day, 1621, William Bradford, governor of the Plymouth Colony, called all the able-bodied men to their work. To most of the colonists, Bradford's request came as no surprise. The Protestant group, later called Pilgrims, to which Bradford belonged did not celebrate Christmas. Christmas to them was a pagan holiday, a part of the Roman Catholic tradition, and was not authorized by the Holy Scriptures. A few of the men who had recently arrived on the ship, the *Susan Constant,* objected to Bradford's order. Their consciences, they informed the governor, forbade them to toil on the day of Christ's birth. Bradford briefly remonstrated with the newcomers, but because they were not yet familiar with the "true way" and there was much work to be done, Bradford excused them. He would try to convince them later. He quickly departed with a group of the original settlers and took up the work at hand.

Bradford's group returned at noon. To the governor's astonishment, the newcomers were shouting, laughing, and running about the single street of Plymouth "openly at play." "Some were pitching the bar," Bradford later wrote, "and some [were playing] at stool-ball and such like sports."[1] Bradford knew well these common folk games of the seventeenth-century English villages. (Stool-ball was an antecedent of modern cricket.) But the doughty governor was angry. He seized the players' "implements" and ordered them off the street. As work on Christmas Day violated the consciences of the newcomers, Bradford said, so it was that sport on Christmas Day violated the conscience of the governor.

This incident in the early history of the English colonies suggests several forces which have shaped American sport. Simply to survive, the little band which settled at Plymouth had to spend much of its energies in conquering the wilderness. For almost three centuries along the advancing frontier, a substantial portion of the American people were engaged in a struggle for existence. The settlers' memory of the English village games, reinforced by a steady stream of new immigrants, encouraged the retention of the sporting life of the mother country. But Bradford, like many of the first colonists, also came with a reforming religious zeal, an enthusiasm hostile to most of the current forms of popular recreation. The Protestant temperament, in both its Puritan and evangelical forms, inhibited the

[1]William Bradford, *Of Plymouth Plantation, 1620–1647,* ed. by Samuel Eliot Morison (New York: Knopf, 1952), p. 97. A similar instance can be found in the early history of the Virginia colony. In 1611, the new governor, Sir Thomas Dale, after witnessing a game of bowls at Jamestown, prohibited all "gaming" on the Sabbath. See George Maclaren Brydon, *Virginia's Mother Church* (Richmond, Va.: Virginia Historical Society, 1947), p. 412.

growth of colonial sports. By the eighteenth century a wealthy gentry class with a religious temperament far more sympathetic to sport than that of the evangelicals or the Puritans had emerged in the American colonies. This class established many of the traditions that would profoundly influence the future of American sport.

ENGLISH VILLAGE PASTIMES

The American colonists inherited from seventeenth-century England a dual recreational heritage. One flourished among the common people of the country villages while the other arose among the privileged upper classes. English upper class pastimes sprang from the courtier traditions of the Middle Ages. Certain sporting activities, along with polished manners, gallantry, gentle breeding, and wealth, marked one as a member of the English gentry. The deer park and deer hunting were especially important privileges reserved to the well-born. The gentry enjoyed all forms of hunting, using both hounds and hawks to ferret out their prey. When the seventeenth century opened, horse racing was in a nascent stage, but it would soon become a major sporting enterprise of the English upper classes. The monarchs themselves usually furnished the leadership for upper-class sporting life. Both as spectators and as participants, most of the Tudor and Stuart monarchs were avid sportsmen. James I, the English king from 1603 to 1625, epitomized the monarch dedicated to vigorous pastimes. He advised his son to banish "the mother of all vice"—idleness— by frequently resorting to running, wrestling, court tennis, and all the field sports. However, the immediate impact of English upper-class games on the American colonists was minimal, for until the eighteenth century, only a few of the settlers had accumulated enough wealth to imitate the recreational life of the English gentry.[2]

In the early years of settlement, the English agricultural villages furnished the American colonists with a far more important recreational tradition. Most of the colonists were of the "middling sort" who emigrated from the small villages of the English countryside. Scattered two or three miles apart, the English villages served as homes for ordinary tradesmen, craftsmen, and farmers. The yeoman farmer often lived in town and tilled the arable land around the village. Residents enjoyed frequent face-to-face contact; they shared common experiences and tried to preserve traditions. With labor abundant in relation to the supply of arable land, there was little incentive for hard work. Only during the harvest season were the demands of labor intense. Then the entire village, including women, children, and artisans, might join the farmers in bringing in the crops. The villagers usually concluded the harvest season with a festival of thanks accompanied by hearty eating, drinking, dancing, and folk games.

[2]See especially Joseph Strutt, *The Sport and Pastimes of the People of England* (London: Thomas Tegg, 1838); Roger Longrigg, *The English Squire and His Sport* (London: Michael Joseph, 1977); and Patricia Ann Lee, "Play and the English Gentleman in the Early Seventeenth Century," *Historian*, 31 (May 1969), 364–80.

The legend of a "merrie ole England" rested on the communal life of these small villages. The festivities, which usually centered around the parish church, expressed and reinforced communal solidarity. The ecclesiastical calendar freed the common people to celebrate the major events in the life of Christ and commemorate numerous saints and martyrs. Yet the manner of celebration combined both Christian doctrine and pagan customs. Christianity had never completely erased the old folk customs that extended back into the mists of English history. For instance, May Day, perhaps the favorite holiday of the villages, originated as a rite of spring. Villagers believed that the return of spring depended upon the proper veneration of a phallic symbol. Accordingly, English young people trekked to the woods after midnight on May first, cut down a tree, and brought it back to the village. There they erected a maypole amid much ceremony, fastened long ribbons to the top of the pole, and danced about it merrily. Puritan critics saw the ancient rite as a form of idolatry and as a source of loose morals. "Of forty, three-score, or a hundred maids going to the wood over night," Phillip Stubbes, a Puritan and an archenemy of the traditional customs, reported, "there have scarcely the third part of them returned home again undefiled."[3]

The villages celebrated many other holidays. One of the most popular holidays of the common people was the annual parish feast, often called a wake or revel. At the wakes the entire village gathered to feast, drink, dance, and engage in the rustic games of their forefathers. Wakes began on Sundays and sometimes lasted the entire week. Seasonal holidays, which were equally popular, included the Christmas season, Plough Monday, Shrove Tuesday, and the Easter season. Country fairs, which mingled business with pleasure, added to the long list of opportunities for the common people in the villages to engage in merrymaking. Combining Sundays, holy days, and the seasonal holidays, the typical seventeenth-century rural village probably celebrated over one hundred days of the year, almost one holiday for each two days of work. No doubt the frequent celebrations relieved some of the grimness of seventeenth-century English life.

Each of the holidays featured a wide assortment of folk games, some of which were quasi-athletic in nature. The villagers played games of chance, games of skill, individual games, team games, games in which most of the residents participated, and games in which most were spectators. Many parishes enjoyed stool-ball, footraces, quoits (in which a contestant attempted to throw an iron ring over a peg), skittles, and ninepins (both

[3]Quoted in Winton U. Solberg, *Redeem the Time: The Puritan Sabbath in Early America* (Cambridge, Mass.: Harvard University Press, 1977), p. 48. On seasonal feasts, holy days, and village pastimes see also Christopher Hill, *Society and Puritanism in Pre-Revolutionary England,* 2nd ed. (New York: Schocken Books, 1967), Chap. 5; E. O. James, *Seasonal Feasts and Festivals* (New York: Barnes and Noble, 1961); Dennis Brailsford, *Sport and Society: Elizabeth to Anne* (London: Routledge & Kegan Paul, 1969); Robert W. Malcolmson, *Popular Recreations in English Society, 1700–1850* (London: Cambridge University Press, 1973); A. L. Rowse, *The Elizabethan Renaissance: The Life of Society* (London: Macmillan, 1971), Chap. 5; E. P. Thompson, "Patrician Society, Plebian Culture," *Journal of Social History,* 7 (Summer 1974), 382–405.

forms of bowling). Unlike modern sports, the rules for these games sprang from unwritten customs and might differ sharply from one parish to the next. Boisterousness, gusto, and even physical roughness often accompanied the playing of all the games. The villagers took special delight in violent games and spectacles, such as bear and bull baiting, cockfighting, football, hurling, and public executions. They relished contests of brute strength, especially wrestling and cudgeling. In cudgeling the contestant used a long, heavy stick with the intention of "breaking the head," or drawing blood from his opponent.

Football was by far the most exciting team game of the villagers. Unlike modern football (soccer), rugby, or American football, all of which are offsprings of the medieval game, the village sport was often an ad hoc affair played by an unspecified number of players. Villagers scheduled impromptu matches in the streets or nearby empty fields. The holidays might feature big matches between the residents of two villages. Depending upon local customs, the game might emphasize kicking, running, or throwing the ball. (The ball was usually an inflated animal bladder which was sometimes encased in leather.) Ostensibly, the object of the game was to move the ball across a previously defined goal line. Once a team had accomplished this feat, the game ended, though darkness also probably halted many matches.

Football vividly illustrates the contrasts between the folk games of the villagers and modern sports. Apart from the absence of referees, standardized rules, well-defined playing positions, and a set number of players on each side, the medieval game, by modern standards, constituted nothing less than a savage brawl. The players kicked, wrestled, struck with their fists, and sometimes bit their opponents. Damaged property, bloodied bodies, torn clothing, broken limbs, and sometimes death accompanied the contests. Between 1314 and 1617 English monarchs and local magistrates banned the game on at least thirty separate occasions, none of which successfully deterred the popularity of football. Apparently football offered the villagers an opportunity to channel their violent tendencies into a form of ritualized combat.[4] It also seemed to promote village unity. "At the seasons of football and cockfighting" many parishes, according to a report in 1712, "reassume their national hatred of each other. My tenant in the country is verily persuaded, that the parish of the enemy had not one honest man in it."[5]

THE PROTESTANT TEMPERAMENT

In the late sixteenth and early seventeenth centuries, even before the first permanent English settlements had been established in North America,

---

[4]See especially Eric Dunning and Kenneth Sheard, *Barbarians, Gentlemen, and Players: A Sociological Study of the Development of Rugby Football* (Oxford: Martin Robertson, 1979), pp. 21–45.

[5]Quoted in Malcolmson, *Popular Recreations*, p. 83.

recreation, especially the rural village customs, had become a major source of religious and political conflict. In England the "industrious sort of people," who "faced unprecedented possibilities of advance" and were often of a Puritan religious temperament, led the crusade for strict Sabbath laws and the suppression of the traditional holidays. The Puritans wanted to purify and reform the established Church of England from within. They thought the Church of England too popish. Too much of the Roman Catholic ritual, pageantry, symbols, the older magical and sacramental modes of thought, and priestly functions remained. Henry VIII, who had made the break from Rome, and the monarchs who had succeeded him had failed to carry the reformation to its full conclusion. The Puritans, in league with those Englishmen who were in general pushing for a new ethic of industriousness and a break with the ways of the agricultural Middle Ages, sought to rid England of all the holy days except the Sabbath. Thus two modes of life clashed. One rested upon the past, the countryside, the old ruling class, and the church hierarchy. The other rested upon the future, the cities, the merchants, and the Puritan temperament.[6]

The key to Puritan antipathy toward the ancient customs of the villages was their belief that God had extended to every man a calling. Glorifying God by diligent pursuit of one's calling ought to be the ultimate, all-absorbing end of man's earthly existence. Every Puritan should strive to become, in Ralph Barton Perry's apt metaphor, a "moral athlete."[7] While play was essentially frivolous and unproductive, close attention to one's calling furthered divine purposes. To do less than one was capable of in pursuit of one's calling constituted a grievous sin against God. Such a temperament resulted in an exceptionally sober and industrious people. Long after the main theological superstructure of Puritanism had collapsed, its heirs continued to experience agonizing guilt from engaging in playful activity. "I was not sent to this world to spend my days in sports, diversions, and pleasures," wrote John Adams in the middle of the eighteenth century. "I was born for business; for both activity and study."[8]

Sunday merriments especially enraged the Puritans and those of an "industrious sort." Throughout England in the early years of the seventeenth century the local magistrates and churchmen of a Puritan temperament mounted a campaign to suppress all recreation on the Sabbath. But they encountered angry opposition from the common people of the villages, high authorities in the Church of England, many of the gentry, and the king himself. In 1618, in response to the growing Puritan assault on Sunday recreation and in order to regularize religious practices throughout England, King James I issued a Declaration of Sports. (Fifteen years later Charles I reissued the proclamation in an extended form.) The

---

[6]In viewing the conflict in wider socio-economic terms rather than simply in terms of religious differences, I am following the interpretation of Hill, *Society and Puritanism*. See especially pp. 168, 208–10.

[7]Ralph Barton Perry, *Puritanism and Democracy* (New York: Harper Torchbacks, 1964), Chap. 10.

[8]Quoted in Philip Greven, *The Protestant Temperament: Patterns of Child-Rearing, Religious Experience, and the Self in Early America* (New York: Knopf, 1977), p. 253. What I have called the Puritan temperament corresponds roughly to Greven's "moderate" temperament.

Book of Sports, which was to be read from every pulpit in England, gave royal sanction to specific village pastimes as well as the custom of holding parish feasts. The King asserted that "after the end of divine service our good people [should] not be disturbed...or discouraged from any lawful recreation, nor from having of May-games, Whitson Ales, and Morris-dances, and the setting up of May-poles and other sports." James rhetorically asked: "For when shall the common people have leave to exercise if not upon Sunday and holidays, seeing they must apply their labor and win their living in all working days?"[9] Those clergymen of a Puritan persuasion who declined to read the royal proclamation from the pulpit found themselves censured, suspended, or deprived of their positions.

The Puritan, middle-class majority in Parliament repeatedly attempted to rescind the Book of Sports, only to be blocked by the monarchs. Finally, in 1641, during the Puritan Revolution, Parliament imposed a rigid Sabbath upon all of England. Restoration of the monarchy and the established church in 1660 brought a partial return of Sunday merriments, the celebration of traditional festivals, and the playing of folk games. Yet the Puritan Revolution had bequeathed to England, Scotland, and the American colonies "the peculiar British Sunday," one devoid of much of the holiday spirit that had prevailed in the England of the Middle Ages and one that stood in sharp contrast to practices of the continental countries of Europe.

As they had in England, those with a Puritan or industrious temperament who fled to the New World tried to legislate a strict observance of the Sabbath, abolish the traditional holy days, and restrict or eliminate the old village recreations. New Englanders celebrated none of the traditional holidays, excluding Sundays. In 1640 Massachusetts imposed a fine upon anyone who fasted, feasted, or refused to work on Christmas day. Unless Christmas happened to fall on Sunday, the churches remained closed. Beginning on Saturday night and ending at sundown on Sunday no labor, recreation, travel, or even "unnecessary and unseasonable walking in the streets and fields" was allowed. In 1656 a Captain Kemble of Boston had to sit in the stocks for two hours for "lewd and unseemly conduct." After being at sea for three years, the indiscreet captain had publicly kissed his wife on the Sabbath. As late as the 1730s, Joseph Bennett, an English traveler, observed that in Boston the Lord's Day was the "strictest kept that ever I yet saw anywhere."[10] Absolutely all trade halted and all taverns closed. Even idle conversation in public on Sunday was subject to fines.

The Middle and Southern colonies also enacted strict Sabbatarian laws. One of the first acts of the Virginia House of Burgesses in 1619 was to ban all forms of amusement on Sunday. Soon, however, many Virginia colonists began to ignore the strictures on Sunday merriments. Similar laws

---

[9]Quoted in Malcolmson, *Popular Recreations,* p. 7. See also the analysis of the Book of Sports in Solberg, *Redeem the Time,* pp. 71–74 and 76–77, and Hill, *Society and Puritanism,* pp. 169–70, 193–95, 199–202, 204–5.

[10]Quoted in John C. Miller, *The First Frontier: Life in Colonial America* (New York: Dell Pub. Co., Inc., 1966), p. 87. Solberg's *Redeem the Time* contains the fullest account of colonial Sabbatarianism.

existed in Maryland. In William Penn's pietistic Quaker colony of Pennsylvania, the assembly in 1682 banned all "rude and riotous sports" and imposed heavy fines on those who persisted in engaging in the popular pastimes of the Mother Country. In New Netherlands, the Dutch in 1656 prohibited dancing, playing ball, cards, "tennis," cricket, and ninepins on Sunday morning. Charleston, South Carolina, reputedly one of the merriest towns in colonial America, observed an equally rigorous Sabbath. A German traveler as late as the 1780s found that "no shop may keep open, no sort of game or music is permitted, and during the church service watchmen go about who lay hold upon any one idling in the streets...and compel him to turn aside into some church or pay 2 shillings and 4 pence; no slave may be required to work on this day."[11] The Sabbatarian legislation of colonial America left an enduring legacy, one that was reinforced by periodic revivals over the next two centuries and continues to exist, albeit in a much more tolerant form, to this day.

While those of a Puritan temperament obtained numerous laws, especially in the New England colonies, preventing the people from engaging in the traditional village forms of play, the doctrine of the calling did not logically lead to the prohibition of all recreation. On the contrary, diversions that clearly contributed to the fulfillment of one's calling were justified and approved. "We daily need some respite and diversion, without which we dull our powers; a little intermission sharpens 'em again," wrote one Puritan minister. Recreation, wrote another prominent divine, "must tend also to glorify God...the scope and end of all recreation is, that God may be honored in and by them."[12] New England parents also allowed their children to play with dolls and toys. When young boys had the leisure time and were orderly, authorities usually permitted them to play informal football, ball and bat, and stool-ball matches. Nonetheless, the conscientious Puritan always worried that recreation would become an end in itself. To the Puritans, play often stimulated the passions, leading to deceit, feasting, dancing, gambling, sexual immorality, and the neglect of one's calling.

Puritanism was not the only major religious temperament in the American colonies. From the earliest days of New England's history a few especially pious settlers—later called the "evangelicals"—departed temperamentally from both the main body of Puritans and from conventional Anglicanism. They rejected the Puritan covenant of grace in which God virtually promised salvation to those men who would believe in Jesus as the Savior and strive to lead pious lives. The evangelicals insisted instead that man could obtain salvation only as a free gift from God; eternal life could be neither guaranteed by belief nor earned by the good works of man. With the Great Awakening, a religious revival that swept through the colonies in the 1730s and 1740s, the evangelicals won thousands of new

[11]J. D. Schoepf, ed., *Travels in the Confederation, 1783–1784*, 2 vols. (Philadelphia: W. J. Campbell, 1911), II, 222. See also Thomas Jable, "Pennsylvania's Early Blue Laws: A Quaker Experiment in the Suppression of Sport and Amusement, 1682–1740," *Journal of Sport History*, 1 (November 1974), 107–21.

[12]Perry Miller and Thomas H. Johnson, eds., *The Puritans: A Sourcebook of Their Writings*, 2 vols. (New York: Harper Torchbacks, 1963), II, 392.

recruits. The revivals divided congregations in the established churches, undermined the authority of the regular clergy, and created giant schisms in the major denominations.

The evangelicals required the absolute submission of the self—first to the parents and then, through a searing conversion experience, to an omnipotent God. Believing that their children had inherited Adam's original sin, parents tried, in the words of John Wesley, to "break their wills, that you may save their souls."[13] The will or self-assertiveness of the child had to be utterly suppressed or annihilated, usually by resorting to shame, guilt, and inner-discipline rather than to the rod. Emerging sexuality and an impulse to rebel against parents and their God during adolescence confirmed the youth's sense of personal unworthiness and corruption. One evangelical after another recalled his youth as a period of shameful rebellion. John Banks, converted in 1654, remembered that when he was about sixteen years of age he was "very much bowed down and perplexed, my sins being set in order before me; and the time I had spent in wildness and wantonness, out of the fear of God, in vanity, sport, and pastime, came into my view and rememberance."[14] Adolescent rebellion typically preceded a dramatic conversion to Christ.

After the rebirth, the evangelicals released their suppressed rage by launching crusades against the evils of the secular world and those who adhered to a more moderate religious persuasion. The evangelicals demanded absolute purity in the church and in individual behavior. They attacked unmercifully the customs, habits, and life styles of the nonevangelicals. For example, George Fox, the founder of the Society of the Friends (Quakers), traveled throughout England "in warning...and in testifying against their wakes or feasts, their May-games, sports, plays, and shows which trained up people to vanity and looseness, and led them from the fear of God, and the days they had set forth for holy-days were usually times wherein they most dishonored God by these things."[15] George Whitefield, a phenomenally successful evangelist during the Great Awakening, stopped in Annapolis, Maryland, in 1739, where he met the governor, local ministers, and several gentlemen. "Some of the company, I believe, thought I was too strict, and were very strenuous in defense of what they called innocent diversions; but when I told them everything was sinful which was not done with a single eye to God's glory, and that such entertainments not only discovered a levity of mind, but were contrary to the whole tenor of the Gospel of Christ, they seemed somewhat convinced...."[16] Although the evangelicals rarely were able to enforce their strict piety in the communities in which they lived, they long remained opponents of sport in any form.

The Protestant temperament, whether in the evangelical or more

[13]John Wesley, "On Obedience to Parents," *The Works of John Wesley*, 14 vols. (Grand Rapids, Mich.: Zondervan, 1958), VII, 103.

[14]Quoted in Greven, *The Protestant Temperament*, p. 57.

[15]Ibid., p. 144.

[16]Greven, *The Protestant Temperament*, p. 145. See also Rhys Isaac, "Evangelical Revolt: The Nature of the Baptist's Challenge to the Traditional Order in Virginia, 1765 to 1775," *William and Mary Quarterly*, 31 (July 1974), 345–68.

moderate Puritan forms, left a profound imprint on the history of American sport. The Founding Fathers, though not as theologically orthodox as their forefathers, could be as suspicious of the consequences of recreation as William Bradford. Even Benjamin Franklin, a quite secular man but one nonetheless influenced by his Puritan heritage, recalled that as a youth "reading was the only amusement I allowed myself. I spent no time in taverns, games or frolics of any kind."[17] Perhaps Dr. Benjamin Rush exemplified advanced moderate thinking about the folk games. While favoring exercise by walking or swimming, he called for an end of Sunday amusements, clubs, cockfighting, horse racing, and fairs. To men like Rush and Thomas Jefferson, a republic of virtue could not be founded on the idle amusements of the decadent monarchies of Europe.

NEW-WORLD FESTIVITIES OF THE COMMON PEOPLE

Despite formidable obstacles, vestiges of the old village holidays survived in the New World. While the New England colonies savagely repressed a few efforts to erect Maypoles, the celebration of all of the holy days, and frivolities on Sunday, they did develop new forms of communal celebration. Irregularly scheduled days of thanksgiving took on some of the features of the old English holidays, though apparently the authorities discouraged the playing of folk games at these festivities. Election days, lectures, commencements, public punishments, and funerals were also popular occasions for the communities to gather in a single place. In the last quarter of the seventeenth century, training days, the days in which colonial militia units mustered, became the first holidays to resemble closely those of the old English parishes. Apparently because training days had no association with the customs of the Church of England and were under the supervision of local authorities, the troops were permitted to play such less violent folk games as foot racing, jumping, and shooting at the mark. In Connecticut, according to a traveler in 1704, the winner of a target-shooting contest on training day won several yards of red ribbon and a "great applause, as even the winner of the Olympic games."[18]

Apart from training days, little is known about the extent to which New Englanders continued to play the old folk games. From the scant evidence available, it appears that from the first settlements in the 1620s to the 1670s, the folk games almost disappeared from New England. After this period a noticeable decline in piety among many of the inhabitants, new immigrants, and the insistence of the British government on religious tolerance all contributed to a somewhat more hospitable climate for

---

[17]Quoted in Greven, *The Protestant Temperament*, p. 216.

[18]Sara Kemble Knight, *The Journal of Madam Knight* (Boston: Massachusetts Historical Society, 1971), p. 20. See also H. Telfer Mook, "Training Day in New England," *New England Quarterly*, 11 (December 1938), 687–97; Mark Van Doren, ed., *Samuel Sewell's Diary* (New York: Russell and Russell, 1963), p. 163; Alice Morse Earle, *Customs and Fashions in Old New England* (New York: Scribner's, 1904), pp. 218–25.

recreation. The repeated passage of nearly identical laws repressing sporting indulgences indicate that at least a few brave inhabitants resisted the laws. Apart from a few reports of boys playing football and other games in the streets of Boston, there is one extant record of an adult male football match between two Massachusetts towns in 1685, but until after the American Revolution there are no other indications of men playing one another in football. Late in the seventeenth and throughout the eighteenth century, authorities usually tolerated inhabitants playing such games as billiards, skittles, and shuttlecock in their homes but not in public places.[19]

The Southern colonies, despite a better climate and a striking absence of organized religious activity in much of the region prior to the 1740s, appear to have been only slightly more successful in preserving the old village pastimes. In neither the Southern nor the Middle colonies did the village pattern of settlement characteristic of England and the New England colonies gain a foothold. Encouraged by the availability of large quantities of cheap land, the settlers tended to spread out along the Atlantic Coast and up the navigable rivers. The new settlers invariably lived on the land they farmed. Because of the sheer distance between settlers in the South, the Anglican Church—the established church in that region—could not recreate the traditional English parish. Thus, observance of the ecclesiastical calendar, along with the timeless rituals, tended to vanish from Southern churches. In Pennsylvania, the Quakers, like the Puritans in New England and the evangelicals everywhere, frowned upon the communal celebrations associated with the Old English parishes.

Nonetheless, the common people did not abandon entirely the village pastimes. In eighteenth century western Virginia, for example, farmers sometimes held harvest festivals. Annual county fairs brought the people of a "middling sort" together with the large planters for communal activities that might include recreation and informal physical contests. The Hanover County Fair, established in 1737, included a great feast accompanied by the music of drums, trumpets, and oboes. The fair sponsored a wide variety of contests: a prize of five pounds for a horse race, a cudgeling match for a hat, a fiddling contest for a fiddle, a quire of ballads to be sung for, a wrestling match for a pair of silver buckles, and a "pair of handsome silk stockings... [to] be given to the handsomest young country maid that appears in the field...."[20] Such fairs, however, did not become commonplace until the nineteenth century.

Of the major colonial towns only New York, which was without the

---

[19]See Nancy L. Struna, "Sport and Societal Values: Massachusetts Bay," *Quest*, 27 (Winter 1977), 40; Albert Bushnell Hart, ed., *Commonwealth History of Massachusetts*, 5 vols. (New York: State Historical Company, 1927–1930), II, 280. For records of football matches in the late eighteenth century see W. Winterbotham, *An Historical, Geographical, Commercial, and Philosophical View of the American United States*, 4 vols. (London: the author, 1976), II, 17; William Bentley, *The Diary of William Bentley, D.D.*, 4 vols. (Gloucester, Mass.: Peter Smith, 1962), I, 253–54.

[20]Quoted in Edmund S. Morgan, *Virginians at Home: Family Life in the Eighteenth Century* (New York: Holt, Rinehart and Winston, 1952), p. 88. For colonial fairs elsewhere see Harry B. Weiss and Grace M. Weiss, *Early Sports and Pastimes in New Jersey* (Trenton, N.J.: Past Times, 1960), pp. 10–13.

strong religious restraints of Boston and Philadelphia, had a recreational history approximating that of Old England. Prior to 1664, when the English acquired the city, the Dutch had bowled, held boat races, and played *kolven,* which some scholars translate as "golf." No descriptions of *kolven* survive. From pictures of the game, it appears that the game was more akin to field or ice hockey than modern golf. Apparently *kolven* was still being played in 1766, for in that year James Rivington advertised for sale "gouff clubs," as well as shuttlecocks, cricket balls, and racquets. The Rivington advertisement suggests that at least a few New Yorkers were engaging in quasi-athletic activities, but the overwhelming majority preferred such recreations as ice skating, sleigh riding, cockfighting, and horse racing. The Dutch seem also to have been responsible for introducing the unique blood sport of "gander pulling" to the American colonies. In this contest the neck of a goose would be liberally greased and the hapless animal would be hung by its feet from a rope stretched between two trees or from a tree limb. Sometimes the goose was hung over a stream and the contestant would, while passing by on a boat, try to jerk the goose's head off. If he failed, a dunking followed. At other times a horseman would attempt the same feat while riding at full gallop. As a prize the winner got the goose. Varieties of gander pulling, which was to become popular in frontier regions, spread southward to Georgia and continued into the nineteenth century.[21]

In all the colonies the many taverns or inns often served as social centers and, except in New England and Pennsylvania, as places for the playing of folk games. (The New England and Pennsylvania colonies specifically prohibited "inn games".)[22] Among the colonists, tippling and regular tavern visits were favorite forms of relaxation. Even Puritan clergymen who assailed drunkenness rarely objected to moderate drinking. Boston itself had 177 innkeepers and retailers of liquor in 1737—roughly one dealer for every twenty-five adult males. "In most country towns," John Adams reported of New England in 1761, ". . . you will find almost every other house with a sign of entertainment before it. . . . If you sit the evening, you will find the house full of people drinking drams, flip, toddy, carousing, swearing. . . ."[23] Rarely, however, did the patrons of the taverns become roaring drunk; they usually consumed small quantities of mild sedatives like beer, ale, and grog. Lively conversation and a variety of games often accompanied drinking. A Virginia clergyman complained in 1751 that taverns had "become the common. . .rendezvous of the very dregs of the people. . .where not only time and money are vainly and unprofitably squandered away, but (what is yet worse) where prohibited

[21]For an interesting picture of "gander pulling" see John Durant and Otto Bettmann, *Pictorial History of American Sports: Colonial Times to the Present* (Cranbury, N.J.: A. S. Barnes, 1965), p. 7. For the survival of the contest into the nineteenth century see Jennie Holliman, *American Sports, 1785–1835* (Durham, N.C.: Seeman, 1931), pp. 146–47.

[22]See Struna, "Sport and Societal Values," 41; Earle, *Customs and Fashions,* p. 238; Alice Morris Earle, *Stage-Coach and Tavern Days* (New York: Macmillan, 1981), p. 5.

[23]John Adams, *The Works of John Adams,* 5 vols. (Boston: Charles C. Little and James Brown, 1850), II, 125–26.

A game of skittles. Published 1801 by J. Wheble, Warwick Square.

and unlawful games, sports, and pastimes are used, followed, and practiced, almost without intermission, namely cards, dice, horse-racing, and cock-fighting, together with vices and enormities of every other kind."[24] The clergyman might have added animal baiting and skittles (a form of bowling) as being among the more popular tavern amusements. Not just places for recreation and convivial drinking, the taverns also served as the center of a crude communications network. Travelers, who used the sleeping quarters furnished by the taverns, brought news from other settlements or sometimes from the mother country. Merchants, artisans, and common laborers often met at taverns to discuss topics of mutual interest.

The games associated with the training days in the North, county fairs in the South, and taverns everywhere hardly constituted an equivalent to the richness of the village recreations of Old England. Training days and county fairs came only once a year. The taverns could not function as effective community-wide social centers, as they typically held only a few

[24]Quoted in Morgan, *Virginians at Home*, p. 87. See also Ruth E. Painter, "Tavern Amusements in Eighteenth Century America," *The Leisure Class in America*, ed. by Leon Stein (New York: Arno, 1975).

patrons and suffered from the increasing antipathy of clergymen, especially those of an evangelical persuasion. The Great Awakening (a religious revival) of the 1730s and 1740s inhibited the potential growth of the old pastimes in all the colonies. In 1774, a Virginia "gentleman" explained to Philip Fithian the effects of the growing evangelical temperament on traditional recreation. "The Anabaptists [an evangelical group] in Louden County are growing very numerous and seem to be growing in afluence [influence?]; and...quite destroying pleasure in the country; for they encourage ardent pray'r; strong and constant faith, & the entire banishment of gaming, dancing & Sabbath-day diversions."[25] Yet, despite the immense handicaps encountered by the common people, a few of them continued to play the traditional folk games.

PASTIMES OF THE GENTRY

In the eighteenth century a separate world of leisure developed among the emerging colonial gentry. Because ascertaining social status in the colonies was fraught with difficulties—no legal aristrocacy existed—wealth was the primary requirement for those claiming to be gentlemen. By the opening years of the eighteenth century two groups possessed the requisite wealth for gentry status: the prosperous merchants in the larger cities and the large planters in the Tidewater Region of the South. The city merchants built lavish homes, retained servants, entertained generously, and often joined the entourage of the royal governor. The planters built large mansions which frequently included a ballroom and sometimes a billiard room, ate with silver decorated with the family's coat of arms, and managed their vast estates with the confidence of Oriental potentates. The gentry also ruled the economic and political life of their respective colonies. They assumed an inherent inequality among men, believing that some were destined to govern while others were foreordained to carry out the meaner tasks required by society. In both England and the colonies almost all social groups accepted the principle that "inferiors" ought to defer socially and politically to their "superiors." By modern standards colonial society was conspicuously deferential. The gentry sought to live by Aristotle's golden mean, a goal of moderation in all things, including religion. Unlike either the Puritans or evangelicals, the gentry, who were almost invariably members of the Church of England, worried less about the fate of their souls. Most of them were supremely confident that God would award them salvation just as he had rewarded them with material abundance.[26]

[25]Hunter Dickinson Farish, ed., *Journal & Letters of Philip Vickers Fithian, 1773–1774* (Williamsburg, Va.: Colonial Williamsburg, 1943), p. 96.

[26]For gentry life see especially Louis B. Wright, *The First Gentlemen of Virginia: Intellectual Qualities of the Early Colonial Ruling Class* (San Marino, Calif.: Huntington Library, 1940); C. Robert Barnett, "Recreational Patterns of the Colonial Virginia Aristocrat," *Journal of the West Virginia Historical Association,* 2 (Spring, 1978), 1–11; Greven, *The Protestant Temperament;* and Jane Carson, *Colonial Virginians at Play* (Charlottesville, Va.: University Press of Virginia, 1965).

The gentry supported their claims to the highest social status in the American colonies by patterning their lives after their counterparts in England. They often sent their children to England to be educated, read the latest literature prescribing gentlemanly behavior, and imported the material fineries that would enable them to ape the tastes of the English gentry. Like the English gentry, the colonial elite sought to distinguish themselves from the "meaner sort" of people by nurturing a specific code of manners and by cultivating skills in a wide variety of activities. Without becoming a specialist in any particular endeavor, the gentleman ideally learned to dance, fence, ride, and converse in a pleasing manner. Certain pastimes identified one as having the leisure time and wealth essential for gentry status. Colonial merchants usually preferred formal dinners, dancing, and card playing to physical contests. But Southern planters not only entertained each other extravagantly, they enjoyed horse racing, cockfighting, gambling, and hunting. They always sought to restrict participation to members of their own class. The case of James Bullocke, a common tailor, provides striking evidence of the gentry's social sensitivity. In 1674 Bullocke scandalized the gentry of York County, Virginia, by presuming to enter his horse in a race for 2,000 pounds of tobacco against a horse owned by a "gentleman," Dr. Matthew Slader. For such a presumption the county court fined the tailor 200 pounds of tobacco and asserted that horse racing was "a sport for gentlemen only."[27]

The experiences of William Byrd II (1674–1744), a prominent Virginia planter, provide insight into the leisure life of the Southern gentry.[28] William Byrd the elder had established the family's wealth by a good marriage, land speculation, political connections, a lucrative trade in guns and rum with the Indians, and tobacco farming in which black slaves furnished the labor. He thought his son should be given every opportunity to acquire the polish and culture of an English gentleman. Thus he sent William the younger to England where he attended the Felsted Grammar School in Essex and the Middle Temple in London. In due course his son was admitted to the bar. Apart from acquiring the tastes and manners of a young English gentleman, the younger Byrd also learned something of business and trade while in Europe. When he inherited his father's vast estate in 1705, at the age of thirty, he was already a man of distinction. He had served in Virginia's House of Burgesses and represented the colony as its agent in London.

Byrd exemplified the most refined qualities of the Southern gentry. He rebuilt the family mansion at Westover, furnished it with the finest Georgian furniture, and constructed an extensive formal garden that fronted the James River. He collected the second largest library in the American colonies, read both Greek and Latin, wrote an urbane account of his expedition to survey the boundary between Virginia and North Carolina, and dabbled enough in science to be admitted to the Royal Society in England. Like most of his fellow planters, Byrd worried much

[27]Quoted in T. H. Breen, "Horses and Gentlemen: The Cultural Significance of Gambling Among the Gentry of Virginia," *William and Mary Quarterly,* 34 (April 1977), 250.
[28]See Wright, *First Gentlemen of Virginia,* pp. 312–47.

less about religious matters than the evangelicals, but he always attended church services and said his prayers regularly.

Byrd participated enthusiastically in all the pastimes common to the English gentry.[29] One of his favorites was billiards. He played with fellow planters, his wife, and his son. He also loved to try his hand at bowls. In 1721 he laid out his own green at his Westover plantation. Every summer for twenty years guests spent pleasant afternoons with Byrd attempting to roll the imperfectly balanced balls—bowls—as near the "jack" as possible. On rare occasions Byrd played ninepins or skittles. However, skittles was usually played only by the lower classes in alleyways or taverns.

Before Byrd had laid out a bowling green, he often played cricket. According to his diary, in the early spring of 1710 he played regularly with neighboring planters on both sides of the James River. The version of cricket played by Byrd and his friends was quite different from the modern game. The wicket was simply two posts about a foot high and a foot apart; the space between was called the "popping hole." The striker ran to the popping hole and tried to hit the ball before the wicket keeper rolled the ball into the hole. In the colonial game as well as the English game of that time, any number of persons could play, and rules of play were passed on orally.

While some of the Southern gentry had an interest in physical contests like billiards, bowls, and cricket, the gentry's involvement in gambling and horse racing had a more profound impact upon the future of American sport. Wherever a few of the great planters gathered, someone always produced a deck of cards, a backgammon board, or a pair of dice. Indeed, these men often risked large sums of money and tobacco—sometimes a year or more of earnings—on almost any proposition that involved an element of chance. While William Byrd II wagered only modest amounts, his intemperate son was an inveterate gambler. As a consequence of his gambling, William Byrd III eventually bankrupted the family's estate and committed suicide.

Above all, the great planters had a passion for wagering on horse races. Until the mid-eighteenth century, the quarterhorse race, a sprint of two horses over a quarter-mile dirt track, excited the most interest. A race might be the result of a regularly scheduled contest on a Saturday afternoon on an established track or an impromptu challenge run on a country road. Each contestant backed his horse with a wager and might make side bets with spectators; likewise, spectators might bet with each other on the outcome. In the last half of the eighteenth century the introduction of English thoroughbreds led to longer races with several heats of a mile or more. Horsemen then organized the first jockey clubs in Virginia, Maryland, and South Carolina.[30] The early jockey clubs were precursors of the nineteenth-century athletic clubs.

[29]See Louis B. Wright and Marion Tinling, eds., *The Secret Diary of William Byrd of Westover, 1709–1712* (Richmond, Va.: Dietz Press, 1941). For a quantitative analysis of the leisure activities of Byrd and other leading colonial figures—based on their diaries—see Thomas Robert Davis, "Sport and Exercise in the Lives of Selected Colonial Americans: Massachusetts and Virginia, 1700–1775," (unpublished Ph.D. dissertation, University of Maryland, 1970).

[30]See Carson, *Colonial Virginians at Play*, pp. 105–32.

   The Southern gentry's passion for horse racing and gambling served social functions similar to the sports of the nineteenth-century elites. Participation in gambling and horse racing visibly identified one as a member of the gentry. Perhaps the provincial gentry cultivated these activities in hopes of establishing a genuine landed or legal aristocracy in the colonies. At any rate, gaming relationships furnished the gentry with a means' of solidifying their dominance over Southern society. They served the gentry as a "safety valve" that allowed the planters to compete with each other without seriously endangering the cohesion of the group. One gained honor and respect only by victories over one's peers, never by competing against inferiors. For the onlookers, which included the common white people and the slaves, horse racing among the gentry was a form of high social drama. By promoting these great public displays, the planters helped convince subordinate groups that the gentry culture was something to be esteemed. By conceding the superiority of gentry culture, the common people were more likely to acquiesce in the gentry's control of the political and economic life of the colonies.[31]

   In a larger cultural sense the American colonies were simply a provincial outpost of the British Empire; the colonists' pastimes were the result of the interaction between the customs the people brought with them and New World circumstances. The gentry, especially the Southern gentry, were able to pattern their leisure activities closely after the models established by the English upper classes. On the other hand, the common people of the colonies sacrificed much of their heritage of village games. The dispersion of the settlers, the need for hard work, and the religious sentiments of many of the settlers had made it impossible for them to transplant the English village customs. The Puritan and evangelical temperaments hampered the growth of sport and shaped the attitudes of future generations. Neither the native Americans (Indians) nor the imported black slaves greatly affected the pastimes of the main body of English settlers. The English colonists, unlike the Spanish and the French in the New World, assimilated little of the native American culture. The severe shock of forced dislocation and slavery insured that the black influence on the recreation of the English colonists would also be minimal.

---

[31]This interpretation follows that of Breen, "Horses and Gentlemen," but for the late eighteenth century see also Isaac, "Evangelical Revolt."

2

Pastimes in the
New Republic

A ratting. Published by Knight and Lacey, 1825.

On May 25, 1825, fifty years after Lexington had witnessed the first shots of the American Revolution, John Quincy Adams, the sixth President of the United States, purchased a secondhand billiard table from a Washington, D. C. merchant for fifty dollars. Adams had the table recovered with a bright green felt cloth and bought additional cues and balls. His costs totaled $104.44. Shortly after the installation of the table in the White House, Adams complained in his diary that he was wasting too much time in the evenings "at the billiard-table."[1] While Adams' youngest son continued to shoot billiards regularly with friends, the President soon stopped playing entirely. A year later, the new piece of White House furniture attracted public notice. In a routine report of items recently purchased for the Executive Mansion, a Congressional Committee included the cost of the billiard table, the new cover, and the accessories. To the surprise of the President and his friends, the purchase of the billiard table aroused a nationwide controversy.

Apparently few Americans perceived the President's billiard table as an innocent source of recreation. Representative Samuel Carson of North Carolina asked: "Is it possible...to believe that it ever was intended by Congress, that the public money would be applied to the purchase of gaming tables and gambling furniture?" The table should, Carson exclaimed, "shock and alarm the religious, the moral, and reflecting part of the community." To most Protestants, at least those of an evangelical temperament, the President was setting a poor moral example. The purchase by Adams seemed to be clear evidence that the President had aligned himself with the "immoral" sporting fraternity rather than the forces of righteousness. One newspaper editor warned: "When we find the fathers and matrons of our country engaged in persuading young men from practices which lead to destruction, we greatly fear that the too frequent answer will be, 'Why, the President plays billiards!'" In Mississippi, claimed one editor, a jury had acquitted the owner of a public billiard room who had been guilty of violating the state's antigambling law. The defense attorney had successfully contended that his client had "as good a right to establish a billiard table as the *President of the United States...*."[2]

The billiard table controversy reveals several of the salient features of American sport during the first half of the nineteenth century. In the first

[1] Quoted in Edwin A. Miles, "President Adams' Billiard Table," *New England Quarterly,* 45 (March 1972), 31n.
[2] Quotations in this paragraph, ibid., 34, 35.

place, it was evident that the public hostility to the table sprang from more than simply the continuation of earlier American attitudes toward leisure, gambling, and sports. The dispute spotlighted the beginnings of a new pattern of culture in the United States. Victorianism (named for Queen Victoria, who reigned in Great Britain from 1837 to 1901) stemmed from the erosion of older social restraints, a revolution in material aspirations, and a reinvigorated Protestantism. The Victorians, who came mostly from the middle-income ranks, praised the values of hard work, religious duty, sexual control, sobriety, and punctuality—values that seemed essential to those who aspired to succeed in the new economy. The values were also useful as a means of social control. Led by the evangelical clergy, the Victorians frequently mounted crusades against drink, gambling, sexual promiscuity, and "idle" amusements. They associated these vices with the "dissolute aristocracy" from above and the "unproductive rabble" from below.

The "unproductive rabble" and the "dissolute aristocracy" formed the core of support for an emerging Victorian subculture or underworld. Largely outside of and opposed to the dominant Victorian culture of the nineteenth century, the members of the subculture wanted to retain preindustrial, preurban patterns of life.[3] The values of the subculture included casual work habits, gusto, extravagance, immediate gratification, and spontaneity. Above all, its members rejected the new emphasis upon time and time-consciousness, an emphasis symbolized by the huge clocks placed atop the newly constructed factory buildings of the nineteenth century. Rather than practicing the virtues of hard work, temperance, frugality, and punctuality held so dear by the Victorians, members of the Victorian underworld might attempt to achieve success—to the extent that they accepted success as a worthwhile goal—through such activities as saloon management, gambling, crime, prostitution, speculative ventures, entertainment, and sport.

Since the commercial-urban-industrial revolution severed the old folk games from their traditional moorings in work, community, and common custom, the subculture offered substitutes—in the form of the saloon, the theatre, gambling halls, and commercial sports (largely in the form of "blood" sports, professional pedestrianism or footracing, prize fighting, billiards, boat racing and the like). Within the subculture, a sporting

---

[3]My formulation of this interpretation is especially indebted in idiosyncratic ways to Melvin Leonard Adelman, "The Development of Modern Athletics in New York City, 1820–1870" (unpublished Ph.D. diss., University of Illinois, 1980); Rowland Berthoff, *An Unsettled People: Social Order and Disorder in American History* (New York: Harper & Row, 1971); Herbert G. Gutman, "Work, Culture, and Society in Industrializing America, 1815–1919," *American Historical Review,* 78 (June 1973), 531–88; Daniel Walker Howe, ed., *Victorian America* (Philadelphia: University of Pennsylvania Press, 1976); J. Thomas Jable, "Aspects of Moral Reform in Early Nineteenth Century Pennsylvania," *Pennsylvania Magazine of History and Biography,* 102 (July 1978), 344–63; Paul E. Johnson, *A Shopkeeper's Millennium: Society and Revivals in Rochester, New York, 1815–1837* (New York: Hill and Wang, 1978); Morse Pecham, "Victorian Counterculture," *Victorian Studies,* 18 (March 1975), 257–76; and Ned Polsky, *Hustlers, Beats, and Others* (Chicago: Aldine, 1967), Chap. 1.

fraternity, often called by contemporaries "the fancy,"* arose to promote these commercial sports. While organized for the interest of spectators and to provide opportunities for gambling, their sports lacked national regulatory bodies. In this sense they were quite unlike modern spectator-centered sports.

In those parts of the new nation relatively untouched by the commercial-urban-industrial revolution—principally the rural areas and along the advancing frontier—the playing of folk games continued much as they had in the past. The sportlike activities found in these regions usually sprang from daily work or common custom. Since fishing and hunting could be vital to survival, such contests as shooting-at-the-mark were especially popular. Prizes might include a jug of whiskey, a turkey, or a side of beef. Other kinds of quasi-athletic contests, such as throwing, running, jumping, rail-splitting, and wrestling often accompanied shooting matches. Vestiges of these informal, individual, and sometimes violent folk games continued to be played in the more isolated rural regions of the United States until well into the twentieth century.

Apart from the folk games of rural America and the world of commercial sport found in the larger cities, another world of sport gradually emerged among those from the middle- and upper-income ranks. In the Revolutionary era, Thomas Jefferson, Benjamin Rush, and Benjamin Franklin, among others, had advocated regular physical exercise while condemning folk games. Beginning in the 1820s a few physicians, ministers of a liberal temperament, and a small contingent of the New England literati promoted exercise for better health and mental acuity. In Massachusetts and a few places elsewhere, the introduction of formal gymnastics and regularized calisthenics (usually by German émigrés created a brief flurry of excitement, but the permanent results were meager.

By 1850 members of the upper- and middle-income ranks in the larger cities began to form numerous voluntary associations or clubs for boating, quoits, racquets, cricket, and baseball. (These clubs will be discussed more fully in Chapter 3.) Gradually the Victorians came to approve of these sports while continuing to condemn sports associated with the underworld, especially those sports featuring violence, gambling, professionalism, and spectatorship. By 1850, the Victorians had even begun to develop a positive sporting ideology, one that defended the playing of certain sports as useful for improved health, as a respite from work, as a surrogate for the vices of the city, and as an instrument for the nurture of proper character traits among the young. Nevertheless, until the opening years of the twentieth century, Victorianism continued to act as a powerful brake upon the overall growth of commerical sport.

---

*Apparently "the fancy" first came into usage in the eighteenth century to describe elegant, perhaps ostentatiously dressed, English "gentlemen" who patronized sporting events, especially prize fights. While the fancy was a widely-used term in early nineteenth-century America, it gradually disappeared in the latter half of the century. The term "fan," which first appeared in the United States in the late nineteenth century to describe baseball enthusiasts, was apparently a derivative of "fanatic" rather than "fancy."

Well before Victorianism could be identified as a cultural style in America, the republican ideology flowing from the Revolutionary era (roughly from 1774 to 1789) had joined forces with both moderate and evangelical forms of Protestantism to reinforce traditional animosities toward the playing of folk games. According to republican ideology, a republic—a political system without a monarchy and with sovereignty residing with the people—could not be founded upon the idle amusements of the decadent monarchies of Europe. For a republic to survive, the citizens had to be especially virtuous. They had to abstain from luxury, practice frugality, and avoid dissipation. The First Continental Congress, meeting in 1774 with a war with the mother country looming on the horizon, resolved that the colonies "discountenance and discourage every species of extravagance and dissipation, especially all horse-racing, and all kinds of gaming, cock fighting, exhibition of shows, plays, and other expensive diversions and amusements."[4] Wherever they could, the Sons of Liberty attempted to impose such strictures on the citizenry for the duration of the Revolution. During the Revolution, all of the states likewise adopted strict sumptuary legislation to restrict personal extravagance and luxury. As Samuel Adams put it, each state ought to strive to be a "Christian Sparta."

Yet many of the citizens of the new republic ignored the spartan demands of republican ideology. John Adams himself, in a rare burst of enthusiam for the pageantry associated with the past, wrote to his wife, Abigail, on July 3, 1776, that American independence "ought to be solemnized with pomp and parade, with shows, games, sports, guns, bells, bonfires and illuminations from one end of this continent to the other from this time forward forever more."[5] After the Revolution, many of the most ardent republican ideologues worried lest the citizens of the new country ape their European counterparts. In Pennsylvania (one of the most restrictive states) Jacob Rush, president of the Third District Court of Common Pleas, reported in 1800 that "So general is disobediance to this law [against Sunday diversions] and so great the contempt of public authority, that a stranger passing through our country, would rather suppose we had a law *enjoining* [requiring] sports and diversions on Sunday, under heavy penalty, than one forbidding them."[6]

In the long run evangelical Protestantism rather than republican ideology furnished the most important source for the emerging Victorian-

---

[4]Henry Steele Commager, ed., *Documents of American History*, 2 vols., 9th ed. (Englewood Cliffs, N.J.: Prentice-Hall, 1973), I, 86. For republican ideology and its implications for personal behavior see Gordon S. Wood, *The Creation of the American Republic, 1776–1787* (Chapel Hill: University of North Carolina Press, 1969).

[5]L.H. Butterfield, ed., *Adams Family Correspondence*, 2 vols. (Cambridge, Mass.: Harvard University Press, 1963), II, 30. See also the incident reported in Edmund S. Morgan, "The Puritan Ethic and the American Revolution," *William and Mary Quarterly*, 24 (January 1967), 31–32.

[6]Quoted in Jable, "Aspects of Moral Reform," 346.

ism as well as for the suppression of public amusements. While organized religion in the United States had suffered a temporary lull in the aftermath of the American Revolution, it rebounded with renewed vigor in the first half of the nineteenth century. Great revivals again swept the country—at the turn of the eighteenth century, in the 1820s, in the late 1830s, and again in the late 1850s. By 1850 the revivals had increased the membership of the Baptist and Methodist denominations, both evangelical in temperament, far beyond that of the more moderate Anglicans and Congregationalists. Far from being fatalistic, the evangelicals promised not only salvation but in many cases personal perfection and a millennium within the lifetime of the convert. Such an optimistic outlook induced strong feelings of personal piety and vigorous campaigns to reform the behavior of others. While the various Protestant denominations competed for members and engaged in bitter theological controversies, they formed a vast network of voluntary associations to promote a common morality. They usually constituted a common front in favor of strict Sabbatarian laws and laws against gambling, "riotous" amusements, and drinking.

The soaring material aspirations of the American people added impetus to the emerging Victorian culture. While the typical colonist had little reason to believe that the future would be very different from the past, many of the post Revolutionary generation came to expect a better standard of living and improved status for themselves and their children. The opening of vast new territories in the West, the construction of a national system of transportation and communication, and the sudden growth of commerce, agriculture, and industry fed the revolution in material hopes. Alexis de Tocqueville, the perceptive French aristocrat who visited the United States in 1831–1832, was astonished. "We are most certainly in another world here," he exclaimed. "Political passions are only on the surface. The profound passion, the only one which profoundly stirs the human heart, the passion of all days, is the acquisition of riches."[7] The quest for wealth received the enthusiastic blessing of many religious leaders, especially those of a more liberal temperament. Horace Bushnell, for example, asserted that "as certainly...as you succeed [in the material world] you will be saved" and that wealth was "a reward and honor which God delights to bestow upon upright people."[8]

Achieving success seemed to require a ceaseless commitment to hard work. "In no country that I know is there so much hard, toilsome, unremitting labor; in none so little recreation and enjoyment of life," wrote one foreign observer.[9] A host of English travelers in the 1830s and 1840s— Frances Trollope, Charles Lyell, Basil Hall, Thomas Hamilton, Frances Wright, and Charles Dickens—reached the same conclusion. "From the time we landed in New England...," Sir Charles Lyell reported, "we seemed to have been in a country where all, whether rich or poor, were

[7]Alexis de Tocqueville, *Democracy in America*, 2 vols., Philips Bradley, ed. (New York: Knopf Inc., 1951), I, 51.
[8]Quoted in Barbara M. Cross, *Horace Bushnell: Minister to a Changing America* (Chicago: University of Chicago Press, 1958), p. 236.
[9]Thomas L. Nichols, *Forty Years of American Life* (London: Longmans, Green, 1874), p. 206.

labouring from morning till night, without ever indulging in a holiday."[10] The foreign observers exaggerated, but, compared to the citizens in their homelands, Americans were an exceedingly hardworking people. This was especially true of the growing middle-income ranks who constituted the main support for Victorian values.

The revolution in material aspirations also undermined older social restraints. The class deference of colonial society was replaced by the egalitarian spirit of the age of Andrew Jackson. (The South remained something of an exception. There, old class relationships lingered with striking vigor.) As champions of the new egalitarianism, the Jacksonian opponents of Adams attacked the President's billiard table as a symbol of aristocratic pretensions. An insensitive defender of the purchase argued that a billiards room was "a common appendage in the houses of the rich and great in Europe, and by no means uncommon as such in the United States."[11] To him, a billiard table was "almost necessary" to maintain the dignity and social status of the White House. But to most Americans, justifying its purchase on the grounds that it was a "common appendage in the houses of the rich and great" reinforced the popular suspicion that Adams thought himself superior to ordinary men. By the 1820s Americans seemed to take literally Thomas Jefferson's happy assertion in the Declaration of Independence that "all men are created equal." By then, the old hierarchy of mutual class obligations had been deeply eroded, thus destroying a key social restraint of the old order.

Even more destructive of these restraints was the massive mobility induced by the pell-mell pursuit of wealth. In the nineteenth century Americans moved in unprecedented numbers, both to the frontiers and the cities; after 1840 old-stock Americans were joined by a massive influx of European immigrants. In colonial times the frontier had inched slowly forward, along the seaboard of the Atlantic coast and up the navigable rivers. A hundred years after the founding of Jamestown in 1607, settlements had advanced only about one hundred miles inland. Suddenly, within the century spanning 1776 and 1876, the settlers burst across the Appalachian Mountains into the Ohio and Mississippi valleys, across the Great Plains, over the Rocky Mountains, and on to the Pacific coast. Physical barriers seemed nonexistent and human barriers, as native Americans and Mexicans soon discovered, were rudely pushed aside or killed. In 1790 no city in the nation had a population of 50,000; by 1870 fifty-one cities exceeded that mark. Urban dwellers also moved frequently; by 1840 about one-third of them changed their residences every year. By 1840 the sheer velocity of life seemed greater. In 1750 it had taken five days to travel from New York to Philadelphia; in 1840 it took less than three hours. Urban Americans, foreign visitors universally reported, always had something to do and were always in a "terrible hurry."

Greater mobility fractured larger kinship groups, corroded links be-

---

[10]Quoted in Allan Nevins, ed., *American Social History as Recorded by British Travellers* (New York: Henry Holt, n.d.), p. 333.

[11]Quoted in Miles, "President Adams' Billiard Table," 36.

tween generations, destroyed close identity with a special place, and encouraged impersonal and abstract relationships among people. As Tocqueville put it, Americans "owe nothing to any man...they acquire the habit of always considering themselves standing alone, and they are apt to imagine that their whole destiny is in their own hands. Thus not only does...every man forget his ancestors, but...hides his descendants and separates his contemporaries from him...."[12] Mobility and the unregulated pursuit of material gain encouraged an emotional disengagement from the past. The transcendentalist, Ralph Waldo Emerson, wrote: "Let us even bid our dearest friends farewell, and defy them saying 'Who are you? Unhand me: I will be dependent no more.'"[13] The traditional community, in which ties founded on family, birthplace, social status, and inherited religion overlapped, was rapidly disappearing. To a remarkable degree, perhaps unparalleled in the annals of human history, the individual in the nineteenth century was cast free of older social restraints. He was now more free to determine for himself his loyalties and enter into them voluntarily.

Since the leaders of early Victorian culture could no longer depend on class deference, an established church, nor the small, close-knit geographic community to insure social order, they frequently turned to the individual conscience. In accordance with their evangelical Protestant religious beliefs, they attempted to instill in each individual an internal set of values so that people would no longer need to be reminded of their duties and could be left to their own volition. Ideally, the individual would be "inner directed," to use David Riesman's terminology,[14] possessing a moral gyroscope that would act as a safe guide through the bewildering changes that were transforming American society. To this end, the cultural leaders gave more attention to child rearing, to the home, and to public education. And they used their superior access to the media to inundate the country with moral exhortation. The Victorians directed much of their exhortation and their laws restricting personal liberties at the sporting fraternity and recent immigrants, two groups who frequently overlapped in membership and behavior. To the Victorians, both groups embodied ways of life that threatened the stability of the existing social order.

THE SPORTING FRATERNITY

A short story written by James Hall in the midst of the billiard table controversy vividly illustrates the conflict in values between early Victorian culture and that of the world of commercial sport. According to Hall, too many unwary young men forsook the "quiet and virtuous comfort" of

---

[12]Tocqueville, *Democracy in America*, II, 99.

[13]Ralph Waldo Emerson, *Emerson: A Modern Anthology*, Alfred Kazin and Daniel Aaron, eds. (Boston: Houghton Mifflin, 1958), p. 168.

[14]David Riesman et al., *The Lonely Crowd: A Study of the Changing American Character* (New Haven, Conn.: Yale University Press, 1950).

home, parents, and wives to visit public billiard rooms. There they found a "stained and dirty floor...strewed with fragments of segars, playbills, and nut shells; the walls blackened with smoke seemed to have witnessed the orgies of many a midnight revel." In the center of the room stood the "gay altar of dissipation" itself, the billiard table. On the benches around the walls sat or reclined the "loungers" who solemnly puffed their "segars" or idly sipped their brandy and water. "Little coteries of gayer spirits" stood around the table, laughing, chatting, and making additional wagers on the match, "while the marker announced the state of the game, trimmed lamps, and supplied refreshments to the guests."[15] The billiard room, as described by Hall, certainly seemed the epitome of human decadence—the neglect and betrayal of parental and marital responsibilities, associations with disreputable men, intemperate smoking and drinking, an immoral use of leisure time, and the dissipation of personal wealth through gambling.

At the same time, Hall unwittingly suggested the main social functions furnished by the sporting fraternity. Apart from the sensual gratification found in smoking, drinking, playing billiards, and wagering, Hall depicted the billiard hall as a refuge from femininity, domesticity, and the demanding routines of the new economy. At the billiard room men need no longer worry about time-thriftiness, their boss, and success or failure in the world of work. Hall also depicted the billiard room as a kind of secular church; he described the billiard table as an altar and noted the more or less ritualistic behavior of the patrons of the parlor. Like the great revivals of the era, the billiard hall and other sporting spectacles amassed people for a shared experience, one that was reminiscent of the communal festivities of the distant past. While the relentless quest for wealth encouraged abstract, impersonal relationships, the sporting experience, even if commercial in nature, facilitated face-to-face communication and interaction.

The lives of the most active members of the sporting fraternity revolved around gambling halls, hotels, volunteer fire departments, barbershops, and saloons. In colonial times gambling had been a popular pastime, especially among the Southern gentry. To the Victorians, the "sin of gambling" led down a one-way road to total degradation. Starting with checkers or whist the traveler passed rapidly through poker to wagering on horses and prize fighters to end his day in "drunken debauches and murder." Nonetheless, gambling grew rapidly in the nineteenth century; by the 1840s almost any coffee house, billiard parlor, or saloon might harbor a gambling establishment.[16] Many of the sporting spectacles arose from spirited arguments over the merits of a horse, a prize fighter, or a pedestrian. A wager and the scheduling of a contest ensued. Spectators wagered on all of the spectacles. For spectator, promoter, and athlete alike,

[15]Quoted in Miles, "President Adams' Billiard Table," 33n. During the controversy, Hall's story was reprinted in many newspapers.

[16]See David R. Johnson, "'A Sinful Business': The Origins of Gambling Syndicates in the United States, 1840–1887," in David H. Bayley, ed., *Police and Society* (Beverly Hills, Calif.: Sage Publications, 1977), pp. 17–47, and Herbert Asbury, *Sucker's Progress: An Informal History of Gambling in America from the Colonies to Canfield* (New York: Dodd, Mead, 1938).

winning a bet might be far more important than the thrill of winning the contest itself.

In earlier times public drinking had been confined largely to taverns which served food and drink, offered temporary lodging to travelers, and functioned as social centers for people of all ranks. While the tavern had enjoyed widespread support, the nineteenth century saloon, which typically featured drinking as its chief activity, incurred the wrath of "respectable" people everywhere. Saloons varied in the richness of their decor and in the wealth of their clientele, but their principal customers were workingmen. (After 1840 Irish and German ethnics were conspicuous for their convivial drinking habits. Consequently the temperance movement often had an antiethnic component.) In the saloons workingmen could communally enjoy upper class comforts. By mid-century the more elegant saloons had brilliantly lighted windows flanked by wicker doors that swung easily open for men of all ages. Inside, the patron might see variegated lampshades, frescoed ceilings, a gilded bar with a glittering mirror behind it, and paintings of famous race horses, prize fighters, and voluptuous, scantily clad women. In addition to the workingmen, the fashionable young men of the sporting set also took delight in the saloons.

The saloon was an ideal retreat for the metropolitan sporting fraternity. The saloon keepers especially courted those interested in politics, sport, and gambling. There, the two extremes of society—young "dissolute" men of some means and the workingmen—could meet to review the latest sport gossip, schedule sporting events, and take bets. The saloons often served as pool rooms; the managers posted the odds on horse races and, later in the century, on baseball matches. In the latter part of the century, saloons often had telegraph hookups so they could post the latest sporting results instantly. Pugilists and their backers almost invariably worked out of local saloons. An advertisement of William Clark summarized some of the social functions of the metropolitan saloon: "Ales, wines, liquors, segars, and refreshments. All the sporting news of the day to be learned here, where files of the *Clipper,* and other sporting papers are kept. Here also may be seen numberless portraits of English and American pugilists.... A room of other facilities are also at all times in readiness for giving lessons in sparring under the supervision of the proprietor. Drop in, and take a peep."[17]

In New York City and in other larger cities the fancy had, by the 1850s, established halls which featured a regular fare of cock fighting, dog fighting, rattings, and other forms of low entertainment. Of the several halls in New York, the best known in the 1860s was Kit Burns' Sportsman Hall. Shaped as an amphitheatre, the hall could seat up to 400 spectators. Apart from watching and wagering upon how long it would take a dog to kill a pit full of rats, the spectator might pay a quarter to see "Jack the Rat" decapitate a rat or a dime to witness him bite off the head of a mouse. Frederick Van Wyck, of a distinguished Knickerbocker family, suggested

[17]Quoted in John Rickards Betts, *America's Sporting Heritage* (Reading, Mass.: Addison-Wesley, 1974), p. 162.

that attendance at such events was a "rite of passage" for certain youth of the upper social ranks. At Tommy Norris' livery stable, he reported seeing a ratting, a cock fight, a goat fight, and a boxing match between two women who were nude above the waist. "Certainly for a lad of 17, as I was," reported Van Wyck, "a night with Tommy Norris and his attractions was quite a night."[18]

The social composition of the sporting fraternity cannot be determined with precision. Generally, the middle-income groups composed of merchants, skilled workingmen, small manufacturers, and professional men avoided any active association with the world of commercial sport. Yet probably few nineteenth-century Amercan males totally resisted the occasional temptation to attend and even wager on a sporting event. "Without intending it by any means," apologized Philip Hone in his diary in 1835, ". . . I found myself with Robert in the barouche [carriage], enveloped in clouds of dust. . . on the road to the [pedestrian] race course, jostled by every description of vehicle conveying every description of people."[19] Even John Quincy Adams attended a few horse races in the nation's capital. The treatment accorded sporting spectacles by the newspapers suggests that there were large numbers of vicarious sportsmen who never deigned to attend a sporting event but nonetheless assiduously followed the sport scene. Newspapers often printed both detailed accounts of spectacles plus pious denunciations of their immorality. The typical Victorian apparently perceived the sporting world with ambivalent feelings; a combination of secret awe and fascination mixed with public horror and disgust.

The majority of the sporting fraternity came from the ranks of the ordinary workingmen. This was partly due to the nature of the nineteenth-century labor market. Few workers could expect a lifetime of stable, full-time employment. Periods of unemployment and underemployment always accompanied the downturns in the ricocheting business cycle; even in prosperous times dock hands, teamsters, and construction crews worked intermittently or by the seasons. And every city had its share of "floaters" who worked only when driven by necessity. Consequently, a surprisingly large portion of the labor force had ample amounts of spare time to engage in sporting activities.

Furthermore, unlike the growing middle-income groups, the ordinary workingmen were slow to acquiesce to the regimen of the new economy. Casual work habits continued into the industrial age. For instance, in Lowell, Massachusetts, one of the birthplaces of modern machine production, protests by workingmen were nonexistent until the 1840s, when the work system was reorganized to achieve greater production. At that point, workers who had known only an irregular pace of work protested vigorously. "Grog" privileges—the tradition of drinking light alcoholic beverages during the work day—remained an accepted pattern in many

---

[18]Quoted in Adelman, "The Development of Modern Athletics," 584.
[19]Allan Nevins, ed., *The Diary of Philip Hone, 1828–1851,* 2 vols. (New York: Dodd, Mead, 1927), I, 156–57.

trades until well into the nineteenth century. The early manufacturers repeatedly complained of the irregular work habits of their employees. Frequent absenteeism, especially on Mondays, plagued employers everywhere. The Pennsylvania iron workers, for example, frequently "took off" from work to hunt, harvest, "frolic," or celebrate weddings, funerals, and holidays.[20] Each newly arrived ethnic group from the peasant societies of Europe (notably the Irish, Italians, and East Europeans) brought with them attitudes toward time-thrift and temperance at odds with the Victorians. The Victorian underworld offered an arena for men to escape—if only temporarily—the demanding routine and discipline of the new economy.

Bachelors, who might also be members of the working class, constituted an especially important contingent of the sporting fraternity. From both the countryside and Europe more men than women swarmed into the growing cities. In New Orleans in 1840, for example, men between the ages of twenty and fifty outnumbered women two to one. Even in 1860, six thousand more males than females resided in the city. Nationwide, the percentage of bachelors in the nineteenth century was much higher than today. By mid-century nearly 40 percent of the men between the ages of twenty-five and thirty-five were unmarried; after that date, the percentages slowly declined.[21] In most cases, bachelors suffered from fewer social restraints than married men. Without ties to wives or traditional homes, many of them sought friendship and excitement at the brothels, gambling halls, billiard rooms, cockpits, boxing rings, or the race tracks.

While most of the sporting fraternity came from the rank and file, a small number of wealthy men sometimes played conspicuous roles in the world of commercial pastimes. A hedonistic fringe of the upper-income ranks might promote and furnish the stakes for sporting spectacles. As in the colonial era, enthusiasm for sporting ventures was much more common in New York than in Philadelphia or Boston. The son of a Boston Brahmin or a Philadelphia "Main Line" family risked social ostracism for wagering at the race track or staking a prize fight. The elites in New York and throughout much of the South, on the other hand, continued to copy English gentry behavior. Sport slumming—participation in the low sports of the common people—had been long popular with a segment of the young gentry in England. Thomas Jefferson blamed the English for the tendency of young American "gentlemen" to gamble, drink excessively, patronize prostitutes, and frequent the sporting activities of the underworld. If the young American "goes to England," Jefferson wrote, "he learns drinking, horse racing, and boxing. These are the peculiarities of English education." In addition, "he acquires a fondness for European luxury and dissipation, and a contempt for the simplicity of his own country.... He is led, by the strongest of human passions, into a spirit of

[20]Gutman, "Work, Culture and Society," 551–53, 554–55.
[21]Paul Jacobson, *American Marriage and Divorce* (New York: Holt, Rinehart, 1959), pp. 34–35; Dale A. Somers, *The Rise of Sports in New Orleans, 1850–1900* (Baton Rouge, La.: Louisiana State University Press, 1972), pp. 52–53. For a description of bachelor boarding-house life in New York, see J.S. Buckingham, *America, Historical, Statistical, and Descriptive*, 3 vols. (London: Fisher, 1841), I, 232–35.

female intrigue...or a passion for whores, destructive of his health, and in both cases learns to consider fidelity to the marriage bed as an ungentlemanly practice...."[22]

Many of Jefferson's worst fears materialized. For England continued to exercise a profound influence over the sporting life of the new nation.[23] Achievement of political independence had not resulted in cultural independence. In questions of taste and style, in the arts, in pastimes, and in fashions and behavior, England remained the model to which many Americans looked for guidance. Throughout the nineteenth century, the English, who preceded the Americans in organizing sporting ventures, virtually dictated the character of American sport. Americans conducted their horse races in strict accordance with the rules at New Market, their prize fights by the London prize ring rules, and copied the latest London modes of wagering on contests. England furnished nearly all of the sporting equipment of the new republic; almost all of the sporting books, magazines, and prints came from England. Even *The Spirit of the Times,* a pioneering sporting sheet founded in New York in 1831, gave extensive space to the latest sporting news from Great Britain and modeled itself after *Bell's Life* in London. By the 1820s a bevy of English athletes regularly visited the United States to demonstrate their skills and compete for stakes; soon American athletes began to frequent English shores for the same purpose. In fact, the American sporting fraternity would come to constitute a part of a larger subculture that extended to both sides of the Atlantic.

COMMERCIAL SPECTACLES

The commercialized diversions of the fancy ranged in respectability from the blood sports and prize fighting at the bottom to pedestrianism at the top, though none of them, of course, won the full approval of proper Victorians. In eighteenth-century England, prize fighting had gained something of a popular following, especially among the younger sons of the nobility and the riffraff, but prize fights in the American colonies had been rare. In the South and along the frontier a few accounts survive of men who engaged in "rough and tumble" fighting, a form of fighting which might involve kicking, biting, kneeing, hair-pulling, "gouging"— tearing the opponent's eye out of its socket—and "balloching" or "Abelarding" (emasculation). There are also several undocumented legends of planters who pitted their best fighting slaves against those of neighboring plantations. One instance may have been Tom Molyneux (spellings vary), allegedly a Virginia slave who won his freedom in about 1800 by defeating a fellow slave. Upon release from bondage, Molyneux eventually appeared in New York City where he fought a few impromptu matches sponsored by

---

[22]Quoted in Henry Steele Commager, ed., *Living Ideas in America,* new ed. (New York: Harper & Row, 1964), pp. 555–56.

[23]See especially, Jennie Holliman, *American Sports, 1785–1835* (Durham, N.C.: Seaman Press, 1931), pp. 5–10.

the free, sporting black men of the city. The American press gave Molyneux some attention in 1810 when he was bested in London by the reigning English champion, Tom Cribb. Molyneux continued to fight in England, but never returned to the United States. From time to time English and Irish pugilists visited American shores for bouts, boxing exhibitions, and to give lessons in boxing for a fee. Efforts of these early pugilists to interest young men of the upper income ranks in learning sparring skills generally failed. Until the 1850s the popularity of formal prize fighting in the United States lagged far behind Great Britain.

Prize fighting, perhaps more than any other commercial sporting endeavor, aroused the ire of Victorians. Respectable people especially condemned pugilism for its brutality. Under the existing Broughton (1743) and London (1838) prize ring rules, fighters fought with their bare fists; wrestling skills and brute strength were more important to success than finesse in boxing. A round ended only when a man was struck down by an opponent's fists, thrown to the turf with a wrestling hold, or deliberately fell to the ground to avoid further punishment. Once downed, a fighter had thirty seconds to recover before "toeing the mark," or "coming to scratch," terms which referred to a line drawn through the center of the ring. A fight ended only when a fighter was unable to come to scratch or conceded defeat. Sometimes the contests were farces with neither fighter forcing the action, but on other occasions the fights could be exceedingly brutal. Philip Hone reported a bout in which two sluggers "thumped and battered each other for the gratification of a brutal gang of spectators" for nearly two hours until, after being floored eighty-one times, one of the fighters fell dead.[24]

The Victorians also condemned prize fighting for the motley, disorderly crowds which it attracted. Fights were illegal everywhere, so the fancy had to schedule them in remote places—in the backrooms of saloons, on barges, or in remote rural areas—and be ever watchful of vigilant legal authorities. In New York City, the center of pugilism, both fighters and spectators typically boarded barges at a secret rendezvous on the harbor; tugs then pulled the barges up the Hudson River to a secluded spot, where a ring was quickly staked. Wagerers often disrupted the match; those who sensed that their bets were in jeopardy sometimes joined the fray by swinging their fists, flashing Bowie knives, or brandishing pistols. Philip Hone reported in 1842:

> The amusement of prize fighting...has become one of the most fashionable abominations of our loafer-ridden city. Several matches have been made lately. The parties, their backers, bettors, and abettors...have been following

[24]Nevins, ed., *Diary of Philip Hone*, II, 620. For early prize fighting see Alexander Johnston, *Ten and Out!*, 3rd ed. (New York: Ives Washburn, 1947), and Nat Fleischer, *The Heavyweight Championship*, rev. ed. (New York: G.P. Putnam's Sons, 1961). The early history of prize fighting is rich in legend but sparse in documentation. Because of the nature of the sources and the tendencies of the standard histories to repeat errors, readers should be especially cautious. Adelman, "The Development of Modern Athletics," 559ff., provides an account of boxing in New York City up to 1870 based upon a careful reading of the newspapers of the day.

the champions to Staten Island, Westchester, and up the North River, out of the jurisdiction (as was supposed) of the authorities of New York; and the horrid details, with all their disgusting technicalities and vulgar slang, have been regularly presented in the New York *Herald* to gratify the vitiated palates of its readers, whilst the orderly citizens have wept for the shame which they could not prevent.[25]

The fancy also patronized commercialized billiards. Billiards developed a dual character, one springing from the "rich and the well-born," the other from the Victorian subculture. As noted in Hall's short story written in the midst of the controversy swirling around the purchase of President Adams' billiard table, public billiard halls attracted mostly the riffraff and a few well-to-do young slummers. The "gentleman's" game, on the other hand, was played in private residences or in exclusive men's clubs.[26]

Beginning in the 1850s Michael Phelan, the sport's "dominant personality and promoter in America," attempted to popularize and improve the image of billiards. Nationwide attention focused on the first billiard "championship" of the United States held in 1859 at Fireman's Hall in Detroit. The two contestants, Michael Phelan and John Seereiter, played before a large "genteel audience," which included several ladies. The terms of the match involved unusually large sums of money, a $5,000 side bet plus $5,000 by the promoters and a portion of the gate receipts to the winner. Play began at 7:30 P.M. and lasted until five o'clock the next morning. Seereiter had the highest run, but Phelan won the match and walked away with a reported sum of $15,000. Phelan, author of several books on billiards, remained the most active promoter of the sport until his death in 1871. Never again did championship billiard matches attract as much public attention or betting. Moreover, public billiard parlors never gained complete respectability among middle-income groups.

A somewhat higher level of respectability was accorded to the activities of John Cox Stevens, the premier of New York City's world of sport in the early nineteenth century. The son of a wealthy New Jersey lawyer, speculator, merchant, and inventor, Stevens married into the "aristocratic" Livingston family of New York. Stevens spent a lifetime being a bon vivant. He, along with a group of fast-moving friends, engaged in a constant round of expensive parties, extravagant balls, and dazzling excursions. Philip Hone compared the elaborate full course dinners given by Stevens with those prepared at the "Palais Bourbon in Paris."[27] Along with good friends, French cuisine, and imported wines, Stevens loved competition. Despite his father's hostility to gambling, Stevens liked to flavor his ventures into yacht, horse, and foot races with heavy wagers. In New York, Stevens helped make the sporting life popular and acceptable among those in the highest strata of society.

Stevens first attracted the attention of the sporting world by his

[25]Nevins, ed., *Diary of Philip Hone*, II, 620.

[26]See esp. Polsky, *Hustlers, Beats, and Others*, Chap. 1.

[27]Nevins, ed., *Diary of Philip Hone*, II, 861. For a biographical sketch of Stevens see *National Cyclopedia of American Biography* (New York: Century, 1928), I, 447.

involvement in horse racing. The American Revolution had temporarily halted racing, but after the war the turf quickly began to resume its traditional popularity. The center of thoroughbred racing gradually shifted from the Tidewater region of Virginia and Maryland to New York City and the Southwest, especially the states of Kentucky and Tennessee. Unlike other sporting spectacles of the era, horse racing by the 1830s was highly organized with regular racing schedules. The Panic of 1837 (a sharp economic downturn) and the increasing sectional tensions between the North and the South severely set back racing, but the turf rebounded in a more prosperous form after the Civil War.

Stevens wagered heavily on American Eclipse in the "race of the century" held at the Union Course on Long Island in 1823. So certain were Stevens and one of his brothers of victory "that, after their purses were exhausted, they took their watches from their pockets and diamond breast-pins from the bosoms, and bet them on the result."[28] Fortunately for Stevens, American Eclipse, a northern horse, bested Sir Henry from the South in two of three four-mile heats. From 50,000 to 100,000 fans had watched the race. Stevens, joined by the Livingstons, purchased Eclipse (for $10,000) and Sir Henry (for $3,000). Stevens put the two horses out for stud at his Hoboken Stables.

In 1831 Stevens and his brother opened a large amusement park, called the Elysian Fields, on their waterfront estate at Hoboken. At a "fête champêtre" given by the Stevens brothers to advertise the fields, two hundred "gentlemen" attended, including the New York City mayor and aldermen. Later in the day the New York and Jersey City boat clubs, their members "dressed in white jackets and trousers, round ship's hats, and checked shirts," came to share the "abundant champagne" and plentiful gourmet food.[29] Conveniently located across the river from New York City, the Elysian Fields became a center of the area's sporting life. It was the home at one time or another of the New York Yacht Club, the St. George's Cricket Club, the country's first organized baseball matches, and the playing area of the New York Athletic Club. Initially, the fields offered a retreat mainly for the rich, but eventually thousands of ordinary pleasure seekers crossed the Hudson every weekend in the summer months to enjoy its delights.

Stevens was also one of the first promoters of professional foot-racing, or pedestrianism, as the sport was then called. In the 1820s a few sportsmen, taking their cues from England, had offered small purses for both long distance runners and walkers. Stevens shocked the sporting set in 1835 by offering $1,000 to any pedestrian who could run ten miles in less than one hour; if only one runner accomplished the feat he would be awarded an additional $300. The race had grown out of a wager between

[28]Archibald Douglas Turnbull, *John Stevens: An American Record* (New York: Century, 1928), p. 486.

[29]Nevins, ed., *The Diary of Philip Hone*, I, 46. See also Brian Danforth, "Hoboken and the Affluent New Yorker's Search for Recreation," *New Jersey History*, 95 (Autumn 1977), 133–44, and Harry B. Weiss and Grace M. Weiss, *Early Sports and Pastimes in New Jersey* (Trenton, N.J.: Past Time, 1960), pp. 92–94, 98.

Stevens and a friend, Samuel L. Gouveneur. Stevens insured that even if he lost his bet and the purse, he would turn a profit. He encouraged the newspapers to report the feats of English runners, advertised freely, attracted an international field of peds, and charged an admission.

The Great Race proved almost as spectacular as earlier horse races. At least 20,000 persons crowded into the stands, the infield, and onto the track of the Union Race Course. Of the nine runners in the field the heavy bettors favored four: Henry Stannard, a farmer from Connecticut who wore black pantaloons and flesh-colored slippers and had been in serious training for a month prior to the event; George Glauer, a Prussian who was attired in white silk and pink shoes; Patrick Mahoney, a butcher from County Kerry, Ireland, who was dressed in a green shirt with black slippers; and Isaac Downes, a young upstate New Yorker. A black athlete, Francis Smith, wanted to run, but was disqualified on the grounds that he had not met the filing date. Mahoney set a torrid pace for the first five miles; five of the nine runners reached the halfway mark in less than one half hour. After seven miles only the four favorite peds were still in the

Deerfoot, the famous Seneca pedestrian, 1835. Lithograph.

field. To the delight of the pro-American crowd, Stannard pulled away from the others and finished in 59 minutes and 48 seconds. Stannard was the only runner to finish in less than one hour. After his victory, he promptly mounted a horse, rode around the track to the cheers of spectators, and made a short victory speech.[30]

The interest aroused by the Great Race of 1835, nationalistic rivalries promoted by pedestrianism, and the wagering potentialities of footracing all helped make pedestrianism the most popular sport of the antebellum era. In 1844 the owners of the Beacon (horse) Race Course in Hoboken, New Jersey, staged a spectacular series of long-distance races that won national and international attention. For the first race, which attracted a large field of peds competing for a purse of $1,000, the New York *Herald* noted that "nothing is talked of now, in the sport circle, but this race," while the *Spirit of the Times* predicted that "all the world and his wife will be assembled." An estimated 30,000 spectators did attend. For the next race the promoters exploited ethnic and nationalistic sentiments. They lured 37 peds into the field, including three Englishmen, three Irishmen, and John Steeprock, a Seneca Indian. To the delight of the spectators, John Gildersleeve, a New York chairbuilder, won. "It was a trial of the Indian against the white man, on the point in which the red man most boasts his superiority," wrote an American newspaper reporter. "It was the trial of the peculiar American *physique* against the long held supremacy of the English muscular endurance."[31] Unfortunately for this interpretation, English peds proceeded to win the next three races at the Beacon course.

The excitement generated at the Beacon Course races of 1844 touched off a nationwide enthusiasm for pedestrianism. "During the next ten to fifteen years," noted an observer, "there were more athletes competing and more races than ever before. People in virtually every state in the union attended professional footraces."[32] Promoters devised all sorts of ingenious races. Sometimes runners ran against time, sometimes against both time and other runners, and sometimes even against a horse (with the human given a headstart). Sprints, hurdle races, and walking contests also took place. Besides prize money offered by promoters, the professional peds issued challenges in the sporting journals. A carnival-like atmosphere usually surrounded the races, and sometimes those wagering on the contests resorted to force in an attempt to insure that their favorite ped won.

Betting, charges of "fixes" or "hippodroming," and general rowdiness gave the sport an increasingly unsavory reputation. The Civil War also set back the growth of the sport. In the 1870s, long-distance running again drew large crowds, especially in New York City. Popularly known as "go-as-you-please" races, the peds attempted to cover as many miles as they could on an indoor track within a set time, usually six days. In six days the peds

[30]See George Moss, "The Long Distance Runners in Ante-Bellum America," *Journal of Popular Culture*, 8 (Fall 1974), 370–82.

[31]Quotations in this paragraph are from Adelman, "The Development of Modern Athletics," 533, 534.

[32]Quoted in ibid., 535.

sometimes covered over 500 miles. In the 1880s, professional footracing declined rapidly, to be replaced in popularity by the amateur track and field contests of the great metropolitan athletic clubs.

Rowing had its origins in the colonial era. Workers in rivers and harbors along the Eastern seaboard sometimes competed, and in the early nineteenth century newspapers began to carry notices of their races. An international race in 1824 stimulated nationwide interest. George Harris, captain of a British frigate, matched his crew of rowers against the Whitehall boatmen of New York City for a stake of $1,000. The British crew, which had won eight races in the West Indies and was supposed to have no rivals on the Thames, lost to the Americans by 300 yards. (Unlike modern shells, the crafts used ranged from eighteen to twenty-seven feet in length and were usually manned by four oarsmen.) Some 20,000 to 50,000 spectators assembled along the Hudson River, and large sums of money exchanged hands among the many wagerers. By the 1830s a virtual boating mania swept the country. "The beauty and the fashion of the city were there," according to an account of a regatta held in Louisville on July 4, 1839, "ladies and gentlemen, loafers and laborers, white folks and 'niggers'. . .and all the paraphernalia of city life. . .formed the constituent parts of the heterogeneous mass that stood jammed and crowded upon the levee."[33]

Unlike pedestrianism, rowing featured both professional and amateur oarsmen. In 1834 New York City amateur clubs, composed exclusively of wealthy "young men of fashion," formed the Castle Garden Amateur Boat Club Association. The association sought to be a regulatory body; it expressly forbade "any club to row for money, or take part in a Regatta or Races with any club or clubs independent of those belonging to the Association." The Association's annual regatta, "attended by the city's elites," Melvin Adelman has concluded, "was as much a display of fashion as it was a display of skill. Each club appeared with its distinct colors and uniforms, and every year the Wave Club, the best crew and quite possibly the wealthiest, came with a new boat constructed by Clarkson Crotus, the leading builder of the day."[34] Nonetheless, enthusiasm for rowing among the city's elites was short-lived; in 1842 the Castle Garden association scheduled its last regatta.

In the mid-1850s rowing was again revived, led initially by professional oarsmen. Professional races usually involved single or double sculls, but regattas in the East sometimes included four-oared barges and six-oared lapstreak gigs. In New York City in the late 1850s, huge throngs, often estimated at 10,000 or more, witnessed the annual regattas of the Empire City Regatta Club and the New York Regatta Club, two organizations formed to promote professional racing. In the East an informal, professional racing circuit of sorts developed. As in the case of the pedestrians,

[33]*Spirit of the Times*, July 10, 1839.
[34]Adelman, "The Development of Modern Athletics," 482. For the early history of American rowing, see, apart from Adelman, Robert F. Kelley, *American Rowing: Its Background and Traditions* (New York: Putnam's, 1932) and Charles A. Peverelly, *Book of American Pastimes* (New York: the author, 1866).

professional scullers often published challenges in the newspapers. After the Civil War, amateur rowing, rooted this time in both private clubs and the nation's colleges, began to supplant professional rowing in popularity.

The existence of commercial spectacles, especially in New York City, is likely to give an exaggerated view of the importance of sport in the life of the new republic. An English guidebook published in 1840 was essentially correct when it reported that prospective immigrants to the United States could expect "none of those sports, pastimes, amusements, and recreation such as he has become accustomed to in his country, as cricket, quoits, rackets, five &c., although many attempts have been made on the part of the 'old country' people to establish them. . . ."[35] James Silk Buckingham, an English traveler, reported from Boston in 1838 that physical training was absent from the schools and that, unlike England, "the vigorous exercise required for the young, in cricket, hoop, foot-ball, running, leaping, wrestling, &c., is almost unknown."[36] For the most part the wealthy of the new republic refused to become a leisure class; they simply declined to live ostentatiously or engage in expensive pastimes. By 1850 many of them had begun to resort to fashionable summer places, particularly in Newport, Rhode Island, and Saratoga Springs, New York. At these "watering holes" they engaged in very little physical activity, the most strenuous being an occasional game of billiards, card playing, cheering at the race track, fishing, and cigar smoking. Women spent much of their time gossiping, crocheting, or, if single, slowly promenading along the sidewalks.

Neither did the members of the middle-income groups endanger their health with too much physical exertion. As the principal supporters of Victorianism, they rarely played cards or danced, for they considered such activities immoral. Women of all social ranks were expected to be models of physical inactivity. In reality, the wives of workingmen put in long, grueling hours of monotonous labor, but this situation did not correspond to the Victorian ideal. One sarcastic commentator summed up the prevailing attitude toward the role of women both as athletes and ministers. "A woman properly educated and with feeling suitable to her sex, would as soon be. . .in the pulpit" as "pitching quoits or engaged in a game of nine-pins." "Womanhood," he wrote, "is as lovely in one place as the other."[37]

Nonetheless, by 1850 the preconditions for a sport "take-off" were present. The nation ranked next to England in terms of per capita wealth, a transportation and communication revolution was underway, the increased application of machinery to production promised more leisure time, and large cities dotted the landscape. The society was exceptionally fluid and impersonal. And already present was a thriving sporting

[35]Quoted in Rowland Tappon Berthoff, *British Immigrants in Industrial America, 1790–1950* (Cambridge: Harvard University Press, 1953), p. 149.

[36]Buckingham, *America*, III, 435.

[37]Quoted in Robert Riegel, *Young America, 1830–1840* (Norman: University of Oklahoma Press, 1949), p. 347.

fraternity that offered an alternate life style to the strictures of Victorianism. The Victorians themselves had begun to reconsider their animosity toward sport. Increasingly they condemned explicitly only those sports which were associated with gambling, drinking, and spectatorship, in short those associated with the sporting fraternity. They came to tolerate "innocent" amusements, at least if the amusements refreshed men for their more important responsibilities. A few Victorians were even beginning to encourage certain forms of sport among the young. After about 1840 a great outpouring of childrearing and moral guidance literature urged exercise and the playing of specific sports (although sport was a minor theme of the guidebooks) as character-building enterprises.[38] In the Age of the Player, the middle-income groups following the leadership of the social elites would eventually find in sport both a means of building subcommunities and of socializing the young. Ironically, sport then became an agency for reinforcing traditional Victorian values.

[38]See Adelman, "The Development of Modern Athletics," Chap. 11; John A. Lucas, "A Prelude to Sport: Ante-Bellum America, 1850–1860," *Quest,* 11 (December 1968), 50–57; Roberta J. Park, "The Attitudes of Leading New England Transcendentalists Toward Healthful Exercise, Recreation and Proper Care of the Body, 1830–1850," *Journal of Sport History,* 4 (Spring 1977), 34–50; Guy Lewis, "The Muscular Christianity Movement," *Journal of Health, Physical Education and Recreation,* 27 (May 1966), 27–28, 42; and Peter Levine, "The Promise of Sport in Ante Bellum America" (unpublished paper delivered at Brockport Conference on the Comparative Social History of Sport and Leisure, October 6–7, 1978).

Part Two

The Age of the Player,
1850-1920

The widespread application of industrial technology to production after 1850 intensified changes that were already underway. More Americans lived in cities, their lives dictated by high-speed machinery and the ticking clock. In the cities they increasingly found themselves segregated by space, ethnicity, race, religion, and income. Communication became even more impersonal. The telegraph, telephone, typewriter, daily newspapers, and interoffice memos all signified the decline of direct oral communication. For many Americans per capita income increased dramatically; they had more money and perhaps more time for leisure. Yet both workingmen and businessmen were more dependent upon the performance of a rapidly growing, ricocheting, unregulated economic system. The Industrial Revolution encouraged the further release of the individual from the oppressive traditions and institutions of the past—from a place, the state, a rigid class system, larger kinship groups, and the church. Individualism triumphed as the dominant social persuasion of the American people.

Yet a new social order emerged, one built largely upon the nurture of individual self-restraint and innumerable voluntary associations. The majority of Americans—middle-income groups with a Victorian temperament—continued to preach and practice prudence, saving, hard work, time-consciousness, and deferred gratification. In addition, many groups found in the "buzzing complex of strictly exclusive, yet voluntary"* organizations a means of establishing small subcommunities within the larger society. Americans formed voluntary societies for every conceivable purpose: for joint political action, social reform, religious worship, social fraternization, and the preservation of occupational prerogatives. Through the formation of voluntary associations, ethnic, racial, and status identities could be preserved or enhanced, children could be socialized in the old ways, and proper group behavior could be defined and enforced. Often local organizations formed national associations of their fellows. It then became possible for a person to find congenial colleagues anywhere in the nation. As the Age of the Player came to a close, yet another emerging order could be identified; it rested largely upon consumption, the mass media, professional expertise, and bureaucratic structures.

Urbanization, technological innovations, rising per capita incomes, and the new social and cultural milieu combined in complex ways to trigger a sports revolution and a new era of American sport, The Age of the Player.

*H. H. Gerth and C. Wright Mills, trans. and eds., *From Max Weber: Essays in Sociology* (New York: Oxford University Press, 1958), p. 310.

A set of dates suggests one dimension of the revolution: New York Knickerbocker Baseball Club organized (1845); first intercollegiate athletic contest (1852); New York Athletic Club founded (1866); first all-professional baseball club (1869); National League of professional baseball formed (1876); Amateur Athletic Union organized (1888); basketball invented by James A Naismith (1891); revival of the modern Olympic Games (1896); first modern "World Series" (1903); Intercollegiate Athletic Association of the United States (NCAA) founded (1905); Johnson-Jeffries prize fight (1910). While the players themselves took the initiative in organizing, managing, and financing many of these sports, separate worlds of sport sprang up for the social elites, the sons of the elites, the "outsiders," and, at the turn of the century, the sons of middle-income groups. Each universe of sport reflected the needs, values, and aspirations of its respective patrons. Thus each has a unique history.

3

The Insiders

The "privileged" spectator at the U.S. Amateur Golf Championships, 1898. *Outing* 33 (November 1898), 136.

In the 1880s the "Old Guard," the original members of the New York Athletic Club (NYAC), angrily protested the decision of the club to "go social." To them, the club, by seeking the admission of the city's most prominent men and by building a lavish clubhouse, had departed from the intentions of the founders. No longer would the club's primary focus be upon athletics. "The social element in the clubs is like 'dry rot'...," exclaimed Frederick W. Janssen. "[It] soon causes them to fail in the purpose for which they are organized.... Palatial clubhouses are erected at great cost and money is spent in adorning them that, if used to beautify athletic grounds and improve tracks, would cause a widespread interest in athletic sports and further the development of the wind and muscles of American youths."[1] The efforts of the Old Guard to stem the growing social orientation of the club were futile. Many of them, including William B. "Father Bill" Curtis, a founder and former president of the NYAC, resigned their memberships.

The conflict between the "social element" and the Old Guard of the NYAC illustrated a source of fundamental tension in the sporting world of the "insiders." The tension arose between an adherence to a player-centered ethos by the Old Guard and the use of sport as a status-enhancing mechanism by the social element. Simply to provide themselves with the opportunity to participate in sports, the players had formed the first clubs, codified the rules, and initially managed the games. Yet in a society characterized by an exceptionally fluid social structure, even the players recognized the potential of sport clubs as agencies of status ascription. Participation in sport, even if only as a "social" member of an athletic club, might assist in marking one as a member of an upper-status set; it could become one means of building a status subcommunity within the larger society. The tension between a player-centered ethos on the one hand and the social functions of the elite athletic clubs on the other provides an important key to understanding much of the history of the sporting world of the insiders.

THE VOLUNTARY ASSOCIATION

The formation of sport clubs by the social elite in the latter half of the nineteenth century was only one phase of the larger rage for voluntary

[1]Frederick W. Janssen, *History of Amateur Athletics* (New York: Charles R. Bourne, 1885), p. 103. See also Bob Considine and Fred B. Jarvis, *The First Hundred Years: A Portrait of NYAC* (London: Macmillan, 1969), pp.18–20.

associations. As early as the 1830s voluntary associations became a striking feature of American society. Alexis de Tocqueville observed that "In no country in the world has the principle of association been more successfully used or applied to a greater multitude of objects than in America...."[2] A contemporary of Tocqueville believed that since Americans had destroyed "classes, and corporate bodies of every kind, and come to simple direct individualism," the vacuum had been filled by the "production of voluntary associations to an immense extent." Although many of the organizations were temporary, designed to accomplish only a specific purpose, they provided a "noble and expansive feeling which identifies self with community."[3] The clubs sorted out persons according to any criteria they chose: it might be common interests, sex, ethnicity, occupation, religion, status, or a combination thereof. Likeminded men found in voluntary associations a milieu by which they could counter the impersonality of the new society.

The voluntary association became one of several means by which Americans sought to replace the old village style of life with new subcommunities. In addition to voluntary societies, important considerations for determining the membership of a subcommunity could be living in a particular neighborhood, marriage into a proper family, belonging to a certain religious denomination, and attending specific educational institutions. For example, essential to becoming a member of a high-status community might be living in a section of the city with others of a similar income range, enjoying a common ethnicity and religious preference (old-stock American and Protestant Episcopal), and attendance at the "right" schools (a New England boarding school and an Ivy League college). Birth into an old family continued to provide a person with advantages in obtaining membership in a status community, but less so than it had in the eighteenth century.

The status community was a product of status equals who wanted to close their ranks to those whom they considered inferior. Withdrawal and exclusion seemed to be the only feasible strategies for the wealthy to demonstrate their achievements and "superior" family connections. In their clubs the elites or would-be elites sought to promote a specific style of life that would exclude outsiders. The style usually included a code of honor, a particular mode of dress and speech, a "proper" education, pursuit of appropriate sports, and a host of in-group behavioral nuances. Men of new wealth were especially avid in seeking membership in the inner circle for themselves and their children. They sent their boys to the schools at which they would meet proper friends and learn the habits appropriate to their status. For example, Edward H. Harriman, the railroad baron, went to work at the age of fourteen but sent his sons to Groton and Yale;

[2]Alexis de Tocqueville, *Democracy in America*, Philips Bradley, ed. 2 vols. (New York: Knopf, 1951), II, 191.

[3]Quoted in Walter S. Glazer, "Participation and Power: Voluntary Associations and the Functional Organization in Cincinnati in 1840," *Historical Methods Newsletter*, 5 (September 1972), 153.

H.J. Heinz, another self-made millionaire, sent his son to Yale; and John D. Rockefeller's children attended Brown and Vassar.

The private clubs served as accurate barometers of different levels of nineteenth-century status communities. At the apex of the status structure in large American cities were metropolitan men's clubs, such as the Philadelphia founded in 1835, the Union in New York (1836), the Century in New York (1847), and the Somerset in Boston (1851). The members of these clubs dominated the social and economic life of their respective cities. Usually composed of older men, these clubs did not promote sport. After the Civil War, the Union Leagues, centers of Republican respectability, and the University clubs, composed of the graduates of prestigious colleges, ranked slightly below the patrician metropolitan clubs. Neither the University clubs nor Union Leagues considered sport an important part of club life. On the third rung of the upper-status layer of the American club structure were the athletic clubs. These clubs originated with younger men who shared a common interest in sports. In due time the athletic clubs, cricket clubs (in Philadelphia), and racquet clubs became important instruments of status ascription and sometimes served as a stepping stone to membership in the metropolitan clubs.

That the American social elite often turned to sport clubs as a means of forming status communities should occasion no surprise. Only those with wealth could play the games that demanded expensive equipment, immense acreage, a staff of assistants, and an abundance of leisure time. Participation in "appropriate" sports helped mark one as a member of an upper status set. Furthermore, participation in sport per se did not threaten any deeply held personal beliefs that might otherwise divide members of the elite. Athletic activity, which is necessarily subordinated to rules, encouraged a temporary equality among the participants; it strengthened the bonds between the athletes and facilitated direct communications. The sport club could also be used to socialize youth in proper behavior and to discipline the membership.

The sudden rise of sport in England in the middle decades of the nineteenth century decisively influenced the American elite. Would-be American aristocrats had always been inclined to ape the latest fashions of the English upper classes. Prior to the 1850s the English gentlemen's leisure activities consisted largely of country weekend excursions, balls, riding to the hounds, a bit of cricket, horse racing, and plenty of gambling and hard drinking. Beginning in the 1850s many of the upper-class Englishmen were caught up in the organized sports movement—forming hundreds of clubs for cricket, athletics (track and field), football, rowing, cycling, yachting, lawn tennis, and eventually golf. In almost every case the English sportsmen preceded the Americans by a decade or so in giving their sports organized form.[4]

---

[4]See George Birmingham, "The American at Home and in His Club," in Henry Steele Commager, ed., *America in Perspective* (New York: New American Library, 1947), p. 175 and Bruce E. Haley, "Sports and the Victorian World," *Western Humanities Review*, 22 (Spring 1968), 115–25.

Of America's three largest cities in the nineteenth century, New York assumed the leadership of the world of elite sports. From colonial times the city's high society had been more tolerant of sport than their counterparts in Philadelphia or Boston. Moreover, in the nineteenth century the New York elites developed in a quite different manner than in the other two cities. In all three places a residue of the colonial elite joined with new men in the late eighteenth and early nineteenth centuries to exploit the immense new opportunities presented in foreign trade, real estate, banking, law, and politics. But unlike New York, the Boston-Philadelphia "mercantile-Federalist" elites founded virtual dynasties. Their descendants managed to perpetuate their inherited status; they continued to dominate the industrial, financial, and cultural activities of their respective cities. To this day the Boston Brahmin and Philadelphia Main Line families retain a large share of the power, property, and prestige of their respective cities. On the other hand, the tremendous surge of population growth, commerce, railroad building, and the growth of the factory system in the latter half of the nineteenth century fractured the old New York elite. "Separate enclaves dominated trade, politics, culture, and fashion, although some common membership existed among these groups."[5] The absence of a clear-cut dynasty or social arbitrator in New York gave rise to the "beautiful people" in the post-Civil War era. The "smart set" or Four Hundred believed that status derived primarily from reputation, that is, upon highly publicized activities available only to the super wealthy. Sport furnished them with one convenient means of self-advertisement.

However, the New York Yacht Club, the first major voluntary sport organization of the city (excluding horse racing as a sport), originated among the families of the older elite. The ubiquitous John Cox Stevens, who was a former president of the Union Club and the city's foremost horseman, founded the yacht club aboard his schooner, *Gimcrack,* on July 30, 1844. After drawing up the bylaws for the club and electing Stevens commodore, the original nine members promptly set sail for Newport, Rhode Island. The wealthy founders were soon joined by a "succession of gentlemen ranking high in the social and financial circles" of the city.[6] Membership in the club came to be equivalent to acceptance in the very top rung of the New York elite. Club members had to pay dues of forty dollars the first year and ten dollars thereafter. Stevens erected a handsome gothic clubhouse at the Elysian Fields in Hoboken, where the club held regular

---

[5]Frederic Cople Jaher, "Style and Status: High Society in Late Nineteenth-Century New York," in Jaher, ed., *The Rich, the Well Born, and the Powerful: Elites and Upper Classes in History* (Urbana: University of Illinois Press, 1973), p. 259. See also Jaher, "The Boston Brahmins in the Age of Industrial Capitalism," in Jaher, ed., *The Age of Industrialism in America: Essays in Social Structure and Cultural Values* (New York: Free Press, 1968), pp. 188–263; Jaher, "Nineteenth-Century Elites in Boston and New York," *Journal of Social History,* 6 (Fall 1972), 32–77; E. Digby Baltzell, *Philadelphia Gentlemen: The Making of a National Upper Class* (New York: Free Press, 1958).

[6]Charles A. Peverelly, *The Book of American Pastimes* (New York: the author, 1866), p. 19.

53

balls and feasts, with turtle being the favorite dish. The club prescribed expensive uniforms and sponsored extensive social cruises to such spots as Bar Harbor, Maine, and Cape Hatteras, North Carolina. Each year the club held a gala regatta off the clubhouse promontory. In the late nineteenth century the club's annual regatta at Newport became the "social event" of the summer season.

In 1851, Stevens, the longtime commodore of the club, organized a syndicate to build a special boat for the express purpose of challenging members of the Royal Yacht Squadron of Great Britain to a race. George Steers, a young shipbuilder, designed and supervised the construction of the yacht, christened *America*. On August 22 the *America* easily defeated eighteen British yachts in a race around the Isle of Wight to win a coveted cup donated by the Royal Yacht Squadron. Queen Victoria visited the yacht and congratulated Stevens on the Yankee performance. The victory by the New Yorkers over the distinguished British yachtsmen encouraged the formation of exclusive clubs in other cities along the Eastern seaboard. In 1857 the syndicate that owned *America* presented the cup to the New York Yacht Club on the condition that it should be contested for by yachtsmen from abroad. Through 1980, twenty-four international challenge matches had been held for the *America's* cup, all, incidentally, won by American yachts. Over the years, yachting has remained one of the most exclusive of American sports.

From the late 1850s to the late 1870s, James Gordon Bennett, Jr., the colorful and eccentric owner of the New York *Herald,* replaced John Cox Stevens as the major-domo of the New York sporting scene.[7] Bennett's father, a recent Scottish immigrant who had built the *Herald* into the world's most profitable newspaper, had been a social outsider. The younger Bennett, however, used his father's vast fortune and sport as levers to lift himself into fashionable circles. A passionate yachtsman, he became a member of the New York Yacht Club in 1857 at the tender age of sixteen. Nine years later, in 1866, he captured the attention of the entire nation by winning the world's first transatlantic yacht race. The large purse of $60,000 won from side bets and the loss of six members of his crew who were swept overboard in a violent storm added immensely to Bennett's reputation for bravado. In the meantime he sponsored Henry Stanley's exotic search for David Livingston who had been missing for several years in the African jungles. Both Europeans and Americans avidly followed Stanley's reports from the heart of Africa. His eventual success in locating Livingston became the stuff of a monumental legend.

Bennett had a direct influence on several sports. Beginning in 1873 he awarded cups and medals to collegiate track and field champions. While visiting England in 1875, he witnessed a game of polo played by English army officers. In 1876 he imported British mallets and balls and hired an English polo player to teach the game to his rich friends. Shortly thereafter Bennett and his friends formed the Westchester Polo Club in New York

[7]See Donald Seitz, *The James Gordon Bennetts* (Indianapolis: Bobbs-Merrill, 1928) and Richard O'Connor, *The Scandalous Mr. Bennett* (Garden City: Doubleday, 1962).

and took the sport to the Newport summer colony. In 1886 Newport hosted the first international match with the Hurlingham Club of England. Bennett's assistance to the sport of lawn tennis had more bizarre origins. According to legend, in 1878 he secured for a British army officer a guest card to Newport's most exclusive club, the Reading Room. He then dared his friend to ride a horse up the steps of the club's front hall. The Englishman accepted the challenge and the Reading Room immediately revoked Bennett's guest privileges for instigating such a provocative act. Miffed, Bennett retaliated by building a lavish sports complex called the Casino a few blocks away. The Casino subsequently became the site for the first thirty-four national tennis championships.[8]

By 1878 Bennett had departed from New York to live in Paris, an exile caused by a gross indiscretion. In mixed company he had relieved himself into a fireplace at his fiancée's New Year's Day party. His fiancée's family immediately broke the engagement; later her brother publicly attacked and humiliated Bennett, and eventually the two men fought a nonlethal duel. Bennett then left America, forever shunned by New York's Four Hundred. He seldom returned to the United States, but his New York *Herald* led the major dailies in reporting sporting news. Later in the century he contributed to the Olympic movement, and he promoted horse, auto, and air races. Bennett was one of the first of a long line of eccentric millionaires, stretching to Ted Turner in the 1970s, who promoted and popularized sport.

For a dozen years or so, New York City's first "athletic" club seemed little concerned with status.* Inspired by the formation of the London Athletic Club in 1863, the first English amateur championship meet in 1866, and the athletic activities of the New York Caledonian Club, three well-to-do young athletes founded the New York Athletic Club (NYAC) in 1866. Apparently the founders simply wanted an opportunity to engage in track and field with men of similar social standing and congenial interests. (The existing world of track and field was dominated by professional athletes, gamblers, and "rowdies.") All three of the founders belonged to local boating clubs, and they induced several of their fellow rowers to join the NYAC. During inclement weather the athletes worked out in the back parlor of a private residence. On fair days they went to the Elysian Fields or some other open space for running, vaulting, and shot-putting. In 1868 the club incorporated with fourteen members and sponsored the first open amateur track and field meet. Having issued the New York Caledonian Club a special invitation, the meet was hailed as "an international match— America against Scotland."[9]

Soon other clubs—among them the Staten Island, American, Manhat-

---

*"Athletics" in the nineteenth century referred specifically to track and field.

[8]See John Hanlon, "A Posh Game in a Posh Town," *Sports Illustrated*, 31 (September 22, 1969), M3–M4. For the early diffusion of polo see J. B. McMahan, "Polo in the West," *Outing*, 26 (August 1895), 385–91. For tennis see Will Grimsley, *Tennis: Its History, People and Events* (Englewood Cliffs, N.J.: Prentice-Hall, 1971).

[9]Janssen, *History of American Amateur Athletics*, p. 35. See also Considine and Jarvis, *The First Hundred Years*.

tan, Pastime, University, and Crescent clubs, all of New York—organized on the NYAC model. By 1879 Baltimore, Buffalo, Chicago, Detroit, and St. Louis had also established athletic clubs. The New York Athletic Club assumed the leadership role for the new clubs. In the 1870s the club expanded its activities by building the first cinder track in the country at Mott Haven, introducing the use of spiked shoes, and sponsoring the first national amateur championships in track and field (1876), swimming (1877), boxing (1878), and wrestling (1878). In 1878 the NYAC transferred the track and field championships to the newly organized National Association of Amateur Athletes of America. In addition to the individual sports, many of the clubs eventually sponsored football and basketball teams.

Beginning in 1882 the New York Athletic Club no longer functioned as a club devoted exclusively to athletics. The club began to depart from a strictly player-centered orientation. In that year Alfred H. Curtis interested two of the city's wealthiest citizens, Herman Oelrichs and William R. Travers, in the club. Both Oelrichs and Travers were members of an exclusive status network supported by prestigious social clubs; they were also prominent in the Four Hundred. Oelrichs, described by a contemporary as a "social leader" of the city, belonged to the Union and New York Yacht clubs as well as eighteen other clubs. He was a leading patron of "gentleman's sports," being himself a capable swimmer, boxer, and polo player. Travers, a stockbroker, bon vivant, and raconteur, was also a member of the Union and the Yacht Club as well as twenty-four other clubs. With his business partner, Leonard W. Jerome, he was a major promoter of horse racing in the city. The decisions of Oelrichs and Travers to support the club drew into the "club's ranks the most prominent and successful men in New York City and vicinity."[10]

By 1885 New York Athletic Club membership had grown to 1,500. For those seeking admission into the Union or Knickerbocker clubs, membership in the NYAC was highly desirable. The NYAC carefully screened membership applicants, and required a written application with pertinent personal information and the signatures of the members proposing and seconding the nominee for membership. With this information the membership committee could place the applicant within the city's status hierarchy. The initiation fee of $100 and annual dues of $50 also helped weed out undesirables. Athletic clubs could impose other strictures. The University Athletic Club, for example, required that all applicants possess a college degree, preferably from an Ivy League school. Membership in the metropolitan athletic clubs became an important link in a web of associations that constituted an exclusive status community.

With Oelrichs and Travers at the helm, the club rapidly expanded its social activities. In 1885 it completed construction of an elegant five-story, Venetian-style clubhouse at a cost of $150,000, which contained a gymnasium, swimming pool, dining rooms, club rooms, a bowling alley, rifle

---

[10]Malcolm W. Ford, "The New York Athletic Club," *Outing*, 33 (December 1898), 251. See also Considine and Jarvis, *The First Hundred Years*, p. 18.

New York Athletic Club Dining Room. *Outing* 33 (December 1898), 255.

range, billiard room, a superb wine cellar, and sleeping rooms. In 1888 the NYAC acquired a country home at Travers Island where it built a track, clubhouse, boat house, and clay tennis courts. Expanding the membership limit to 2,500 in 1892, the club constructed an even more lavish facility at the corner of 59th Street and 6th Avenue. Several of the other New York clubs attempted to emulate the opulence of the NYAC. Each club established an elaborate social calendar, and most of them sponsored activities for women. "Wine, women, and song," according to the historians of the NYAC, "became more than a catch phrase—they were woven into the texture of NYAC activities."[11] Perhaps the ultimate in social snobbery by the clubs was the practice of allowing spectators at some athletic events by invitation only.

The 1880s and early 1890s marked the heyday of the athletic club. In 1887 an observer reported: "Athletic clubs are now springing into existence in the United States in such profusion as to baffle the effort to enumerate them. Scarce a city can be found having a population of more than 30,000 inhabitants, in which there is not at least one club of this class."[12] While the clubs in smaller cities enjoyed far less commodious facilities than the metropolitan clubs, they were usually made up of the community's wealthiest citizens. In most cases they also sponsored annual track and field competition, although their athletes rarely competed successfully with the larger clubs.

Clubs in Boston, New Orleans, Chicago, and San Francisco rivaled the New York clubs in terms of facilities and membership. In 1893 the Chicago

[11]Considine and Jarvis, *The First Hundred Years*, p. 43.
[12]Henry Hall, ed., *The Tribune Book of Open-Air Sports* (New York: Herald Tribune, 1888), p. 332.

Club, for example, built a nine-story clubhouse costing nearly one million dollars, a structure more costly than any of the New York clubs. Sometimes the clubs sponsored exotic and extravagant shows. In 1895 the Olympic Club in San Francisco put together a detailed reconstruction of Greek and Roman games, complete with a Caesar, courtiers, senators, gladiators, and vestal virgins. Over 4,000 persons attended the event, which cost $2.50 per seat.[13] But the 1890s also brought severe financial problems to many of the clubs. Some had overbuilt and the economic depression of that decade brought about their collapse. After the 1890s the metropolitan athletic club movement never fully recovered, but the early twentieth century witnessed the formation of many less pretentious, smaller clubs whose energies were devoted primarily to sport rather than social exclusion.

Ironically, as the metropolitan athletic clubs became more effective as agencies for the establishment of status communities, their sporting activities became less player-centered. It was this trend that so alarmed the Old Guard of NYAC in the 1880s and led many of them to resign from the club. The active athletes in all of the clubs witnessed a steady diminution in their power. Increasingly, responsibilities for staging and management of athletics shifted from the active players to the social element. (The social element consisted of those club members who were more concerned with the fate of the club as a whole rather than sport per se.) Thus the wider social interests of the clubs began to supersede the interests of the players; the social element tended to view the active players as simply representatives of the clubs. To the social element, sport was primarily a means of enhancing the prestige of the club, not something to be pursued for its own sake. While continuing to espouse a player-centered pristine amateurism, the clubs, in fact, began to engage in intense rivalries with one another, charge gate receipts, and even extend thinly disguised subsidies to star athletes.[14]

The evolution of amateurism reflected the subtle, conflicting forces at work within the sporting world of the insiders. Initially, the clubs seemed unconcerned about insisting upon an amateur-professional distinction. In the early days, many of the club members competed for bets of several hundred dollars. An athlete might run in a match for a $500 side bet one week and compete in his club's closed games a week later for a medal. Threatened with the possibility of an invasion by "professional" athletes and athletes with "inferior" social credentials—working class, ethnics, and blacks—the clubs gradually placed strictures on participants at their meets. For their fall games in 1876, NYAC defined an amateur as "any person who has never competed in an open competition for public or admission money, or with professionals for a prize...nor has at any period in his life taught or assisted in the pursuit of athletic exercises as a means of livelihood."[15] The National Association of Amateur Athletes of America,

[13]See John W. Hipwell, "The Chicago Athletic Club," *Outing*, 33 (November 1898), 145–52 and Arthur Inkersley, "Graeco-Roman Games in California," *Outing*, 25 (November 1898), 145–52.

[14]See Janssen, *History of American Athletics*, p. 103 and Considine and Jarvis, *The First Hundred Years*, pp. 18–20.

[15]*Spirit of the Times*, September 2, 1876.

commonly called the N4A, formed in 1879 by the most exclusive clubs (mostly from metropolitan New York), essentially copied the NYAC definition. At least one athletic club member regretted the exclusion of the less privileged. Frederick Janssen wrote: "The youths who participate in health-giving competitions, as a rule, cannot afford the expense of membership in the so-called Athletic Clubs, and they retire in favor of the wealthy young man whose sole claim to athletic distinction is his connection with a 'high-toned' club."[16]

The more typical opinion was that of Caspar W. Whitney, the dignified sports editor of *Harper's Weekly.* "And what drivelling talk is all this that prates of ignoring the poor 'laborer,'" wrote Whitney, "...and wants to drag him into *our* sport, putting him under restrictions with which he has no sympathy, and paying him for the time he may lose from his trade! What sporting 'Coxeyism'* is this that has neither rhyme nor reason to warrant it serious consideration by intelligent mankind?"[17] If the clubs permitted open professionalism, as Whitney recognized, they could no longer serve as effective agencies of status communities. In short, the clubs had an important vested interest in discrimination. William B. "Father Bill" Curtis, a founder of the NYAC, asserted in 1886 that while the amateur-professional distinction discriminated against lower income groups "the practical point is that under existing laws there has grown up a system of clubs and associations whose best interests, pecuniary and social, would partially or wholly lose their value were the amateur fence to be taken down or even materially lowered. So that, in advocating any radical change, one must fight—not abstract right or wrong—but these interests."[18]

Nonetheless, the amateur code was less restrictive in practice than it was in principle. The American amateur code, unlike its English counterpart, rested neither upon a body of established customs or the sponsorship of an inherited aristocracy. In England centuries of tradition and the perquisites of old wealth had prescribed behavior appropriate to a gentleman and a sportsman. To win at all costs, in particular to exert oneself unduly to obtain victory, was bad form. Work and play were distinctive spheres of gentlemanly activity; no gentleman could claim such a status if he made his living from sport. In contrast to the English upper strata, members of the American athletic clubs, especially those in New York, were often men of new wealth. They usually brought with them the acquisitive values of the marketplace. While paying lip service to the concepts of "fair play" and amateurism, defeating one's rivals by any means within the rules was perfectly consistent with their experiences in the world of commerce and industry. Thus the major metropolitan athletic clubs engaged in intense rivalries to field the strongest bevy of athletes possible and in many cases extended subsidies to the most outstanding athletes. A superior athlete,

---

*In 1894 Jacob Coxey, a self-appointed "General," led an army of a few hundred unemployed men to Washington to support a roads bill that was supposed to put people back to work. The army was quickly dispersed and the leaders arrested on a technicality. But the incident alarmed conservatives everywhere.

[16]Janssen, *History of American Amateur Athletics,* p. 103.

[17]Caspar W. Whitney, *A Sporting Pilgrimage* (New York: Harper & Bros., 1895), p. 208.

[18]Quoted in "General Athletics," *Outing,* 6 (May 1886), 251.

unless he be black, a recent immigrant, or too crude in social demeanor, could expect little difficulty in finding a club that would grant him membership and perhaps other valuable perquisites as well.

Lawrence E. "Lon" Myers, "the world's greatest runner," is an example of the gap between principle and practice.[19] Born in Richmond, Virginia, of Jewish ancestry, Myers had moved with his family to New York where his father had become a successful businessman. Plagued by sickness as a youth, Myers had been urged by a physician to take up athletics. For most of his amateur career, extending from 1878 to 1885, he ran for the Manhattan Athletic Club. His appearance—he stood a mere five feet, seven and three-quarters inches and weighed only 114 pounds—belied his speed. As an amateur, he won fifteen American championships plus several English and Canadian titles. At one time or another he held every American record in all distances from fifty yards to the one-mile run. When he died in 1899, he still held records in five distances. As late as 1929, fifty years after Myers had been in his prime, his time in the quarter mile was superior to that of the winner of the American National Championships. Myers dominated his era as no runner had done before or since.

In 1884 James Waston, a reporter, charged Myers with violating the N4A amateur code. The executive committee of the Association heard that Myers had received payments for directing the construction of the new grounds of the Manhattan Athletic Club, for serving as secretary of the club, and for editing a portion of a sporting sheet. Waston also accused Myers of selling and pawning some of his medals. While the charges were apparently valid, the executive committee formally upheld Myers' amateur standing. In the next year, 1885, the Manhattan Club, without any apparent embarrassment, scheduled a benefit for Myers which netted the athlete some $4,000. Shortly afterward Myers became an announced professional, but the N4A continued to founder on the problems that arose from his example.

Rivalry between the clubs for athletic supremacy, especially between the NYAC and the Manhattan Club, and disputes over the amateur standing of athletes resulted in the demise of the National Association. Amidst bitter charges and countercharges, the NYAC withdrew from the association in 1886 and led a group of clubs in forming the Amateur Athletic Union (AAU) in 1888. By prohibiting any athlete from participating in AAU games who had competed in games governed by the Association, the AAU succeeded by the summer of 1889 in destroying the N4A. But formation of the AAU did not eliminate conflicts between clubs or eligibility controversies. By offering more generous expense and traveling allowances and superior facilities to athletes, the larger clubs continued to "steal" the better athletes from the smaller clubs. Since the larger clubs controlled the Board of Governors of the AAU, the smaller clubs had no recourse in solving their grievances. Likewise the affiliates of the AAU, especially the colleges,

---

[19]For a description of the feats of Myers, see Joe D. Willis and Richard G. Wettan, "L. E. Myers, 'World's Greatest Runner,'" *Journal of Sport History*, 2 (Fall 1975), 93–111.

resented the power of the AAU. In the first two decades of the twentieth century, the AAU, the colleges, the American Olympic Committee, and other athletic organizations started a running battle for control of amateur sports. Since each organization had an important stake in the athletes or the activities sponsored by the others, there was no simple solution to the conflicts.[20]

Despite a history of controversy, social discrimination, and blatant hypocrisy, the athletic clubs and the AAU played a significant role in the promotion of track and field in the United States. Prior to 1900 the clubs produced most of the outstanding performers in running, jumping, pole vaulting, and shot-putting. At a celebrated international meet in 1895, the Americans swept to victory in every event. Bernard J. Wefers equalled the world record in the 100-yard dash at nine and four-fifths seconds and broke the 220-yard mark with a run of twenty-one and one-fifth seconds.[21] The clubs also assisted in the development of collegiate track and field. Beginning in the 1870s the collegians gained valuable experience by competing in club meets and most of the early intercollegiate meets were held on the superior grounds of the athletic clubs. In the first two decades of the twentieth century, the exclusive clubs continued to sponsor major amateur meets. (Until the 1970s, the NYAC's annual indoor meet was the single most prestigious winter track and field event.) But increasingly, a larger share of the athletes of championship caliber came from the colleges, the YMCAs, and ethnic clubs like the Irish-American Athletic Club of New York.

The revived Olympic Games never had an entirely player-centered orientation. According to the official ideology of the Olympic movement, the Games were held solely for the benefit of the players, and only amateur athletes could compete. Pierre de Coubertin, the aristocratic French Anglophile who founded the modern games, repeatedly asserted that the Games were a forum for the young men of the world to unite in peaceful competition through sport. Yet even the official ideology of the Games included more than simply participation for the sheer joy of the experience. The Games would also, Coubertin argued, expose athletes to people with different values, broaden their horizons, and contribute to pacific international relations. Unofficially, Coubertin, who smarted deeply from the humiliating defeat that the Germans had administered to the French in

[20]See Richard Wettan and Joe W. Willis, "Effect of New York Athletic Clubs on American Amateur Athletic Governance, 1870–1915," *Research Quarterly*, 47 (October 1976), 499–505; Eric Danhoff, "The Struggle for Control of Amateur Track and Field in the United States," *Canadian Journal of History of Sport and Physical Education*, 6 (May 1975), 43–85; Robert Korsgaard, "A History of the Amateur Athletic Union of the United States," Ed.D. project (Teachers College, Columbia University, 1952); Arnold Flath, *A History of Relations between the National Collegiate Athletic Associations and the Amateur Athletic Union of the United States, 1905–1963* (Champaign, Ill.: Stipes, 1964).

[21]See "International Track and Field Contests of 1895," *Outing*, 26 (September 1895), 454–61; John A. Lucas, "The First Great International Track Meet," *Sports Illustrated*, 33 (August 23, 1972, Midwest ed.) M6–M8. Although technically a meet between NYAC and the London Athletic Club, both clubs recruited the best athletes from the other clubs of their respective countries.

1870, also hoped the example of the Games would strengthen the national character of the French people. Moreover, responsibilities for the management of the Games and the national teams rested with committees of nonathletes. Finally, forces external to the Olympic movement (including national pride, commercial consideration, and boosterism) shaped much of the history of the Games.[22]

Until 1912 the Olympic Games remained a minor event in American track and field competition. The Americans made no concerted effort to field a strong team at the first Games held at Athens in 1896. College athletes sponsored by the Boston Athletic Association reinforced by a few others who paid their own expenses comprised the total American delegation. Harbingers of the use of the Games for nonathletic purposes were evident even at Athens. The Greek royal family blatantly exploited the Games to enhance their power, and the first Games initiated the practice of raising the national flags of the winning athletes at a victory ceremony. The next three Games were essentially sideshows to other more publicized attractions: The Paris Exposition of 1900, the World's Fair held in St. Louis in 1904, and the Franco-British Exposition of 1908 held in London. In addition, the Greeks scheduled what has been called a "rump" Olympics at Athens in 1906.[23] Only fifteen countries competed in the 1900 Games, and only eleven nations participated in the third Olympics held at St. Louis in 1904. Rivalries between the large and patriotically motivated American and British teams marred the London Games of 1908. For the first time, Olympic officials required that all competitors perform as part of a national "team." By 1908 American track and field officials took the Games seriously. They had organized a national Olympic committee which selected teams of first-rate athletes and subsidized them for their trips abroad. At each of these early Games, American athletes tended to dominate track and field, but fared poorly in other forms of competition.

In the 1912 Olympic Games held at Stockholm, Sweden, the Games "arrived," at least as far as the Americans were concerned. Unlike earlier Games, nothing overshadowed the event, and American newspapers gave the Games detailed coverage. The Americans went all-out to win the track and field events. The American Olympic Committee selected the best athletes available, including a native American and several blacks. Jim Thorpe, the great athlete from the tiny Carlisle (Pennsylvania) Indian School, emerged as the hero of the Games. Already well known for his football feats, Thorpe captured the pentathlon and decathlon. He won four of the five individual events in the pentathlon and scored a 700-point margin over his nearest competitor in the decathlon. Unfortunately, Thorpe became a victim of the amateur code. The following year, a

[22]On the founding and early history of the Olympic movement see Richard D. Mandell, *The First Modern Olympics* (Berkeley: University of California Press, 1976). The standard histories of the Olympic movement are John Kieron, Arthur Daley, and Pat Gordan, *The Story of the Olympic Games, 776 B.C. to 1976*, rev. ed. (Philadelphia and New York: J. B. Lippincott, 1977) and John Lucas, *The Modern Olympic Games* (South Brunswick and New York: A. S. Barnes, 1980).

[23]Mandell, *The First Modern Olympics*, p. 167.

Massachusetts newspaper accused Thorpe of playing professional baseball for a minor-league team during the summer of 1909. Thorpe admitted the transgression, and the AAU revoked his amateur status. The International Olympic Committee then deprived him of his Olympic medals. The IOC selected Berlin as the host for the 1916 Games, but the eruption of World War I in 1914 resulted in their cancellation.

CRICKET CLUBS AND COUNTRY CLUBS

The elite used sports other than track and field as a means of building status communities. In Philadelphia but not in other American cities, old-stock Americans became enthusiastic cricketeers. The popularity of cricket among Philadelphia's elite appeared to spring largely from chance. Unlike the instances of New York and Boston, cricket gained a following among Philadelphia's elite before the Civil War. In the 1840s a group of young Philadelphians residing in the Manheim region became acquainted with cricket from the English textile workers employed at the nearby Wakefield Mills. William Wister, one of the youngsters, played a pivotal role in teaching and organizing the sport on the Manheim estates. In the 1850s three clubs were organized; one, the Young America Cricket Club, explicitly excluded from membership anyone who was foreign-born. By so doing, the club helped dissociate itself with the "steak and ale" style of cricket played among the English workingmen. Yet in the 1850s no clear distinction had yet evolved between amateur and professional cricketeers nor had the clubs yet constructed fancy clubhouses and playing fields. The main purpose of the clubs was simply to provide a means by which wealthy young men of similar social origins could play cricket. But even in the 1850s the sport's major sponsors in Philadelphia came from families of impeccable social standing. Without their support, cricket in Philadelphia would probably have followed the path of cricket in other cities and remained primarily a sport of English immigrants.[24]

After the Civil War, each club built elaborate clubhouses and acquired spacious grounds. All five of the major clubs were located in the most socially prestigious neighborhoods of Philadelphia. By the 1890s, within a ten-mile radius of Philadelphia, there were four beautifully kept, sumptuous grounds with lavish clubhouses; London, by comparison, had only two grounds of equal stature. Membership in the five "first class" clubs ranged from 500 to 1,300 persons. In 1874 a team picked from the Philadelphia clubs accepted an invitation to play a series of matches at Halifax, Nova Scotia, with British and Canadian elevens for an international prize. After

[24]See John A. Lester, ed., *A Century of Philadelphia Cricket* (Philadelphia: University of Pennsylvania Press, 1951); Melvin Leonard Adelman, "The Development of Modern Athletics in New York City, 1820–1870," (unpublished Ph.D. dissertation, University of Illinois, 1980), Chap. 5; Charles Blancke, "Cricket in America," *Harper's Weekly*, 35 (September 26, 1891), 732; and George Stuart Patterson, "Cricket in the United States," *Lippincott's Magazine*, 50 (November 1892), 650.

the Philadelphia eleven won the cup, it became the object of intense competition among the major clubs of the city. By 1891, Philadelphia teams had played touring professional and amateur teams from the British Isles at least seven times, Australian clubs twice, and Canadian teams on numerous occasions. In both 1884 and 1889 the "Gentlemen of Philadelphia" visited England. They acquitted themselves well, winning four, losing three, and drawing five matches against top-flight English competition.

The Philadelphia cricket clubs became part of an elite status community. Not only the expense of membership but the time required to play cricket automatically excluded the ordinary workingman. As the "national game" of England, cricket also appealed to status-conscious Americans who were intrigued with emulating the habits of English sportsmen. The clubs assumed a wide array of social functions similar to the metropolitan athletic clubs. The report of the Board of Governors of the Germantown Cricket Club in 1891 reveals the social character of the typical first-class club:

> That the grounds are socially a success is now an undisputed fact, and too much credit cannot be given to the Ladies' Committee for their untiring efforts to promote the welfare of the club in this direction. Ladies' teas have been served every Tuesday; Thursday has been made music day, and Saturday match day, so that the entire week has been made attractive, and the attendance consequently large. It is proposed that these attractions shall be continued and new ones added during the coming year.[25]

The Germantown club enjoyed a new clubhouse, designed by the distinguished New York architectural firm of McKim, Mead, and White. Like the other clubs, it also sponsored an elaborate program of cricket for juniors. Club leaders believed that playing cricket inculcated the young with gentlemanly values.

While the Philadelphia cricket clubs continued to thrive in the twentieth century, cricket as a sport declined rapidly. As the clubs became agencies of social exclusion, cricket tended to be only a by-product of the clubs' main function. Other diversions such as lawn tennis, golf, and swimming could serve the club membership equally well. Since tennis required less space and could be played much more quickly than cricket, it became, in time, the rage of the cricket clubs. Two members of the Merion Club, William Jackson Clothier and Richard Norris Williams, were United States doubles champions in 1906, 1914, and 1916. And William "Big Bill" Tilden, the country's greatest player in the 1920s, learned his tennis on the courts of the Germantown Cricket Club. By the 1920s the cricket clubs could hardly be distinguished from any other super-wealthy metropolitan country or golf club.

The metropolitan athletic and cricket clubs were forerunners of the great country club movement that has flourished since the 1920s. The country club was, in effect, a substitute for the English country home of the aristocracy or monied gentry. "It is a banding together for the purpose of making available to the group facilities which previously had been the

---

[25]Quoted in Lester, ed., *A Century of Philadelphia Cricket*, p. 313.

privilege of the wealthy aristocrat," declared the official historians of the original Country Club at Brookline, Massachusetts.[26] While in England the upper strata of society usually lived in the country and belonged to clubs in the cities, rich Americans normally resided in the cities and sought an approximation of the English country home with the aristocratic privileges of servants and exclusive outdoor sports. The main activities of the early clubs centered on hunting, fishing, horseback riding, and other activities which in England were reserved to those able to afford country estates.

The first "Country Club," founded in 1882, was far more exclusive than later imitators. "For many years after 1882 Boston had that of which it was very proud—its Society," wrote the country club historians. "Everybody was either in it or out of it; and those who were in it were proud of the fact and guarded its boundaries jealously. They played with each other, not with others; they competed with each other, not with others; above all, they married each other only, and so their children carried on the good (?)* tradition."[27] The Brookline Country Club was one of the primary agencies for preserving the exclusiveness of Boston "Society." In the twentieth century, the country club became a haven for those seeking to establish status communities in the smaller cities and the suburbs of metropolises. Some ethnic groups—Jews, for example—established country clubs, but most clubs were composed of status-conscious, old-stock Americans.

Country clubs were far less significant as constituents of status communities in England than in the United States. The contrasts between the functions of the clubs were sharply drawn by George Birmingham, an Englishman.

> There are also all over England clubs especially devoted to particular objects, golf clubs, yacht clubs, and so forth. In these the members are drawn together by their interest in a common pursuit, and are forced into some kind of acquaintanceship. But these are very different in spirit and intention from the American country club. It exists as a kind of center of the social life of the neighborhood. Sport is encouraged by these clubs for the sake of general sociability. In England sociability is a by-product of an interest in sport.
>
> The country club at Tuxedo [New York] is not perhaps the oldest, but it is one of the oldest institutions of its kind in America. At the proper time of year there are dances, and a debutante acquires, I believe, a certain prestige by "coming out" at one of them. But the club exists primarily as a social center of Tuxedo. It is in one way the ideal, the perfect country club. It not only fosters, it regulates and governs the social life of the place.[28]

*The question mark in parentheses appears in the original quotation and suggests that the official historians of the first country club either had some doubts about the merits of the traditions of the Boston "Society," or were attempting to be humorous.

[26]Frederic H. Curtiss and John Heard, *The Country Club, 1882–1932* (Brookline, Mass.: privately printed for the Club, 1932), p. 4.

[27]Ibid., p. 139.

[28]Birmingham, "The American at Home and in His Club," p. 175. For articles on the country clubs see Caspar W. Whitney, "Evolution of the Country Club," in Neil Harris, ed., *The Land of Contrasts, 1880–1901* (New York: George Braziller, 1970), pp. 134–46; Edward S. Martin, "Country Clubs and Hunt Clubs in America," *Scribner's Magazine*, 18 (December 1895), 302–21; Robert Dunn, "The Country Club: A National Expression," *Outing*, 47 (November 1905), 160–74.

While golf did not furnish the initial impetus for the formation of the first country clubs, it was the most potent of all sports in encouraging the spread of the clubs throughout the country. Historians of golf credit Joseph M. Fox, a member of Philadelphia's Merion Cricket Club, and John Reid, a transplanted Scot and an executive of an iron works in Yonkers, New York, with introducing modern golf from Scotland into the United States. In 1887 Reid organized the first modern golf club, the St. Andrews Club, named after the historic club in Scotland. In the early 1890s golf caught the fancy of the super-rich tycoons in New York, Boston, Philadelphia, and Chicago. In 1891 William K. Vanderbilt brought over Willie Dunn, famed Scottish golfer, to build the first professionally designed links, the Shinnecock Hills course, located at Southampton, Long Island, where many wealthy New Yorkers had summer homes. The Shinnecock Hills Golf Club hired Stanford White, the noted architect, to design an opulent clubhouse. The clubhouse and course became models for wealthy men interested in forming golf clubs elsewhere. By 1900 rich golfers could follow the seasons. When the cold winter winds began to blow, they left their courses at Newport, Brookline, Yonkers, Long Island, and Chicago for sumptuous golfing resorts built for them in Georgia, Florida, or North Carolina. In 1894 both the St. Andrews Club and the Newport Golf Club scheduled national tournaments. The formation of the United States Golf Club Association led to the scheduling of a single tournament. Initially, Scottish and English immigrants dominated championship play. Theodore A. Havermeyer, the "Sugar King" and prominent member of the

Lawn tennis. Lithograph by L. Prang & Co. after Henry Sandham, circa 1887. Courtesy of the Library of Congress.

Newport summer colony, became the long-time president of the association. With but few exceptions, a reporter wrote in 1898, golf "is a sport restricted to the richer classes of the country."[29]

Yet in the first two decades of the twentieth century, golf began to appeal to active business and professional men who were a notch or two below the super-rich. By 1917, 472 courses had been built, a few of which were even public courses. About two-thirds of the links were in the Northeast. Golf served paradoxical if not contradictory functions for harried white-collared Americans. Apart from being a conspicuous status mechanism, it furnished them with an escape from the close confinement and annoying details of their downtown offices. They could presumably retreat to the open, verdant, serene, pastoral countryside. There, according to the promoters of the game, the golfer could release his overtaut nerves. Yet the game itself was intrinsically frustrating. The golfer competed not only against other golfers but the course itself and his earlier scores. Moreover, the white-collar golfers brought their business with them to the links. The golf course often became a substitute for the conference room where the groundwork for future transactions or the completion of old agreements would be reached. And sometimes playing golf seemed to be only a pretext for convivial gatherings at the "nineteenth hole," the clubhouse bar.[30]

Lawn tennis flourished at first in the cricket clubs and in the summer resorts of the elite. At Newport, where the nation's wealthiest families constructed huge palaces of stone for summer homes and entertained each other royally, tennis became the "in" sport. Dixon Wector captured the flavor of Newport in the late nineteenth century when he wrote that: "Other than social consciousness, the only bond which drew this summer colony together was sport—which might consist of sailing around Block Island, or having cocktails upon one's steam yacht reached by motor-boat from the landing of the New York Yacht Club, or bathing at Bailey's Beach or the Gooseberry Island Club, or tennis on the Casino courts."[31] The posh Newport Casino Club became the home of the United States National Lawn Tennis Association (1881) and was the site of the national champion-

[29]H. L. Fitz Patrick, "Golf and the American Girl," *Outing*, 32 (December 1898), 294–95. For the diffusion of golf in the 1890s, see a series of articles in *Outing*, 34 (May-August 1899), 260–68, 354–65, 443–57 and Herbert Warren Wind, *The Story of American Golf*, 3rd rev. ed. (New York: Knopf, 1975).

[30]See Jesse Frederick Steiner, *Americans at Play* (New York: McGraw-Hill, 1933), pp. 70–71; Samuel G. Blythe, "Golf and the Government," in Harry T. Paxton, ed., *Sport U.S.A.: The Best from the Saturday Evening Post* (New York: Thomas Nelson and Sons, 1961), pp. 48–51; and Wind, *The Story of American Golf*, pp. 35–37, 39.

[31]Dixon Wector, *The Saga of American Society: A Record of Social Aspiration, 1607–1937* (New York: Scribner's, 1937), p. 457. Apparently modern lawn tennis evolved most directly from the ancient game of court tennis. In 1873 Major John Wingfield, an avid court tennis player from England, popularized a game of lawn tennis which he called "Saphairstike," named for an ancient Greek sport. Soon thereafter the Marlebone Cricket Club in England and the All England Croquet Club at Wimbledon took up the game. Wimbledon held the first of its famous tournaments in 1877. Some dispute surrounds the first introduction of the sport in the United States, but apparently two courts—in Staten Island, New York, and Nahant, Massachusetts—were built in 1874.

ships until 1913 when the tournament was moved to the West Side Tennis Club at Forest Hills, New York. Lawn tennis long remained a sport dominated by clubs of impeccably high status aspirations.

The sponsorship of tennis and golf by the elite clubs expanded the opportunities for women to participate in sport. While the aggressive physical activity essential to success in most sports violated the Victorian image of femininity, women from wealthy families were less inhibited than those from middle-income families. Many of the first tennis courts were built specifically for the wives and daughters of club members. During the first decade or so of the development of American tennis, many observers believed that tennis would remain primarily a sport of women. In the early years the women preferred doubles to singles, possibly because they were encumbered by bustles and full-length skirts. The women held a few tournaments as early as 1881 and in 1887 scheduled the first women's national tennis championships. The task of breaking the sex barrier in golf was more difficult. In the closing years of the nineteenth century, the golf clubs along the Atlantic Coast began reluctantly to set aside the links on certain afternoons for female players. Only thirteen women participated in the first national tournament held on the Meadowbrook course on Long Island in 1895. In 1898 H. L. Fitz Patrick announced—prematurely—that "the American golf girl has arrived!"[32] The golfing women helped initiate a more liberal style of dress. By 1898 a few brave ladies were playing without hats and with sleeves extending only to the elbows. But compared to men, the number of women athletes remained exceedingly small. Most of the women engaged only in the social life of the clubs.

If we posit player-centered and spectator-centered sports as opposites, then by the early twentieth century the sports of the insiders could be treated on a spectrum between these two poles. The games of the metropolitan athletic clubs had begun with an athlete-centered ethos but soon shifted toward a fan-centered orientation. Management and finances of track and field competition soon came under the control of the social element of the clubs; the clubs began to charge admissions to their meets and the athletes drifted toward increased specialization and professionalization. Yet the clubs continued to adhere nominally to an amateur code; the ideals of amateurism acted as a brake, preventing the complete triumph of a spectator-centered ethos. Polo, golf, and tennis, reserved almost exclusively to men of the highest social ranks, stood nearest to the player-centered archetype. In the decision-making processes of these sports, the athletes themselves played pivotal roles. They usually had responsibility for rule changes, scheduling tournaments, and management. Golf and tennis attracted few spectators; golf charged no admissions, even for national tournaments, and tennis only began to take in gate receipts at its national tournament in 1913. Moreover, with the exception of a few golf-teaching professionals, no golf nor tennis players could be considered full-time athletes.

[32]Fitz Patrick, "Golf and the American Girl," 294.

4

The Sons of the Elite

Football: Cornell vs. Rochester, October 19, 1889. Photograph by Seneca Roy Stoddard. Courtesy of the Library of Congress.

A jerky little train loaded with students steamed out of Princeton, New Jersey, early on the morning of November 6, 1869. Upon arrival at the sleepy town of New Brunswick, New Jersey, the students from Princeton received a warm welcome from the youngsters of the College of Rutgers. During the rest of the morning, the Princeton lads strolled about the town with their hosts; a few played billiards at a local parlor. That afternoon at three o'clock perhaps two hundred spectators gathered on the Rutgers Common. The milling fans did not have to purchase tickets; there were no seats for comfort nor refreshments to satisfy hunger or thirst. Before play commenced, the students burst forth with a few college songs as the nation's first intercollegiate "football" contest got underway. Twenty-five young men lined up on the Common for each side. Rutgers soon demonstrated its superiority at "dribbling"—kicking the ball along the ground with short strokes—and won the game by six goals to four. (To a modern football fan, the game they played could more aptly be described as soccer.) That evening the Rutgers players treated their visitors to a festive supper and the guests joined their hosts in song and good humor.

Those present on the historic occasion of America's first intercollegiate football match had no idea that the nation's colleges would become major centers of sport. Until 1869, football had been essentially a folk game, played mostly by young men and boys. The rules of play sprang from oral traditions. The players did not prepare for the contests, and none of them specialized in a particular aspect of the game. They learned the sport simply by playing it. But the 1869 game pointed the way to a new stage in the evolution of the sport. After 1869, collegians organized clubs, formulated written rules, appointed officials to regulate the sport, and eventually formed a national regulatory association. Football and other intercollegiate sports were ostensibly player-centered affairs, but by the 1890s several colleges, led by Yale, initiated steps that would make football a spectator-centered sport. By then the sport had begun to be characterized by rationalization, athletic specialization, and commercialization.[1]

---

[1] For general treatments see Guy Maxton Lewis, "The American Intercollegiate Football Spectacle, 1869–1917" (Ph.D. dissertation, University of Maryland, 1965); Parke H. Davis, *Football: The American Intercollegiate Game* (New York: Scribner's, 1912); and Alexander M. Weyand, *American Football: Its History and Development* (New York: D. Appleton & Co., 1926). For a cultural interpretation of football rule changes see David Riesman and Reuel Denney, "Football in America: A Study in Culture Diffusion," in Riesman, ed. *Individualism Reconsidered* (Glencoe, Ill.: Free Press, 1954), 242–57.

Even before 1869, rowing, or crew, the first intercollegiate sport, had indicated the general direction of college sports from folk games to player-oriented and finally to fan-centered contests. Rowing probably owed its beginnings to the experiences of students in private boat clubs and the publicity surrounding the intermittent English matches between Oxford and Cambridge that were held after 1826. As early as the 1830s, young men in the Northeast, some of whom were collegians, had formed clubs to race on nearby lakes and rivers. By 1846 both Harvard and Yale had small, informal clubs that sometimes engaged in intramural contests or competed against noncollegiate clubs. In several instances Harvard clubs even competed in Boston regattas for cash prizes. That the students exhibited no reluctance in accepting the prizes indicates that strict amateurism was as yet not an accepted convention of college sport.* Rather than distributing the proceeds to crew members, however, the students apparently used the meagre prize money to pay club expenses.

The first rowing match between American colleges actually resulted from a promotional venture of a small New England railroad. The railroad persuaded Harvard and Yale to send crews to race at Lake Winnepesaukee in 1852 as one of several festivities to promote the area as a summer resort. "The clubs with other students afterwards passed a very pleasant week at the Lake, and returned together to Concord, New Hampshire, where, amid much good feeling and many fraternal adieus, they finally separated."[2] The approach of the student athletes toward the contest was quite casual. Neither winning nor potential profits motivated the early rowers. They took up rowing principally for exercise and recreation. The clubs hired no coaches or trainers, maintained no training tables, nor did they engage in systematic preparation for the regattas. Prior to the Yale-Harvard contest in 1852, the Harvard crew, according to one report, had "only rowed a few times for fear of blistering their hands."[3]

In the late 1850s the convergence of new attitudes toward sports by certain members of the elite and publicity of the exploits of English boys intensified the interest of American collegians in sport. In particular, Thomas Hughes' popular novel, *Tom Brown's School Days,* which combined a muscular Christian perspective with a vivid account of the sporting life of the Rugby School in England, excited American students. Because of Hughes, wrote a Harvard student in 1858, a "multitude from every class are playing at base [ball] or cricket, in a manner that would excite the

---

*Neither was the receipt of money prizes frowned upon by English collegians. Cash prizes were awarded at the first track and field competition between Oxford and Cambridge in 1864, though there is no evidence that the practice continued after that date. See C. Turner, "The Progress of Athletism," *Outing,* 13 (November 1888), 114.

[2]Quoted in John A. Blanchard, ed., *The H Book of Harvard Athletics, 1852–1922* (Cambridge, Mass.: Harvard University Press, 1923), p. 26. See also Guy Lewis, "The Beginning of Organized Collegiate Sport," *American Quarterly* (Summer 1970), 222–29.

[3]Blanchard, *The H Book of Harvard Athletics,* p. 24.

admiration, even if it shocked the taste, of Tom Brown and his fellows of Rugby."[4] Within two years sport had become so disruptive at Harvard that the president, Cornelius C. Felton, resorted to repression. He reported to the Overseers that "The language of some of the recent discussions seems to imply that muscular development is identical with moral, intellectual, and religious progress. It seems to be thought the panacea for all the evils under which humanity labors."[5] Little did Felton dream that the athletic involvement of the students would soon overshadow their moral, intellectual, and religious interests.

Reports of the Oxford-Cambridge rowing contest in 1858 revived the interest of American students in rowing. Correspondents who covered the race seized the opportunity to laud the English students for their physical prowess while expressing their dismay at "the entire disregard for exercise among Americans." Angered by these reports, the editor of Harvard's student magazine proposed a grand regatta of all New England colleges. "What say ye, Yale, Dartmouth, Brown, Columbia, Harvard," he asked, "shall we introduce a new institution in America?"[6] Representatives from four colleges responded by forming the College Union Regatta Association in 1858. The association sponsored successful races in 1859 and 1860 on Lake Quinsigamond, but the Civil War temporarily disrupted its activities. From 1864 to 1871 only Yale and Harvard competed in the intercollegiate regatta.

The race of Harvard against Oxford in 1869 on the Thames River in England, the race that "will be henceforth ever immortal in Anglo-American annals," declared the London *Times,* indicated the increasing seriousness with which the collegians approached the sport. The Harvard crew practiced a full month before the event, and American newspapers speculated that the defeat of the Harvard rowers might have been due to their "soft food" diet of too much milk and fruit rather than beef and ale, the diet of the hardy Oxford crew. Though the Americans had lost the momentous race of 1869, it stimulated a renewed interest in crew among the other northeastern colleges. In 1870 they formed the Rowing Association of American Colleges. Up to sixteen colleges participated in the regattas of the new organization.[7]

Rowing, more than any other sport, reflected the perceived difference in status among the various colleges. In the mid-1870s both Harvard and Yale withdrew from the association, pleading that the regattas had become too unwieldy. Apparently the real reason sprang from the humiliating defeats that the two schools had suffered at the hands of smaller, less prestigious institutions. The victory of the "bucolics" over the "intellectuals," wrote a Harvard student after the Massachusetts Agricultural College defeated Brown and Harvard for the Championship in 1871, "was a bitter

[4][Henry G. Spaulding], "Mens Sana," *Harvard Magazine,* 4 (June 1858), 201.
[5]*Annual Report of the President of Harvard College to the Overseers, 1859–60* (1860), p. 22.
[6]"Editor's Table," *Harvard Magazine,* 4 (May 1958), 178.
[7]See Joseph J. Matthews, "The First-Harvard-Oxford Race," *New England Quarterly,* 33 (March 1960), 74–82 and Guy M. Lewis, "America's First Intercollegiate Sport: The Regattas from 1852 to 1875," *Research Quarterly,* 38 (December 1967), 637–48.

pill for us to swallow...."[8] Several newspapers accused the clubs of snobbery, but the charges did not deter Harvard and Yale from rowing almost exclusively against each other for the rest of the century. For over twenty years Yale and Cornell engaged in a rancorous dispute over the merits of their respective crews. Yale refused to accept Cornell's repeated challenges, claiming that the Cornell men had been ungentlemanly in accusing them of cowardice. Whatever the reason, the old saying that "the Cabots speak only to the Lowells and the Lowells speak only to God" had its counterpart in the rowing history of Harvard and Yale. The two schools refused to join the new Intercollegiate Rowing Association, formed in 1883 by seven northeastern schools. But they continued to hold their own regatta.

By the 1870s the student bodies of several northeastern schools had a large emotional stake in winning the regattas. Victory meant far more to many students than their studies. The clubs went all-out to win. They hired professional coaches and trainers to prepare the crews for the major regattas. Training for the regattas was spartan; often the crew was put on a strict diet (consisting largely of meat) and required to row from three to five miles before breakfast and about four miles every afternoon. The crews gave up "their pleasures: they resigned their very will to the control of others," all for "twenty thrilling minutes of the race."[9] Because of the general superiority of English rowing, the clubs looked to England for coaches, the latest strokes and shells, and for international matches.

The regattas likewise became an important date on the social calendars of alumni and the fashionable set of the larger cities. Of the 1875 regatta, *Outing* reported: "The moneyed aristocracy which assembles yearly at Saratoga gilded the grand stand and the shore of the lake, outshown in turn by the kaleidoscopic ribbons of the intent, excited, uproarious mob which represented the thirteen colleges."[10] Large sums of money exchanged hands among the wealthy wagerers present at the regatta. Newspapers carried whole pages of "special dispatches" plus extended discussions of the social leaders who graced the regattas by their presence. It was not until the mid-1880s that football replaced rowing as the favorite intercollegiate sport of students and the social elite.

Track and field as an intercollegiate sport had its beginnings as an offshoot of crew. In 1873 James Gordon Bennett, Jr. of the New York *Herald* offered a challenge cup for a two-mile race as part of the Saratoga intercollegiate regatta. Only three men, one each from Amherst, Cornell, and McGill College of Canada, competed in the first meet. The next year an expanded program included a 100-yard dash, 120-yard high hurdles, one-mile and three-mile runs, and a seven-mile walk. The desultory character of this meet can be gathered from the fact that most of the contestants had rowed for their varsity crews the day before. In 1876 the

---

[8]Quoted in Lewis, "America's First Intercollegiate Sport," 643.

[9]J. R. W. Hitchcock, "The Harvard-Yale Races," *Outing*, 6 (July 1885), 403. See also B. W. Dwight, "Intercollegiate Regattas, Hurdle-Races, and Prize Contests," *New Englander*, 35 (1876), 253.

[10]Hitchcock, "Harvard-Yale Races," 393.

collegians and their sponsors formed the Intercollegiate Association of Amateur Athletics of America, commonly known as the IC4A, to supervise the track and field events at the Saratoga regatta. By that date, athletes from seven or so colleges competed regularly in the annual meet. In the 1880s the annual games of the New York Athletic Club at Mott Haven, open to all amateurs, became the premier college track and field event. With the rise of the state universities, the popularity of college track and field spread rapidly to other parts of the country.

Until the 1880s, track and field training varied widely. In the northeastern colleges, an aspiring sprinter or walker might hire a professional trainer. As the professional coaches vied with one another for the services of college athletes, unseemly disputes arose which were not "in keeping with the spirit of a gentleman's sport."[11] In 1882 Harvard hired J. G. Lathrop as a general trainer and supervisor of track and prohibited any association of the collegians with professional coaches. These reforms represented one of the earliest instances of college administrators assuming control of the management of athletics.

Apart from rowing and track, baseball was the only other intercollegiate sport to generate much interest prior to 1869. Boys from the eastern academies introduced a version of baseball to college campuses in the 1840s and 1850s. The first recorded intercollegiate match between Amherst and Williams in 1859 failed to stimulate an immediate college rivalry in the sport. But baseball was popular in the 1860s as an intramural sport, and college nines did engage in contests with nearby local clubs. Beginning in about 1862, a group of boys from Phillips Exeter Academy converted fellow Harvard students to the New York Knickerbocker version of the sport. Until the 1880s, the Harvard Base Ball Club, organized in 1862, fielded the strongest college nine in the country. For a seven-year span they did not lose a single intercollegiate game. In the summer of 1870 they took an extended road trip through the West, playing all of the major amateur and professional teams in the country. They won forty-four of fifty-four matches, and even frightened Harry Wright's powerful Cincinnati Red Stockings. In the words of a contemporary: "The game was remarkably close, the Harvards outplaying their opponents at bat and in the field; but at a critical moment in the last inning, professional training showed its superiority over amateur excitability, and the Red Stockings won by 20 to 17."[12]

While intercollegiate baseball continued to be widely played, after 1870 it was superseded in popularity by rowing and finally football. In 1879 Harvard, Princeton, Brown, Amherst, and Dartmouth formed a college association, but provided for no regular schedule of games nor for the naming of a champion club. The association folded in 1887, to be replaced that year by the short-lived Eastern College League. Compared with rowing and football, college baseball suffered from several handicaps.

[11]Samuel Crowther and Arthur Ruhl, *Rowing and Track Athletes* (New York: Macmillan, 1905), pp. 275–76.

[12]J. Mott Hallowell, "American College Athletics: I. Harvard University," *Outing*, 13 (December 1889), 241.

Inclement weather limited the number of games that could be played during the regular academic year, and college authorities usually prohibited summer tours. By joining the numerous semiprofessional and professional teams during the summers, the college ball players could earn money. For almost a century college authorities tried to prevent this practice, but without much success.

THE SOCIAL MILIEU OF FOOTBALL

In the last three decades of the nineteenth century, football evolved from a simple, informal diversion of a few young "gentlemen" in northeastern academies and colleges into a serious enterprise involving the student bodies, college authorities, alumni, and thousands of spectators. In the 1870s the students organized clubs, scheduled the contests, managed the finances (such as they were), and determined the rules of the game. No professional coaches existed; the team captain decided who would play, the deployment of the players, and the nature of team strategy and training. Then within two decades the nature of the game changed radically. By the 1890s, as many as 40,000 fans watched the annual Thanksgiving Day championship contest in New York City. Newspapers covered the game on their front pages, and receipts from the contests mounted to thousands of dollars. Although college football was ostensibly played for the sake of the game itself, merely for the fun that accrued to the players, winning took precedence over moral scruples and amateur principles. The emphasis on winning was the key determinant in shaping the rules of the game, schedules, finances, and team organization.

The changing character of American higher education after 1870 facilitated the "take-off" of football. Unlike England, where only Oxford and Cambridge competed for eminence, literally dozens of institutions in America scrambled for recognition. None of them, save perhaps Harvard, could take their status for granted. Since what constituted preeminence in higher education remained rather nebulous, the college authorities tended to equate success with bigness and public attention. Thus they strove to increase enrollments, expand endowments, and develop new programs. Captains of industry, such as Johns Hopkins, Leland Stanford, Jr., and John D. Rockefeller, responded with munificent grants for the founding of new private universities. Likewise, the older colleges of the Northeast became the beneficiaries of the largesse of the nation's industrial and commercial leaders. By the end of the century, federal land grants and more generous appropriations of state legislatures inaugurated the era of the large state universities.

The college authorities soon came to believe that football contributed to their drive for larger student bodies and more liberal benefactions. With an excess of colleges, the competition for students was intense. Even the older, more prestigious institutions of the Northeast turned to football as a means of recruiting students. As early as 1878 President James McCosh of Princeton wrote an alumnus in Kentucky: "You will confer a great favor on us if you will get...the college noticed in the Louisville papers.... We must persevere in our efforts to get students from your region.... Mr. Brand Ballard has won us [a] great reputation as captain of the football team which has beaten both Harvard and Yale."[13] Football seemed an even more potent weapon in the battle for students among the land-grant institutions and numerous sectarian colleges of the West. Upon securing Princeton's Hector R. Cowan as "coach" in 1895, Kansas University president Frank Snow was ecstatic. "I repeat, this is an immense thing at U. K. and will tend to develop the green eyes rapidly of other Kansas institutions."[14] Faculty, students, and the townspeople of Lawrence enthusiastically joined in raising the money necessary to pay Cowan's salary.

Upon assuming the presidency of John D. Rockefeller's newly endowed University of Chicago in 1892, William Rainey Harper, a Yale graduate, immediately set out to publicize the new university by establishing a winning football team. Harper hired Amos Alonzo Stagg, a famed Yale player, as coach, making Stagg the first coach with professorial rank in the country. Harper gave Stagg unambiguous instructions. "I want you to develop teams which we can send around the country and knock out all the [other] colleges," he explained to the new coach. "We will give them [the players] a palace car and a vacation too."[15] Stagg responded with enthusiasm. "If Chicago University places a team in the field it must *be a winning team* or one which will bring honor to the university."[16] According to Stagg, during the halftime of a game in which Chicago trailed Wisconsin 12–0, Harper delivered an impassioned plea to the Chicago players. "Boys, Mr. Rockefeller has just announced a gift of $3,000,000 to the University," the President declared. "He believed that the University is to be great. The way you played in the first half leads me to wonder whether we really have the spirit of greatness in ambition. I wish you would make up your minds to win this game and show that we have it."[17] Chicago bounced back the second half to win 22–12.

College authorities also found that football developed an alumni loyalty that was far more profound than fond memories of chapels, classrooms, pranks, or professors. "You do not remember whether Thorpwright was valedictorian or not," wrote a young college alumnus in 1890, "but you can never forget that glorious run of his in the football game." The alumni continued to identify with the football team long after their official connection with the college had been severed. The lament of a Bowdoin alumnus in 1903 could be heard in countless variations from alumni everywhere. Referring to a 16–0 defeat of Bowdoin by the University of Maine, he declared: "In my day the University of Maine was a standing

[13]Quoted in Frederick Rudolph, *The American College and University: A History* (New York: Vintage Books, 1962), p. 385.
[14]Quoted in Guy Maxton Lewis, "The American Intercollegiate Football Spectacle," pp. 158–59.
[15]Ibid., p. 141.
[16]Stagg to Harper, March 18, 1892, quoted in Kooman Boycheff, "Intercollegiate Athletics and Physical Education at the University of Chicago, 1892–1952" (unpublished Ph.D. dissertation, University of Michigan, 1954), p. 19.
[17]Amos A. Stagg and Wesley W. Sterit, *Touchdown!* (New York: Longmans, Green, 1927), p. 203.

joke.... We got licked to-day because we hadn't the stock—the stock sir...Old Bowdoin must fling open her gates and get some—some stock sir."[18]

In the closing years of the century football encouraged the growth of an alumni subculture. Alumni in cities remote from their college campuses organized chapters, sponsored elaborate homecoming events, and printed bulletins listing the achievements of their classmates and the latest exploits of the football team. "The feeling of solidarity and loyalty in the student body that intercollegiate contests develop is a good thing," ex-President William Howard Taft explained in 1915, "it outlasts every contest, and it continues in the heart and soul of every graduate as long as he lives."[19] College authorities tried to convert the alumni's new-found enthusiasm into generous contributions. But the alumni demanded a price, one that the colleges seemed quite willing to pay. They wanted a winning team and a substantial voice in the management of the school's football program. By the turn of the century, alumni were recruiting athletes, raising money for sports, and assisting in the administration of college athletics.

College football, whether it be in the small college town of Ames, Iowa, or the metropolis of New York City, especially attracted social climbers. Whether alumnus or not, by becoming football devotees they could identify with a college. Increasingly, identification with a college was essential to those who wanted to be in upper-status communities. As early as the mid-1880s, the wealthy social aspirants in New York City went to great lengths to display conspicuously their allegiance to a college. After Yale's defeat in 1889, the New York *Herald* reported, "Mr. Cornelius Vanderbilt [who had never attended a college] and his son William went back to the big house on Fifth Avenue and sadly removed the Yale flag that had floated so bravely all day."[20] Thereafter, at each of the Thanksgiving Day battles the Vanderbilts and Whitneys hung blue and white Yale banners between their mansions across Fifth Avenue. Other wealthy families—the Sloanes, the Alexanders, and the Scribners—displayed the colors of Old Nassau (Princeton) with equal pride.

Aspirants to the inner social circle of New York City and elsewhere basked in the attention given to them by the newspapers. Reporters always provided their readers with detailed lists and accounts of the fashionable set who attended the games. The New York *Herald,* referring to those present at the Yale-Princeton game of 1892, reported that "Mrs. William C. Whitney had a conspicuous box, trimmed profusely in Yale colors and beautifully decorated with a bevy of young girls." In another box "His Luminous Magnificence the Sun was patted pleasantly on the back by Mrs. Elliott Shepard when she stepped into the Shepard-Vanderbilt box and remarked, 'what a perfect day; what glorious sunshine.' And, indeed, the sun reciprocated thankfully to the compliment and smiled full and bright in her lovely face."[21]

---

[18]Quoted in Rudolph, *The American College and University*, p. 383.

[19]William H. Taft, "College Athletics," *Proceedings of the Tenth Annual Convention of the National Collegiate Athletic Association* (1915), p. 67

[20]Quoted in Lewis, "The American Intercollegiate Football Spectacle," p. 92.

[21]Ibid., pp. 119–20.

Not only could hungry newspaper readers find that the sun smiled warmly on the rich, they could even discover what the fashionable wore. "Mrs. Shepard wore a burr brown broadcloth tailor made suit, with a soft Scotch turban of velvet and a spotted veil." On the other hand, Mrs. Douglas Stewart "might have posed as the Goddess of Yale, for she wore a Yale gown, real university style, with trimmings of blue and her wrap and toque were of blue velvet."[22] Little wonder that Richard Harding Davis concluded in 1893 that "the sporting character of the event has been overwhelmed by the social interest...which has...made it more of a spectacle than an athletic contest."[23]

Until the advent of college football, women had usually been forbidden by the dictates of Victorian decency from attending the more disreputable sporting spectacles. Football was different. The annual fall horse show and the Thanksgiving Day contest in New York launched the city's winter social season; debutante balls and banquets soon followed. The antics, cheering, and enthusiasm of the younger ladies at football games led G. Stanley Hall, the psychologist-president of Clark University in 1900, to conclude that "while the human female does not as in the case of many animal species look on complacently and reward the victor with her [sexual] favor, military prowess has a strange fascination for the weaker sex, perhaps ultimately and biologically because it demonstrates the power to protect and defend."[24] Only an academic could have put the matter so delicately.

The wealthy accounted for much of the color, ritual, and social activity that accompanied college football contests. By the 1890s the pageantry of the annual Thanksgiving Day game between the two top college teams in New York City equalled or surpassed any other spectacle offered to the American people. On Wednesday, an advanced contingent of collegians arrived in the city. By evening "the sidewalks of Broadway flashed with blue and orange ribbons and the buildings along the way resounded with the impact of many and diverse college cheers, for the occasion was a convocation for all." By ten o'clock the next morning a parade of horsedrawn coaches, "a feature that was second only to the game itself," slowly made its way through the heart of the city to Manhattan Field. Style required that each coach be pulled by at least four horses, that the horses be ornately decorated, and that each carriage have a coaching-horn and hornsman. Lavish banners featuring the school colors hung from many residences and hotels along the way. The sight of each brought forth "salvos of cheers from the collegians whose colors were displayed."[25]

Festivities continued at the field of play. Many of the carriages had reserved spaces overlooking the field. From atop their coaches, parties ate their lunches and drank champagne. During the game the fans were regaled by vivid displays of school colors, vociferous school cheers led by "yell captains," and boisterous songs. Fans might see Yale's indomitable

[22]Ibid., p. 120.

[23]Richard Harding Davis, "Thanksgiving Day and Football in New York," *Harper's Weekly*, 37 (December 9, 1893), 1170.

[24]Quoted in Rudolph, *The American College and University*, p. 393.

[25]Quotations from Davis, *Football*, pp. 103–4.

mascot, a prize English bulldog that had cost the students the princely sum of $300. After the game, the great crowd, perhaps as many as 40,000, boarded the coaches or the elevated train for the return trip downtown. Soon happy parties crowded every restaurant for a bacchanalian Thanksgiving Day feast. During the evening many of the celebrants attended the theatres where they more often than not interrupted performances with raucous displays of school spirit.

Neither the college authorities, the alumni, nor social climbers furnished the initial impetus for the growth of football. It came from the students. College enrollment spurted upward, more than tripling in the last three decades of the century. A few of the new students came to prepare themselves for specific careers; many more had no clear educational goals. The sons of the new rich often sought a degree as a means of achieving a social position commensurate with their father's wealth. Increasingly, a college degree, particularly from an Ivy League school, was perceived as a passport to polite society or as a requisite to membership in a high-status community. By the 1890s, young men from families of middling status came to believe that the college experience was also valuable in developing the personality traits essential for success in the world of corporations. The corporate managers, who gradually replaced the individual business leaders in the late nineteenth century, looked to the college campuses for men who had social poise, demonstrated success in competition, and had experience in decision-making under fire. Football, they came to believe, steeled young men in the qualities essential for successful corporate managers. Whether motivated by status ambitions or hopes of becoming corporate managers, higher education for such students was a social rather than an intellectual or spiritual investment.

Confronted with a more impersonal academic setting and the apparent need to make their college years more worthwhile as social experiences, the new students made extracurricular activities the center of college life. Earlier, their social life had revolved around the class with which they entered college. But the elective curriculum—initiated by Harvard and gradually emulated by other colleges—plus burgeoning enrollments gradually undermined the class as a social unit. Students replaced it with a host of social organizations that sliced across class lines. Greek letter societies in particular tried to bring together as a small subcommunity the most urbane young men on campus, offering them a type of communal experience and institutionalized escapes from the monotony of collegiate life—more or less ritualized drinking, smoking, card playing, and seducing. To the fraternity man, polished manners and *bon homie* were far more important than cultivating spirituality or intellectual endowments.

The number of college athletic organizations also burgeoned in the new academic setting. Apparently the first clubs were simply composed of students with a common interest in sport. Sometimes they modeled themselves after the private clubs of the larger society. Any freshman who wanted to join the Yale Navy in 1862, for example, had to pay an entry fee of ten dollars and be elected to membership by upper classmen. The organization of the navy closely resembled that of an exclusive yacht club.

But as the rowing and football fevers mounted in the 1870s, the students organized college-wide athletic associations. Everyone was invited to join; after all, student subscriptions were an important means of financing the early teams. Furthermore, the football teams sponsored by the associations were anxious to attract the best potential athletes on the campus. By the 1890s a husky youth with athletic promise was likely to experience intense pressure from his peers to try out for the team.

Apparently football instilled a sense of community to the college as a whole. Student riots, rebellions, hazings, and drunkenness declined with the advent of football at Yale, according to professor of mathematics Eugene L. Richards, for football had created a common bond among the students. Football cultivated "a sense of friendship among the students— not fellowship in mischief, but fellowship in pluck and manliness, in generous admiration of their mates. . . ."[26] Students might be divided by social background, personal values, and the lack of common curriculum, but football, in the words of President Arthur T. Hadley of Yale, took "hold of the emotions of the student body in such a way as to make class distinctions relatively unimportant," and made "the students get together in the old-fashioned democratic way."[27] In short, football promoted a college-wide community of cheerleaders rather than scholars. College presidents welcomed the change, for football assisted in making the peer group the principal force for orderly student behavior rather than the college authorities themselves.

Paradoxically, football appealed to both the potential for individual heroism and the desire of the students to conform to group values. The student newspapers became major proponents of the sport, editorially condemning "slackers" who failed to attend games or display adequate enthusiasm. "School spirit," expressed in terms of loyalty to the football team, was often a necessity for acceptance by one's peers. The average man at Oxford or Cambridge, Caspar Whitney reported in 1895, evinced only a "lukewarm" interest in the football team's prospects "compared with the spirit with which a Harvard, Yale, or Princeton undergraduate will discuss his eleven, and grow eloquent over the brilliant rushes of the half-back, or sorrowfully deprecate the slowness with which an end rusher gets down the field under a kick." English students did not take the outcome of matches "so seriously." "The sight, familiar to us, of members of a defeated eleven throwing themselves prostrate on the ground in agony or bitter disappointment would indeed make Englishmen stare in wonderment."[28]

WALTER CAMP AND THE TRANSFORMATION OF THE RULES

The first football games on college campuses—the interclass matches— had been essentially "free-for-alls," or general melees. At several colleges in the early nineteenth century, students utilized the annual interclass football

[26]Eugene L. Richards, "Athletic Sports at Yale," *Outing*, 6 (July 1885), 453.

[27]Arthur Twining Hadley, "Wealth and Democracy in American Colleges," *Harper's Monthly*, 93 (August 1906), 452.

[28]Caspar Whitney, *A Sporting Pilgrimage* (New York: Harper & Bros., 1895), pp. 90, 92.

contests as a means of initiating freshmen into the rigors of college life. Beginning in 1827, freshmen and sophomores at Harvard began to square off on the first Monday of each school year. As early as 1840, Yale took up the practice. Invariably the class matches resulted in black eyes, bruised and bloodied faces, sprained limbs, and shredded clothes. The ferocious interclass matches apparently promoted class unity. According to a Brown periodical, "The result of it all is that one class is *beaten* collectively, each class individually. It affords talk for the winter; and the bruised limbs, black eyes and cracked heads are carefully treasured up by the Freshmen as spoils of the battlefield, to be du(al)ly handed down to the incoming class the following year."[29] College authorities generally disapproved of the violent rite so that by 1860 it had been abolished at both Harvard and Yale.

Perhaps partly because of the popularity of *Tom Brown's School Days*, a number of New England academies enthusiastically took up football in the 1860s. The school boys played without written rules, but they brought a measure of respectability to the sport and reintroduced it into northeastern colleges. Shortly after the first intercollegiate contest between Rutgers and Princeton in 1869, students formed football clubs at several colleges. The first clubs tended to be exclusive; one became a member by invitation only. All of the clubs except those at Harvard played under some variation of the London Football Association rules (essentially soccer), usually with twenty-five players on a side.*

A series of games played at Cambridge, Massachusetts, between clubs from McGill University of Montreal, Canada, and Harvard in 1874 proved to be a decisive turning point in the history of college football. In the first three games—all played on the same day—the two schools engaged in a contest peculiar to Harvard which combined features of both association football and rugby. The next day, the clubs met under the Rugby Union rules favored by McGill. After struggling to a scoreless tie, the Harvard athletes became immediate converts to rugby, a game which allowed the players to carry the ball and engage in more direct physical contact. With surprising swiftness the other northeastern colleges adopted the new "Rugby game." In 1876, student delegates from Princeton, Columbia, Yale, and Harvard founded the Intercollegiate Football Association and adopted rules closely resembling those of the Rugby Union. Initially the association counted touchdowns as one point and kicked goals as four. A modern observer would be especially surprised by the "drop kicks," which involved the kicker dropping the ball and, as it bounded up, kicking it through the goal. As the ball became more oblong in shape and the points for touchdowns increased, the drop kick disappeared from football. From 1884 to 1897 the numerical values for scoring plays were: safety–2, touchdown–4, goal following touchdown–2, and goal from the field–5. The delegates set up a schedule and decided to name a champion team at the end of the season. The latter decision was an important one, for it encouraged an emphasis on winning and an abrupt departure from the amateur traditions of English universities.

*The term soccer was derived from the term "association."
[29]Quoted in Blanchard, ed., *The H Book of Harvard Athletics*, p. 328.

   Although Yale did not formally join the association until 1879, its club
determined immediately to make football a serious enterprise. Led by
Captain Eugene V. Baker, the Yale athletes engaged in systematic
workouts with one hour for practice each afternoon and a three-mile run
required of all players at nine o'clock in the evening. Hard work paid
dividends, for Yale upset favored Harvard in 1876 before about 100
spectators and defeated Princeton in the championship game on Thanksgiving Day at the St. Georges Cricket Grounds in Hoboken before a crowd
of about 1,000. By 1878 the football fever had captivated the student body
at Yale. While it was still unfashionable at Harvard to take the game
seriously, large numbers of Yale students spent their leisure time watching
daily practice. At the Yale-Princeton championship game of 1879, some
6,000 spectators watched a heroic "push and pull" contest. Some of the
flavor of the contest is captured in a *New York Times* account. "For nearly 10
minutes the men struggled without gaining 10 feet either way, the 'backs'
of each side being nothing but interested on-lookers.... Writhing and
twisting the men rolled about until Yale made a very hot kick...."[30] Yale,
as usual, emerged victorious.
   Walter C. Camp (1859–1925), a member of the Yale squad from 1875
to 1882, was the architect of the modern game of American football. Frail
and rather gawky as a youngster, Camp developed a taste for outdoor
sports while a student at Hopkins Grammar School in New Haven,
Connecticut. Upon entering Yale, he participated in intercollegiate
baseball, crew, track, lawn tennis, and football. After obtaining his
bachelors degree in 1880, he continued at Yale as a medical student and
football player for two more years, allegedly withdrawing from medical
school because he could not tolerate the sight of blood. He then took a
position with a watch manufacturing company and after 1888 became a
permanent resident of New Haven. From the 1880s to about 1910 much of
the development of football revolved around Walter Camp.
   Camp played a large role in gradually undermining the student control
of football. In the early years of the sport the captain of the team, who was
annually elected by the students, supervised all aspects of the squad's
training and strategy. In the 1880s the clubs began to invite former
graduates of their schools to return and assist in the preparation of teams
for key games. Since the graduate "coaches" appeared irregularly and
received no salaries, their influence over the club was far less than that of a
modern full-time, professional coach. In the 1880s Yale began to depart
from the informal pattern of coaching. Around 1885 Walter Camp, while
an employee of a local watch company, became a regular advisor of Yale
captains; from 1888 to 1906 he was the unpaid "advisory head coach" and
supervisor of Yale athletics. (Later Camp did receive a salary for his
services, drawing $1,750 in 1897, for example.) Although Camp could
rarely attend practice sessions, his wife, Alice, observed the players in
action and carefully noted the team's progress. In the evenings Camp
coached the "coaches," and sometimes the captain and other players as

[30]Quoted in Lewis, "The American Intercollegiate Football Spectacle," p. 36.

well. Camp, as the "Czar" of the Yale system, provided continuity from game to game and season to season.

Other schools tried to imitate the Yale system, but without the same success. The record established by Yale in intercollegiate football from 1872 through 1909 has never been equalled. In those years the Yale elevens recorded 324 victories, 17 losses, and 18 ties. From 1883 through 1898, Yale produced nine undefeated teams and from the final game of the 1890 season to the ninth game of 1893 Yale scored 1,265 points to none for its opponents. Yale so dominated archrival Harvard that "Harvard felt a certain loss of manhood in not winning a single football game with Yale in the eighties and only two in the nineties."[31] Among the prominent Yale athletes were Amos Alonzo Stagg (the future coach of the University of Chicago team), W. W. "Pudge" Heffelfinger (who revolutionized line play), and Lee "Bum" McClung (who scored 500 points in four seasons). Perhaps Frederic W. Remington, who became a renowned painter and illustrator, typified the spirit of the Yale football player. In preparation for the Harvard game of 1878, Remington took his football jacket to a local slaughterhouse and dipped it in blood to "make it more businesslike."

Yale partisans felt that the more democratic spirit at New Haven accounted for their unparalleled success on the gridiron. Frank Merriwell, the fictional Yale football hero, explained that at Harvard:

> A man's real worth does not carry him so far as in Yale or Princeton. Here [Yale] a man is accepted for just what he proves himself to be; there, he is accepted for what he has the reputation of being. Aristocracy cuts a mighty small figure at Yale, but in Harvard the bloods are the ones who play ball, row and so forth. A fellow whose parents are nobodies has a poor show in Harvard, but here he gets just where he is able to place himself by merit. That is why Yale has triumphed over Harvard so often, and that is why Harvard receives so little sympathy when she meets defeat.[32]

Whatever the aristocratic pretensions of Harvard or the democratic claims of Yale, shortly after the turn of the century Harvard joined the other colleges in its unbridled enthusiasm for football.

Camp was also football's most successful promoter. The early clubs had financed their games by student subscriptions, but Camp, as the treasurer of the Yale Field Association, saw the possibilities of making college football a profitable sport. He urged that the major matches be scheduled in New York City with an admission fee of at least fifty cents. Boxes could cost as much as $150. Camp flooded the newspapers and periodicals with feature stories about games, summaries of seasons, inside knowledge of football fundamentals, and trivia that fascinated the dedicated football fan. Altogether, he wrote twenty books on sports—boys' novels, histories, and

[31]Samuel Eliot Morison, *Three Centuries of Harvard, 1636–1936* (Cambridge, Mass.: Harvard University Press, 1936), p. 410.

[32]Burt L. Standish, pseud. [Gilbert Patten], *Frank Merriwell's Loyalty* (New York: Street and Smith, 1904), p. 29. See the interpretation of Allen L. Sack, "Yale 29–Harvard 4: The Professionalization of College Football," *Quest*, 19 (Winter 1973), 24–34.

coaching manuals. In 1889 he devised an ingenious promotional gim-mick—the naming of an "All-America" football team. Each year until 1924 Camp personally decided the composition of a hypothetical team of the nation's best players. In due time, football fans everywhere waited anxiously to see if their local heroes would be enshrined by Camp in the immortality of the All-America team. Camp's genius for promotion would have engendered the jealousy of Madison Avenue's best hucksters.

Camp made other important contributions to the game. Beginning in 1878 he served for forty-eight years on nearly every collegiate group charged with revising the rules. Camp believed that the rugby game could be improved by reducing the element of chance and providing for sustained offensive action. Play in rugby started with the scrum, in which the ball was set down on the field. Players from both teams huddled around the ball, trying to drive it free with their feet so that a "back" could pick it up or kick it. Sometimes several minutes transpired before the ball squirted out of the struggling mass of players. Neither team knew until the ball had emerged out of the scrum which team would take the offensive. Once a "back" was downed with the ball, another scrum took place.

In 1880 the collegiate association accepted Camp's suggestion for a revolutionary new means of putting the ball into play. The new rule provided for the replacement of the scrum with a line of scrimmage.* Unless the ball was fumbled or punted to the opposing side, the offensive team could continue to put the ball into play from the line of scrimmage without any interference from the defensive team. Unfortunately, Camp failed to make any provision for the offensive team to surrender the ball when they were unable to move it forward. Much to the disgust of the fans and the players alike, the Yale-Princeton game of 1881 turned into a fiasco. Princeton repeatedly lost yardage but retained possession of the ball the entire first half; Yale did likewise the second half. The next year Camp came forward with an ingenious solution to such tactics.** The offensive team had to give up the ball if it was unable to gain five yards after three attempts. This rule required the liming of lines across the field at five-yard intervals, from which the term "gridiron" is derived. The implementation of the scrimmage line and the down-yardage system marked a fundamen-tal departure from rugby and the emergence of American football as a distinctive sport. In 1882 the convention also established an annual Thanksgiving Day game to be played in New York City.

The rule changes widened the opportunities for advancing new tactics and strategies. Soon teams began to employ offensive signals. (The use of the offensive "huddle" did not become a feature of football until the 1910s.) At first the quarterbacks simply used sentences in which one word or another might be omitted, but by 1885 complex numerical signals began

---

*The 1880 convention also reduced the number of players on each team from fifteen to eleven.

**The idea of a down-yardage system apparently stemmed from an item that first appeared in a metropolitan newspaper. The author was anonymous, but he entitled his piece, "Letter of an Englishman." See Parke H. Davis, *Football: The American Intercollegiate Game* (New York: Charles Scribner's Sons, 1912), p. 80.

to supersede prior systems. In the 1880s the offensive line typically stretched across the entire field, forcing the defense to do likewise. The backs also lined up across the field several yards behind the scrimmage line and received long sideline passes from the quarterbacks. Forward passes, that is, passes across the line of scrimmage, were illegal. Prior to 1888, the game featured wide-open offensive action with fast, dodging backs, pitchouts, open-field runs, and expert kicking.

The adoption of Camp's suggestion in 1888 that tackling be allowed below the waist—another major departure from rugby—destroyed the open style of play and led to the substitutions of plays emphasizing mass and momentum. Already officials had been permitting offensive players to run between the ball carrier and potential tacklers, a violation of rugby rules. As early as 1884 Pennsylvania had initiated their offensive action with the famous "V Trick," which involved the players forming a V with their arms encircling the players ahead of them. Formed some ten yards behind the ball, the V moved forward, enclosing the ball carrier within the apex of the V. Breaking the fearsome formation was not easy. Without any protective gear, defensive men had to hurl themselves directly in front of the V or try to crash its flanks. The low tackle encouraged a host of variations in power plays. For a short time the rules permitted a "flying wedge" in which the offensive line started action some twenty-five yards behind the line of scrimmage. In 1895 formations which involved the entire offensive team moving forward before the ball was put into play were outlawed. While this rule change reduced the terrific collisions between the lines, it failed to open up the offense. Tight formations in which teams tried to squeeze out the five yards needed for a first down by sheer physical power continued into the next century.

With the heavy emotional stake of students, social climbers, alumni, and college authorities in football, the commercialization of the sport was probably inevitable. Exactly what year the students first charged for admissions to a game is unknown, but as early as 1873 Yale and Rutgers shared gate receipts of ninety dollars for a game which attracted some 500 spectators. By the 1890s the annual Thanksgiving Day game in New York regularly generated over $10,000 for each team. By 1903, Yale, probably the most successful team commercially in the nation, generated $106,000 from football, a figure that represented one-eighth of Yale's gross income or the equivalent of the combined budgets of the medical, divinity, and law schools at Yale. While gate receipts furnished most of the funds for athletics, athletic associations also resorted to dues from members, general student assessments, contributions from faculties, and bequests from business concerns.[33]

By the 1890s, the intercollegiate football in the Northeast had begun to take on all of the characteristics of a full-blown spectator sport. All the colleges depended largely upon admission charges to fund their athletic

[33]Andrew M. F. Davis, "College Athletics," *Atlantic Monthly*, 51 (May 1883), 682; Clarence Deming, "The Money Power in College Athletics," *Outlook*, 80 (July 1905), 570.

programs. Guaranteeing adequate gate receipts often depended upon a winning record or beating an arch-rival. To win, teams began to approach football as a science. Amos A. Stagg and Henry L. Williams, two coaches, revealingly entitled their 1893 treatise on coaching, *A Scientific and Practical Treatise on American Football for Schools and Colleges.* Winning, the coaches argued, required planning, careful organization, and specialization, in short, "system" and "order." Yet, while coaches might be able to impose system and order upon their own teams, hostile intercollegiate athletic relations threatened to lead to the demise of college football.

5

The Outsiders

Harper's Weekly, 23 (March 23, 1889), 244.

Recent immigrants, blacks, displaced males in the larger cities—the social "outsiders"—constructed separate worlds of sport. One centered around voluntary associations. Like the social elite of the major cities, ethnics and blacks often formed voluntary associations in which sport was a conspicuous activity. Such organizations facilitated the formation of ethnic and black subcommunities, in some measure helped to counteract dislocations which accompanied the Age of the Player, and assisted in the preservation of traditional cultural patterns. A second world of sport centered around the Victorian subculture. The outsiders joined the "slummers" from the elite as the principal patrons and promoters of the sporting fraternity. By sponsoring professional billiards, bowling, cycling, wrestling, and boxing, the outsiders, especially the Irish-Americans, profited from the growing urban appetite for "illicit" amusements. Moreover, ethnic athletes sometimes found in professional sports, particularly prize fighting and baseball, opportunities to improve their social and economic position. Blacks, on the other hand, usually encountered barriers in professional sports as impenetrable as those they faced in the skilled professions.

In the Age of the Player massive waves of immigration from Europe played a primary role in shaping the sporting activities of the outsiders. From the 1840s to the 1880s most of the immigrants were northwestern Europeans: Irish Catholics, German Protestants and Catholics, and Protestants from both England and the Scandinavian countries. The second wave, extending from the 1880s to the outbreak of World War I in 1914, brought fewer Protestants but millions of Catholics and Jews from southern and eastern Europe. By 1914, immigrants and their offspring accounted for over 70 percent of the population of the nation's five largest cities. Ethnicity and religious affiliation often determined the social texture of urban America. Ethno-religious considerations provided valuable clues, usually far more reliable than one's income level, to whom one would marry, one's personal associates, and how one would vote on election day. Added after 1865 to the urban mosaic was an increasing number of Afro-Americans who had been released from legal bondage by the Civil War.

The ethnics and blacks usually found themselves at the bottom of the urban social ladder. Industrial technology undercut the need for many of the old handicraft artisans. Most of the millions who immigrated after 1880 took jobs as unskilled industrial workers; by 1900 some 57 percent of the factory force was foreign born. The machine dictated the pace of work, and it often killed or maimed. Although precise data on industrial safety do not exist for the late nineteenth century, the available statistics are chilling. The ethnics and blacks crowded into the tenement districts of the cities, aggravating the problems of housing, public health, and crime. The tenements were notoriously unhealthy; in 1900 three of every five babies born in Chicago ghetto failed to reach their first birthday. Facing insurmountable handicaps, ethnics and blacks struggled to claw their way out of the slums and find a place in an alien society.

The ethno-racial-religious mix rarely fulfilled the American dream of a "melting pot." In the 1840s and 1850s, riots repeatedly erupted in the larger cities. In the early forties, Protestant mobs in widely scattered locations attacked Catholic churches and convents. In the fifties, as urban immigrants began to vote in ever-larger numbers, election-day riots became commonplace. Though no urban resident was totally exempt from ugly mob violence, the free blacks suffered even more severely than recent immigrants. Between 1832 and 1849, Philadelphia alone witnessed five antiblack riots. In New York City in 1863, immigrant workers rioted for days against the Union draft, killing several hundred people (mostly free blacks) and terrorizing the city until quashed by federal troops. Although mob violence declined after the Civil War, it was symptomatic of the breakdown of the old social order and of deep conflicts between the cultural values of American social groups. Throughout the Age of Player and into the Age of the Spectator, ethnic, racial, and religious groups viewed each other with suspicion, anxiety, and often bitter hatred. Despite grandiloquent claims to the contrary, sport was not immune to the ethno-racial-religious conflict.

ETHNIC AND BLACK SPORTS CLUBS

The need of immigrant groups to form separate ethnic communities depended upon a host of variables including their nationality, religious beliefs, language, and status. The majority of old-stock Americans were likely to be least discriminatory toward immigrants who were most like themselves. Immigrants from England, Scotland, and Wales tended to assimilate more rapidly than those from other parts of Europe. The history of nineteenth- and early twentieth-century sport clubs reflected the process of acculturation by distinctive ethnic groups. The Scottish Caledonian clubs and the English cricket clubs, for example, functioned briefly as distinctive ethnic communities. But as Scottish and English immigration declined and they adopted the old-stock, largely Victorian-American culture, the need for ethnic communities subsided. The German Turner societies began as ethnic communities, and, as the clubs assimilated, they sometimes became status communities.[1]

[1] For an example of the transition of a Turner group from an ethnic to a status community, see Noel Iverson, *Germania, U.S.A.: Social Change in New Ulm, Minnesota* (Minneapolis: University of Minnesota Press, 1966).

The Scottish Caledonian clubs may have been the most significant ethnic community in encouraging the growth of nineteenth-century American sport. Back in the mists of Scottish history, rural communities had held annual track and field games. During the 1850s, these games began to provide one of the bases for organizing Caledonian clubs in America. Eventually, well over one hundred clubs formed. Wherever a few Scots settled, they usually founded a Caledonian club. In 1887, for example, the *Scottish-American Journal* reported that "A Caledonian Club has been organized at Great Falls, Montana, with a membership of 37 enthusiastic Scots."[2] The clubs restricted membership to persons of Scottish birth or descent.

Although the evidence is not conclusive, it appears that the Caledonian clubs functioned as a major agency for the formation of a Scottish ethnic community in many American cities. The purpose of the clubs, as one of the founders of the Boston organization put it, was to perpetuate "the manners and customs, literature, the Highland costume and the athletic games of Scotland, as practiced by our forefathers."[3] Apart from sport, the clubs sponsored extensive social activities, such as dinners, dancing, and bagpipe playing. In short, the clubs provided a sense of community in a strange society.

Old-stock Americans exhibited an unexpected enthusiasm for the annual Caledonian games. Huge crowds, as many as 20,000 in New York City, turned out to view competition in footracing, tug o' war, hurdling, jumping, pole vaulting, throwing the hammer, and putting the shot. The clubs quickly recognized the potential for financial gain. They opened competition to all athletes regardless of nationality or race, charged admission, and offered lucrative prizes to winners. From the 1850s to the mid-1870s, the Caledonians were the most important promoters of track and field in the country. The success of the games helped to stimulate the formation of the old-stock American athletic clubs and the growth of intercollegiate track and field. In fact, by the 1880s, the wealthy old-stock American clubs had seized basic control of American track and field from the Caledonians. The Caledonians then began to decline rapidly as promoters of sport, but they continued to serve as the focal point of Scottish communities. With the slackening of Scottish immigration and the rapid assimilation of Scots into American society, most of the clubs had disappeared by 1900. Most of the Scots no longer felt a compelling need for distinctive ethnic communities.

For a brief time, cricket clubs may have assisted English immigrants in establishing ethnic communities. By the 1840s, when a new influx of immigrants arrived in the United States, England was already in the midst of a sporting revolution. Cricket was popular in both the southern downs and the industrial north of England. The skilled textile workers from the North brought the sport with them to the mills at Lawrence and Lowell,

---

[2]Quoted in Gerald Redmond, *The Caledonian Games in Nineteenth-Century America* (Rutherford, N.J.: Fairleigh Dickinson University Press, 1971), p. 45.
[3]Ibid., p. 39.

Massachusetts, and to the Manheim district of Philadelphia. Their version of cricket often included a rough-and-tumble style of play, strictly male companionship, and hard drinking. After the matches, the immigrant workingmen gathered at a favorite drinking establishment to recount matches of the past and swap stories of the homeland. In New York, Brooklyn, and Boston, English merchants and professional men founded formal cricket clubs. Their version of cricket was only somewhat more decorous. They usually wagered for side bets and hired professional players if they could afford it, but they might also interrupt matches for a dinner, and the matches might continue over two or three days. Both types of cricket helped preserve old English traditions and customs in a new environment.[4]

In the 1850s, cricket rivaled American baseball as a team sport spectacle. The St. George's Cricket Club of New York, which employed a professional cricketer from England as a trainer and was the premier club in the United States until the Civil War, attracted large crowds in the 1840s and 1850s to its matches with clubs from Montreal, Toronto, and Boston. New York newspapers regularly gave its matches more coverage than the city's baseball games. In 1859, over 24,000 attended a cricket match at the Elysian Fields in Hoboken between an all-star American team and a touring professional English eleven. Extra ferries had to be engaged to handle the crowds who crossed the river from Manhattan. By 1860, there were ten clubs in New York and Brooklyn. Several pioneers of American baseball, such as Harry Wright and Henry Chadwick, came from the ranks of the English cricket clubs. For a decade or so after 1850, old-stock American clubs sometimes played both cricket and baseball.[5] The Civil War dealt cricket in New York and Brooklyn a blow from which it never fully recovered.

In the last half of the nineteenth century, teams from the British Isles, Australia, and Canada regularly toured the United States, playing both the ethnic clubs and the powerful old-stock American clubs of Philadelphia. By 1887, there were at least fifty clubs scattered throughout the larger cities of the country. For a few years in the 1890s, clubs in Chicago, Detroit, Pittsburgh, New York, Philadelphia, Boston, and Baltimore played in the Inter-City Cricket League, an amateur circuit, and on the Pacific Coast clubs engaged in lively competition for the Harrison Championship Cup. But in the early twentieth century, as English immigration declined sharply and later generations assimilated into the host society, the English cricket clubs rapidly faded from the sporting scene.

Unlike the Scottish Caledonian and the English cricket clubs, the Turner societies had first been organized in their native land. In reaction

[4]See E. Digby Baltzell, *Philadelphia Gentlemen: The Making of a National Upper Class* (New York: Free Press, 1958), pp. 358–61; John A. Lester, ed., *A Century of Philadelphia Cricket* (Philadelphia: University of Pennsylvania Press, 1951); and Melvin Leonard Adelman, "The Development of Modern Athletics in New York City, 1820–1870," (unpublished Ph.D. dissertation, University of Illinois, 1980), esp. pp. 286–87.

[5]See Harold Seymour, *Baseball: The Early Years* (New York: Oxford University Press, 1960), pp. 14–15. In the 1880s and 1890s, *Outing* magazine is an excellent source for cricket.

to the rule of Napoleon, the power of the German aristocracy, and the disunity of the German states, Friederick Ludwig Jahn formed the first Turner society in Berlin in 1811. From the start, the Turners had a strong ideological cast. By establishing universal education and a systematic program of gymnastics (the latter modeled after the ancient Greeks), Jahn hoped to create a united Germany ruled by the people. Young men of the middle class—petty officials, intellectuals, journalists, and students—flocked to Jahn's new society. The Revolution of 1848 brought disaster for the Turners in Germany; many of them emigrated to the United States.

The Turner immigrants faced a different challenge in America, for the Americans had already achieved several of the Turner goals. The United States had no hereditary aristocracy to combat, and a representative democracy was accepted as the ideal political form. Yet the Turners were utopian, free-thinking, and socialistic. They sought an organic community. American individualism ran counter to their deepest social instincts. They also arrived during the heyday of the Know-Nothing movement, a nativist movement of the 1850s. Though the nativists directed their energies primarily at the Catholic Church and Irish immigrants, the Turners bore the brunt of mob action in several American cities. Perhaps even more crucial in driving the Turners together was the fierce antagonism they experienced from the "church" Germans. The haughty anticlericalism and superior cultural achievements of the Turners made it impossible for them to find refuge in the larger German ethnic communities. Consequently, the Turner societies formed distinctive subcommunities in many American cities, sharply separated from those Germans whose lives centered around their churches.

Shortly after their arrival in the New World, the revolutionary émigrés of 1848 began to organize Turner societies. Friedrich Hecker, a hero of the Revolution in Baden, erected a gymnasium in Cincinnati in 1849 to cultivate "rational training, both physical and intellectual." The Turner halls provided a complete social center with lectures, libraries, and usually a bar. Here the Turners tried to preserve the speech, songs, and customs of the Fatherland. They often formed separate militia companies. In 1851 the Turners held a national gymnastics festival in Philadelphia. This competitive event became an annual affair, with gymnasts from over 150 societies participating. After the Civil War, the Turners abandoned most of their radical political program and began to assimilate more rapidly into the host society. In 1881, by competing in a gymnastics festival held at Frankfurt on the Main, a group of Turners from the Normal School of the *Turnerbund* located at Milwaukee, initiated irregular competition between Turner teams from the United States and Germany that continued until World War I. One of the striking features of the Chicago World's Fair of 1893 was a mass exercise performed by 4,000 German-American members of the national *Turnerbund*. In 1898, the United States Commissioner of Education declared that the introduction of school gymnastics in Chicago, Kansas City, Cleveland, Denver, Indianapolis, St. Louis, Milwaukee, Cincinnati, St. Paul, and San Francisco was due to the Turners and that "the directors of physical education [in these cities] are graduates of the Seminary or

Normal School of the North American Turnerbund."[6] Moreover, modern Olympic gymnastics originated primarily from the Turner societies.

Baseball appealed to almost all nineteenth-century ethnic groups, but particularly to the Irish and the Germans. Since baseball could be played relatively quickly, any open space could be used as a playing area, and equipment requirements were cheap, it did not long remain an exclusive sport of the status-conscious old-stock American clubs (see Chapter 6). Beginning in the 1850s, the Germans and the Irish took up the sport with alacrity. In New Orleans, for example, the Germans founded the Schneiders, Laners, and Landwehrs, and the Irish formed the Fenian Baseball Club. The Irish volunteer fire departments, saloons, and political clubs of the nineteenth and early twentieth centuries frequently sponsored baseball clubs. Baseball invariably accompanied the ethnic picnics of the Germans, Irish, French, and later, Italians. As late as the 1920s, a French-Canadian faction in Woonsocket, Rhode Island, "resorted to the archetypical American game" as a means of preserving their community from the forces of assimilation.[7] While immigrant groups adopted baseball as one way of identifying with the host society, the sport could also be used to preserve and coalesce the old cultural patterns. It assisted in blurring the status, ideological, and economic differences within the ethnic communities.

Inadequate evidence makes it difficult to reach more than tentative conclusions about the black experience in nineteenth-century sport. Newspapers and sporting journals rarely reported the sporting activities of Afro-Americans. Until 1865, slavery obviously curtailed the athletic opportunities for blacks. In the antebellum era, planters sometimes promoted boxing bouts among their slaves and used them as crews for boating regattas. To the extent that they had equal leisure time and funds, free blacks in the urban areas probably were as active in sport as their white counterparts. In the New York City area, blacks sponsored occasional prize fights and scheduled a few professional pedestrian races. In New Orleans, where the largest aggregation of free blacks lived in the antebellum era, Afro-Americans formed two sport clubs—Bayou and LaVille—for the playing of raquette. Apparently borrowed from the Choctaw Indians, raquette was a team game roughly resembling lacrosse. The Sunday matches between two black clubs in the 1850s sometimes attracted as many as 4,000 spectators from all social ranks and both races. For a brief interval

[6]Quoted in A. E. Zucker, ed., *The Forty-Eighters: Political Refugees of the German Revolution of 1848* (New York: Columbia University Press, 1950). p. 109. See also Henry Metzner, *A Brief History of the American Turnerbund,* rev. ed. (Pittsburgh: National Executive Committee of the American Turnerbund, 1924); Horst Uberhorst, *Turner Unterm Sternenbund* (Munich, 1979). Equally striking as sport organizations that promoted ethnic communities were the Czech Sokols. Eventually some 184 Sokols were organized in the United States. Most had large buildings in which calisthenics, gymnastics, athletic contests, singing, and other social activities took place. Training in the Sokol system included Czech youth and women as well as men. See *Panorama: A Historical Review of Czechs and Slovaks in the United States of America* (Cicero, Ill.: Czechoslovak National Council of America, 1970), pp. 133–52.

[7]Richard Sorrel, "Sports and the Franco-Americans in Woonsocket, 1870–1930," *Rhode Island History,* 31 (Fall 1972), 112. Sorrel believes that baseball both encouraged and discouraged the acculturation of the French Canadians in Woonsocket.

after the Civil War, a few interracial raquette contests were held, but interest in the game soon gave way to other sports.[8]

After the Civil War, many ex-slaves fled the plantations for the cities. Little is known of their athletic activities. But it is clear that prize fighting within the black communities was common, that a few black athletic clubs existed, and that many black baseball teams were organized. Baseball was by far the most popular team sport of the urban blacks. In New Orleans, for example, several clubs scheduled a city-wide "Negro championship" series in the 1880s. As in other parts of the country, it was not unusual for black and white amateur or semiprofessional teams to play against one another. A newspaper account of a game played in 1887 at New Orleans, in which a black nine defeated a white club, noted: "The playing of the colored club was far above the average ball playing and elicited hearty and generous applause from the large crowd in attendance, which was about evenly divided between white and colored."[9] From the scanty evidence available, it appears that the black athletic organizations served as agencies for promoting the formation of subcommunities of blacks.

ETHNICS AND BLACKS IN PROFESSIONAL SPORTS

Professional sports have long been regarded as the very symbol of democratic opportunity. Presumably, ethnic and racial minorities found in sport that only their athletic skills counted. Education, ethnicity, skin color, and parental status were irrelevant, for on the athletic field all men competed on an equal basis. For the athletically talented ethnic or black, professional sport purportedly offered an easier exit out of the ghetto than other possible careers. John K. Tener, president of baseball's National League and former governor of Pennsylvania, probably reflected the self-perception of professional sportsmen when he declared: "I tell you that baseball is the very watchword of democracy. There is no other sport or business or anything under heaven which exerts the leveling influence that baseball does. Neither the public school nor the church can approach it."[10]

For aspiring athletes of whatever social origin, professional baseball offered far more jobs than the other sports combined. The rosters of major-league teams suggest that baseball did indeed measure men more by their athletic talent than their ethnic origins. Contemporary observers often commented on the large number of German and Irish players in the major leagues. One expert estimated that about one-third of the major leaguers in the early 1890s were of Irish origins. There were "so many Irish in the game that some thought they had a special talent for ball playing. Fans liked to argue the relative merits of Irish as against those of German

[8]See Dale A. Somers, *The Rise of Sports in New Orleans, 1850–1900* (Baton Rouge: Louisiana State University Press, 1972), pp. 71–72, 208–9.

[9]Quoted in ibid., p. 120. For blacks in baseball, see also Robert Peterson, *Only the Ball Was White* (Englewood Cliffs, N.J.: Prentice-Hall, 1970).

[10]Quoted in Seymour, *Baseball*, p. 83.

extraction."[11] Apparently well over half of the big-league ball players in the 1880s and 1890s were either of German or Irish origins. The hostility of middle- and upper-status old-stock American groups toward professional baseball as a career choice undoubtedly increased opportunities for ethnics.

The story of the black in professional baseball was another matter. As early as 1867, the National Association of Base Ball Players, composed of "amateur" athletes, specifically excluded black players and clubs from membership.[12] The professional association of the early 1870s did not formally ban blacks—at least one black played briefly in the association— but apparently did practice exclusion by a "gentleman's agreement." Informally, the National League, organized in 1876, enforced a "color ban" from its founding. In the 1880s, a few clubs in other professional leagues experimented with integrated teams. In 1883, Moses Fleetwood Walker, a former Michigan and Oberlin College student, signed with Toledo. The next year Toledo entered the American Association, then a major league, with Walker behind the plate. Later in the season, Weldy Walker, Moses' younger brother, played in six games with Toledo. Neither of the Walkers obtained a contract in 1885, but Moses Walker along with seven or eight other blacks continued to play on white minor-league teams.

The experiment with integrated professional baseball was brief. Racial antagonism intensified in the 1880s, and the white players deeply resented the competition with blacks for playing positions. In 1887, Adrian C. "Cap" Anson, the player-manager of the Chicago White Sox, refused to allow his team to play an exhibition game with Newark until Moses Walker and another black were removed from the Newark lineup. In the same year, the St. Louis Browns team successfully petitioned their owner to block a match with the Cuban Giants, a black professional team. (In an effort to escape discrimination, black players and teams often tried to use the ploy of advertising themselves as Cubans.) Also in 1887, several of the best white players in the International League threatened to quit unless blacks were dropped from the circuit. According to the *Sporting News* in 1889 "race prejudice exists in professional baseball ranks to a marked degree, and the unfortunate son of Africa who makes his living as a member of a team of White professionals has a rocky road to travel."[13] Indeed, he did. Black players had to withstand withering ridicule from fellow players, their managers, and the white spectators. In the 1890s, total segregation became the rule, corresponding in time with the passage of a new array of Jim Crow laws and the increased disenfranchisement of blacks by state legislatures. The "color ban" remained in the major leagues and their affiliates until 1945, when Jackie Robinson signed with the Montreal Royals, a minor-league club owned by the Brooklyn Dodgers.

In the 1880s, blacks themselves organized several professional baseball teams. Apparently each of the major metropolitan areas had one or more

---

[11]Ibid., p. 334.
[12]For the official statement of the NABBP see ibid., p. 42.
[13]Quoted in Peterson, *Only the Ball Was White*, p. 41.

black clubs. In 1889 and 1890, the powerful Cuban Giants of New York City belonged to the Middle States League, which, apart from the Giants, was composed of white clubs located mostly in smaller cities along the East Coast. When the league folded in 1890, the Giants joined the Connecticut State League, only to witness its demise after one year. A few professional teams regularly barnstormed the country in the 1890s, playing each other, amateur black and white teams, and white professional teams in exhibition matches. During the next two decades, blacks formed many more touring professional teams, most of which were financially marginal operations. Moreover, the black players generally earned far less than their professional white counterparts.

Sometimes blacks found opportunities in professional sports other than baseball. A few became pedestrians and competed on both sides of the Atlantic Ocean, but after the 1870s, professional running nearly disappeared. Blacks enjoyed more success in prize fighting (see the final section of this chapter). Prior to the 1890s, many blacks served as jockeys. The bicycling rage of the last decade of the nineteenth century reflected the typical problems confronted by blacks in sport. Prior to 1890, when the cycle was expensive, the question of black membership in the amateur League of American Wheelman (LAW), organized in 1880, was practically nonexistent. But in the early 1890s, the manufacturers perfected inexpensive "drop frame," or "safety" bicycles, which opened the sport to nearly all income groups. To protest black membership in the LAW, southern affiliates in the early 1890s began to withdraw from the league. In response, the 1894 LAW convention adopted a "whites only" membership policy. "There is no question of our accepting the negro in preference to the white wheelman of the south," wrote a LAW official. "If it should be narrowed down to a question such as that, we should undoubtedly decide that we want our southern brothers in the league in preference to the negroes of the country."[14]

Only Marshall W. "Major" Taylor, a black man from Indianapolis, Indiana, succeeded in breaking the racial barrier in professional bicycle racing.[15] Hailed as the "Fastest Bicycle Rider in the World," Taylor, who won the national sprint championships in 1898, 1899, and 1900, broke many national and world records before retiring in 1910. From the beginning of his career as a "scorcher," as bicycle racers were dubbed, at the tender age of fourteen, Taylor experienced nearly every conceivable form of discrimination from white racers. Apart from frequent racial slurs, white riders often colluded in throwing him from his cycle or "boxing" him in, and, in at least one instance, he was physically attacked by a white rider after the completion of a match. Promoters prohibited Taylor from racing on all southern and several northern tracks. In 1897, fellow riders tried to exclude him from all "white" tracks, but the conspiracy collapsed, attribut-

---

[14]Quoted in Somers, *The Rise of Sports in New Orleans*, p. 223. See also Robert A. Smith, *A Social History of the Bicycle: Its Early Life and Times in America* (New York: American Heritage, 1972).

[15]See especially Marshall W. "Major" Taylor, *The Fastest Bicycle Rider in the World* (Battleboro, Vt.: Green-Stephen, 1972).

able largely to the influence of the bicycle manufacturers and racing promoters. Despite the hostility of the other scorchers toward Taylor, the bike makers and race promoters had a stake in keeping Taylor on the tracks. For the black scorcher attracted larger crowds than any other single performer. Apart from Taylor, however, few other blacks competed in "white" events. Most of them raced only in an all-Negro league. In the early years of the twentieth century, the popularity of cycle racing rapidly declined, to be replaced in part by automobile racing.

IRISH-AMERICANS AND PRIZE FIGHTING

During the Age of the Player, Irish males were an especially important segment of the sporting fraternity. In the first place, the Victorian subculture offered Irish youths what Daniel Bell has called in another context "one of the queer ladders of social mobility in American life."[16] This "queer ladder" became available to the Irish because Victorian America placed severe strictures on human appetites, branding as illicit gambling, drinking, prostitution, and prize fighting. These Blue Laws ran counter to a growing urban demand for the satisfaction of such hungers. Given their moral scruples and opportunities for profit in other careers, old-stock Americans hesitated to satisfy the demand. The Irish Catholic culture, on the other hand, was not so encumbered by these Victorian inhibitions. Finding avenues of opportunity blocked in respectable occupations, many of the Irish naturally turned to careers that satisfied the urban hunger for gaming, drink, and sport. Such careers required little education and could produce quick rewards in a society that placed a high value on material success. A close connection necessarily existed between these careers and urban politics, for, in order to be successful, the Irish sportsman had to reach an understanding with local political authorities.

In the second place, the prominence of a "bachelor" subculture within the larger Irish population encouraged the growth of the sporting fraternity. A high percentage of bachelors, delayed marriages, rigorous norms of premarital chastity, and traditions of segregation of the sexes made all-male groups far more important to the Irish-Americans than to any other ethnic group. Whether married or unmarried, a male's status within the larger Irish community tended to rest on his membership and active participation in the bachelor subculture. Thus many of the "bachelors" were technically married men, although they spent nearly all of their leisure time with other males. The subculture furnished a refuge against loneliness, a substitute for the conjugal family, and served as an agency of social cohesion. The bachelors usually gathered at saloons to drink, gossip, tell stories, exchange information, and engage in political and business transactions. They performed the rites of passage for Irish

[16]Daniel Bell, *The End of Ideology: On the Exhaustion of Political Ideas in the Fifties,* rev. ed. (New York: Collier Books, 1962), pp. 128–29. Bell's application of the "queer ladder" is to organized crime in the twentieth century.

male youths that symbolized the passage from adolescence to adulthood. They promoted the ideas of a gay, irresponsible, carefree life; they placed a high premium on feats in drinking, sports, politics, violence, and storytelling, all of which were conducive to the growth of a flourishing sporting fraternity.[17]

The bachelor subculture held fighting ability in the highest esteem. Even as youngsters, survival and status of an Irish boy in the slums might depend more on his ability to use his fists than his intelligence. Fisticuffs was a favorite means of settling disputes in the ghetto and a way to maintain one's standing among fellow juveniles. Street fighting prepared ghetto boys for future careers as pugilists, criminals, or policemen. Local Irish political machines, especially early in the century, employed "pugs" in their battles with other political factions. If the boy became a successful prize fighter, he furnished a role model for other slum youths. To the youngsters in the tenement districts, the prize fighter embodied not only the survival values of the slum but received handsome rewards as well. In the last half of the nineteenth and in the early twentieth century, Irish boxers dominated the world of the ring; they were replaced in turn by Jews in the 1920s, Italians in the 1930s, and blacks and Latin Americans in the 1940s and since. The prize ring perfectly reflected the order of ascent for ethnic groups from the urban ghettos.[18]

The career of John Morrissey (1831–1878) epitomized the successful Irish combination of politics, gambling, and prize fighting.[19] Born in Ireland as one of eight children, he emigrated with his impoverished family to Troy, New York. His rise to fame and fortune embodied all of the main ingredients of the success myth. As a boy, he became a gang leader and skilled street fighter. Upon arriving in New York City, he immediately invaded the Empire Club, a leading saloon, and challenged all comers to a free-for-all fight. Although severely beaten by the local saloon brawlers, Morrissey was undeterred. Shortly, he became a "pug" for a Tammany Hall faction and hurled challenges to Tom Hyer and Yankee Sullivan, two major prize fighters of the day. Unable to obtain a match, he "bummed" his way across the country to California in hopes of exploiting the gold rush. Morrissey soon returned to the East and prize fighting. In 1853 he defeated Yankee Sullivan at Boston Four Corners, New York, in thirty-seven rounds for $2,000 in prize money. Claiming the national championship, Morrissey began to branch out into gambling and politics. He did not fight again until 1857, when he bested James C. Heenan, another Irish-

[17]See Richard Stivers, *A Hair of the Dog: Irish Drinking and American Stereotype* (University Park and London: Pennsylvania State University Press, 1976), especially Chaps. 5 and 6, and Patrick McNabb, "Social Structure," in *The Limerick Rural Survey, 1958–1964,* ed. by Jeremiah Newman (Tipperary, Ireland: Muintir Na Tire Rural Publications, 1964). The Irish bachelor subculture also existed in Ireland at the time of large-scale Irish immigration to the United States. Both Stivers and McNabb refer to it simply as the "bachelor group." Stivers believes the bachelor group had essentially disappeared in the United States by the 1940s.

[18]See S. Kirson Weinberg and Henry Arond, "The Occupational Culture of the Boxer," *American Journal of Sociology,* 57 (March 1952), 460–69.

[19]See especially the account of Alexander Johnston, *Ten—and Out!*, 3rd rev. ed. (New York: Ives Washington, 1947), Chap. 4.

American, at Long Point, Canada, in eleven rounds. Morrissey then retired from the professional prize ring.

Thereafter, he devoted his full attention to politics and the development of his gambling enterprises. From the earnings of his first fight he established a gaming house in New York City which by 1860 had become the most celebrated parlor in the city. It became a second home of the city's wealthy fancies. "His table, attendants, cooking and company," wrote a contemporary, "are exceeded by nothing on this side of the Atlantic."[20] In 1867, he built an equally lavish gambling parlor and restaurant at Saratoga Springs, New York. He also combined with a syndicate to build the first horse racing track at Saratoga Springs. Morrissey now hobnobbed with the rich and counted Cornelius Vanderbilt as a personal friend. Since the 1850s he had retained a close association with the Tammany Hall political machine and was rewarded by being elected to Congress in 1866. He won reelection in 1868. By the time he died in 1878, he had won a fortune and demonstrated the opportunities in sport, gambling, and politics for a young Irishman who enjoyed both brains and brawn.

After Morrissey's retirement from the ring, James C. Heenan assumed the championship title. Few challengers stepped forward, so Heenan traveled about the country giving exhibitions with theatre troupes. In 1860 he met Tom Sayers, the English champion, in a match near London that excited far more public interest than any prior prize fight. The American newspapers and magazines sent a large corps of reporters and artists to cover the event. In England the fight attracted low and high alike; members of the English aristocracy joined the riffraff in witnessing a two-hour blood bath. In the seventh round, Sayers, who weighed only 150 pounds compared to Heenan's 190 pounds, pulled a muscle in his right arm but continued to stage a masterful defense. Finally, with both fighters bloody and exhausted, the crowd out of control, and the police about to stop the fight, the referee called the match a draw.

In the 1880s, several circumstances joined to bring a new era in prize fighting. One was *The National Police Gazette* published and edited by Richard Kyle Fox.[21] Printed on shocking pink paper and distributed at discount rates to such all-male preserves as barbershops, livery stables, saloons, private men's clubs, and volunteer fire departments, the notorious weekly *Gazette* exploited to the fullest the nation's racial bigotry, secret sexual lusts, and thirst for the sensational. Repeated libel suits and efforts by the authorities to suppress the *Gazette* only served to increase its circulation. In the mid-1880s, subscriptions mounted to over 150,000 copies, and each issue circulated through several hands. Fox defined sport broadly, managing to include practically every form of bizarre human behavior imaginable. He offered championship belts and other prizes for, among other things, the world's championship heavyweight boxing,

[20] Quoted in Herbert Asbury, *The Gangs of New York: An Informal History of the Underworld* (New York: Capricorn Books, 1970), p. 100.

[21] See Gene Smith and Jayne Barry, eds., *The Police Gazette* (New York: Simon & Schuster, 1972) and Edward Van Every, *Sins of America As Exposed by the Police Gazette* (Philadelphia: J. B. Lippincott, 1930).

teethlifting, hog butchering, "one-legged clog dancing," female cycling, and female weightlifting. But his favorite sport was prize fighting. With little success, he repeatedly pleaded for the legalization of the fight game. By launching a campaign to unseat John L. Sullivan as heavyweight king and by more or less arbitrarily awarding belts and naming champions in different weight divisions in boxing, Fox attracted national attention to pugilism and even brought a modicum of order to the intrinsically chaotic sport.

Key metropolitan saloons supplemented Fox's efforts to promote the new era of prize fighting. The most important was Harry Hill's saloon, located on notorious Bleeker Street in New York City. Politicians, elite slummers, professional gamblers, show people, promoters, fight managers, and pugilists made Hill's their headquarters. Hill's place was more than simply a saloon; it was a house of entertainment, for it consisted of a long serving bar upstairs, a standing bar downstairs, a wine room, a concert hall, and a room with a boxing and wrestling ring. "Ladies" never went to Hill's, but it was a favorite haunt of dashing young "gentlemen" looking for "illicit" entertainment and excitement. "If you were anybody at all in New York night life of the late seventies and early eighties," wrote one observer, "you got into Harry Hill's as often as possible. Here boxing and wrestling were held and articles were signed for bigger matches elsewhere, shows were cast, large bets were made."[22] Prize fighting was illegal in New York at the time, but boxing "exhibitions" were permitted. In the early eighties, both William Muldoon, the most renowned Greco-Roman wrestler of the day, and John L. Sullivan, the prize fighting champion, worked out of Hill's saloon. Harry Hill himself was the best-known and most esteemed stake-holder and boxing referee in the country. Though usually less lavish, saloons in other large cities served the sporting fraternity in a similar fashion.

Athletic clubs, whether those of an elite character or those composed specifically of fight promoters, also contributed to the new era of ring history. A growing interest in boxing by a few members of elite athletic clubs, especially in New York, New Orleans, and San Francisco, improved the public image of the fight game. Several clubs even hired boxing "professors"—invariably of Irish extraction—to teach interested members the finer arts of pugilism. Sometimes the slummers from the athletic clubs joined in an uneasy alliance with Irish politicians in efforts to repeal or modify state laws or city ordinances that banned prize fighting. In an effort to placate a hostile public, the supporters of legalized fighting invented ingenious ruses. In New York, for instance, the Horton Law of 1896 permitted fights under the auspices of bona fide athletic clubs. A coterie of fight enthusiasts, which included well-to-do old-stock Americans and Irish-Americans, promptly formed the Twentieth Century Athletic Club as a front, leased Madison Square Garden, and began to hold public prize

[22]Donald Barr Chidsey, *John the Great: The Times and Life of a Remarkable American, John L. Sullivan* (Garden City, N.Y.: Doubleday, Doran, 1942), p. 13. See also Alexander B. Callow, Jr., *The Tweed Ring* (New York: Oxford University Press, 1966), pp. 56–57.

fights. This law, like similar laws in other states, resulted in the formation of a host of smaller fight clubs as well. A public outcry against this devious tactic in New York led to the repeal of the act in 1900, but in 1910 the fight fans invented yet another artifice. The Frawley Act allowed no decision, no knock-out, ten-round "exhibitions." Thus began an era of "newspaper decisions," a situation in which newspapers announced "unofficial" winners. Bettors then wagered on the newspaper winners. Despite rampant chicanery under the new law, prize fighting flourished.[23]

The entrance of athletic clubs into the fight game altered the nature of the sport. The clubs prompted the growing acceptance of the Marquis of Queensberry rules. Drafted under the patronage of the Marquis of Queensberry in 1867, the rules required the use of gloves, limited rounds to three minutes, provided for ten-second knockouts, and prohibited wrestling holds. A major breakthrough in the use of the new rules was a New Orleans city ordinance passed in 1890 which permitted gloved fights sponsored by athletic clubs. The ordinance paved the way for the first gloved heavyweight championship fight between John L. Sullivan and James J. Corbett, held in 1892. The clubs also encouraged the practice of fighting for a specified number of rounds, though round limitations did not become a universal practice until the 1920s. Moreover, the clubs joined Richard Kyle Fox in promoting weight divisions for pugilists. By the mid-1880s, Fox was naming national champions, often with very shadowy claims, for six distinct weight divisions. Finally, by bringing the matches indoors, charging admissions, and offering specific purses to the winners, the clubs altered the traditional decor and modes of fight promotion.[24]

Into the new era of prize fighting stepped a new champion heavyweight whose contribution to pugilism may have exceeded that of Fox, the saloons, and the fight clubs.[25] Born in Boston of Irish immigrant parents, John L. Sullivan, unlike Morrissey, ignored politics and gambling and devoted his large energies mostly to fighting and drinking. As a teenager, he began boxing occasional exhibition matches in Boston theatres, where he soon developed a reputation as a slugger. In 1882 he finally got a match with the reigning champion, Paddy Ryan, whom he knocked out in the second round at Mississippi City, Louisiana, for a stake of $5,000 and a side bet of $1,000.

The public adored the new champion. Shortly after winning the title, Sullivan toured the country offering the astonishing sum of $1,000 to anyone who could stand up to him for four rounds. Only one person performed the feat; some fifty challengers suffered knockouts from Sullivan's mighty blows. Sullivan used gloves in these exhibitions. Unlike previous titleholders who avoided defending their crown as long as possible while profiting from sparring matches in vaudeville acts, Sullivan

---

[23]No adequate account of New York prize fighting exists, but see Barry Nagler, "Boxing," in *Madison Square Garden: A Century of Sport and Spectacle on the World's Most Versatile Stage*, ed. by Zander Hollander (New York: Hawthorn, 1975), pp. 93–107.

[24]See especially Somers, *Rise of Sports in New Orleans*, pp. 188–90.

[25]See especially Chidsey, *John the Great* and John L. Sullivan, *Life and Times of a 19th Century Gladiator* (Boston: Jas. A. Hearn, 1892.)

liked to fight. Between 1884 and 1886 he added fourteen official victories to his record. The tour, Sullivan's love of fighting, and his flamboyant lifestyle raised the "Boston Strong Boy" to the pinnacle of national popularity. Among the patrons of the sporting underworld and proper Victorians alike his name became a household word.

In the mid-1880s Richard Kyle Fox became a pivotal figure in Sullivan's career. Fox recognized in Sullivan an opportunity to increase the circulation of *The National Police Gazette.* The newspaper ran story after story depicting Sullivan in the stereotypical terms with which old-stock Americans tended to perceive the Irish generally. Sullivan was a dissolute bully who, according to the *Gazette,* went on drunken benders that lasted several weeks and left the champion with "delirium tremors." His brute strength and uncontrollable temper made him a dangerous man. "The wonder is," reported the *Gazette,* "that he has never killed anyone, for he has such a terrific wallop that the head and shoulders of his victim sometimes hit the canvas before the buttocks."[26] Fox launched a national campaign ostensibly in quest of a challenger that could rid boxing of the menace of the Boston Strong Boy. Fox's tactics presaged techniques that would become commonplace in the promotion of later boxing matches.

Fox generated widespread interest in the personal life of Sullivan and the world of professional boxing. By the late 1880s there were several

John L. Sullivan knocks out Jake Kilrain. Photograph by George Barker, 1889. Reproduced from the Collections of the Library of Congress. Courtesy of the Library of Congress.

[26]Quoted in John Durant, "Yours Truly, John L. Sullivan," *American Heritage,* 10 (August 1959), 59.

willing challengers for the championship mantle. Sullivan avoided only the black boxers, one of whom—Peter Jackson—might have sent him to an early defeat. In 1889 Sullivan finally found a worthy opponent in Jake Kilrain. In the last bout of the bare-knuckle era, Sullivan and Kilrain dueled under the Richburg, Mississippi, sun for seventy-five rounds before the referee finally awarded the match to the Boston Strong Boy. Sullivan's seconds reportedly fortified him regularly with copious drafts of tea mixed with whiskey. In the 45th round, Sullivan began to heave up the concoction. One wag claimed that the champion's stomach "rejected the tea but held the whiskey." The reign of Sullivan ended in his bout with James J. "Gentleman Jim" Corbett in New Orleans in 1892. In the 21st round, Corbett "shot his right across the jaw and Sullivan fell like an ox."[27] The fight inaugurated the use of gloves in heavyweight championship fights, employment of the Marquis of Queensberry rules, and a more "scientific" style of boxing. Despite the stories of Sullivan's excesses, the champion had helped make boxing a more respectable sport.

Sullivan was probably the first truly national sports hero. His climb to fame embodied the mythology of rugged American individualism and the gospel of self-help. Without the assistance of superior birth or presumably external advantages, he had fought his way to the top of the savage world of boxing sheerly through his own efforts. He had succeeded in the sport which was becoming symbolically the ultimate test of masculinity. Perhaps the aura which surrounded Sullivan is best summed up in a story told by William Lyon Phelps. "In 1892 I was reading aloud the news to my father," Phelps wrote. "My father was an orthodox Baptist minister. . . . I had never heard him mention a prize fight and did not suppose he knew anything on the subject, or cared anything about it. So when I came to the headline CORBETT DEFEATS SULLIVAN I read that aloud and turned the page. My father leaned forward and said earnestly 'Read it by rounds!'"[28] Sullivan remained a hero of his own time long after his loss to Corbett. He performed theatrically in numerous vaudeville acts and plays—he played Simon Legree in a traveling production of *Uncle Tom's Cabin*—and, after 1905 he became a popular temperance speaker.

Yet neither the popularity of Sullivan, the reforms instituted by the athletic clubs, nor the propaganda of Richard Kyle Fox completely erased the traditional stigma associated with prize fighting. The sport remained illegal almost everywhere; respectable women did not regularly attend fights until the 1920s. Compared to professional baseball or even the college football of the era, prize fighting was a disorderly sport without a rational system for scheduling matches or determining champions. Heavyweight champions, with the noteworthy exception of Sullivan, invariably avoided meeting the leading contenders unless they could be assured of a large stake—"win or lose." Young fighters with dreams of reaching the top also sought out "patsies" who would leave their records unblemished. And the bottom line for any fight was the anticipated profits of promoters.

[27]Quoted in Somers, *Rise of Sports in New Orleans,* p. 184.
[28]William Lyon Phelps, *Autobiography with Letters* (New York: Oxford University Press, 1939).

Regardless of other considerations, for promoters, a proposed fight had to attract enough public interest to promise profits. "Carrying an opponent," "taking a dive," and "fixing records"—these and other fraudulent tactics were endemic to the fight game. Despite the increased attention that rich slummers gave to prize fighting, the ambience of boxing continued to be working class and ethnic, shrouded in turn by the shady world of bookies, thugs, and racketeers.

BLACK VS. WHITE

Although opportunities in the prize ring did not extend equally to blacks in the Age of the Player, boxing was somewhat less discriminatory than other sports. If pitting a black against a white could be profitable, the sporting fraternity was not averse to promoting such a battle. In the 1890s, George Dixon, a black who fought in a large number of interracial bouts, claimed both the bantam and featherweight championships. For a time, both Joe Gans and Joe Walcott held titles in the lower weight divisions. Peter Jackson, winner of the Australian championship in 1886 and the leading black heavyweight in the 1880s and early 1890s, was not so fortunate. Sponsored by the (white) California Athletic Club in San Francisco, Jackson fought and defeated several prominent white heavyweights in the United States. In 1891, the year before the Sullivan-Corbett bout for the championship, Jackson fought Corbett to a sixty-one-round draw in San Francisco for a purse of $10,000. The California Athletic Club offered a $20,000 purse for a Sullivan-Jackson match, but the Boston Strong Boy declined.[29] The white successors to Sullivan—Corbett, Bob Fitzsimmons, and James J. Jeffries—also drew the "color line."

In 1908, under rather unusual circumstances, a black heavyweight, Jack Johnson (1878–1946), widely but not universally acknowledged as the greatest of all heavyweights, finally obtained a shot at the title. Johnson literally pursued Tommy Burns, the reigning champion around the world from New York to London, to Paris, back to London, and then Sydney, Australia. Along the way, he issued challenges to the titleholder. The press in Australia, burning with indignation at the refusal of earlier white champions to meet their favorite, Peter Jackson, took up the cry in Johnson's behalf. Hugh McIntosh, a wealthy Sydney businessman, clinched the decision of Burns to meet Johnson. McIntosh guaranteed Burns $30,000, win or lose, a guarantee far larger than any previous one. Johnson was to receive $5,000. In addition, Johnson agreed to allow Burns' manager to referee the match. Ex-champion John L. Sullivan probably expressed the typical response of American whites to the decision of Burns. "Shame on the money-mad champion! Shame on the man who upsets good American precedents because there are Dollars, Dollars, Dollars, in it."[30] Johnson easily battered Burns into submission.

[29]*New York Clipper*, May 3, 1890.
[30]Quoted in Al-Tony Gilmore, *Bad Nigger! The National Impact of Jack Johnson* (Port Washington, N.Y.: Kennikat, 1975), p. 27.

Almost at once, ex-champions, fight promoters, and newspapermen launched a hunt for a "Great White Hope" to retake the crown from Johnson. As Johnson disposed of several second-rate white hopefuls, the demand grew for James J. Jeffries, a popular former heavyweight champion, to come out of retirement and rid boxing of the "black menace." Finally, in 1910, Jeffries agreed to battle Johnson at Reno, Nevada, the winner to receive about $60,000. Jeffries himself interpreted the fight in racial terms. "That portion of the white race that has been looking for me to defend its athletic superiority may feel assured," he said, "that I am fit to do my best."[31] Jeffries' best was not enough, for Johnson knocked him out in the 15th round. Johnson's victory ignited black celebrations across the country which were in some instances accompanied by racial violence.

The victories of Jack Johnson stunned white America. To both white and black, Johnson's ascension to the heavyweight throne possessed incalculable symbolic significance. For in the most primeval of American sports, the ultimate metaphor of masculine conflict, the best of the black men had defeated the best of the white men. Newspaper columnist Max Balthazer wrote of the prospective Jeffries-Johnson fight: "Can the huge white man [Jeffries]...beat down the wonderful black and restore to the Caucasians the crown of elemental greatness as measured by strength of blow, power of heart and being, and, withal, that cunning or keenness that denotes mental as well as physical superiority?"[32] To both races the fight could signify or suggest racial equality or even black superiority; above all, to whites, it might suggest a potential threat to the status quo in American race relations. While Johnson personally ignored organized efforts for greater racial justice in America, his feats might inspire blacks to mount formidable challenges to white supremacy. To many whites, Johnson represented an enormous threat to the entire superstructure of racial segregation.

Never had a heavyweight champion been more controversial than Johnson. Johnson's demeanor resembled a combination of Muhammad Ali and John L. Sullivan. In an age in which racial animosity had reached a fever pitch, Johnson exacerbated deep-set white fears. In the ring, while smiling broadly, he badgered, taunted, and jeered his white opponents. He was a big spender who loved the high life—flashy dress, champagne, night clubs, large cars, and women of questionable character. To most whites and some blacks he was the embodiment of the "uppity Nigger." He defied age-old racial customs; he married three white women and had sexual relations with many others. By openly flaunting this taboo, Johnson intensified white sexual anxieties. Deeply embedded in black-white mythology was a gnawing suspicion of black sexual superiority and the silent fear that white females fantasized about sexual liaisons with black men. Speaking at the annual governors' conference in 1912, the governor of South Carolina described Johnson as a "black brute." "If we can not protect our white

[31]Quoted in Finis Farr, *Black Champion: The Life and Times of Jack Johnson* (New York: Charles Scribner's Sons, 1964), p. 107.

[32]Quoted in Randy Roberts, "Jack Dempsey: An American Hero in the 1920's," *Journal of Popular Culture*, 8 (Fall 1974), 412.

women from black fiends, where is our vaunted civilization?" he asked rhetorically.[33]

Johnson's enemies struck back. Local and state governments barred the showing of the Johnson-Jeffries fight films in American theatres; in 1912 Congress cooperated by prohibiting the transportation of all moving pictures of boxing matches in interstate commerce. Johnson inspired the introduction of miscegenation laws in half of the twenty states then free of such restrictions. Johnson himself became the victim of legal attacks. In 1912 the mother of one of Johnson's consorts charged him with abducting her daughter across state lines for immoral purposes, which, if true, would have constituted a federal crime under the Mann Act of 1910. But the young woman in question, Lucille Cameron, refused to substantiate her mother's accusation, and Johnson was acquitted. Shortly afterward Johnson married Cameron. In the meantime, a federal grand jury returned to Judge Kenesaw Mountain Landis a charge against Johnson for another violation of the Mann Act. Belle Schreiber, a "high-class" white Chicago prostitute, confessed that she had earlier lived and traveled with Johnson and was paid to engage in immoral and "unnatural" acts. In 1913 a Chicago jury found Johnson guilty, and the judge sentenced him to jail for one year and a day. During the stay of execution to appeal the decision, Johnson jumped bail and fled the country, first to Canada and then to Europe.

Johnson's flamboyant career then careened toward a climax. While the search continued in the United States for a "Great White Hope," in Europe the champion met a few nondescript challengers, performed in vaudeville, and saw his financial resources dwindle away. Finally, in 1915, a year after war had erupted in Europe, Jess Willard, a giant farm boy from Kansas, knocked Johnson out in Havana, Cuba, in the 26th round. Willard promptly announced that he would reimpose the "color line." In return for an exemption from his prison sentence and $50,000, Johnson later claimed that he threw the Havana fight.[34] A famous photograph of Johnson on the canvas during the "knockout" appears to lend some credence to his claim, for the champion seemed to raise his glove over his face to shield his eyes from the blinding Havana sun. Charges of "taking a dive" and a "fix" frequently accompanied fights in this era, but in this case, boxing authorities present at the fight and Johnson's biographer have concluded that Johnson was indeed the victim of a genuine knockout. American officials refused in any case to rescind Johnson's sentence. In 1920 he returned to the United States and served his sentence at Fort Leavenworth. Afterwards, he performed in vaudeville, appeared in a few fights, and engaged in sparring exhibitions until 1945, when he was sixty-eight years old. The next year Johnson died from injuries suffered in an automobile accident. Thus ended perhaps the most dramatic and symbolically significant athletic career in the annals of American sport.

---

[33]Quoted in Gilmore, *Bad Nigger!*, p. 107.
[34]Jack A. Johnson, *Jack Johnson is a Dandy: An Autobiography* (New York: Chelsea House, 1969), pp. 100–102.

6

Baseball

Baseball. Lithograph by L. Prang & Co. after Henry Sandham, circa 1887. Reprinted from the Collections of the Library of Congress. Courtesy of the Library of Congress.

Baseball, which had its origins in simple, informal folk games played mostly by boys on empty lots or village greens, evolved into a formally organized sport of young gentlemen, and then, within a few decades, into a spectator-centered sport.[1] Contrary to the myth propagated by Organized Baseball, General Abner Doubleday had nothing to do with the invention of baseball (see Chapter Seven). In the 1840s and 1850s young men in several of the larger cities simply formalized the bat and ball games that had been played by boys for decades, if not centuries. They adopted written rules, formed private clubs, and initially placed a higher priority upon playing for their personal pleasure than upon playing for the benefit of spectators. The early clubs had a player-centered orientation, but soon local patriotism, the desire to display advanced baseball skills, and potential monetary rewards induced intense rivalries among the clubs. By and large, baseball then became a spectator-centered sport. Many of the clubs built grandstands, charged admission, recruited players mostly on the basis of talent rather than social standing, and paid the best players. Although many of the traditions of the player-centered era lingered on, baseball completed its transformation into a full-fledged spectator sport with the formation of the National League in 1876.

It is unclear why a group of young businessmen, clerks, professional men, brokers, and assorted "gentlemen" in New York City began playing what had been formerly a child's game. Perhaps it was simply an extension of their childhood experiences or of the social activities of the volunteer fire company to which they belonged. At any rate, beginning in 1842, they gathered regularly to play baseball at 27th Street and 4th Avenue in Manhattan. In 1845, Alexander Cartwright, co-owner of a stationery and book shop, urged the group to form a socially exclusive club and secure a permanent playing site. Once organized, the Knickerbocker Base Ball Club restricted membership to forty, charged annual dues of five dollars, and

[1]The standard scholarly histories of baseball in this era are Harold Seymour, *Baseball: The Early Years* (New York: Oxford University Press, 1960) and David Quentin Voigt, *American Baseball: From Gentleman's Sport to the Commissioner System* (Norman: University of Oklahoma Press, 1966). See also the important revisions in Melvin Leonard Adelman, "The Development of Modern Athletics in New York City, 1820–1870," (unpublished Ph.D. dissertation, University of Illinois, 1980), Chaps. 6 and 7. For a contemporary but not always trustworthy account, see Albert Spalding, *America's National Game* (New York: American Sport's Pub., 1911). For the early origins and rules of the game see Robert W. Henderson, *Baseball: Notes and Materials on Its Origins* (New York: New York Public Library, 1940); Henderson, *Ball, Bat and Bishop: The Origins of Ball Games* (New York: Rockport, 1947); Harold Peterson, *The Man Who Invented Baseball* (New York: Charles Scribner's Sons, 1973).

required members to attend "Play Days" every Monday and Thursday. The members also had to purchase common uniforms of blue woolen pantaloons, white flannel shirts, and straw hats. Obviously one had to be a man of some means and leisure, though not a member of the city's top elite, to meet the Knickerbocker standards of membership. The Knickerbocker was the first organized baseball club, at least for which any records survive, in the world.

The Knickerbocker and other early baseball clubs imposed a strict code of personal behavior upon their members. In sharp contrast to the unrestrained emotions that often accompanied folk games, the clubs levied fines on those members who disobeyed the captain, disputed an umpire's decision, or used profanity. Players were supposed to treat opponents with the respect due to gentlemen. After each contest, the home club often sponsored a gala dinner for visiting club members. After-game festivities could be rather extravagant. In 1858, for example, "the Excelsior Club was escorted to Odd Fellows Hall, Hoboken, by the Knickerbocker Club, and entertained in splendid style, covers being laid for over two hundred gentlemen. Dodworth's band was in attendance to liven the scene, and all the arrangements were exceedingly creditable to the taste and liberality of the committee who had charge of the festive occasion."[2] In the off-season, the clubs often scheduled additional social gatherings that included wives or girlfriends. The clubs expected their members to be as skillful in the social graces as in wielding a bat or throwing a ball. To them, winning was secondary to the maintenance of the values and behavior befitting gentlemen.

Apparently in 1845 Alexander Cartwright set down the first written rules for baseball. Until then, several versions of baseball, labeled variously as "base ball," "town ball," and the "Massachusetts game," all of which were derivatives of the English game of rounders, competed for popularity. Cartwright's rules, with some important exceptions, resembled rounders. They stipulated that the infield be diamond-shaped with four bases at each corner. He located the bases ninety feet from one another. Tagging a runner between bases replaced "soaking" or "plugging," a painful feature of rounders in which base runners could be retired by striking them with a thrown ball. In another departure from rounders, Cartwright limited the team at bat to only three outs. A game ended when a team scored twenty-one "aces," or runs, in any number of equal innings for both teams. Fielders could obtain outs by catching a batted ball on the first bounce, in the air, throwing to first base ahead of the runner, or tagging the runner between bases.

For today's observer, a baseball match in the 1840s and 1850s would be both familiar and strange. He would be surprised to see the umpire seated at a table along the third base line, perhaps dressed in tails and a tall black top hat. From this position, the umpire, who was selected by the team captains, resolved all disputes and kept a careful record of the violations of club rules. The captains called a coin to see which team batted first. When

[2]Quoted in Seymour, *Baseball,* p. 21.

the losing side took the field, all infielders except the "short" fielder (the shortstop) usually stood atop their respective bases. The shortstop probably played inside the baseline. The fielders wore no gloves, and the catcher used no protective gear. Hoping to catch pitches on the first bounce, the catchers stood several feet behind the "striker," or batter. The pitcher tossed the ball gently underhanded from a distance of forty-five feet. Since the umpire called no strikes, the batter could wait patiently for a pitch to his liking. No spectators observed the earliest matches except those especially invited by the clubs. Often the clubs assured the comfort of their guests by providing plenty of refreshments and tents to shade the ladies from the sun.

In 1858, the early clubs formed the National Association of Base Ball Players (NABBP) which in the early 1860s had a membership of some forty or fifty clubs, mostly from the East but a few from the Midwest. The association assumed responsibility for rulemaking and attempted to bar professional players from the sport. In 1860, for example, the Washington, D.C. club members jealously guarded their amateur standing by refusing to take payments for their travel expenses. As late as 1866, Charles A. Peverelly, an expert on the contemporary sporting scene, reported that for the Knickerbockers, "the same standard still exists, and no person can obtain admission to the club merely for his capacities as a player; he must also have a reputation as a gentleman...."[3] Some but certainly not all of the association clubs tried to enforce their exclusiveness by refusing to play clubs whom they considered to be less than their social equals.

The game soon spread to a wide array of social groups. The exciting nature of the game, its capacities to feed upon urban rivalries, the experience of American boys in playing ball games, the brevity of the playing time (compared to cricket, baseball's major rival for popularity), the desire to emulate the leisure habits of an upper-status group, and improved transportation (particularly railroads) and communication (telegraph and newspapers) all combined to insure baseball's rapid growth. Any group of men who enjoyed a working schedule that left a few daylight hours free and had the wherewithal to rent playing space could easily form a club. In the late 1850s, a casual reader of the sporting journals would find clubs in the New York area composed of butchers, firemen, policemen, dairymen, schoolteachers, physicians, barkeepers, and even clergymen. In 1858 the star players from the clubs in Brooklyn challenged the stars of New York. For over a decade the "Fashion Course all-star series" between the two cities generated an immense amount of public interest. By 1860, on the eve of the Civil War, the "New York" or Knickerbocker game, as baseball was sometimes called to indicate differences with rounders and other ball games, could be found in all the larger cities in the country. The Civil War, far from impeding the growth of the sport, encouraged the introduction of baseball by veterans returning to every hamlet in the

---

[3]Charles A. Peverelly, *The Book of American Pastimes* (New York: the author, 1866), p. 341. Adelman, "The Development of Modern Athletics," p. 237, argues that the original Knickerbockers had no desire to monopolize baseball, but he also found that almost none of the early ball players came from the unskilled working class.

nation. By the 1870s, baseball had truly become a national game, if not *the* national game.

By then, baseball had developed many of the auxiliary activities familiar to the modern fan. In the 1850s, newspapers began to give the sport cursory coverage; in the next decade the papers devoted two or three full-length columns to major matches. In 1867, Henry Chadwick, the dean of baseball publicists and a longtime member of the NABBP's rules committee, founded and edited the *Chronicle,* a weekly sheet given over mostly to baseball. Chadwick also edited the annual baseball guidebook, which by the mid-1860s claimed to have a circulation of over 65,000. The guidebooks enabled the avid fans to keep abreast of the latest rules, franchises, and statistics, as well as other news of the diamond. Finally, Chadwick invented the box score and batting averages, quantitative devices which enhanced the appeal of the sport.

Baseball throve upon urban rivalries. Determining urban supremacy in terms of population growth, community leadership, or the quality of life might be difficult, but baseball games offered an unambiguous test of urban supremacy in the form of a symbolic contest. A city's baseball team often rallied the citizens behind a common cause as nothing else short of a natural disaster could do. When the St. Louis Brown Stockings played and defeated the Chicago White Stockings in 1875, the Chicago *Times* captured the emotional dimensions of the contest for the city's residents:

> For weeks nothing was talked of in business circles save the approaching contest which was to decide the superiority between the two cities in the most intellectual, refined and progressive pursuit ever entered upon by man.... When the result was announced deep gloom settled upon the city. Friends refused to recognize friends, lovers became estranged, and business was suspended. All Chicago went to a funeral, and the time, since then, has dragged wearily along, as though it were no object to live longer in the world.[4]

The victory of the Brown Stockings in 1875 was not accidental. A year earlier, St. Louis businessmen had started to form a professional team. (The Chicago club was already a semiprofessional, if not a professional team.) They had even imported star players from outside the city to strengthen their roster. Fierce local patriotism had overridden any surviving amateur sentiment.

A COMMERCIAL ENTERPRISE

Well before the 1870s, a player-centered ethos had begun to give way to professionalism and a spectator-centered orientation. By 1860, inviting the general public to attend games and charging admissions had become

---

[4]Quoted in Gregg Lee Carter, "Baseball in Saint Louis; 1867–1875: An Historical Case Study of Civic Pride," *Missouri Historical Bulletin,* 31 (July 1975), 257. See also Steven A. Riess, *Touching Base: Professional Baseball and American Culture in the Progressive Era* (Westport, Conn.: Greenwood Press, 1980), pp. 18–21.

commonplace. At first, the clubs used the gate receipts simply to cover club expenses, but soon clubs and promoters of matches began to distribute part of the proceeds to the players. In 1863, the Brooklyn *Eagle* reported that "ball matches have of late years got to be quite serious affairs and some have even intimated that ballplaying has become quite a money making business, many finding it to pay to play."[5] Apparently, many clubs flagrantly violated the association rules against paying star players. The social decorum of the game also changed. Unlike the early days of "gentleman's" baseball, the "cranks," or fans, cheered wildly for their heroes, heckled umpires and opposing players, and sometimes even rioted. Gradually, working-class youth, often of German or Irish extraction, began to replace old-stock Americans on the team rosters of many of the quasi-professional and professional teams. As winning became the main objective of the teams, the clubs abandoned all efforts at maintaining social pretensions.

In the late 1860s and 1870s, critics of semiprofessional and professional baseball insisted that the sport had close ties to the Victorian underworld. The players often consorted with gamblers and show people. In 1872, *The New York Times* vilified the typical player as a "worthless, dissipated gladiator; not much above the professional pugilist in morality and respectability." The players spent their off-seasons, according to the *Times,* "in those quiet retreats connected with bars, and rat pits, where sporting men of the metropolis meet for social improvement and unpremeditated pugilism."[6] Hotels often refused to rent rooms to ball players, fearful that the players would drive away respectable guests.

Patrons of the Victorian underworld found in baseball a sport to satisfy the widespread hunger for gambling. In all the larger cities, pool rooms determined odds, kept records of bets, and assured payments—all for a commission. At some parks, gamblers openly hawked their odds. Justifiably, fans suspected that some games were fixed. New York gamblers, for example, controlled the Troy, New York Haymakers, a team that enjoyed a notorious reputation for "hippodroming," or fixing games. In California, just as a fielder was about to catch a fly ball, the gamblers, who had placed wagers on the side at bat, would fire their six-shooters. On several occasions, bettors even mobbed playing fields to prevent the completion of games in which they stood to lose money. "So common has betting become at baseball matches," complained a *Harper's Weekly* editor in 1867, "that the most respectable clubs in the country indulge in it to a highly culpable degree, and so common...the tricks by which games have been 'sold' for the benefit of the gamblers that the most respectable participants have been suspected of baseness."[7]

The defenders of baseball launched a counterattack. When the sport first attracted a popular following, proponents had to overcome the criticism that baseball was merely a boy's game and thus unsuited for adult

---

[5]Quoted in Adelman, "The Development of Modern Athletics," p. 391.
[6]*New York Times,* March 8, 1872.
[7]*Harper's Weekly,* October 26, 1867.

men to play. Baseball's supporters responded by repeatedly insisting upon the "manliness" of the sport. Responding to the charge that baseball lacked manliness, widespread agitation developed in the mid-1860s to require that the fielders catch the ball "on the fly" rather than on the first bounce for a putout. Defenders of the game also argued that, whether one be a fan or a player, participation in baseball improved one's health and furnished a much-needed respite from work. Play by boys, according to the Brooklyn *Eagle,* kept the youngsters "out of a great deal of mischief....[Baseball] keeps them from hanging around [fire] engine houses, stables, and taverns." Henry Chadwick concluded that the game merited "the endorsement of every clergyman in the country" because it was a "remedy for the many evils resulting from the immoral associations [that] boys and young men of our cities are apt to become connected with."[8] While such arguments by no means stilled public criticism of semiprofessional and professional baseball, they did relieve some the hostility directed at the sport.

The question of a proper moral image did not curb the popularity of the sport or the trend toward increased professionalization. In 1869, the Cincinnati Red Stockings became the first avowed professional team. For the Cincinnati team to become publicly professional, Albert Spalding later wrote, "required a great deal of moral courage," for many Americans still believed baseball ought to be an amateur activity of gentlemen.[9] Led by Harry Wright, a former cricket player who recruited five eastern stars, the Red Stockings swept through the 1869 season of fifty-eight games without a loss and but one tie. Over 23,000 fans watched their six-game series in New York, the center of the baseball world. Some 15,000 saw a single contest in Philadelphia. In Washington, D.C., President Ulysses S. Grant welcomed the western "Cinderella" team and complimented them on their excellent play. *Harper's Weekly* published a page of pictures of the "picked nine;" visages of the players revealed serious young men with full beards and sideburns. In September, the club crossed the United States on the newly completed transcontinental railroad to play a series of games in California. Altogether, the Red Stockings traveled 11,877 miles by rail, stage, and boat, and over 200,000 fans witnessed their games.

Despite the fantastic success of the team on the playing field, Wright experienced several headaches in managing the touring Red Stockings. Sometimes the gate receipts did not meet team expenses. For example, at Mansfield, Ohio, the club grossed only $50, and in Cleveland $81. Then the team arrived in Syracuse, New York, to find no opposition. Like players of later years, Wright's young men were hard to discipline. At times they cut practices, missed trains, and drank far too much alcohol. Wright's pitcher, Asa Brainard, was a hypochondriac and eccentric. During one game, a wild rabbit ran across the infield in front of Brainard. He impulsively turned and hurled the ball at the frightened bunny. He missed,

[8]Quoted in Adelman, "The Development of Modern Athletics," p. 439. See also Adelman's discussion of this topic.

[9]Spalding, *America's National Game,* p. 133.

and the ball rolled into the crowd, allowing two rival runners to score. All was not lost, for the Red Stockings proceeded to win the game anyway.[10]

The success of the Red Stockings encouraged the formation of the first all-professional league, the National Association of Professional Base Ball Players (NAPBBP) in 1871. The association (1871–1875) bore only a faint resemblance to a modern professional sports league. It did assure that in the future professional baseball would dictate rule changes and the style of play. (The amateur association collapsed in 1872.) But the league allowed any team that could muster a mere ten-dollar entry fee to join. Consequently, many teams located in smaller cities, joined but quickly dropped out of the NAPBBP. Teams scheduled their own matches; a team could qualify for the championship pennant by playing all other clubs at least five times during the season. To maximize profits, big-city clubs attempted to avoid playing more than the minimal number of games in the smaller towns. While the clubs were nominally joint-stock companies, the NAPBBP was a players' "paradise." The players controlled the league, were free to move from one club to another at the end of each season, and enjoyed salaries two or three times higher than the ordinary workingmen of the era.

Harry Wright and most of his team departed from Cincinnati for Boston after the 1870 season. Wright's mastery of the game, ability to handle players, and business acumen assured Boston's domination of the new loop. Although narrowly losing the pennant to Philadelphia in 1871, the Reds then won the next four consecutive championships. George Wright, Harry's brother, was the club's superb fielding, hard-hitting shortstop. Young Albert Spalding was the most baffling pitcher in the league, and Roscoe Barnes was the perennial batting champion. In 1875 Boston had the top four hitters in the circuit and ran away with the league pennant, winning seventy-one games while losing only eight.

THE NATIONAL LEAGUE

In 1876 a few men, led by William A. Hulbert, president of the Chicago club, conspired to overthrow the national association and found a new professional league that would be profitable to investors. After secretly obtaining the support of the western clubs that resented the eastern domination of the NAPBBP, Hulbert called a meeting in February, 1876, with representatives of five eastern clubs. When assembled, as a dramatic gesture, Hulbert reportedly locked the hotel door and dropped the key into his pocket. After reviewing the weaknesses of the association, he proposed a new league, "The National League of Professional Base Ball Clubs."* Significantly, the term "Clubs" had been substituted for "Players." The constitution of the new National League gave the owners complete

*Charter members of the new league were Boston, Chicago, Cincinnati, Louisville, Hartford, St. Louis, Philadelphia, and New York.
[10]See Voigt, *American Baseball*, p. 31.

control of the management, regulations, and the resolution of disputes. To project an image of integrity and respectability, the league forbade Sunday games and betting in ball parks. In time, the league assumed full responsibility for scheduling games, setting uniform game admission rates, and paying umpires.

The National League pioneered in developing a business structure that would become standard for all twentieth-century team sports. In economic terms, the league was a loosely organized cartel, an arrangement among the clubs designed to restrict competition among franchises for players. Although the founders did not initially have enough foresight to devise a reserve clause to bind players to one team for their entire playing careers, the league did forbid negotiations with players from another team while the season was in progress. In 1879 the owners secretly agreed to "reserve" five players, a policy later expanded to include virtually every player on a club's roster. Such a system prevented competitive bidding among the teams for the services of players. The National League also essentially prohibited the planting of more than one franchise in each market area, regardless of population. Clubs could be located only in towns of 75,000 or more persons. Finally, the league established an entry monopoly. Two blackballs by existent franchises barred new applicants from the league. Thus in order for an aspiring baseball owner to obtain a league franchise, he either had to purchase an existing club, win the vote of the owners of existing clubs to add a franchise, or form a competing major league.

Yet the National League, like most arrangements based upon gentlemen's agreements, often failed to function as a genuine cartel. Ownership and management decisions of the individual franchises remained largely free of league authority; the league had only one employee, a secretary-treasurer. Ultimately, restrictive agreements could be enforced neither by the league nor the courts. Consequently, each club owner tended to place the economic interest of his franchise before that of the welfare of the league. As Albert Spalding, a shrewd observer of baseball history explained: "The [baseball] magnate must be a strong man among strong men, else other club owners in the league will combine in their own interests against him and his interests...."[11]

For its first six years, William Hulbert did offer the National League strong, albeit sometimes questionable, leadership. He immediately cracked down on the loose player behavior that had blemished the integrity of professional baseball in the past. In 1877 he dramatically expelled four Louisville players for taking bribes from gamblers. He levied stiff fines upon players for using profanity or threatening umpires. Under Hulbert's direction, the league made other decisions that were more debatable. The charging of a uniform admission price of fifty cents when the daily wages of workingmen ranged from one to three dollars led opponents of the loop to describe it as a "rich man's" league. When both the Philadelphia and New York teams failed to take their final road tours of the 1876 season, Hulbert led the movement to expel them from the league. Hulbert

[11]Quoted in Seymour, *Baseball,* p. 206.

stubbornly refused to permit either city to field teams in the league while he was alive. Thus, until Hulbert's death in 1882, the league sacrificed potential revenue from the nation's two most populous cities. When the Cincinnati club persisted in selling beer at its park and playing Sunday games, Hulbert also forced them out of the league in 1880. Hulbert's high-handed and dictatorial methods may have kept the league intact and improved the moral image of professional baseball, but when he died, the league directors made certain that none of his successors obtained similar powers.

The expulsion of Cincinnati led to a direct challenge to the National League. In 1881 Cincinnati called together delegates from cities that had been excluded from the league to form the American Association of Base Ball Clubs, which was dubbed by critics as the "Beer Ball League" since four of the six directors of association clubs owned breweries.* By charging only a twenty-five-cent admission fee, selling liquor at games, and playing on Sunday, the association hoped to profit from the strictures of the older league. The association openly invited league players to jump to the new circuit, and several did. The success of the association caused the leaderless National League to call for a strategic surrender. In 1882, the presidents of the two leagues plus the head of the Northwestern League (which operated in Michigan, Ohio, and Illinois) signed a tripartite National Agreement. At the heart of the agreement was the mutual recognition of reserved players and the establishment of exclusive territorial rights.

The booming prosperity of the 1880s resulted in whirring turnstiles at the parks of both the National League and the American Association. With the implementation of an informal post-season series between the two circuits, interest in professional baseball increased phenomenally. On the playing field, the Association clubs proved to be fully equal to the senior loop. The powerful St. Louis Browns, managed by young Charles Comiskey (later owner of the Chicago White Sox), won four consecutive Association pennants and two world series from National League opponents. For the first time, most of the clubs made profits, but competition for player talent drove up salaries. To obtain an advantage over opponents, clubs in both leagues from time to time violated the spirit if not the letter of the National Agreement of 1882.

Association club owners, in particular, found cooperation difficult to achieve. Brooklyn and St. Louis fought each other regularly for both the pennant and for domination of the management of the circuit. When the Association chose a puppet of the St. Louis Browns as president in 1890, Brooklyn and Cincinnati resigned from the Association and joined the National League. To accommodate the two new clubs, the league conveniently ignored the National Agreement, indicating that it was prepared to resume an all-out war with the Association. The formation of the Players' League in 1890 added to the woes of the Association. Attendance dropped drastically. At the end of the 1891 season, the Association surrendered to

---

*Charter franchises were located in Baltimore, Cincinnati, Louisville, Philadelphia, Pittsburgh, and St. Louis.

the National League. The league then absorbed four Association clubs—making the National League a twelve-member loop—and bought out the four other clubs.

The players posed another major challenge to the National League magnates. Employer-employee relations in professional baseball reflected the general industrial unrest of the 1880s and 1890s. To the club management, the salaries of players was their single largest expense; some two-thirds of the expenditures of the clubs went into salaries. Shrewd management of salaries could mean the difference between the club's financial success or failure. To keep salaries at a minimal level, club owners devised several ingenious methods, all of which involved some form of collusion that violated the principles of free-market theory. From its beginning in 1876, the National League clubs had employed the dreaded "blacklist." Once a player had been dismissed by another club or the league for whatever reasons, no other club could negotiate with him. In 1879 the owners secretly agreed that each club could "reserve" five players; by 1887, clubs were reserving fourteen men, which in that day practically meant the entire team. Finally, in the mid-1880s, the club owners introduced a salary classification plan by which they agreed to uniform salary limits. All of these strictures on the players depended on the mutual cooperation of club owners. Often when a particular club saw that the league rules failed to benefit its interests, they successfully ignored them.

At the backbone of the owner control of the players was the reserve clause in contracts. As long as a club kept a player on the reserve list, no other club was supposed to negotiate with him. In effect, the club that first signed a player had a lifetime option on the player's services. Negotiating individually, the player had only two weapons at his disposal: he could "hold out" or quit baseball. Neither was a very attractive option. For the player of ordinary ability, holding out would probably mean a loss of income for the playing time that he had cost the club. And most players could not find jobs outside of baseball that paid equally well. The reserve clause also proved vital in increasing the worth of players to the owners, for it made it possible to "sell" players to other clubs.

The player-control measures of the clubs and major-league baseball's prosperity in the 1880s triggered a players' revolt. By the mid-1880s, the players probably earned an average of $1,750 annually, about three times the wages of an industrial worker, but the rising expectations of the players collided with the salary ceilings of the league. In 1885, John Montgomery Ward, who was a lawyer as well as a star player, founded the Brotherhood of Professional Base Ball Players. Initially, the secret order functioned more like a fraternal group than a labor union. Late in 1887 a National League committee accepted the basic outlines of Ward's "model contract" but refused to abandon the salary system. Instead, in 1889, the league set a $2,500 limit on salaries of all players. Angry players demanded a strike, but Ward advised caution. He presented the league with an ultimatum: the league had to abandon the salary ceiling system and stop selling players or face competition from a brotherhood league in 1890.

Ward carried through with his threat by forming the Players' League.

To challenge the National League directly, the new circuit invaded seven cities of the older league. The capacity of the brotherhood to deliver most of the best players attracted enough financial backing to insure the initial success of the league. The Players' League combined features of both private and cooperative enterprise, for both the workers and the capitalists were to share league management and profits. The brotherhood's published "manifesto" in 1889 appealed for public support and summarized their grievances.

> There was a time when the League stood for integrity and fair dealing. Today it stands for dollars and cents.... Players have been bought, sold and exchanged, as though they were sheep, instead of American citizens. 'Reservation'...became for them another name for property right in the player. By a combination among themselves, stronger than the strongest trusts, they [the owners] were able to enforce the most arbitrary measures, and the player had either to submit or get out of the profession in which he had spent years in attaining a proficiency.[12]

The National League called upon a former player—now a sporting goods entrepreneur and stockholder in the Chicago club—Albert Spalding, to head a war committee to suppress the player uprising. Spalding employed every "legal" method at his disposal. He denounced the players as "hot-headed anarchists" who were bent on a "terrorism" characteristic of "revolutionary movements." While the newspapers happily printed Spalding's scorching press releases, he had less success in prosecuting players for violating the reserve clause. Just as Ward had predicted, the courts held that the league contracts containing reserve clauses lacked equity. Bribery of star players to stay in the loop was also less successful than the magnates had hoped. Spalding offered Mike "King" Kelly, a National League superstar, a "blank check" to remain in the league, but Kelly refused, saying "I can't go back on the boys."[13] The league did manage to retain two popular heroes, Adrian "Cap" Anson of the White Stockings and Harry Wright, manager of the Philadelphia team, but about 80 percent of the players jumped to the new circuit, including the entire Washington team.

Other techniques of harassing the Players' League brought more success. The National League deliberately scheduled its games so that teams from the two circuits competed on the same day in the same city for the same customers. The strategy cost the clubs of both leagues heavily. With its superior financial resources, the National clubs were in a better position to take the losses. They raised a "war fund" to assist the weaker clubs. By giving away numerous tickets, National clubs hoped to keep fans from attending the Player games. On a lesser scale, the Players also provided fans with free tickets. Both leagues grossly exaggerated their attendance figures. But since the brotherhood provided a much superior brand of baseball, they outdrew the senior circuit. At the end of the 1890

[12]Quoted in Spalding, *America's National Game*, p. 272.
[13]Ibid., p. 297. See also Lee Lowenfish/Tony Lupien, *The Imperfect Diamond: The Story of Baseball's Reserve System and the Men Who Fought to Change It* (New York: Stein and Day, 1980), Part I.

season, the Players were reasonably optimistic. Their losses had been less than those of the National League. But the brotherhood members failed to take into account their financial backers and the defection of some of their members. By threats and payments, the National League induced one after another of the backers to capitulate. The short-lived experiment in cooperative-capitalistic baseball ended in failure after one season.

LIFE ON THE DIAMOND

Most fans had little interest in the squabbles taking place in the executive suites; they were far more excited by the action on the diamond. To increase the attractiveness of baseball as a public spectacle, the league experimented with numerous rule changes. When the National League began in 1876, pitchers threw from below the hip at a distance of forty-five feet from home plate. While three strikes constituted an out, the hitter could call for a strike above or below the waist. Fouls did not count as strikes until 1901. Nine balls delivered outside the zone designated by the hitter gave him a free base on balls. Finally, in 1887, the batters lost their "high-low" privilege, and in 1889 the number of base on balls was reduced to four. In 1884, pitchers received the right to throw overhanded, but the pitching distance was gradually extended until it reached the modern figure of sixty feet, six inches in 1893. Since the turn of the century, baseball rules have essentially remained the same.

During the 1880s, managers developed most of the tactics familiar to the modern fan. Infielders played away from their respective bases, and catchers were moved closer to the plate. Fielders learned to back each other up in case of wild throws or muffed balls. Unlike modern professional baseball, most of the fielders played several positions, even within a single season. Initially, players sporting gloves were subjected to pitiless ridicule from the fans, but in the 1880s, catchers began to don primitive masks and use mitts. In the 1890s, the other fielders were gradually converted to gloves. Underhanded pitchers supposedly threw curves as early as the 1860s. They also worked every game in the entire season. Overhanded pitching resulted in a wide assortment of new pitches but placed a tremendous stress on the pitcher's arm. By the end of the 1890s, most teams rotated at least three pitchers, though sometimes one pitcher would work several games in a row. Unless injured, the pitcher was expected to throw the entire nine innings.

The managers were beginning to stress offensive teamwork. Most batters swung freely in the 1880s, though a few were known as "place hitters." Sometimes a hitter bunted the ball, but such a move would likely draw the ire of the fans who considered it unmanly. From time to time, the league considered making the bunt illegal. A few clubs used the "hit-and-run" play in the 1880s, but it was not perfected nor regularly employed until the late 1890s. The psychological warfare of the players was developed into a brutal art. Verbal and physical harassment drove more than one player out of the league. A notorious case was that of Lou "Chief"

Sockalexis, a Penobscot native-American, who was greeted at each game with war whoops, "Ki Yi's," insults, and threats. Although batting .413, Sockalexis, after two months in the league, was suspended for drunkenness. By the 1890s, ragging opponents was commonplace—a far cry from the gentlemanly origins of the game.

To the modern fan, the baseball park of the 1880s and 1890s would be both familiar and strange. Most of the parks were surrounded by wooden stands and a wooden fence. A roof protected some of the stands while the others were unprotected wooden seats of sun-bleached boards (hence the term bleachers). A crowd of 4,000 was considered large. As late as the early 1900s, clubs sometimes allowed patrons to park their carriages or automobiles in the outfield, though by this time middle- and upper-income groups could reach the park by fast trolleys. When the stands had been filled, spectators crowded around the infield and stood in the outfield. At a Baltimore-Boston game in 1897, over 25,000 fans appeared, far exceeding the park's capacity. The outfielders stood only a few feet behind the infielders, and any ball hit into the crowd was ruled an automatic double. (Incidentally, Boston triumphed by a score of 19–10.) Scorecards and concessions could be purchased at all parks, but the lack of a public address system or numbers on the players' uniforms challenged the fans' ingenuity in following the action. Often a brass band played during lulls in the action. Since the owners wanted to maximize profits, a fan could sometimes encounter his favorite player taking tickets at the gate.

Until the 1890s, the Chicago White Stockings, under the leadership of Adrian C. "Cap" Anson, dominated National League play. Anson, who stood six feet, two inches and weighed over 200 pounds, was for that era a veritable giant. He could play any position but finally settled on first base. As a hitter he won four league batting crowns and in twenty-two seasons failed to hit .300 only twice. Anson became the playing-manager of the Stockings in 1880, a position he retained for nineteen years. Under Anson's capable command from 1880 to 1886, Chicago won five pennants. Another player, Mike "King" Kelly, competed with Anson for the adoration of the Chicago fans. A colorful player both on and off the field, Kelly excelled at hitting and baserunning. "Slide, Kelly, Slide!" later became a hit song title. Apart from baseball, Kelly also loved race horses and liquor. In 1887 Chicago shocked the baseball world by selling Kelly to the Boston Red Sox for the astronomical sum of $10,000.

"As Celtic as Mrs. Murphy's pig," Kelly inspired many legends. Most of them centered around his opportunism and trickery. It was Kelly who allegedly took advantage of a rule that permitted a substitute to enter the game at any time by simply notifying the umpire. In Boston, he leapt from the dugout bench shouting, "Kelly now catching," and caught a foul fly which the regular catcher could never have reached. On another occasion, as the sun began to set in the last of the 12th inning in Chicago, Kelly pulled an even more startling stunt. With two out and the bases full, Kelly, as the rightfielder, leapt into the twilight trying to catch a mighty drive that would win the game. As he came down, he held his glove high in the air and jauntily jogged to the dugout. The umpire yelled, "Out number three! Game called on account of darkness!" "Nice catch, Kell," his teammates exclaimed. "Not at all, at all," Kelly responded. "'Twent a mile above my head."[14]

For youth with lower socioeconomic origins, baseball offered a glamorous career opportunity. Most of the 240 big-league players of the 1880s advanced from the unstable minor-league professional teams; others came from amateur teams or directly from the sandlots. Only a handful of players ever attended college, and only a few enjoyed professional careers outside of baseball. Most had short playing careers and when released, became either blue-collar workers or workers employed in jobs provided by the Victorian underworld. An unusually large number of German and Irish names appeared on club rosters, suggesting that to these ethnic groups, major-league baseball may have represented a means of social mobility. (See Chapter Five on ethnics and blacks in professional baseball.) Almost all of the big leaguers came from cities, particularly the large metropolitan areas of the Northeast. In 1897, only three of 168 National Leaguers were from as far south as Virginia and only seven came from the Far West. Over one-third of the players were born in either Massachusetts or Pennsylvania.

Most of the players were genial, fun-loving, big spenders. Albert Spalding, as manager of the White Sox, once hired a Pinkerton detective to follow his players. Seven of the players, the detective reported, spent almost every night going "up and down Clark Street [in Chicago] all over the tenderloin districts, through the whole roster of saloons and 'speakeasy' resorts." After Spalding had the report read to the team, King Kelly broke the long silence by saying: "I have to offer only one amendment. In that place where the detective reports me as taking a lemonade at 3 a.m. he's off. It was straight whiskey; I never drank a lemonade at that hour in my life."[15] Spalding fined each of the offenders $25 to cover the costs of hiring the Pinkerton man, but such actions failed to curb player misbehavior.

Baseball promoted itself as a democratic sport, claiming to reach all social classes and ethnic groups. "The average American boy," wrote a reporter in 1888, "although he may be rather ignorant as to how delegates are elected to national [political party] conventions, the number of electoral votes apportioned to the different states of the Union, or the date of Lee's surrender, can call the names of eminent professional ball players offhand, or with equal ease give the principal events of Captain John Ward's history as pitcher and short-stop, and Adrian C. Anson's record from the date he left Philadelphia...."[16] Yet, while lower-income groups may have been aware of the actions of the big leaguers and played baseball themselves, it appears that few of them attended major-league games. The fifty-cent admission charge of the National League probably excluded most workingmen, who rarely earned more than three dollars per day. Since games were always played in the daylight hours, usually beginning at 3:30 or so in the afternoon, most workers could not attend weekday games. The starting time, on the other hand, was quite convenient for clerks and

[14]As told to and quoted in Tristram Potter Coffin, *The Old Ball Game in Folklore and Fiction* (New York: Herder and Herder, 1971), pp. 36–37.

[15]Quoted in Spalding, *America's National Game*, p. 184.

[16]Harry Palmer, "America's National Game," *Outing*, 12 (July 1888), 351.

professional men. Most fans therefore probably came from the sporting fraternity, show people, gamblers, and those middle-income groups who were uninhibited by Victorian attitudes.

The American elite, the leading proponents of a player-centered ethos, tended to consider professional baseball a crude, ungentlemanly sport. As one of them wrote: "Our professional baseball, with its paid players and its thousands of smoking, and sometimes umpire-mobbing spectators, is doing more harm than good. The players are devoting their lives, instead of their spare time, to diversion instead of duty; and the spectators are wasting two or three hours of fresh air and sunshine looking at what they ought to be doing."[17] The sporting tastes of the most elite groups leaned toward actual participation or, if spectators, to watching club games or intercollegiate football matches. Henry Chadwick sarcastically described them as a "shoddy class of Anglomaniacs."[18] Nevertheless, the baseball magnates made special efforts to attract both "respectable" men and women. They believed women would improve crowd behavior. Early photographs suggest, however, that less than one-tenth of those attending professional games were women. Baseball was essentially a masculine sport. Despite its best efforts, until the twentieth-century professional baseball was unable to rid itself completely of its association with the Victorian underworld of entertainment.

For the committed fan, baseball had become something more than a simple diversion from daily routines. The game brought overwhelming feelings of exhilaration or depression. The last stanza of "Casey at the Bat" expressed the emotional power of baseball to the nineteenth-century fan.

> Oh! somewhere in this favored land
> the sun is shining bright;
> The band is playing somewhere,
> and somewhere children's hearts are light.
> And somewhere men are laughing,
> and somewhere children shout;
> But there is no joy in Mudville—
> mighty Casey has Struck Out.

After the mighty Casey had struck out, Mudville no longer had room for joy, laughter, shouting children, brass bands, or bright sunshine. A kind of pall hung over the village. The baseball game had reenacted in a capsulized and symbolic form the "game of life."

> 'Tis the old game of life, with its conquest
> and strife,
> With its wonderful outings and innings;
> Where the umpire of fate forever doth wait
> Giving gladness and sorrow for winnings.[19]

---

[17]Price Collier, "Sports' Place in the Nation's Well Being," *Outing*, 32 (July 1898), 384–85.
[18]Quoted in Seymour, *Baseball*, p. 333.
[19]S. P. Richardson, "Base Ball," reprinted in Spalding, *America's National Game*, p. 457. For a full text on "Casey at the Bat," see ibid., pp. 450–51.

7

The Quest for Order

Dean Hill, *Football Thru the Years* (New York: Gridiron Publishing Co., 1940), p. 56.

In the three decades prior to 1920 the owners of professional baseball teams and the custodians of college football struggled to resolve perplexing problems. On the one hand, the barons of baseball wanted to permit the individual franchise holder maximum freedom to operate his ball club as he saw fit. Yet, if all or most of the franchises in baseball were to prosper, collusive agreements and a tightly constructed central bureaucracy seemed to be essential. Consequently, professional baseball attempted to devise means to avoid direct competition among franchises for players, to prevent the formation of rival big leagues, and to restrict the total number of big-league teams. Furthermore, the owners sought to bring the minor leagues under major-league control, thereby creating an entity known as Organized Baseball, which was, in essence, to become one large, rather unwieldy cartel. Order was also important to college football. Regional and national governing bodies were founded to equalize the conditions of competition, prevent quarrels, preserve the sport's image of pristine amateurism, and, above all, to make the sport more attractive to spectators. Such organizations eventually brought a modicum of order and stability to the previously chaotic world of intercollegiate football.[1]

ORGANIZED BASEBALL PROSPERS

Baseball's quest for order began inauspiciously. Despite the collapse of both the Players' League in 1890 and the American Association in 1891, the decade of the 1890s was a grim one for the National League. Burdened by the debts accumulated from the brotherhood war and the purchase costs of four American Association clubs, the league faced a general economic depression, public disillusionment due to the brotherhood war, and growing competition from other forms of entertainment. Moreover, the new twelve-team loop proved to be a disaster. Teams with poor records,

[1]On baseball see Steven A. Riess, *Touching Base: Professional Baseball and American Culture in the Progressive Era* (Westport, Conn.: Greenwood Press, 1980); Harold Seymour, *Baseball,* 2 vols. (New York: Oxford University Press, 1960, 1971); David Quentin Voigt, *American Baseball,* 2 vols. (Norman, Oklahoma: University of Oklahoma Press, 1966, 1970); and Lee Lowenfish/Tony Lupien, *The Imperfect Diamond: The Story of Baseball's Reserve System and the Men Who Fought to Change It* (New York: Stein and Day, 1980), Part II. No adequate history of the quest for order in college football exists, but see especially Guy Maxton Lewis, "The American Intercollegiate Football Spectacle, 1869–1917," (unpublished Ph.D. dissertation, University of Maryland, 1964).

124

such as the Louisville and St. Louis franchises, which between them occupied last place five of eight years that the circuit existed, attracted few fans at home or on the road, and the New York Giants, who were vital to the success of the league, failed to field a strong team. Because of vicious infighting, the barons of baseball were unable to agree to reduce the size of the circuit or set up the league into two six-team divisions. Either action might have generated more fan interest and profits. Finally, in 1899, the league returned to eight clubs. The new circuit, composed of Boston, Brooklyn, Chicago, Cincinnati, New York, Philadelphia, Pittsburgh, and St. Louis, would remain intact until 1953, when the Boston Braves moved to Milwaukee.

But the woes of the National League were not over. The return of prosperity at the turn of the century, the elimination of the four "weak" franchises, and the conflicts within the league's counsels encouraged a challenge by a formidable rival—the American League led by the indomitable Byron Bancroft "Ban" Johnson. When the National League dropped the four franchises and returned to an eight-team loop, Johnson, as president of the Western League (a minor league), convinced his followers to plant franchises in the abandoned cities. In 1901 he claimed major-league status for the western circuit, renamed the loop the American League, formed plans to invade New York, and began to raid National League player rosters. With Johnson in firm control of the American League franchises and the National League owners divided, the senior loop finally sued for peace.

The peace settlement, known as the National Agreement of 1903, became the centerpiece of professional baseball. The leagues agreed to recognize each other's reserve clauses and established a three-man National Commission to govern all of Organized Baseball. Composed of the presidents of the two leagues and a third member chosen by them, the National Commission served primarily as a judicial body to resolve disputes between the leagues and controversies involving the minor leagues. In the National League, the owners retained nearly absolute power to manage their franchises as they saw fit; in the American League, Ban Johnson continued to rule with a firm hand until the 1920s. The 1903 agreement also recognized the territorial monopolies of minor-league teams, granted them reserve rights in players, and set up a system by which the major leagues could draft players from the minors.

In the pre-1920 era, the club owners confronted two major challenges to the 1903 agreement: the appearance of a new players' union and yet another contender for big-league status. The reserve clause allowed the owners to limit salaries to less than the players would have received on the open market. As attendance and club profits rose rapidly in the early years of the century, player salaries slowly drifted upwards. Better players sometimes effectively "held out"—refused to play until they obtained higher pay. Probably as many as ten superstars received salaries of $10,000 or more by 1910, but players with ordinary talents might continue to receive as little as $1,900 for a season of play. When a third major circuit, the Federal League, threatened the cartel between 1912 and 1915, the salaries of superior players jumped markedly. Ty Cobb's salary, for example, leaped from $9,000 in 1910 to $20,000 in 1915. Nonetheless, some owners refused to capitulate to the external pressure. Connie Mack, the owner-manager of the 1914 champion Philadelphia Athletics, sold or released all of his high-priced stars. With the demise of the Federal League at the end of the 1915 season, the magnates held the line on salaries until after World War I.

Salary conflict, capricious owner actions, and several other grievances led to the formation of a new players' union, the Base Ball Players' Fraternity, in 1912. Organized by David Fultz, a former big-league player who had become an attorney, the fraternity grew to 700 members (including minor leaguers). After instituting a number of lawsuits against various clubs for contract violations, the players presented the National Commission in 1913 with seventeen demands, most of which concerned the standardization of contracts, player releases, and severance payments. Faced with the Federal League war, the commission reluctantly granted a few minimal concessions. The commission agreed that the players should be able to see their contracts, that waiver lists should henceforth be public, and that big-league veterans of ten years could negotiate with any club they pleased. Except for the last provision, the fraternity made no effort to challenge the reserve clause nor the right of the clubs to sell players. For several years, the union continued to file lawsuits in behalf of both major- and minor-league players, but the collapse of the Federal League in 1915 and the lack of adequate player support weakened the bargaining position of the fraternity. Not until the post-World War II era would the players again mount an organized movement against the owners.

The owners worried more about the Federal League. In 1914, James A. "Long Jim" Gilmore, a Chicago iron manufacturer, aligned wealthy capitalists in Chicago, New York, and St. Louis to reorganize the old Federal League into a circuit claiming major-league status. The Federals offered established major-league stars fantastic salaries to jump to the new league. The major-league owners responded as they had during the Player's League war of 1890; they blacklisted players who had abandoned the majors, obtained court injunctions, and raised the salaries of their players.

Even though high salaries and low attendance plagued the Federal League in both 1914 and 1915, the major league owners panicked and settled for an expensive peace. In effect, the major-league magnates sabotaged the new loop by bribing the wealthiest Federal League owners. For example, Albert Sinclair, who later gained notoriety in the Teapot Dome scandal, received permission to buy a controlling interest in the Chicago Cubs at a bargain price. In addition, Sinclair received a regular payment of $10,000 for ten years from the major leagues. On the other hand, those owners of Federal League clubs which were not in direct competition with the majors received nothing except the revenues from player sales. The settlement may have cost the major leagues as much as $5 million, tarnished the image of the owners, and brought disaster to many minor-league clubs.

Despite the problems professional baseball confronted in establishing order within its ranks, the sport enjoyed an unparalleled popularity in the first two decades of the twentieth century. Big-league attendance doubled between 1903 and 1908. Attendance as a percentage of the population of the areas served by big-league clubs was not only higher than ever before but higher than it would ever be in the future. Every city, town, and village of any consequence had one or more amateur or professional teams. Minor-league baseball grew from thirteen circuits in 1903 to over forty in 1913. Over 300 cities, many of them with less than 25,000 inhabitants, had professional baseball teams by 1913. Baseball had at last gained social respectability, even among proper Victorians. Women began to attend games in larger numbers. William Howard Taft established the precedent for the President opening each season by throwing out the first ball in 1909. This ritual in effect made the President a promoter of professional baseball. The major leagues produced a galaxy of super-heroes, and the World Series became an annual fall rite. At no other time in baseball history did the game enjoy such an emotional grip on the American people.

Myth and Reality

To fans, baseball in the early twentieth century offered both tangible and intangible attractions. Among the less tangible was baseball's marvelous capacity to generate symbols and myths. One of the sport's most potent myths was the notion that the game was solely of American origins. Such a myth appealed strongly to nationalistic sentiments.

The legend that baseball had been invented by Abner Doubleday at Cooperstown, New York, in the summer of 1839 took "official" form in 1907 with the report of a special commission of men of "high repute and undoubted knowledge of Base Ball" which had been appointed to investigate the origins of the sport. The commission apparently engaged in no research but did send out letters of inquiry to old-timers who had been associated with the sport. (Later scholars have totally discredited the work of the commission and traced the origins of the game to various English ball games.) The myth helped free baseball, as Albert Spalding put it, "from the trammels of English traditions, customs, conventionalities," in short, free it from the artificiality and decadence of the Old World.[2] In 1939 the major leagues celebrated the "centennial" of baseball with impressive ceremonies at Cooperstown. They dedicated the Hall of Fame, presented a pageant showing the Doubleday contribution, and staged an all-star game featuring former all-time-great players. The United States government joined the festivities by issuing a commemorative stamp, marking 1839 as the date of the birth of the "National Game." Even today the legend of Doubldeay and Cooperstown is often repeated by ignorant sportswriters and more circumspectly by Hall of Fame publicists.

The Doubleday-Cooperstown myth helped establish baseball as a secular, peculiar American religion. As Mohammedans have their Mecca and

[2]Albert Spalding, *America's National Game* (New York: American Sports Publishing Company, 1911), p. 4.

Christians have their Jerusalem or Bethlehem, baseball followers have their Cooperstown, New York. Each year, thousands of Americans make the "pilgrimage" to the "shrine" at Cooperstown, the site of the Hall of Fame and museum. There they can see statues and pictures of their former heroes and observe the "relics" used by them—old, discolored bats, balls, and uniforms. They can visit the "hallowed ground" of Doubleday Field, where the young Doubleday "immaculately conceived" the game. Coopers-town is rich in religious terminology: "shrine," "pantheon," "sanctuary," and "relics." Each year, sportswriters dutifully select great players of the past for "enshrinement," after which they become "immortals."[3] No doubt baseball mythology provided solid links between the past and the present, between generations, and between men divided by values, skin color, and social class.

The ballparks themselves had rustic qualities, thus reminding the fans of the nation's simple agrarian past. For the urban spectator, surrounded as he was by noise, dirt, and squalor, entering a major-league ball field could be an exhilarating experience. Suddenly he was transported into another world, one characterized by vistas of green grass and clean, white boundaries. The owners gave their edifices pastoral-sounding names: Ebbets Field, Sportsman Park, the Polo Grounds. Such nomenclature remained popular until 1923, when Yankee Stadium was built. Parks built since then have more urban names: Shea Stadium, Astrodome, Superdome. Perhaps the change from rustic names to urban names reflected the growing urbanization of the country. Whatever they were called, the massive baseball parks, built of concrete and steel, bore mute testimony to the values Americans placed upon baseball. To the fans, they were more than simply a place for commercial amusement; the park was a kind of civic, religious sanctuary representing the entire community.[4]

Baseball was allegedly a vehicle for promoting social integration, for building social solidarity through support of local teams, and for the assimilation of new immigrants. As Morgan Bulkeley, one-time president of the National League put it, "There is nothing which will help quicker and better amalgamate the foreign born, and those born of foreign parents in this country, than to give them a little good bringing up in the good old-fashioned game of Base Ball." Baseball would help prevent revolutionary conspiracies. "They don't have things of that kind on the other side of the ocean," declared Bulkeley, "and many spend their hours fussing around in conspiring and hatching up plots when they should be out in the open improving their lungs."[5] Yet as Steven A. Riess has demonstrated, "baseball was not a democratic spectator sport." Lower-income groups generally did not have the financial wherewithal and leisure time to attend big-league games. Organized Baseball excluded blacks, and the newer immigrants from southern and eastern Europe apparently found no greater opportu-

[3]For these parallels I am especially indebted to Seymour, *Baseball,* I, 4.
[4]See Steven A. Riess, "Baseball Myths, Baseball Realities, and the Social Functions of Baseball in the Progressive Era," *Stadion,* 3 (1980), 273–311.
[5]Quoted in Seymour, *Baseball,* II, 4.

nities for advancement in baseball than they did in other professions.[6]

Among the most tangible attractions of baseball in the early twentieth century was the annual World Series. The National Agreement of 1903 had not provided for a championship playoff, but in 1903 the pennant winners of the two leagues did agree to play a nine-game "World Championship" series. No postseason games were played in 1904, but in 1905 the World Series became a permanent feature of big-league baseball. The series furnished an exciting conclusion to the regular baseball season; the entire nation soon became absorbed in the outcome. Fans congregated in the city streets to watch the play-by-play progress of the series as reported on the boards posted in front of newspaper offices. Reportedly, the series sometimes even delayed the proceedings of the United States Supreme Court.

The sheer drama of baseball was yet another attraction. Baseball had a cast of well-defined heroes and villains, familiar plots, comedy, and the unexpected. Since most of the fans had played the sport as youths and watched many contests, they understood the intricacies of the plot—the purpose of bunting, the hit-and-run play, a deliberate base on balls, the removal of a struggling pitcher, and the appropriate place for the insertion of a pinch-hitter. Baseball was a rational sport, one in which means were specifically related to ends. "Baseball, year by year, [has] grown more scientific, more a thing of accepted rules [of tactics], of set routine," wrote F. C. Lane, a baseball reporter. "This slow evolution of the sport displayed itself in batting, in the form of the bunt, the place hit and various other manifestations of skill."[7] Every fan could be a grandstand manager, but the rationality of the game had severe limits, for baseball was also governed by uncertainties.

Like the melodrama, baseball seemed unusually well suited to present a marvelous set of type characters. "You know, there were a lot of characters in baseball back then," recalled Samuel "Wahoo Sam" Crawford in the 1960s. "Real individualists. Not conformists, like most ball players—and most people—are today."[8] The fans noticed and adored the special physical traits and idiosyncratic behavior of the players. Their colorful nicknames—Bugs, Babe, Rube, Wahoo Sam, Mugsy, Chief, Muddy, Kid, Hod, Dummy, Dutch, Stuffy, Gabby, and Hooks, to list only a few— suggested baseball's capacity to produce stock characters. And, of course, the umpire continued to serve as the chief villain.

The players seemed to take a special delight in spicing the game with comedy and the unexpected. Perhaps none equalled the feat of Herman "Germany" Schaefer. He stole first base! With the score tied in a late inning, Schaefer was on first base and Davy Jones on third. Schaefer gave

[6]Riess, "Baseball Myths," 292–309; Riess, "Race and Ethnicity in American Baseball, 1900–1919," *Journal of Ethnic Studies*, 4 (Winter 1977), 39–55.

[7]Quoted in Leverett T. Smith, Jr., *The American Dream and the National Game* (Bowling Green, Ohio: Bowling Green University Popular Press, 1975), p. 190.

[8]Lawrence S. Ritter, *The Glory of Their Time: The Story of the Early Days of Baseball Told by the Men Who Played It* (New York: Macmillan, 1966), p. 49.

the sign for a double steal and broke for second. The catcher, fearing that
Jones would steal home if he threw the ball, simply held it. In the words of
Jones:

> So now we had men on second and third. Well, on the next pitch Schaefer
> yelled, 'Let's try it again!' And with a bloodcurdling shout he took off like a
> wild Indian *back to first base,* and dove in headfirst in a cloud of dust....
>   But nothing happened. Nothing at all. Everybody just stood there and
> watched Schaefer, with their mouths open, not knowing what the devil was
> going on. Me, too. Even if the catcher *had* thrown to first, I was too stunned to
> move....But the catcher didn't throw. He just stared!...
>   So there we were, back where we started, with Schaefer on first and me on
> third. And on the next pitch darned if he didn't let out another war whoop
> and take off *again* for second base. By this time the Cleveland catcher
> evidently had enough, because he finally threw to second to get Schaefer,
> and when he did I took off for home and *both* of us were safe.[9]

Equally zany behavior was common off the field. Like show business
personalities, the drinking and sexual escapades of the players were
notorious. Reportedly, Rube Waddell, a superb pitcher, accomplished all
of the following feats in a single year:

> He began that year sleeping in a firehouse at Camden, New Jersey, and
> ended it tending bar in a saloon in Wheeling, West Virginia. In between those
> events he won twenty-two games for the Philadelphia Athletics, played left
> end for the Business Men's Rugby Football Club of Grand Rapids, Michigan,
> toured the nation in a melodrama called *The Stain of Guilt,* courted, married,
> and became separated from May Wynne Skinner of Lynn, Massachusetts,
> saved a woman from drowning, accidentally shot a friend through the hand,
> and was bitten by a lion.[10]

This account fails to mention Waddell's heroic drinking binges. *Sporting
News* called him "the leading sousepaw" in baseball.

THE "DEAD BALL" ERA

In terms of the delicate balance between the offense and the defense,
during the three decades preceding 1920 superb pitching held the
limelight. The pitchers enjoyed several advantages over the hitters. Until
1910 they worked with a rubber-centered ball which had less resiliency
than the modern cork-centered baseball. The umpires used only a few new
balls per game; consequently, a ball might become soft, lopsided, and
stained with dirt, grass, or tobacco juice before it was thrown out of play. A
variety of legal "trick" pitches added to the repertoire of several hurlers.

[9]Ibid., pp. 44–45.
[10]Quoted in Seymour, *Baseball,* II, 105–6.

Especially difficult to hit was the spit ball. By applying saliva to the fingers, the pitcher could remove the natural spin from the ball, causing it to behave much like a knuckle ball, dipping and breaking sharply in unpredictable ways as it approached the plate.

While a few pitchers had successful careers built on the spitball, most of the best hurlers relied on fast balls and curves. Cy Young, Grover Cleveland Alexander, "Smoky Joe" Wood, Joe "Iron Man" McGinity, Christy Matthewson, and Walter Johnson—the pitching heroes of the era—all threw blazing fastballs. Walter Johnson, who pitched for the lowly Washington Senators from 1907 to 1927, was perhaps the greatest pitcher of all times. He won 414 games for a team that usually resided in the league's second division; he struck out 3,497 batters and pitched 113 shutouts during his career, both marks that no other hurler has approached. His strikeout record is all the more remarkable considering that the hitters in the deadball era carefully guarded the plate rather than swinging freely. For ten years in a row Johnson won twenty or more games. In one incredible pitching span he shut out the Yankees three times in four days, then after three days' rest won two more consecutive games, for a total of five wins in nine days. Many stories have inspired the legend that Johnson, because of the speed of his pitches, deeply feared that he might hit a batter and kill him. But in fact, Johnson hit 204 batters over his long career, more batters than any other pitcher in the history of the game.

Given the superiority of the pitchers, managers tried to perfect the "scientific" or "inside" baseball strategy made famous by the Boston Beaneaters and the Baltimore Orioles in the 1890s. Most of the hitters choked the bat, trying simply to meet the ball squarely so that it could be driven through the infield or bunted. Managers often fined free swingers. Of the few home runs hit prior to 1910, almost all were inside the park. Since the outfielders of that day played very shallow, inside-the-park homers occurred more frequently than today. The bunt was another favorite weapon of the managers, being used to obtain hits, to cause errors, and to sacrifice runners into scoring position. The deadball could be bunted much more effectively than the modern cork-centered ball. Manager Joe McCloskey of the St. Louis Cardinals once required his hitters to bunt seventeen consecutive times. The strategy produced the two runs needed to win the game. With the introduction of the cork-centered ball in 1910, batting averages shot upward phenomenally, but the managers continued long afterwards to employ the "scientific" strategy.

John J.McGraw, the colorful, controversial, and longtime manager of the New York Giants, was a master of the nuances of deadball strategy. After nine years of play with the famed Baltimore Orioles in the 1890s, McGraw came to New York to take the helm of the Giants in 1902, a post he held for the next thirty years. He led the Giants to ten National League pennants and four "world championships." Like most of the managers of the era, McGraw concentrated upon the acquisition of good pitchers. Other than such pitchers as McGinity, Matthewson, and Rube Marquand, the Giants had no outstanding stars, but they always had speed, aggressiveness, and the peerless McGraw.

Perfectly suited to the nation's center of commerce, high finance, show business, the media, and a multiplicity of ethnic groups, McGraw attracted headlines both on and off the field. He epitomized the martinet managers of the day who exercised harsh discipline through stiff fines and scathing verbal reprimands. Over and over he drilled his team in the fundamentals of the game, in covering bases, place hitting, bunting, sliding, and base running. He brawled with fans, opposing players, umpires, and league presidents. Quick-tempered, McGraw was always ready to use his fists no matter who crossed his path. Fans in the other National League cities came out in droves in hopes of seeing the hated Giants defeated. McGraw took with equal ardor to New York's glamorous social life. He liked the theatrical world, horse racing, gambling, parties, and highballs. New Yorkers loved him for all these things, for his frequent scrapes with the law, his association with both gamblers and the President of the United States, for his belligerency as well as his endearing Irish charm.

Had it not been for Tyrus "Ty" Raymond Cobb (1886–1961), long-time star of the Detroit Tigers, the pre-1920 era would probably be remembered only for its pitching heroes. Part of Cobb's greatness can be measured by comparative statistics. In a career that spanned twenty-four years (1905–1928), he played in more games than any other player in baseball history (3,033), had the highest lifetime batting average (.367), won the league batting championship the most seasons (12)—he won the title nine times in succession—and had the most hits (4,191). Statistics, of course, fail to do Cobb full justice. He had no peer as a master of the deadball tactics. With his spread-handed grip he would bunt if the infield played deep; if the infield tightened up, he would slash the ball through the holes or over the fielders' heads. Moreover, his dazzling speed and recklessness on the base paths terrorized opponents.

Ty Cobb personified, in an exaggerated form, the rugged individualism of the nineteenth century. Lacking the exceptional physical attributes of a Babe Ruth, Cobb relentlessly drove himself to excel. To Cobb, baseball was a form of warfare. "When I played ball," Cobb wrote in his autobiography in 1961, "I didn't play for fun.... It's no pink tea, and mollycoddles had better stay out. It's a contest and everything that implies, a struggle for supremacy, a survival of the fittest."[11] Given such a view, Cobb ignored the old amateur traditions of the sport. Since the 1880s, players had engaged in brawling but usually within a framework of understood conventions that involved a bit of shoving and a great deal of verbal warfare and rarely slugging, but Cobb used every weapon at his disposal—his spikes, fists, bat, and his tongue—all in an effort to intimidate and defeat his opponents. The other players and the fans soon recognized that Cobb was deadly serious, that he was a man driven by internal demons that even left his sanity in question.

Instances of Cobb's aggressive behavior off the field were equally legion. Throughout the league he verbally challenged and sometimes fought

[11]Ty Cobb and Al Stump, *My Life in Baseball: The True Record* (Garden City: Doubleday, 1961), p. 280.

taunting fans; in one case he leaped into the stands and struck a fan who happened to be physically handicapped. In 1914 he got into several scrapes. In one instance Cobb's wife got into an argument with a butcher over twenty cents' worth of spoiled fish. Believing that his wife had been insulted, Cobb went to the butcher's shop, pulled out the revolver that he always carried, and demanded that the butcher telephone his wife to apologize. The butcher, naturally, complied, but the butcher's young assistant appeared and dared Cobb to resolve the issue without the pistol. Cobb was quite willing to accommodate and proceeded to beat the boy insensate; the boy's life may have been saved only by the quick arrival of the police. Cobb was particularly brutal to blacks; on at least two occasions he struck black women. At the Pontchartrain Hotel in Detroit he allegedly kicked a black chambermaid in the stomach and knocked her down the steps because she had objected to being called a "nigger." Repeated warnings, fines, and suspensions by Ban Johnson, president of the American League, failed to curb Cobb's violent temper.

Cobb never became a popular hero in the mold of a Babe Ruth or even a Cap Anson. Almost everybody thoroughly disliked him, including his own teammates. He evoked fear and respect, but never affection; he never had a close, personal friend among the big-league players or managers. He ate alone, roomed alone, and for years at a time did not speak to certain of his teammates. The depth of the feeling against Cobb by fellow players was exemplified clearly in 1910 when Cobb appeared to have won the American League batting championship. In the final doubleheader of the season Napoleon Lajoie, the leading contender for the title, made eight hits in eight times at bat. Six of the hits came from bunts toward third base, which the notoriously slow-footed Lajoie had somehow beaten out. It soon became clear that the St. Louis Browns had deliberately tried to deny Cobb the crown by "giving" Lajoie free access to first base. (Incidentally, the strategy failed, for Cobb was able to retain the title by a single percentage point.) Fans everywhere came out to see the rampaging Cobb, partly in awe of his playing ability, but also in hopes of seeing him stymied by the local club or of witnessing a brawl in which Cobb would be the principal victim.

Cobb's ugly behavior and intense drive apparently arose from a combination of circumstances. Born of a proud family in Georgia that had once owned slaves, Cobb was inordinately defensive of his origins and the South. Teammates discovered this sensitivity. As a rookie he became the natural butt of unmerciful hazing. Teammates broke his bats, nailed his uniform to the clubhouse wall, hid his clothes, locked him in the bathrooms, and tried to get him into a fight with the biggest man on the club. Cobb responded violently, eventually intimidating the rest of the players. Likewise, fans enjoyed ragging the superstar. At every league park except Detroit fans threw a steady barrage of verbal insults at Cobb. Sometimes the insults turned to violence, and Cobb had to be escorted by the police. It is little wonder that Cobb believed he was the target of a conspiracy.

Cobb was also obsessed with the bizarre circumstances of his father's death. He explained in his autobiography that "I did it for my father, who was an exalted man. They killed him when he was still young. But I knew he was watching me and I never let him down."[12] The mysterious "they" referred to by Cobb was his own mother. Cobb's father had suspected his wife of unfaithfulness and had gone to her bedroom window to investigate. Apparently mistaking him for an intruder, she had shot him with a shotgun. The tragic incident occurred just as Cobb was entering the big leagues. "I had to fight all my life to survive," Cobb later wrote. "They were all against me...but I beat the bastards and left them in the ditch." As Cobb grew older, the symptoms of insanity grew more pronounced. He talked frequently of a vague conspiracy to take away his life. When he died in 1961, only three people from Organized Baseball attended his funeral. Never had a more successful, a more violent, and more maladjusted personality passed through the annals of American sport.

FOOTBALL'S CRITICAL ERA

The three decades preceding 1920 marked the most critical era of intercollegiate football's history. By then, the game had largely been transformed from a student activity on the campuses of a few private schools in the Northeast into a nationwide commercial spectacle. While the sport was being institutionalized within the confines of the colleges, the custodians of the sport confronted grave obstacles in developing orderly relationships among themselves. The emphasis upon winning and the absence of a body of established amateur traditions permitted large outlays of money for football, the open recruitment of player talent, fierce training schedules, and clear cases of premeditated brutality. The eligibility problem, professionalism, deaths and serious injuries from football, the lack of gentlemanly behavior, and the issue of whether to make football even more financially rewarding as a spectacle all contributed to a virtual state of anarchy among the nation's colleges. Consequently, football became the subject of a vigorous nationwide debate which eventually involved college presidents, faculties, the press, and even the President of the United States.

The transition of football from a player-centered to a spectator-centered sport offers a key to understanding the quest for order in college football. Students, alumni, college authorities, and social climbers all had an important stake in promoting a winning college team. The requirements of fielding winning teams led the American collegians to adopt the rhetoric of English amateurism without its substance. Like their fathers in the athletic clubs, the sons of the elite had no established customs that inhibited commercialization or the turning of the sport into a deadly serious activity. The collegians and the professional coaches (whom they eventually hired) hailed the ideals of amateurism but brought with them to the gridiron the values of the marketplace. They wanted above all else to win. "The spirit of American youth, as of the American man, is to win, to 'get there,' by fair

[12]Quoted in Seymour, *Baseball,* II, 111.

means or foul," observed a *Nation* writer in 1890, "and the lack of moral scruple which pervades the struggles of the business world meets with temptations equally irresistible in the miniature contests of the football field."[13] The absence of a body of amateur traditions encouraged endless quarrels over the eligibility of athletes, player behavior, and the rules of the game.

Some of the disenchantment with college football flowed from the growing realization that the sport was no longer a student-centered activity. Everywhere, but especially in the Midwest and the South, student control of football diminished. Administrators sought control of finances and management; professional coaches determined schedules, supervised practices, and selected players. In short, the professional coach became a virtual dictator. "What has become of the natural, spontaneous joy of the contest," asked Owen Johnson through a fictional character early in the century. "Instead you have the most perfectly organized business systems for achieving the required result—success. Football is driving slavish work."[14] Indeed, football coaches usually drove their men harder than did professional baseball managers. Coaches subjected their players to countless repetition of the same plays, verbal harangues, and controlled diets. When the legendary Glenn S. "Pop" Warner took his first coaching job at Iowa State College in 1895, he required his young charges in preseason practice to do five miles of roadwork each morning, three hours of practice in the afternoon, and to be in bed by 6:00 p.m. The athletes universally hated the practices but loved the adoration heaped upon them on Saturday afternoons. No doubt Yale athletes also enjoyed their training table, which featured a choice of beefsteak or mutton for dinner, to be washed down with ample quantities of milk, ale, or sherry.

Early in the twentieth century, Harvard, which had attempted more than most other schools to imitate the English system of athletics, resorted to a full-time professional coach. In hopes of reversing their abysmal record against Yale, the Harvard Athletic Association hired Percy D. Haughton in 1908. Prior to the Haughton era, graduates had returned to campus to give haphazard instruction in the finer points of the game. Sometimes techniques taught by one coach in one week would be contradicted by a new coach a week later. Haughton implemented a new discipline, one modeled along the lines of a military hierarchy. A chain of command led from Haughton through the assistant coaches and the captain to the players. Haughton coordinated a staff of coaching specialists and imposed an iron discipline upon all the participants in the program. Players who failed to perform according to expectations often found themselves cursed or physically disciplined. Haughton drilled the players repeatedly in the fundamentals. His dictatorial methods brought success. During his tenure at Harvard from 1908 through 1916, the Crimson lost

[13]"The Future of Football," *Nation*, 51 (November 20, 1890), 395. See also Allen L. Sack, "Yale 29–Harvard 4: The Professionalization of College Football," *Quest*, 19 (Winter 1973), 24–34.

[14]Quoted in Brooks Mather Kelley, *Yale: A History* (New Haven: Yale University Press, 1974), p. 298.

only one game to Yale. Against the best of the eastern colleges, Harvard went unbeaten in thirty-nine straight games in 1911 through 1915 and garnered the mythical national championship in 1910, 1912, and 1913. Other successful coaches copied the "Haughton System."

With the emphasis upon winning, amicable intercollegiate relations repeatedly foundered, especially over the question of the eligibility of players. Initially, American colleges, following the precedents of the English universities, allowed almost anyone connected with the college to play. As late as 1900 in some parts of the South and West, townspeople and younger faculty members sometimes joined the teams as players. In the 1898 southern championship game, Virginia accused North Carolina of employing two professional stars but raised no objections to Professor Edward V. Howell, who scored the lone winning touchdown for the North Carolina eleven. Some students "grew old" as football players. After playing four years while pursuing a baccalaureate degree, they might continue to play indefinitely while enrolled in professional or graduate programs. To place some limits on this practice, in 1882 members of the Intercollegiate Football Association restricted players to five years of competition.

In 1889, Wesleyan and Yale called for a special convention to treat "questions of amateur standing." Recognizing the gravity of the situation, Walter Camp attempted to head off a revolt of the smaller colleges by submitting a resolution barring subsidized and part-time students from competition. Princeton promptly tried to amend Camp's resolution to include any student who had transferred from another college, but the convention ruled the amendment out of order and proceeded to pass Camp's original resolution. Harvard's delegate then presented protests questioning the eligibility of fifteen Princeton players; Princeton responded by filing complaints against four Harvard men. Tempers flared. Amid angry and "undignified" charges and countercharges, the convention adjourned for ten days to give the protested players an opportunity to defend themselves. When the convention reassembled with a "great crowd of collegians and newspaper men" present, the delegates had to retreat behind closed doors. Wesleyan and Pennsylvania joined Princeton in successfully tabling all the protests; Harvard and Yale cast negative votes. To add to Harvard's humiliation, two days later Princeton defeated the Crimson football team. Angry Harvard students held a mass meeting and voted to withdraw from the Intercollegiate Football Association, a move that led to rapid disintegration of the association. Within five years, the association folded completely.

ETHICS OF RECRUITING

In the 1890s and the first years of the twentieth century, the recruitment and extension of thinly disguised subsidies to football players became something of a national scandal. While no college athletic association employed the professional coach-recruiter who would become a familiar feature of college football in the 1950s, team captains, the managers of athletic associations, alumni, and the voluntary "coaches" sought by flattery, promises of glory, special favors, and outright subsidies to secure the best athletes they could from private preparatory schools, other colleges, and public high schools. The elite northeastern colleges recruited mostly from the prep schools; thus Harvard's teams, for instance, abounded with the sons of old-stock, wealthy families of New England— the Appletons, Cabots, Cushings, Peabodys, and the like. But in the 1890s several Irish and German names began to dot the lineups of northeastern schools. In 1892 and 1893 Walter Camp even named William H. Lewis, a black player from Harvard, to his "All-America" team. State universities tended to recruit more frequently from public high schools or simply from their general student bodies.

Although difficult to document, it was obvious that many college athletic associations offered generous subsidies to football players. On campuses across the country, but especially in the South and West, the so-called "tramp" athlete, who each fall essentially offered his services to the highest bidder, was commonplace. In most instances, the tramp athlete only vaguely pretended to be a student; he might play for several years beyond the expected four years for graduation. Caspar W. Whitney exaggerated only slightly in 1895 when he reported that in the Middle and Far West "men are bought and sold like cattle to play this autumn on 'strictly amateur' elevens."[15] Ten years later, according to a report in *McClure's Magazine,* conditions had hardly improved. James J. Hogan, the renowned captain of the Yale team, reputedly lived in a style befitting a prince. He enjoyed free tuition, a free suite in the swank Vanderbilt Hall, free meals at the University Club, a $100 scholarship, a ten-day vacation to Cuba paid for by the Yale Athletic Association, a monopoly on the sale of scorecards at games, and the exclusive commission to handle the products of the American Tobacco Company on the Yale campus. Apparently, the students took Hogan's good fortune in stride, for they affectionately spoke of smoking "Hogan's cigarettes."[16]

FORMATION OF CONFERENCES

Preventing the subsidization and unsavory recruitment of student athletes proved to be a formidable task. Since the colleges were reluctant to acknowledge the commercial character of football, they did not organize tightly governed economic cartels which could have imposed and enforced a uniform set of athletic rules or equalized the conditions of competition. Instead, each school, perceiving itself to be an honorable institution and happily oblivious to the commercial dimensions of football, wanted to

[15]*Literary Digest,* 12 (November 30, 1895), 128.
[16]Henry Beach Needham, "The College Athlete," *McClure's Magazine,* 25 (June–July 1905), 115–28, 260–73.

govern its own sports. Internally, the colleges by 1900 had instituted three main types of self-control: student control with little or no external interference from the faculty but often a strong alumni influence (examples were Yale and Princeton); joint faculty-alumni-student control (example Harvard); faculty control with various groups often exercising a strong influence (for example, most of the colleges in the Midwest and South). Since the self-imposed controls often failed to curb the worst abuses, the colleges could resort to another method; they could threaten to sever relationships with those schools which blatantly ignored the conventions of amateur sport. Apparently such an informal regulatory system did check some of the worst excesses of the college football programs.

External ly, the colleges increasingly turned to the formation of athletic conferences as a means of regulating sports. Students had formed the first intercollegiate association in 1858 when Harvard, Yale, Brown, and Trinity organized the College Rowing Association. Eventually the students also formed associations in baseball, football, and track and field. Beginning in 1895 with the organization of the Intercollegiate Conference of Faculty Representatives, later known as the Western Conference, and even later as the Big Ten, which was initially composed of the large midwestern universities of Chicago, Illinois, Purdue, Michigan, Minnesota, and Northwestern, college presidents took the initiative in attempting to bring a higher degree of order to intercollegiate athletic relations.[17] From its founding, the conference conceived of itself as the "anchor of amateur athletics in America." The conference pioneered in the establishment of rules of eligibility, prohibition of subsidies to student athletes, and the faculty supervision of athletes—measures subsequently copied by other conferences. The conference of faculty representatives had one major weakness: it left enforcement in the hands of faculty committees of the member institutions.

Faculty athletic committees by no means guaranteed that a college's sports program would be exempted from abuses or a strictly commercial orientation. Edward S. Jordan, after an examination of college football in 1905, flatly asserted that "faculty control is a myth."[18] In the first two decades of the twentieth century at the typical college, the faculty, regardless of its stated powers, shared the actual supervision of sports with coaches, presidents, trustees, and the alumni. Any of these groups might block or thwart faculty control. Moreover, for the most part, the faculties were just as interested in the success of the football team as any other group. Frequently, presidents handpicked sympathetic faculty members to sit on athletic committees and to represent the university at conference meetings, and even when a committee member had a firm commitment to player-centered ideals, he faced the problem of familiarizing himself with

[17]See Howard Roberts, *The Big Nine: The Story of Football in the Western Conference* (New York: G. P. Putnam's Sons, 1948); Carl D. Voltmer, *A History of the Intercollegiate Conference* (New York: George Banta, 1935).

[18]Edward S. Jordan, "Buying Football Victories," *Collier's*, 36 (November 18, 1905), 23. See also Howard J. Savage et al., *American College Athletics* (New York: Carnegie Foundation, 1929), pp. 100–101 and Lewis, "The American Intercollegiate Football Spectacle," p. 197.

the bewildering complexities of the institution's athletic programs while fulfilling his regular obligations. Finally, for a faculty representative to challenge prevailing athletic practices usually meant subjecting himself to exceptionally hostile reactions from football fans both inside and outside of the college.

An instance involving the University of Michigan and its football coach, Fielding H. "Hurry Up" Yost, graphically illustrates the problems of faculty control. Before coming to Michigan, Yost had won a reputation for his recruiting talents. He liked experienced players. The star of his undefeated Kansas team of 1899, for example, had played five years at the University of West Virginia and one year as a professional before joining the Jayhawker squad. A Kansas "purity" campaign resulted in Yost's ouster after the 1899 season. Then Yost went to Stanford. David Starr Jordan, the president of Stanford, later related the following story:

> A young fellow came in from the mines who wanted to study mining engineering—a tremendously big and strong fellow. He was admitted because of certain symptoms of earnestness he showed—admitted as a special student.... [He] failed in his studies, and was dropped. Yost carried him to Michigan, where he has become the center of the strong team which is the pride of Michigan University; and this man, who was not able to pass any examinations [while at Stanford]... has been playing some ten or fifteen games a year at Michigan.... All of us who have ever had a Yost or any Yost-like man about are not to be counted as sinless.[19]

Yost recruited for Michigan other players besides the "tremendously big and strong fellow" from the mines. When he came to Michigan in 1901, he brought with him several experienced western players, including Willie Heston, a college graduate of San Jose State who was later to be named to many all-time, all-American teams. Heston, as a law student, played four seasons with the Wolverines, finally retiring after seven years in the college ranks. The enthusiastic alumni of Michigan cooperated fully with Yost in recruiting, keeping the football players eligible, and providing sub rosa subsidies to the star athletes, all of which violated the spirit of Western Conference rules and the player-centered tradition. The results were phenomenal. From 1901 through the 1905 season Michigan lost only one contest. "The words 'Yost' and 'Michigan' were synonymous," concluded one historian of the university. "The newspapers regarded the whole institution as the backdrop for the football squad."[20]

A new set of conference rules in 1906, adopted in response to the national football crisis and apparently as a means of curbing the abuses of Michigan, threatened to emasculate Yost's high-powered program. (Ironically, President James G. Angell of Michigan was a major proponent of change.) First, the conference restricted the eligibility of the players to three years, which, since the rule was retroactive, would have excluded

---

[19]*School Review*, 11 (May 1903), 344. See also Wilfred B. Shaw, "Michigan and the Conference: A Ten Year Argument Over the University's Athletic Relations," *Michigan Alumnus*, 54 (December 6, 1947), 34–48.

[20]Quoted in Lewis, "The American Intercollegiate Football Spectacle," p. 211.

several of Yost's top performers. Second, the conference limited competition to "undergraduates," which would have prevented one of Yost's favorite ploys, the use of experienced students in professional or graduate schools at key positions. Third, the conference required that coaches be regular members of the staff with a salary commensurate with their professional rank. Yost was not a regular member of the staff and was paid more than any professor on the Michigan campus.

The Michigan faculty quickly approved the rule changes, but the students and alumni protested bitterly. They believed that the conference rules had been designed specifically to curtail the success of the Michigan football team. The university regents responded by abolishing the faculty committee responsible for athletics and substituting a new Board of Athletic Control. The new board was solely responsible to the regents. Since games with Michigan produced lucrative revenues, the other Western Conference schools were reluctant to enforce the new rules. They relented on most of the rule changes, but they refused to sustain the action of the Michigan regents in totally denying the principle of faculty control. With neither side willing to concede on this issue, Michigan withdrew from the conference in 1908.

Michigan's experience outside the Western Conference and its subsequent readmission in 1917 reflected the power and influence of the commercial interests in football. After dropping out of the conference, Michigan had difficulty scheduling games with major opponents. Receipts from football and the prestige of the team declined sharply. In 1917 Professor Ralph W. Aigler, an ardent Michigan football enthusiast, explored ways by which the university might be readmitted to the Western Conference. After visiting most of the conference schools, Aigler reported that what constituted faculty control varied widely from one university to the next. Michigan should be able to meet conference rules, he suggested, by giving the Faculty Senate veto power over the actions of the regents' Board of Athletic Control. The regents acquiesced. Recognizing the potential revenue growth that would accompany Michigan's readmission to the conference, the other schools quickly welcomed the Wolverines— complete with Yost as head coach—back into the fold.

Violence Under Fire

The commercialization, the intense seriousness, and abuses in eligibility and recruitment did not arouse as much public controversy as the issue of brutality. Since the 1880s, football had periodically been the subject of public outcries against its physically violent character. Deliberate slugging and kicking, both representing abrupt departures from the gentlemanly traditions of English Rugby, plus the widespread use of mass plays in the 1890s intensified public criticism. In 1897 the state legislature of Georgia, after the death of a player in a college game in that state, abolished football. The governor, however, vetoed the measure. Criticism of football reached a peak in 1905 and 1906, when muckraking journals—especially *McClure's, Collier's, The Nation,* and *Outlook*—published a series of scathing exposés, revealing in shocking detail the absence of gentlemanly behavior and the "insidious" role of money in the sport. In order to insure victories, according to the journals, teams often tried to "knock out" key opposing players early in the game.

In 1905 President Theodore Roosevelt decided to intervene in the controversy. The President had long been obsessed with physical fitness. Apparently he tried to compensate for his feelings of personal physical inadequacy by repeatedly displaying unusual stamina and reckless courage—he captured a gang of rustlers in Dakota Territory, killed a Spanish soldier in Cuba, and stalked lions in Africa. He feared above all else that boys born into luxury would be effeminate. Football was a healthy antidote, teaching "pluck, endurance, and physical address." Roosevelt had a special interest in the Harvard eleven. His son was a member of the squad, and the President often sent the team letters of encouragement. Endicott Peabody, the distinguished headmaster of Groton School, was the immediate stimulus for Roosevelt's action. The masters of the elite prep schools along the East Coast were concerned that their boys tended to emulate the improper behavior of the college players. Peabody urged the President to "get the coaches of Harvard and Yale and Princeton together, and persuade them to undertake to teach men to play football honestly."[21]

Roosevelt agreed, but he had no intention of opening the conference to a full-fledged debate on the merits of college football. He invited only selected coaches, faculty, and alumni from the Big Three—Harvard, Yale, and Princeton—to attend the conference. His expressed hope was "to get them to come to a gentlemen's agreement not to have mucker play." Those who wanted a more open style of play and those who wanted to eliminate or reduce the commercial dimensions of the sport found themselves excluded from the conferences. Walter Camp of Yale, leader of the forces demanding essentially the status quo in college football, immediately took charge of the conference. The delegates submitted to the President a mild statement promising to eliminate unnecessary "roughness, holding, and foul play." The President, satisfied with the resolution, urged its immediate release to the press.*

The White House football conference failed to still the critics of the sport. While the *New York Times* hailed Roosevelt's accomplishment as a feat equal to his success in mediating the Russo-Japanese War, President Charles W. Eliot of Harvard noted that those who drafted the resolution were the very persons most responsible for the abuses of the sport. And

---

*There is a legend that Roosevelt threatened to abolish college football by executive order. Apart from the dubious constitutionality of such an action, there is no contemporary documentation that Roosevelt made such a threat. Moreover, such a threat would have been inconsistent with the President's numerous statements praising college football.

[21]Quoted in ibid., 223–24. See also Lewis, "Theodore Roosevelt's Role in the 1905 Football Controversy," *Research Quarterly*, 40 (December 1969), 717–24, and John Hammond Moore, "Football's Ugly Decades, 1893–1913," *Smithsonian Journal of History*, 2 (Fall 1967), 49–68.

play in the 1905 season continued to be as brutal as ever. The *Chicago Tribune* dramatically reported that eighteen college and secondary students had lost their lives and 159 men had been injured in the 1905 season. The issue of brutality helped coalesce the forces demanding reform.

Several colleges took drastic action. Columbia and the Massachusetts Institute of Technology abolished the sport; Stanford and California substituted Rugby for football. The Western Conference limited schools to five games, outlawed training tables, and restricted competition to undergraduates who had been in residence for at least six months. Even Harvard, Yale, and Princeton banned freshmen and graduate students from varsity play. The final blow came late in the 1905 season when Harold P. Moore, a Union College player, died in a game with New York University. Henry B. McCracken, the chancellor of New York University, promptly called for a conference of college presidents representing schools on New York University's schedule. McCracken recognized that fundamental changes in football would not come from Walter Camp's rules committee. "I would not intrust the reformation of the game to the present Rules Committee," he flatly asserted.[22]

At this point, the proponents of a more open style of play seized upon the reform impulse in an effort to make football an even more exciting sport for spectators. The world of college football had for some time been split into two warring factions. One wanted to retain the sport as it existed and the other sought rule changes that would encourage more offensive action. Walter Camp's Intercollegiate Rules Committee, a self-constituted body representing a select group of northeastern schools plus the University of Chicago, staunchly defended the status quo. They conceded only the need to reduce foul play and brutality. The midwestern faction, led mostly by professional coaches whose tenure depended upon the financial returns from football, advocated radical rule changes that would increase the appeal of the sport to spectators. They wanted a game that featured long runs, more scoring, and the greater likelihood of upsets. Only the desire to schedule interregional contests had prevented a complete rupture with the Intercollegiate Rules Committee prior to 1906.

The representatives of the thirteen colleges that attended McCracken's conference on December 8, 1905, in New York did not even debate the possibility of abolishing the sport. Instead, they called for a national college convention and the formation of a new rules committee. Delegates from sixty-two colleges, representing all sections of the country, save the West Coast and the member colleges of Walter Camp's Rules Committee, met in New York on December 28, 1905. The convention quickly organized the ·Intercollegiate Athletic Association (IAA) with Captain Palmer E. Pierce of West Point as chairman and appointed their own rules committee. In 1910 the IAA became the National Collegiate Athletic Association (NCAA). The delegates gave no legislative or executive powers to the IAA, but did allow it to formulate standards of conduct for member colleges and the various conferences. Until the post-World War II era, the most important function

---

[22]Quoted in Lewis, "The American Intercollegiate Football Spectacle," p. 234.

of the NCAA was the creation of rules committees for college sports rather than regulation of the institution's athletic behavior.

The IAA convention still had to contend with Walter Camp. Creating a separate rules committee would not only offend the most powerful figure in college football, but might prevent the scheduling of interregional games. After a "stormy" nine-hour session, the convention agreed to explore the possibility of an amalgamated rules committee. With the urging of Roosevelt, delegates from Harvard and Navy finally broke ranks with the Intercollegiate Rules Committee. On January 12, 1906, the two rules committees held separate sessions in New York. After an exchange of notes, Camp's committee reluctantly acquiesced to a joint committee in which each group had equal representation. Although the new system failed to provide equal representation for all schools, it was more equitable than the former one. The joint arrangement continued until 1915, when Yale finally joined the NCAA.

In 1906, the new rules committee adopted a series of changes that it hoped would give the offense more freedom of action and reduce brutality. Rather than three attempts to gain five yards for a first down, the new rule provided for three downs to make ten yards. Supposedly, the additional yardage required for a first down would encourage teams to abandon the fashionable mass plays designed for short yardage gains. The committee also approved the forward pass, but placed severe restrictions on its use. The ball had to pass over the line of scrimmage five yards or more to the right or left of where it had been put into play, and an incomplete pass resulted in an automatic fifteen-yard penalty. With such strictures, only a foolish coach would make more than an occasional use of the forward pass. Whatever the consequences of these rule changes, the "Revolution of 1906," as it has been hailed, represented a ringing victory for those promoting football as a spectator-centered sport rather than those concerned with the preservation of the player-centered ideals of the sport. The midwestern coaches had taken a major step in making college football a bigger and more attractive spectacle.

The rule changes of 1906, however, failed to lead to an open game of wide end runs and numerous forward passes. The ten-yard rule and the limited utility of the pass led teams to engage in an even more conservative style of play. Most teams did not even bother to mount sustained offensive drives in their half of the field, but often kicked on first downs hoping for a mistake by the opposition. Almost all scoring came from drop kicks. Play remained as brutal as ever. In 1909 thirty players (eight of them college men) lost their lives, and the 1910 rules committee took more drastic action. They abolished interlocking interference and required at least seven offensive men on the line of scrimmage. Over Camp's opposition, the committee liberalized the forward pass, allowing the ball to cross the line of scrimmage at any point. Two years later, the offense was given four downs to make ten yards, and the value of a touchdown was increased from five to six points.

The cumulative rule changes brought the "modern" game of football into existence. Slowly, the coaches, particularly in the West, began to exploit the potential of the forward pass. In 1913, when Notre Dame came East to play Army, the astonishing passes of Gus Dorais to Knute Rockne resulted in a stunning upset victory for the Irish. Later in the season the cadets profited from the disaster by using the "Western" passing game to defeat archrival Navy. After the 1913 season, coaches everywhere began to experiment with the forward pass. The custodians of college football had finally created an immensely exciting sport and had even brought a degree of order to the ranks of the college game.

8

American Sporting Ideology and Youth Sports

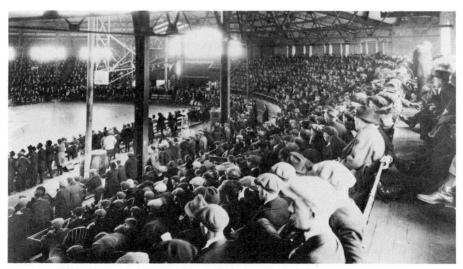

High school basketball tournament, interior of Coliseum, University of Nebraska, circa 1921. Reprinted by permission of the Nebraska State Historical Society.

In the three decades between 1890 and 1920, the nation exhibited a new activist mood. The mood found expression in an aggressive nationalism, an intense interest in untamed nature, muscular music (ragtime), realistic fiction, the emergence of the "New Woman," and a boom in sports and recreation. Theodore Roosevelt, the "dandy" Easterner turned cowboy, the "Rough Rider" of the Spanish-American War, and the supercharged President of the United States between 1901 and 1909 personified the nation's fascination with new forms of strenuosity. Reacting against the excessive refinement, the femininity, and the enervating tendencies of modern life, even the middle-income Victorians, once suspicious of both the rough outdoor sports of the social elite and the commercial spectacles of the sporting fraternity, became apostles of the strenuous life. Bicycling seemed to touch off the new sporting craze. The number of bicycles leaped from one million in 1893 to ten million in 1900; cyclists formed clubs, organized a national association, and scheduled races which attracted millions. College football caught on everywhere. It spread from the eastern colleges across the Midwest and on to the Pacific Coast; several schools erected large stadiums of steel and concrete. Baseball, long a favorite sandlot sport, reached the pinnacle of its popularity in the first two decades of the twentieth century. Even boxing, once shunned by all the proper Victorians, began to lose some of its unsavory reputation after 1892, when "Gentleman Jim" Corbett used padded gloves to dispose of John L. Sullivan.[1]

One of the central aspects of the new vigor and vitality was the development of a national sporting ideology and the emergence of mammoth programs of adult-managed sport for youth (especially boys). Before 1890, youths had competed in sport, but nearly always on teams and in games that they themselves had organized or they played on teams composed largely of adults. Except in the colleges and the private boarding schools of the Northeast, no sharp line divided youth from adult sport. After 1890 the Young Men's Christian Association, the Public Schools Athletic Leagues, the city playground associations, and the public high schools, all of which reflected old-stock, Protestant, middle-class concerns, became major sponsors of boys' sports. Females in the colleges and high

[1]See the discussion of the activist mood in John Higham, "The Reorientation of American Culture in the 1890's," in Higham, *Writing America's History: Essays on Modern Scholarship* (Bloomington: Indiana University Press, 1970), pp. 73–102. On the bicycling rage see Robert A. Smith, *A Social History of the Bicycle: Its Early Life and Times in America* (New York: American Heritage, 1972).

schools also joined the boom in youth sport, but without the enthusiastic support of adults.

The drive for adult-directed boys' sport was an integral part of a larger movement to organize and manage the spare-time activities of the nation's youth. The thrust for this larger movement to control the environment of youth stemmed from a heightened concern that the traditional agencies of socialization no longer satisfactorily prepared youth for adult roles in the community. Boys' sports, the leaders of the movement believed, could be an important surrogate for a rural upbringing, the disappearance of the household economy, the absence of early work experience, the weakened authority of religion, and the breakdown of the small geographic community. Muscular Christianity furnished the initial rationale for the movement; later, professional "boy-workers" added to the existent defense of boys' sport a theory of play that was grounded in evolutionary theory. The combined ideas of a virile Christianity and an evolutionary theory of play constituted a new sporting ideology; these ideas also shaped the content and institutional structure of the adult-managed boys' sport movement.[2]

Those most concerned for the fate of youth in the 1890–1920 era, believed that the new urban-industrial society had dealt harshly with the old ways of child-rearing. In particular, the new society had weakened the family as a nurturing institution. Earlier in the nineteenth century, the family had often constituted a household economy. Children had lent assistance to their parents in spinning thread, weaving cloth, making garments, fabricating tools, constructing furniture, baking bread, or perhaps in helping their father pursue his trade. But by 1890, all save the most wretched families purchased many of their essential items in the marketplace. No longer was the home a place for creating new goods nor the location for the father's trade or business. Father now toiled away from home, and the children were left at best with dull, routine chores, with "make-work" that failed to exercise their "constructive impulses in a wholesome way." Relieving the children of productive work in the home, most youth observers believed, had fatal consequences for healthy moral growth. Habits of good conduct could best be nurtured in a family jointly engaged in creative, essential work, not simply from proper moral instruction. "The transmission of morals is no longer safe in the family," Luther Gulick glumly concluded, "because the activities out of which morals arise have been taken away."[3]

---

[2]For the larger movement to organize and manage the spare-time activities of youth, see Joseph F. Kett, *Rites of Passage: Adolescence in America, 1790 to the Present* (New York: Basic Books, 1977), and Paul Boyer, *Urban Masses and Moral Order in America, 1820–1920* (Cambridge, Mass.: Harvard University Press, 1978). For boys' sport, see Lawrence A. Finfer, "Leisure and Social Work in the Urban Community: The Progressive Recreation Movement, 1890–1920" (unpublished Ph.D. dissertation, Michigan State University, 1974), and Dominick Joseph Cavallo, "The Child in American Reform: A Psycho-history of the Movement to Organize Children's Play, 1880–1920" (unpublished Ph.D. dissertation, State University of New York at Stony Brook, 1976). For organized sport among boys since 1920 see Jack W. Berryman, "From the Cradle to the Playing Field: America's Emphasis on Highly Organized Sport for Preadolescent Boys," *Journal of Sport History*, 2 (Fall 1975), 112–31.

[3]Luther Halsey Gulick, *A Philosophy of Play* (New York: Scribner's 1920), p. 219.

Neither could numerous casual contacts with other adults shape the youth's character. Increasingly, the new society segregated teenagers from the general work force. In the early nineteenth century, children fourteen or younger had been expected to leave the family and strike out on their own. Sometimes they became apprentices learning a skill, or they might experiment with a variety of jobs and sporadically attend local academies. But the growing reliance on machinery in the nineteenth century gradually undermined the apprenticeship system. Countless youths were left with "dead-end" jobs that required few if any skills and offered even fewer opportunities for a better future. While the sons of workingmen had no choice but to continue taking jobs in industry at a tender age, middle- and upper-status parents began to encourage their sons to enter the growing white-collar sector of the economy. The key to becoming a lawyer, doctor, accountant, engineer, or business manager seemed to be an extended education, lasting until age sixteen or even longer. Parents who could afford to do so began to withdraw their children from the job market and send them to school.

The push by middle- and upper-status parents for longer periods of formal education coincided with the passage of state laws that had the effect of barring younger adolescents from the work force. In the first two decades of the twentieth century, most of the states, as part of the "Progressive" reform impulse, increased the length of the school term from four months to nine months, extended compulsory school attendance to the age of fourteen or longer, and prohibited children from working at full-time jobs until they were fourteen or even sixteen. "The whole tendency of the times, therefore, is to drive children under sixteen out of work and into school," noted the Fall River, Massachusetts, school board in 1914.[4] Not only did this legislation deny younger adolescents opportunities for employment, but is also made long periods of seasonal work combined with school attendance impossible.

The separation of teenagers from the general work force undermined a traditional source of socialization. Instead of numerous casual contacts with adults through early work experience, youths now spent most of their time in school with other youngsters or in leisure activities that were unsupervised by adults. The school tended to restrict youth-adult interaction to the highly formal student-teacher relationship. The abundance of unmanaged spare time that younger adolescents increasingly enjoyed was a cause of deep concern for parents and youth observers alike. Unless offset by morally uplifting activity organized by adults, the ethical growth of the urban youth was endangered by the pervasive wickedness of the city. Urban children, declared one youth worker, "watch the drunken people, listen to the leader of the gang, hear the shady story, smoke cigarettes, and acquire those vicious habits, knowledge, and vocabulary which are characteristic" of the worst denizens of the city.[5]

Profound suspicions of the burgeoning cities and deep nostalgia for the countryside shaped the attitudes and values of the "boy-workers" in the

[4]As quoted in Kett, *Rites of Passage,* p. 235.
[5]Henry S. Curtis, *The Play Movement and Its Significance* (New York: Macmillan, 1917), pp. 119–20.

YMCA, the playgrounds, the Scouts, and the high schools. To them, the cities seemed to symbolize the triumph of the values of the marketplace over the older values of the church, the family, and the small community. Furthermore, the city was the principal home of alien peoples who held strange beliefs and often violated the behavioral codes of old-stock Americans. Traditional social restraints seemed to evaporate in the cities. Boys were vulnerable to a host of new "perversions"—"the mad rush for sudden wealth," the impulse to mature too quickly, the emulation of the "reckless fashions set by gilded youth," membership in juvenile gangs, impure sexual thoughts and practices, the "secret vice" (masturbation), and fornication. While the city was an unmitigated college of vice for youth, the country had furnished a wholesome, natural environment. "The country boy roams the hills and has free access to 'God's first temples,'" asserted F. D. Bonyton, the superintendent of Ithaca schools in 1904. "What can we offer to the city boy in exchange for paradise lost? His only road to paradise regained is thru the gymnasium, the athletic field, and the playground."[6] Sport, many of the boy-workers came to believe, could serve as an effective surrogate for the lost rural experience.

To the advocates of the new sporting ideology, modern life had become too soft and effeminate. Frontiers and battlefields no longer existed to test manly courage and perseverance. Henry W. Williams observed that the "struggle for existence, though becoming harder and harder, is less and less a physical struggle, more and more a battle of minds."[7] Apart from sports, men no longer had arenas for proving their manliness. Theodore Roosevelt worried lest prolonged periods of peace would encourage "effeminate tendencies in young men." Only aggressive sports, Roosevelt argued, could create the "brawn, the spirit, the self-confidence, and quickness of men" that was essential for the existence of a strong nation.[8] In the view of the sport advocates, no game (unless it be boxing) rivalled football in its capacity to instill manliness. The football field "is the only place where masculine supremacy is incontestable," concluded an *Independent* editorial.[9]

MUSCULAR CHRISTIANITY AND THE YMCA

Well before 1890, Protestants, partly in response to the changing place of youth in the new urban-industrial society, had begun to reconsider their traditional animosity toward sport for boys. By launching a crusade for the

[6]F. D. Bonyton, "Athletics and Collateral Activities in Secondary Schools," *Proceedings and Addresses of the National Education Association* (1904), 210. The antiurban bias runs throughout all of the literature of the boy-workers. A few of them explicitly asserted that adolescent sexuality was the principal problem of the city. For instance: "I believe that sex-perversions are the most common, subtle and dangerous foes that threaten modern life." William Byron Forbush, *The Boy Problem: A Study in Social Pedagogy* (Boston: Pilgrim Press, 1901), p. 147.

[7]Henry W. Williams, "The Educational and Health Giving Value of Athletics," *Harper's Weekly* (February 16, 1895), 166.

[8]Quoted in Joe L. Dubbert, *A Man's Place: Masculinity in Transition* (Englewood Cliffs, N.J.: Prentice-Hall, 1979), pp. 116, 117.

[9]"The Uncultured Sex," *Independent* (November 11, 1909), 1100.

practice of muscular Christianity in the 1850s, eastern patricians prepared the way for a general conversion of Protestant attitudes. New England clerics and essayists, joined by many newspaper editors, and influenced by the examples of Thomas Hughes and Charles Kingsley in England, tried to convince the eastern elite of the compatibility of "physical vigor and spiritual sanctity." The tireless American champion of muscular Christianity, Thomas Wentworth Higginson, asked for a renaissance of the Greek ideal of a symmetrical life that gave equal attention to both physical and spiritual growth. "Physical health," Higginson added, was ". . . a necessary condition of all permanent success."[10] In linking success to a strenuous boyhood, Higginson introduced a major motif of advice-to-boys books after the Civil War. In the latter half of the nineteenth century and during the first two decades of the twentieth century, Christian manliness grew into something of a cult among old-stock patricians. It was often an ally of patriotism, group loyalty, and national pride. An exaggerated concern for manliness—or so it appears in retrospect—also accompanied the rising imperialistic and jingoistic spirit of the 1890s.

Sport fiction furnished the most popular vehicle for the transmission of Christian manliness to boys. Thomas Hughes' classic, *Tom Brown's School Days,* published in 1857, inaugurated the new genre of boys' sport fiction. *Tom Brown's School Days,* immensely successful throughout the English-speaking world, spawned a few pale imitations over the next quarter century. Then the 1890s witnessed a virtual flood of boys' sport novels. Beginning in 1896, Gilbert Patten, writing under the the the nom de plume of Burt L. Standish, introduced the Merriwell series. Over the next twenty years Patten produced 208 Merriwell books, all of which revolved around boyhood manliness. Although a pious man, Patten refrained from preaching explicit Christian doctrines. Instead, he attempted to convince his youthful readers that vigorous participation in athletics would result in personal moral improvement and enhance one's probability of material success. Edward Stratemeyer, the inventor of the Rover Boys along with seven other series, was even more popular than Patten. Stratemeyer and his stable of hack writers stressed adventure, action, humor, and suspense at the expense of moral instruction. By 1920 most of the authors of boys' sport fiction had removed all overt moralizing from their novels, but the "manliness" of Thomas Hughes's original formula remained intact.[11]

The words "manliness" and "manly" incorporated a variety of character traits not always easily comprehended by the modern reader, particularly

[10]Thomas Wentworth Higginson, "Saints and Their Bodies," *Atlantic Monthly,* 1 (March 1858), 585–86. See also Guy Lewis, "The Muscular Christianity Movement," *Journal of Health, Physical Education and Recreation,* 37 (May 1966), 27–28, 42; John A. Lucas, "A Prelude to the Rise of Sport: Ante-Bellum America, 1850–1860," *Quest,* 2 (December 1968), 50–57; Melvin Leonard Adelman, "The Development of Modern Athletics in New York City, 1820–1870" (unpublished Ph.D. dissertation, University of Illinois, 1980), Chap. 11.

[11]See John Levi Cutler, *Gilbert Patten and His Frank Merriwell Saga* (Orono: University of Maine Studies, Second Series, No. 31, 1934); Walter Evans, "The All American Boys: A Study of Boys' Sport Fiction," *Journal of Popular Culture,* 6 (Summer 1972), 104–21; Russell B. Nye, "The Juvenile Approach to American Culture," in Ray B. Browne et al., eds., *New Voices in American Studies* (West Lafayette, Ind.: Purdue University Press, 1966), pp. 67–84.

since the terms had no connotations of machismo. The manly youth, above all, practiced sexual continence and resisted the "secret vice." Masturbation especially alarmed youth advisors, for they believed that its practice depleted the body of vital energy and resulted in a host of other dire consequences. The manly youth cultivated self-command and absolute candor; he abhorred display, pretension, sentimentality, and capitulation to pain. He insisted on justice and was quick to defend honor with physical prowess; he was physically active, striving to develop to the utmost robustness, animal energy, and personal courage. His spirit found its truest expression in the out-of-doors, in the refreshing vigor of the countryside, and on the athletic field.

In the last quarter of the nineteenth century, the popularity of Christian manliness began to extend beyond the eastern elite to middle-status Protestants, even to those of an evangelical temperament. The favorable response of these groups to muscular Christianity reflected a growing anxiety with the alleged "feminization" of American Protestantism and the excessive decorousness of Victorian life. Church leaders had long been concerned with their inability to reach both adolescent boys and young men. Women and girls made up the large majority of most Protestant congregations. Furthermore, to those who advocated a virile Christianity, the churches overemphasized the feminine virtues of humility, submission, and meekness. "There is not enough of effort, of struggle, in the typical church life of today...," declared Josiah Strong, a popular exponent of a manly Christianity. "A flowery bed of ease does not appeal to a fellow who has manhood in him.... Eliminate heroism from religion and it becomes weak, effeminate."[12]

By the 1890s, the Young Men's Christian Association had emerged as the outstanding institutional expression of muscular Christianity among evangelical Protestants. Founded by laymen in England in 1851 and subsequently transplanted to the United States before the Civil War, the original purpose of the YMCA had been to offer spiritual guidance and practical assistance to the young men who were flooding into the nineteenth-century cities. But after the Civil War, the local YMCAs began to broaden their program. To attract young men and boys to their spiritual work they offered classes in physical culture, largely in the form of gymnastics and calisthenics. Instead of young displaced males, the main clientele of the YMCAs became stable young men from the "clerical classes"—bookkeepers, stenographers, clerks, and salesmen—businessmen, a few skilled workingmen, and boys from the middle- and

[12]Quoted in Gilman Ostrander, ed., *The Evolutionary Outlook, 1875–1900* (Clio, Mich.: Marston Press, 1971), p. 61. See Barbara Welter, "The Feminization of American Religion: 1800–1860," in William L. O'Neil, ed., *Insights and Parallels: Problems and Issues in American Social History* (Minneapolis: Burgess, 1973), pp. 305–55; Ann Douglas, *The Feminization of American Culture* (New York: Alfred A. Knopf, 1977). Note the following books published early in the twentieth century: Carl Case, *The Masculine in Religion* (Philadelphia: American Baptist Pub. Co., 1906); Robert Conant, *The Virility of Christ* (Chicago: the author, 1915); Harry Fosdick, *The Manhood of the Master* (New York: Association Press, 1911); Jason Pierce, *The Masculine Power of Christ* (Boston: Pilgrim, 1912); Fayette Thompson et al., *Men and Religion* (New York: Y.M.C.A., 1911).

upper-income ranks.[13] By 1892 the YMCA membership had leaped to nearly a quarter of a million, and the organization had 348 gymnasiums directed by 144 full-time physical leaders. The stage was set for the YMCA to become the leader in the adult-managed sport movement for young men and boys.

One man, Luther Halsey Gulick, Jr., who began his career with the YMCA, played a preeminent role in all phases of the adult-directed boys' sport movement. Born of missionary parents in Honolulu, Hawaii, Gulick waged a "determined war" against the "subjective type of religion" traditionally fostered by pietistic Protestants.[14] While he rejected the formal religious doctrine of his parents, he retained a zest for embarking on crusades. He discovered his equivalent to a spiritual "calling" by becoming in turn the champion of muscular Christianity within the YMCA, a major proponent of a new theory of play, the founder of the Public Schools Athletic League in New York City, an organizer and the first president of the Playground Association of America, a leader of the American Boy Scout movement, and the cofounder with his wife of the American Campfire Girls. According to Gulick, he turned to the strenuous life partly as a way of compensating for his personal feelings of physical and psychical inadequacy. Throughout his life he suffered from severe migraine headaches, periods of dark depression, and a weak physical constitution, all of which he attributed to his father, who had been the victim of a nervous breakdown.

Although Gulick obtained a medical degree, he found far more exciting work than medicine in 1887 as an instructor in the physical department of the International Young Men's Christian Association Training School (later renamed Springfield College) in Springfield, Massachusetts. Since most of the general secretaries and physical directors of local YMCAs passed through the regular two-year curriculum or summer school of the training school, Gulick had found an ideal position for reaching a national and even an international audience. In journals he edited for the training school, in numerous articles and books, and in speeches delivered throughout the country, Gulick unrelentingly preached the same gospel: the spiritual life of man rested on the equal development of the mind and the body. Gulick invented the famous emblem of the YMCA, the inverted triangle which symbolized the spirit supported by the mind and the body. Unlike prior YMCA leaders, Gulick welcomed the introduction of sport into YMCA programs. "We can use the drawing power of athletics a great deal more than we are doing at present," he wrote in 1892, but he cautioned that "...we must work along our own lines and not ape the athletic organizations, whose object is the development of specialists and the breaking of records."[15]

[13]See Luther Gulick, "Young Man of the Cities, II," *Athletic League Letters*, (February 1899); Forbush, *The Boy Problem*, p. 67; Forbush, "Can the Y.M.C.A. Do All the Street Boys' Work?" *Work With Boys*, 4 (July 1904), 182; Boyer, *Urban Masses*, pp. 115–16.

[14]Forbush, *The Boy Problem*, p. 70. See Ethel Josephine Dorgan, *Luther Halsey Gulick, 1865–1918* (New York: Teachers College, Columbia University, 1934).

[15]Gulick, "State Committees on Athletics," *Young Men's Era*, 18 (October 27, 1892), 1365.

Under Gulick's aegis, competitive sport, despite formidable opposition, began to supplant gymnastics in YMCA physical programs. The Springfield training school itself furnished an example of athletic activism to the local YMCAs. Throughout the 1890s the school fielded a baseball team that competed regularly with college and amateur nines. From time to time the college also sponsored competition with outside institutions in track and field, swimming, gymnastics, basketball, and volleyball. In 1890 Amos Alonzo Stagg, a famed Yale football player of the 1880s, enrolled at Springfield. He promptly gathered a team of faculty and students, about half of whom had never played football before, and challenged all the prominent northeastern colleges to games. That fall, "Stagg's Stubby Christians" almost upset mighty Yale before succumbing 16 to 10 in the country's first indoor football game in Madison Square Garden. The vigorous sport program at Springfield and the experience of the students there inspired YMCAs everywhere to organize their own athletic teams.

While the physical curriculum of the training school continued to center on traditional subjects such as anatomy and motor development, Gulick added a pioneering course in the psychology of play as well as training in specific sport skills. Students learned how to give instruction in all the major track and field events, football, swimming, lawn tennis, baseball, basketball, rowing, and volleyball. Gulick, in his psychology of play course, asked students to experiment with new games and sports that could be played in the confined space of gymnasiums and that would be appropriate to a certain level of maturity. The invention of both basketball and volleyball resulted from Gulick's inspiration and suggestions. In 1891, James A. Naismith, a young minister from Canada who was a student and part-time instructor at Springfield, put together the essentials of the game of basketball. And in 1895, William G. Morgan, while serving as physical director of the YMCA at Holyoke, Massachusetts, invented volleyball especially for older men who found basketball too strenuous.[16]

The unbridled enthusiasm of the young men and adolescent boys for basketball and other forms of athletic competition presented the YMCA leadership with a trying dilemma. On the one hand the organized games obviously increased membership, interest, and the physical prowess of the participants. On the other hand, basketball threatened to convert the YMCAs into full-fledged athletic clubs. As early as 1892, Gulick had warned the association of the dangers of a spectator-centered orientation. Nonetheless, by the mid-1890s, in one local YMCA after another, basketball threatened to drive all other forms of physical activity off the gymnasium floor. The YMCA basketball players usually imbibed the spirit of winning at all costs with as much ardor as the collegians. "In several places," Gulick reported in 1895, "the game was played with such fierceness last year, the crowds who looked on became so boisterous and rowdyish, and the bad feeling developed between teams so extreme that

[16]For the diffusion and early history of basketball see Bernice Larson Webb, *The Basketball Man, James Naismith* (Lawrence: University Press of Kansas, 1973). YMCA athletic activities can be followed in the following journals: *Men, Physical Education, Triangle, Young Men's Era,* and *Athletic League Letters,* as well as the *Yearbooks of Young Men's Christian Association.*

the game has been abolished in toto."[17] Yet most YMCAs took far less drastic steps. In 1895, the YMCA formed the Athletic League of North America with Gulick as secretary. To curtail athletic "excesses" the league joined the Amateur Athletic Union, published a monthly newsletter, and developed an extensive body of rules and sanctions.

Ultimately, the league failed to insure the "purity" of YMCA athletic programs. By 1905, YMCA teams regularly played over 2,000 games with outside competitors. In their contests with the collegians and athletic clubs, the Y athletes enjoyed remarkable success, whether it was in track and field, swimming, or basketball. For example, for over a dozen years the Buffalo German YMCA team totally dominated championship basketball. They won the Buffalo Exposition tournament in 1901 and won the gold medal at the 1904 Olympic Games in St. Louis. Eventually, much to the relief of YMCA officials, the Germans became an avowed professional team. The spirit of rivalry, athletic specialization, and even professional tendencies of YMCA athletics equalled that of the athletic clubs and the colleges. Local YMCAs, despite the repeated admonitions of the Athletic League officials, were guilty of extending to star athletes special privileges such as free memberships, room and board, and generous traveling allowances to compete away from home. Many of the local secretaries and physical directors tried to resist "excessive" athleticism, but others capitulated to the demands of their membership.[18]

In 1911, several years after Gulick had resigned as secretary of the Athletic League and as an instructor at the training school, the YMCA changed the entire focus of its athletic programs. Henry F. Kallenberg, the new physical director at Springfield, recommended a radical break from past practices. The YMCA should, Kallenberg argued, promote a comprehensive sport program that would reach the "mass of young men and boys, [and] discourage prize winning and overtraining."[19] Competition should be restricted to males of a similar age and weight and be restricted to local teams. At Kallenberg's initiative, the league severed its relationship with the Amateur Athletic Union and began to organize local amateur athletic federations composed of Ys, high schools, churches, Turners, and other groups. By 1920 the YMCA had essentially completed Kallenberg's reform agenda. Never again would the YMCA's attempt to compete at championship levels in athletics.

THE EVOLUTIONARY THEORY OF PLAY

In the 1890s, G. Stanley Hall, a pioneer in genetic psychology at Clark University, and Gulick, once a student of Hall's summer school, began to

---

[17]Gulick, "Basket Ball," *Physical Education*, 4 (November 1895), 1200. See also Gulick, "Abolish Basket Ball," *Men*, 5 (January 30, 1897), 687.

[18]In addition to *Athletic League Letters*, 1896–1911, see William H. Ball, "The Administration of Athletics in the Young Men's Christian Association," *American Physical Education Review*, 16 (January 1911), 12–22.

[19]*Athletic League Letters*, June 1911, 1.

work out an evolutionary theory of play that exercised an immense influence on every phrase of the early twentieth-century boys-work. Hall and Gulick believed that man had acquired the fundamental impulse to play during the evolution of the "race." Each man, as he passed from birth to adulthood, recapitulated or rehearsed in an approximate way each epoch or stage of human evolution. The play activities of early childhood—spontaneous kicking and squirming in infancy and running and throwing when a bit older—corresponded to the play of man's primal ancestors. The track, field, and tag games common to children between the ages of seven and twelve sprang from the hunting instinct acquired during the presavage stage of evolution. Games at this stage were individualistic. Finally, the complex group games of adolescent boys—baseball, basketball, football, and cricket—rested on a combination of the earlier hunting instinct and the new instinct of cooperation, the latter having emerged during the savage epoch of evolution, when savages hunted and fought in groups while subordinating themselves to the leadership of a chief.

That each person recapitulate the history of the race through sports was essential to proper physical, moral, and neural growth. Complex motor behavior became "reflexive" through repetition. Bountiful physical activity in childhood not only developed muscles but also spurred the growth of neural centers in the spinal cord and brain. Directed motor behavior was also the primary agency in shaping moral "reflexes." When the youth repeated via games the evolution of man, he engaged in physical activities that embodied moral principles. "Life for others is rendered far more probable, natural and tangible," Gulick wrote, "when it comes as a gradual unfolding and development of that instinct that has its first great impulse of growth in the games of adolescence."[20] Too often, however, the instincts from which group games sprang could result in the ripening of wicked reflexes, such as the juvenile gang of the city, "the most perilous force in modern civilization," rather than team contests supervised by adults.

Team sport, then, offered an unparalleled opportunity for adults to encourage in boys the healthy growth of moral and religious reflexes. Stemming from the instinct for cooperation, team sports required the highest moral principles—teamwork, self-sacrifice, obedience, self-control, and loyalty. "These qualities appear to me," Gulick wrote, "to be a great pulse of beginning altruism, of self-sacrifice, of that capacity upon which Christianity is based."[21] The churches and the YMCA sought to deemphasize the teaching of feminine traits to boys and present Jesus in terms of his "noble heroism...his magnificent manliness, his denunciation of wickedness in public places, [and] his life of service to others...."[22] Gulick's conception of Christian manliness hardly squared with the injunction of Jesus to turn the other cheek when wronged. On one

[20]Luther Gulick, "Psychological, Pedagogical, and Religious Aspects of Group Games," *Pedagogical Seminary*, 6 (March 1899), 144. See also Gulick, "Physical Aspects of Muscular Exercise," *Popular Science Monthly*, 53 (October 1898), 793–805, and "The Psychology of Play," *Association Outlook*, 8 (February 1899), 112–16.

[21]Gulick, "Psychological, Pedagogical, Religious Aspects," 142.

[22]*Athletic League Letters*, June 1901, 65.

occasion, he advised that a boy should have the ability and the courage to "punch another boy's head or to stand having his own punched in a healthy and proper manner."[23] Gulick's theory implied a far more radical departure from orthodox Protestantism than he probably recognized. For his ideas not only made the religious and moral life almost exclusively a matter of vigorous activity—almost activity for activity's sake—but also suggested a naturalistic explanation for the origins of man's religious sentiments.

In one version or another, the evolutionary theory of play became part of the conventional wisdom of the boy-workers in the first two decades of the twentieth century. G. Stanley Hall repeated it almost verbatim in his classic two-volume work on adolescence published in 1905.[24] Joseph Lee, a prolific writer on play, took as his major premise the notion that play arose from an earlier stage of man's evolution, from the "barbaric and predatory society to which the boy naturally belongs."[25] Henry S. Curtis, a pioneer in both the playground and Boy Scout movements, wrote that athletics "are the activities of our ancestors conventionalized and adapted to present conditions. They are reminiscent of the physical age, of the struggle for survival, of the hunt, of the chase, and of war."[26] William Forbush, an ardent disciple of Gulick and Hall, may have reached the largest audience of all in his *The Boy Problem,* an advice manual reprinted eight times between 1901 and 1912. Each boy, Forbush wrote, repeated the "history of his race-life from savagery unto civilization."[27]

The acceptance by the boy-workers of an evolutionary theory of play had important implications for the use of sport as a socializing agency. First, it seemed to require the creation of special institutions for boys that would be closely supervised by adults. Unregulated activity would fail to encourage desirable social traits. Second, the theory encouraged boy-workers to relinquish the extreme forms of piety associated with the evangelical temperament and emphasize activity at the expense of spirituality or intellectuality. The YMCA became increasingly secular in its programs. Many of the "institutional" or "social gospel" Protestant churches in the larger cities abandoned explicitly spiritual programs for boys in favor of organized activities ranging from dances to baseball matches. Beginning in Brooklyn in 1904, one city after another organized Sunday School athletic leagues. In 1916, through the creation of the Boys' Brigade, Catholics also joined the boys' sport movement. Third, the play theory permitted boy-workers to subordinate ethnic, religious, and social class differences to a presumably universal experience of maturation. Thus the boy leaders saw no need to fashion special programs for boys with distinctive social or cultural characteristics. Finally, the evolutionary theory of play furnished a rationale for the sexual segregation of organized play, a

[23]Gulick, "The Alleged Effeminization of our American Boys," *American Physical Education Review,* 10 (September 1905), 217.

[24]G. Stanley Hall, *Adolescence,* 2 vols. (New York: D. Appleton, 1905), I, 202–23.

[25]Joseph Lee, *Play in Education* (New York: Macmillan, 1915), p. 234.

[26]Curtis, "The Proper Relation of Organized Sports on Public Playgrounds and in Public Science," *Playground,* 3 (September 1909), 14.

[27]Forbush, *The Boy Problem,* p. 9.

rationale that would influence youth workers and physical educators until past the middle of the twentieth century.[28]

THE PSAL AND THE PLAYGROUND MOVEMENT

In the first two decades of the twentieth century, Gulick, Hall, and their followers found ample opportunities to put their theory of play into practice. After leaving the YMCA training school in 1900 and serving for three years as principal of Pratt Institute High School in Brooklyn, Gulick, in 1903, became the director of physical training of the public schools of Greater New York City. Rather than relying exclusively on traditional gymnastics and calisthenics to nurture physical and moral growth, Gulick quickly determined that "*all* the boys in the city needed the physical benefits and moral and social lessons afforded by properly conducted games and sport."[29] Consultations with General George W. Wingate, James Sullivan, Secretary of the Amateur Athletic Union, and William H. Maxwell, the Superintendent of the Schools of Greater New York, led to the formation of the Public Schools Athletic League (PSAL) in 1903. Although the PSAL was financially independent of the school system, it depended upon the city's 630 schools for implementing its program. It won the immediate plaudits of the city's press and the endorsement of such czars of industry and finance as Andrew Carnegie, John D. Rockefeller, J. Pierpont Morgan, S. R. Guggenheim, and Henry Payne Whitney, who contributed munificently to the league's finances.

Underlying the enthusiastic reception of the league was a manifest fear of the city's foreign-born population. The founders were not only concerned with the absence of play experience by immigrant youths, recalled General Wingate, the long-time president of the league, but they "also found the morals of the boys were deteriorating even more than their bodies."[30] The school boys joined marauding street gangs, engaged in criminal acts, and defied the authority of their teachers. Above all, the ethnic youngsters exhibited a lack of understanding of American values and institutions. A carefully managed sport program, the founders believed, would reduce juvenile delinquency and "Americanize" the ethnic youth of the ghettos. By 1910, the PSAL, which was hailed as "The World's Greatest Athletic Organization," had at least seventeen imitators in other large American cities.[31] Moreover, in 1905, the league had added a Girls' Branch. But, unlike the boys' division, the Girls' Branch did not permit public interschool competition.

[28]See George D. Pratt, "The Sunday School Athletic League," *Work With Boys,* 4 (April 1905), 131–37; "Recreation in the Church," *Literary Digest,* 53 (July 29, 1916), 256; Richard A. Swanson, "American Protestantism and Play, 1865–1915" (unpublished Ph.D. dissertation, Ohio State University, 1967).

[29]Gulick, "Athletics for School Children," *Lippincott's Monthly Magazine,* 88 (August 1911), 201.

[30]George B. Wingate, "The Public Schools Athletic League," *Outing,* 52 (May 1908), 166.

[31]Albert B. Reeve, "The World's Greatest Athletic Organization," *Outing,* 57 (October 1910), 107–14; Luther Gulick, "How to Start a Public School's Athletic League," *Work With Boys,* 4 (October 1905), 232–35.

The league's comprehensive athletic program embodied the latest wisdom of the play theorists. To insure maximum participation of the school boys, the league included three separate forms of competition. By reaching a minimum level of performance in several physical feats, every boy could win the Athletic Badge. A widely heralded means of encouraging overall physical development, the badge test served as a model for a similar program implemented by the Playground Association of America in 1913 and for the President's physical fitness drive which began in the 1960s. The second form of competition, class athletics, pitted the average performance of one school class in certain track and field events against the average of another. Finally, the league sponsored district and city championships in more than a dozen sports. Baseball was especially popular. In 1907, 106 teams competed, and over 15,000 fans attended the championship game held in the Polo Grounds. Class, district, and city champions received expensive trophies.

The introduction of rifle-shooting competition among the high school boys by the PSAL suggested the special fondness that most of the boy-workers had for martial virtues. By 1908, over 7,000 boys competed for marksmanship badges. Each year, President Theodore Roosevelt wrote a letter of commendation to the boy receiving the highest marks, and the E. I. du Pont de Nemours Powder Company awarded prizes to the school team having the highest scores. General George W. Wingate declared that none of the sports conducted by the league "was likely to have as important an influence on the country at large as the system of instruction in military rifle shooting."[32]

"Duty," "Thoroughness," "Patriotism," "Honor," and "Obedience"—these were the official mottoes of the Public Schools Athletic League. To inculcate such values, the league consciously exploited the athletic interests of the students. Each year General Wingate wrote an open letter to the boys warning them of a host of dangers that might adversely affect their athletic performances. Above all, "you must keep out of bad influences of the street if you want to be strong," he wrote.[33] While it may be doubted that Wingate's advice had much influence on the behavior of the boys while they were away from school, the teachers quickly recognized that the PSAL could be used effectively to promote discipline in the classroom. "All of the little imps in my class have become saints," wrote one teacher, "not because they want to be saints, but because they want to compete in your games."[34] No student could compete without a certification from his teachers that his deportment and class performance had been satisfactory. Peer group pressure also encouraged student conformity. "Many a big, vigorous boy out of sympathy with his school work," reported another source," is driven to his lessons by his mates so that he can be eligible to represent his school."[35] Perhaps it was little wonder that the city's teachers volunteered to spend long hours after school and on weekends in planning and supervis-

[32]Wingate, "The Public Schools Athletic League," 174.
[33]Ibid., 169.
[34]Reeve, "The World's Greatest Athletic Organization," 110.
[35]Clarence Arthur Perry, *Wider Use of the School Plant* (New York: Charities Pub. Committee, 1910), p. 308.

ing every aspect of the league's program. The improvement by the student "on the side of ethics, school discipline, and *esprit de corps* is even greater," concluded a report in 1910, than in athletic proficiency.[36] Nonetheless, the PSAL failed to alter the lives of over two-thirds of the city's adolescent boy population. For these older boys did not attend school and in most cases had already entered the labor market.

The early twentieth-century movement for city playgrounds furnished Gulick and his followers with even broader opportunities for implementing their evolutionary theory of play. Prior to 1900, a few private citizens and charity groups had organized playgrounds—usually consisting of sandpiles and simple play equipment—for preadolescent children in the slums of the larger cities. A turning point came in 1903 when the voters of the Chicago South Park District approved of a $5 million bond issue for the construction of ten parks. Unlike previous efforts, the Chicago system included field houses at each park with a gymnasium for both boys and girls. Moreover, the Chicago authorities hired a professional physical educator, Edward B. de Groot, as director and furnished each park with two year-round instructors to supervise play activities. The managers of the new system sponsored a host of activities ranging from organized athletic leagues to community folk dances. Inspired by the Chicago example and driven by anxieties arising from modern cities, middle- and upper-income taxpayers exhibited a remarkable enthusiasm for supervised recreation programs. Between 1906 and 1917 the number of cities with managed playgrounds grew from 41 to 504.[37]

The same concerns and values that shaped the PSAL also guided the work of playground leaders. The evolutionary theory of play furnished them with ready-made formulas for supervising playgrounds. For example, among the questions on the standard examination administered to all candidates for employment with the New York playgrounds was: "What is meant by the 'club or gregarious instinct?' How can it be developed and utilized with beneficial results on the playground? What athletic events are appropriate for boys aged 10–14?...for boys aged 14 to 16?"[38] Not only were prospective playground leaders expected to master the principles and practical implications of play theory, they also had to be able to exercise the subtle psychological techniques essential for managing youth without resorting to harsh repression. Edward B. de Groot summed up the prevailing conception of the ideal playground director. "The men or women employed for playground service...should not be regarded as mere instructors, play bosses, or leaders of games, but rather as thoughtful managers, interpreters of child and adolescent life, chemists of human

---

[36]Reeve, "The World's Greatest Athletic Organization," 108.

[37]See Clarence E. Rainwater, *The Play Movement in the United States: A Study in Community Reaction* (Chicago: University of Chicago, 1922); Richard F. Knapp, "Play for America: National Recreation Association, 1906–1950, Part I," *Parks & Recreation*, 7 (August 1972), 14–19, 44–52, and "Part II," ibid., 7 (October 1972), 20–27, 43–49; Mark A. Kadjielski, "'As a Flower Needs Sunshine:' The Origins of Organized Children's Recreation in Philadelphia, 1886–1911," *Journal of Sport History*, 4 (Summer 1977), 169–88; Bernard Mergan, "The Discovery of Children's Play," *American Quarterly*, 27 (October 1975), 339–420; Boyer, *Urban Masses*, esp. Chap. 16.

[38]"Questions for Teachers to Answer," *American Gymnasia*, 2 (March 1906), 149.

desires, and captains of the marching legions of young people on the way to a 'square deal' citizenship."[39] The playground leaders abhorred the unsupervised, unstructured play that arose from the spontaneous impulses of children. Henry S. Curtis, in the leading textbook for playground supervisors, wrote that "scrub play," that is, play which the children themselves initiated, "can never give that training either of body or conduct, which organized play should give; for in order to develop the body, it must be vigorous, to train the intellect, it must be exciting, to train the social conscience, it must be socially organized. None of these results come from scrub play."[40]

Despite the enthusiasm of municipal governments for organized recreation, the playgrounds usually failed to extend their control over spare-time activities to those who presumably needed it the most—the ethnic youth in the slums. According to the sweeping claims of the playground leaders, supervised recreation sharply reduced the incidence of juvenile delinquency, but even Henry Curtis admitted that less than 10 percent of the urban youngsters regularly used available playgrounds. The playgrounds appealed most to the children of old-stock families of the middle- and upper-income ranks, youngsters who had been shaped by the same values espoused by recreation leaders. The children of the slums tended to admire physical prowess—particularly as expressed in streetfighting— spontaneity, and defiance of authority rather than the values of self-restraint and cooperation so dear to the playground leaders. Conflicts between recreation supervisors and ghetto youths were inevitable. To attract such youths, the leaders had to make compromises with the values of the slum subculture and remove heavyhanded, detailed supervision. Yet the absence of direction not only ran counter to prevailing playground theory, it could result in the transformation of the playground into an asphalt jungle in which the strongest and most vicious boys ruled the grounds by intimidation. Even in 1920 there were clear harbingers of the typical inner-city playground of the mid-twentieth century, which, except for a few of the toughest adolescent boys in the neighborhood, often stood empty.[41]

HIGH SCHOOL SPORTS

Like the YMCA, the PSAL, and the playgrounds, the demand for the adult management of public high school athletics arose from several sources. In the first place, in order to preserve the moral image of their institutions, educators eventually felt compelled to extend their authority

---

[39]Edward B. de Groot, "The Management of Park Playgrounds," *Playground*, 8 (November 1914), 273. Italics added for emphasis.

[40]Curtis, *The Play Movement and Its Significance*, p. 81.

[41]See ibid., pp. 31, 83; Howard R. Knight, *Play and Recreation in a Town of 6000* (New York: Russell Sage Foundation, n.d.), p. 25; L. H. Wier, "Playgrounds and Juvenile Delinquency," *Playground*, 4 (May 1910), 37–40; Gulick, *A Philosophy of Play*, pp. 223–45.

over interscholastic competition. High school sport had begun in the nineteenth century at the initiative of the students themselves; students had formed the first athletic organizations, scheduled the first games, managed the finances, and hired seasonal coaches. By the 1890s, the rage for football in the larger high schools equalled or surpassed that of the colleges. High school authorities could no longer ignore interscholastic sport, for sport imposed on the academic functions of the school. High school sport not only absorbed student interest at the expense of their study; it was guilty of all the same "abuses" as college sport—winning at all costs, use of "ineligible" players, and financial mismanagement. "Athletic contests between different high schools," declared one irate principal in 1905, "cause a reduction in the class standing of the students participating, teach boys to smoke cigarettes, loaf in the streets during school hours, and use unfair methods in order to win, and make liars out of many teachers and students."[42] To curtail such evils, high school educators across the country tried to increase their authority over interscholastic sport. By 1902, when the Fifteenth Educational Conference of Academies and High Schools met, the faculties had already gained basic control of interscholastic sport in Wisconsin, Illinois, and at several of the boarding schools of the Northeast. That year, the conference recommended strict faculty supervision, the limitation of interscholastic athletics to bona fide students, and the formation of associations to regulate competition. By 1923, only three states were without state-wide interscholastic athletic organizations.[43]

The emergence of the "comprehensive" high school in the twentieth century encouraged both the extension of adult control and the growth of school sport. In the three decades before 1920 the comprehensive high school gradually supplanted the academic-oriented high school. In 1893, the Committee of Ten, chaired by President Charles W. Eliot of Harvard, had called for a continuation with only slight modifications of the classical curriculum, a course of study that featured Greek, Latin, mathematics, oratory, and writing. The committee visualized the high school as an academic institution designed to prepare students for entrance into the colleges. In the years following, the committee's position came under heavy attack, especially from middle-income parents who wanted their sons to develop the social poise required of white-collar occupations and from "social" educators who believed the school ought to be a major agency for the preparation of youth for adulthood. By 1917, when a special committee of the National Education Association published *The Cardinal Principles of Secondary Education,* the social educators and middle-income parents had routed the defenders of the classical curriculum.[44]

[42]"Public School Notes," *American Gymnasia,* 1 (April 1905), 215.

[43]"The Question of School and College Athletics," *School Review,* 10 (January 1902), 4–8; Lewis Hoch Wagenhorst, *The Administration and Cost of High School Interscholastic Athletics* (New York: Teachers College, Columbia University, 1926), p. 9. See also James A. Montgomery, "The Development of the Interscholastic Athletics Movement in the United States, 1890–1940" (unpublished Ed.D. dissertation, George Peabody College for Teachers, 1960).

[44]See Kett, *Rites of Passage,* pp. 235–36; Joel H. Spring, *Education and the Corporate State* (Boston: Beacon Press, 1972), esp. Chap. 6.

The proponents of the comprehensive high school shared many of the perceptions and ideas of the boy-workers. They believed that modern industrial life had eroded the traditional socializing institutions. According to *The Cardinal Principles:* "In connection with home and family life have frequently come lessened responsibility on the part of the children; the withdrawal of the father and sometimes the mother from home occupations to the factory or store; and increased urbanization resulting in less unified family life. Similarly, many important changes have taken place in community life, in the church, in the State, and in other institutions. These changes in American life call for extensive modifications in secondary education."[45] To meet these changes the committee recommended two goals for the high school: prepare the students for vocations and teach them the social values essential for coping with modern life. By social values the committee meant "those common ideas, common ideals, and common modes of thought, feeling, and action that make for cooperation, social cohesion, and social solidarity."[46] Vocational preparation required that the school offer a wide range of subjects, expert guidance, and a differentiated curriculum. Inculcating the social values necessary for establishing a genuine community was a much more difficult task, for the students lacked a common curriculum, represented different "racial stocks," and had "differing religious beliefs." Like Gulick, the social educators believed that activity rather than the teaching of moral precepts was the key to developing proper social or moral traits. Thus they advocated that the high school give special attention to the "participation of pupils in common activities. . . such as athletic games, social activities, and the government of the school."[47]

Underlying the attention of the social educators to the extracurricular activities of their students was an acute awareness of adolescent sexuality, a subject that was approached with excruciating obliqueness. For example, a report of the National Educational Association of 1911 argued that high school moral training had to be different than grammar school because the teen-age years were a "time of life when [sexual] passion is born [and] which must be restrained and guided aright or it consumes the soul and body." In common with the proponents of the evolutionary theory of play the educators believed that the sexual drives of adolescents could be husbanded to nurture moral growth. "It is a time when social interests are dominant and when social ideals are formed."[48] Exclusive reliance on formal classwork failed to channel sexual energy into high ideals or encourage cooperative social habits. Only team sports were ideally suited to encourage these traits.

Educational leaders also recognized that interscholastic athletics could be used in solving an important problem of the school—the problem of

[45]*Cardinal Principles of Secondary Education*, Bul. 1918, no. 35 (Washington, GPO, 1918), pp. 7–8.

[46]Ibid., p. 21.

[47]Ibid., p. 23.

[48]"Tentative Report of the Committee on a System of Teaching Morals in the Public Schools," *National Education Association Proceedings* (1911), 360.

controlling the behavior of a heterogeneous mass of potentially rebellious students. Apart from interscholastic athletics, the public high schools had no common goals that could inspire the allegiance of the student body as a whole. Many of the students attended school only because of parental or legal compulsion. Few students found in grades alone an adequate motive for a positive identification with the high school. Grades tend to encourage individual achievement, student competition rather than cooperation. But varsity sport could rally the student body in a common cause; it could create an *esprit de corps,* "a mass spirit in which each individual surrenders himself" to a common goal.[49] Such a communal spirit encouraged a positive attitude toward the high school and a peaceful acquiescence of the students to adult direction.

Moreover, high school sports helped give an identity and common purpose to many neighborhoods, towns, and cities which were otherwise divided by class, race, ethnicity, or religious differences. These geographic entities, like the schools without interscholastic games, lacked collective goals. Varsity sport could coalesce them into a united front. High school sport could become a community enterprise; the entire community might celebrate victories or mourn losses in concert. The result of this identification of the community with school sport was quite evident in teachers' salaries, for school boards typically paid the coach more than any other teacher. "You know that, if a principal is looking for a teacher, one of the first questions he asks frequently is: 'Can this man be of use in connection with athletics?'" reported Edwin H. Hall as early as 1905, "and the man who can be of use in connection with athletics gets more money, gets the place sooner, than another man."[50] Likewise, school boards invariably placed a higher priority on the construction of a gymnasium or a football field than they did a laboratory or a library. In the 1920s, high schools, both small and large, built expensive athletic facilities. In Indiana, a hotbed of high school basketball, the seating capacity of the school's gymnasium sometimes exceeded that of the town's population.

The large stake of the community in interscholastic sport tended to subvert the ideals of the comprehensive high school. The actual participation of the student body at large in athletics, according to the principles of the social educators, was essential to the growth of desirable social habits. But school boards, reflecting the will of the community, placed a far higher priority on fielding a strong varsity team. They were reluctant to furnish the coaches and facilities required for mass student participation, particularly since, unlike interscholastic sport, financing would have to come largely from additional taxes. While intramural sport did experience a minor boom in the late 1910s and physical education instructors increas-

[49]Webster Cook, "Deportment in the High School," *School Review,* 10 (October 1902), 629. On occasion the social educators and boy-workers advocated an explicitly repressive school atmosphere. For example, Luther Gulick asserted that the modern school required the "complete obliteration of individual differences." Gulick, "The Alleged Effemination of Our American Boys," 28.
[50]Edwin B. Hall, "Athletic Professionalism and Its Remedies," *School Review,* 13 (December 1905), 761.

ingly substituted athletics for gymnastics and calisthenics, the results were pitifully small in terms of the goals of the social educators. Within the high school, varsity sport tended to glorify athletic success at the expense of other forms of possible achievement. James Naismith unwittingly suggested this point while praising the democratizing function of varsity sport. The athlete "who will perfect himself physically for the good of the institution is respected, regardless of his ancestry or his financial standing," wrote Naismith. "Mere manhood is recognized, while lack of it is sufficient to bar a student from the honors of his fellows."[51] In the high school status structure, the athlete almost always dwelt in the upper ranks, usually higher than the most outstanding academic students.

The identification of the community with interscholastic sport presented yet another problem to the conscientious social educator. The pressures to win resulted in varsity athletics developing a code of ethics independent of the values of the social educators. Cooperation and fair play might extend to teammates but rarely extended to the opposing team. "Like the unscrupulous lawyer," wrote Alfred E. Stearns, a former school football coach, "the football player has seemingly come to believe that his business is to circumvent the laws of the game, not to obey them." Football coaches, hired above all to win games, subordinated ethical principles to fielding a strong team. Often the football coach "is vulgar and profane," declared Stearns. "Sometimes he is brutal. Seldom does he exhibit, on the football field at least, those qualities demanded of a gentleman."[52] Stearns feared that the high school athlete would carry with him into adulthood the unethical habits developed on the football field. Perhaps the views of Stearns represented the excessive decorum of the old-fashioned gentry. Nonetheless, the requirements of winning rarely allowed the high school coach the freedom to utilize varsity athletics as a training ground for the values of the social educators.

SPORTS FOR GIRLS AND YOUNG WOMEN

Neither men nor women perceived an urgent need for adult-managed sports for girls. Both Victorian sentiment and the evolutionary theory of play tended to promote a feminine stereotype inconsistent with the physical vigor required of sport. The play theorists assumed that males and females had acquired distinctive instincts or propensities over the course of human evolution. Of utmost importance to the survival of males had been an adeptness in fighting, hunting, and running—activities recapitulated in the games of boys. Those females, on the other hand, who had cared best

---

[51]James Naismith, "High School Athletics and Gymnastics as an Expression of the Corporate Life of the High School," in Charles Hughes Johnston, ed., *The Modern High School: Its Administration and Extension* (New York: Scribner's, 1914), 434–35.

[52]Alfred E. Stearns, "Athletics and the School," *Atlantic Monthly*, 113 (February 1914), 148–52. See also Wagenhorst, *The Administration and Cost of High School Interscholastic Athletics*, pp. 77, 97.

Midget basketball team, Lincoln, Nebraska. Director: Anne Spurek; Captain: Edith Schwartz (later Mrs. F. E. Clemments); Adeleyd Whiting (later Mrs. Williams), and Grace Broady. Reprinted by permission of the Nebraska State Historical Society.

for the home were more likely to survive and produce offspring. "So it is clear," Gulick wrote, "that athletics have never been either a test or a large factor in the survival of women; athletics do not test womanliness as they test manliness."[53] Thus the play activities of girls should be guided toward the acquisition of talents essential for the management of the home.

The great social changes of the nineteenth century encouraged a new image of femininity that reduced the likelihood of a large commitment to girls' sport. More and more women began to enjoy the financial resources and leisure time necessary to cultivate a genteel image of femininity. Status-conscious middle-income husbands encouraged their wives to lead lives of enforced idleness. Consistent with this notion, women donned numerous petticoats, tightly fitted corsets, and floor-length dresses. Victorians in turn gave women increased responsibility for managing the home and for the moral instruction of the children. They developed the cult of motherhood; they taught women to think of themselves as being superior spiritual and moral leaders. A certain etherealness, passivity, delicacy, and fragility furnished evidence of the female's superior moral sensibilities. Such ideal images hardly stimulated women to embark upon vigorous physical activities.

Popular literature and medical opinion reinforced these Victorian ideals of femininity. The large circulation magazines, sentimental literature, and endless tracts encouraged women to conform their behavior to Victorian

[53]Gulick, *A Philosophy of Play*, p. 92.

expectations. While physicians and physical educators recommended light exercises for women, they universally feared the consequences of strenuous physical activity. They considered the menstrual period to be the equivalent of an illness. Strenuous sport during menstruation, they believed, could lead to displaced or contracted uteruses and a reduction in childbearing capacities. Physicians believed that women were especially subject to excessive emotions. Highly competitive sports might induce in women nervous breakdowns. Such opinions regarding the physiological and psychological capacities of women remained part of the conventional belief of the medical profession until well into the twentieth century. As late as 1953, the Amateur Athletic Union, in a study of the effects of athletics upon women, quoted a woman doctor as saying that competition during a woman's menstrual period might adversely affect her ability to be "a normal mother."[54]

Consistent with these conceptions of femininity, the Victorians imposed two major constraints upon women's participation in sports: sport should be nonstrenuous and nonspectator-centered. Women's and girls' sports requiring large bursts of physical energy or physical contact between players received universal condemnation. Individual sports such as croquet, tennis, golf, bowling, and cycling were much more likely to fit these criteria than the team sports of basketball, baseball, football, or field hockey. Furthermore, sport should be played only for personal pleasure or the improvement of one's health, never for personal prestige, financial gain, or the plaudits of spectators. As long as the women confined their physical contests to the athletic clubs, the YWCAs, and the colleges, they encountered little opposition. But contests between such groups held in the presence of spectators were incompatible with the Victorian constraints.

The evolution of women's basketball in the colleges and high schools vividly illustrated the dynamics of these two constraints. While Victorian women played croquet, golf, and tennis without causing much controversy, basketball threatened the Victorian image of femininity. Soon after Naismith invented the game in 1891, it became the most popular sport of college women. Previously restricted to gymnastic exercises and rather sedate games, the women loved the freedom of movement, rapid changes of pace, and vigorous competition provided by the new sport. In most cases, the women played on intramural teams or in physical education classes, but a substantial number of colleges at one time or another had varsity teams. Varsity basketball was even more widespread at the high school level. Prior to about 1925, probably over half of the states had high school championships for girls. Upon returning home from winning the Michigan state championship in 1905, the town of Marshall welcomed their heroines with "bonfires, 10,000 Roman candles, crowds, noise, Supt. Garfield, ex-mayor Porter, and all red-corpuscled Marshall."[55]

Yet as varsity basketball for women grew in popularity, opposition

---

[54]*A.A.U. Study of Effect of Athletic Competition on Girls and Women* (New York: Amateur Athletic Union, 1953), p. 8.

[55]Quoted in Deobald B. Van Dalen and Bruce L. Bennett, *A World History of Physical Education,* 2nd ed. (Englewood Cliffs, N.J.: Prentice-Hall, 1971), p. 451.

mounted from several quarters. College trustees, administrators, and faculties often objected to the sport. College officials conceived of themselves as the special custodians of the Victorian ideal of womanhood; the colleges should act as parents in absentia for female students and strive to complete the training in the delicate social graces essential for fulfilling the ideal of womanhood. (Until the middle of the twentieth century, long after public attitudes toward proper female roles and behavior had begun to change, the nation's colleges continued to reinforce traditional images of femininity.) Varsity sport hardly seemed consistent with these responsibilities. The young female athletes had to travel for road games, perhaps without "adequate" supervision and under the direction of a male coach; the athletes often performed before audiences of both sexes; they might sacrifice modesty to the excitement of the game; and above all, they might exhibit aggressive behavior suited only to men. A former University of Nebraska student recalled that it was "not an unheard of thing to meet at a promenade a proud coed blushing behind a black eye received in the afternoon's practice."[56] Perhaps it was little wonder that nearly all college officials frowned upon female varsity sports.

Women's physical educators also played a key role in bringing about the demise of varsity basketball for women. Whereas men's varsity sports had grown up largely independent of male physical educators, female physical educators from the beginning exercised much more control over the evolution of women's sports. Rather than the girls themselves organizing, managing, and writing the rules for sports, the initiative had usually come from professional educators. Confined by the Victorian stereotype of femininity and committed to player-centered ideals, they sought to prevent women's basketball from becoming a facsimile of the men's game. Moreover, they found in women's sport an opportunity to advance the professionalization of their occupation. By insisting that only trained women could properly manage women's sports, they carved out for themselves a restricted occupational domain.

Control of the rulemaking process assisted the educators in limiting the strenuosity of the game and reducing the tendencies toward the spectator domination of women's basketball. In the 1890s, Senda Berenson, director of physical education at Smith College, developed a modified set of rules for women. The rules of the men's game, she decided, encouraged too much rough play, too much physical exertion, and the domination of play by the better athletes. Assuming that women did not possess the physical capacity to play on all of the court, that roughness might endanger them physically, and that all girls should benefit from play, she prohibited players from snatching the ball out of an opponent's hands and divided the court into playing areas. The women players could not move out of their designated areas. In 1899 a committee of female physical educators led by Berenson induced A. B. Spalding Company to publish these modified rules as the "Official Rules" of women's basketball. Several other sets of rules competed with Berenson's and probably as late as 1914, one half of the

---

[56]Quoted in Robert N. Manley, *The Centennial History of the University of Nebraska: I. The Frontier University, 1869–1919* (Lincoln: University of Nebraska Press, 1969), p. 305.

girls in the country played by men's rules. Nonetheless, despite the apparent opposition of the players and the fans, a distinctive women's game eventually triumphed and prevailed in educational institutions until the 1960s.[57]

Gradually the women educators developed a stance opposed to all intercollegiate and interscholastic competition for females. Pressure came from the negative example of men's athletics. Emulation of the intensely competitive, commercial, spectator-centered character of men's college athletics would patently violate the prevailing images of proper femininity. "We must avoid the evils which are so apparent...in the conduct of athletics for men," declared Lucille Eaton Hill, Director of Physical Training at Wellesley College in 1903. Senda Berenson warned in 1901: "The greatest element of evil in the spirit of athletics in this country is that one must win at any cost—that defeat is an unspeakable disgrace."[58] To reduce the likelihood of such evils in women's basketball, the educators urged the use of female coaches and the prohibition of spectators at the contests. Increasingly, they simply opted for the abolition of varsity sport for women.

Apart from the player-centered ideals which the educators attempted to uphold, their acceptance of sport as a useful agency for the socialization of girls reinforced their hostile view of varsity sports. Sharing concerns similar to those of the boy-workers in the early twentieth century, they thought that sports, if properly managed by trained adult women, could nurture desirable social traits in girls. Reacting against the extreme individualism of the nineteenth century, they saw team sports as especially suitable for teaching the values of cooperation. But to succeed in accomplishing its goals, sport should be played within the strictures of traditional femininity and be available to all girls. Varsity sports, which placed a high priority on winning and the achievements of the individual players, interfered with this purpose.

By the early 1920s, all educational groups directly concerned with female sports had reached a consensus. In 1923, the Women's Division of the National Amateur Athletic Federation composed of colleges, high schools, athletic associations, YWCAs, and women's clubs and headed by Lou Henry (Mrs. Herbert) Hoover, went on record against varsity competition. The 1923 platform of the division served as the guiding principle for women's athletics until the 1960s. It stated that women's athletics should "be protected from exploitation for the enjoyment of the spectator, the athletic reputation, or the commercial advantage of any school or other organization." Emphasis upon "individual accomplishments and the winning of championships" should be subordinated to universal participation.[59] Varsity competition in the colleges and high

[57]See Ronald A. Smith, "The Rise of Basketball for Women in Colleges," *Canadian Journal of History of Sport and Physical Education, 1* (December 1970), 18–36.

[58]Both quotations from ibid., 24.

[59]Quoted in Ellen Gerber, "The Controlled Development of Collegiate Sport for Women, 1923–1936," *Journal of Sport History,* 2 (Spring 1975), 11. See also Mabel Lee, "The Case For and Against Intercollegiate Athletics for Women and the Situation as It Stands Today," *Mind and Body,* 30 (Nov. 1923), 246, 25.

schools dropped sharply. A probably not uncommon notice appeared in the New York *Herald Tribune* in 1931: "Acting on the suggestion of...[the] girls' physical education instructor...the [school] board last night voted unanimously to withdraw the sport [of girls' basketball] from the interscholastic calendar."[60] From the 1930s to the 1960s high school basketball for girls nearly disappeared.

In the 1920s and 1930s, female physical educators developed closely supervised substitutes for interscholastic and intercollegiate athletics. The substitutes took four principal forms: intramurals, telegraphic meets, play days, and sports days, all of which had a player-centered orientation. A survey of seventy-seven colleges taken in 1936 indicated that 74 percent had been involved in a telegraphic meet, 70 percent in a play day, and 41 percent in a sports day.[61] Telegraphic meets curbed the competitive spirit between schools by replacing face-to-face competition with telegraphed reports of performances and excluding spectators. Frequently, the colleges competed in only one activity. Play days, which brought together all of the girls from several schools to a single site, minimized competitiveness by arbitrarily selecting girls from several schools to form teams. The play days also featured a wide array of informal contests and placed a high emphasis on social interaction between the girls. Sport days, on the other hand, did permit teams representing the colleges to play. However, to insure a player-centered orientation, the educators altered the rules of such games as basketball and refused to announce winners.

Women educators, unlike their male counterparts, succeeded in exercising a decisive influence over girls' sport in the colleges and high schools. In large measure they had been able to impose upon the girls' programs that were consistent with their philosophical position. Yet the net effects were not all that the women hoped for. The women themselves appeared to be ambivalent and divided on the question of how competitive girls' sport ought to be. Frequently, the leaders of women's physical education left the impression that they were opposed to competitive sports in any form. Consequently, physical education programs in the schools often substituted dance or dainty, nonstrenuous contests and exercises for highly competitive sports. Moreover, by refusing to permit girls' sport to become spectator-centered, the educators reduced the likelihood of tapping community resources necessary to realize their motto of "A game for every girl and every girl in a game." Finally, their ideology prevented them from providing opportunities for girls of unusual athletic abilities to excel.

[60]Quoted in Gerber, "The Controlled Development," 10. According to a survey taken in 1938 only nine states scheduled state-wide basketball tournaments. See Alice Allene Sefton, *The Women's Division National Amateur Athletic Federation* (Stanford University, Calif.: Stanford University Press, 1941), p. 44.

[61]Cited in Gerber, "The Controlled Development," 3.

Part Three

The Age of the Spectator (1920 to the Present)

By the 1920s, industrial technology had transformed the United States into a consumer's paradise. The automobile, the most prized of all the new consumer goods, emancipated millions of Americans from a restricted network that consisted of their homes, neighborhoods, and places of work. Electricity revolutionized the home. By 1940, four of five Americans could plug in electric lamps, washing machines, vacuum cleaners, refrigerators, and toasters. The Great Depression of the 1930s and World War II temporarily set back the national buying spree, but in the 1950s, plastics, aluminum, and transistors became the staples of a new round of consumption. The consumption bonanza extended to communications—movies and radio in the 1920s and television in the 1950s. To encourage Americans to buy, salesmen and advertisers unrelentingly assaulted the older virtues of thrift and prudence. The new consumer ethic rested on immediate gratification—"buy now, pay later," and "live for the moment." Consequently, more and more Americans abandoned their age-old habits of saving, avoidance of debt, and judicious buying.

The social order in the Age of the Spectator rested on both the old and the new. Individual inner restraint, preached so vigorously by the Victorians, weakened, but subcommunities based on neighborhoods, ethnicity, religious affiliation, and sometimes income remained surprisingly strong. In a less tangible sense, consumption itself, the mass media, and large bureaucracies promoted social stability. The national communication centers presented a new model of the "good life," one in which consumption rather than production was the vital core. Evanescent and nonideological, "consumption communities" helped unite and reassure Americans of the goodness of their society.[1] The radio, movies, and television nationalized sights, sounds, and common experiences. Most Americans, whether in business, government, or the professions, found themselves working for vast bureaucracies. Specialized skills became more important than ever to success, but one also could no longer flaunt one's initiative or idiosyncracies. To be successful at the managerial level, one needed to be an expert in human relations—in the skills of manipulating others and in being manipulated by others. Frederick W. Taylor, an apostle of the new bureaucratic order, put it succinctly: "In the past the men had been first; in the future the system must be first."[2] The swashbuckling

---

[1]Daniel Boorstin, *The Americans: The Democratic Experience* (New York: Vintage Books, 1973), Part Two.

[2]Quoted in ibid., p. 363.

pioneer and lone business tycoon gave way to the "organization man" dressed in a grey flannel suit.

In the Age of the Spectator technological breakthroughs, especially in the media, a new set of values associated with consumption, and the accompanying changes in the social order altered the contours of American sport. To be sure, Americans continued, as they had in the Age of the Player, to find in sport the sheer joy of play, a vehicle for building subcommunities, and a means of instilling proper character traits in the young. But the most marked feature of the new sporting landscape was the ascendancy of "big-time" spectator sports, that is, sports that attracted and were designed for mass audiences. After 1920 the fans virtually dictated the character of American sport history. Even the ethos and structure of "amateur" sports like Little League Baseball and high school football resembled their professional counterparts more than the player-centered sports of an earlier era. In principle, if not in practice, amateur sport had been for the pleasure and benefit of the players; in short, the athletes "played." But with the ascendancy of the spectator, the athletes "played" for the fans; sport then became a form of "work." Specialization, bureaucratization, expert coaching, careful preparation, hours of grueling training, and the application of scientific methods to improve performances accompanied the growth of spectator-centered sports. Finally, full-time administrators rather than the players decided matters of policy and directed the actual playing of sports.

9

The Modern Sports Hero

Red Grange as the "Ice Man." Reprinted by permission of United Press International Inc.

The decade of the 1920s, often hailed as the Golden Age of American Sport, teemed with sport heroes. "Never before, nor since, have so many transcendent performers arisen contemporaneously in almost every field of competitive athletics as graced the 1920s," concluded veteran sports reporters Allison Danzig and Peter Brandwein in 1948.[1] Each sport had its magic name: George Herman "Babe" Ruth in baseball, William Harrison "Jack" Dempsey in boxing, Harold "Red" Grange in football, Robert T. "Bobby" Jones in golf, and William T. "Big Bill" Tilden in tennis. Many others stood close to the magic circle.

Why sport idols in the 1920s? The public acclaim accorded star athletes sprang from something more than performance, though indeed their athletic feats were often phenomenal. The same skill and shrewd promotion which successfully hawked automobiles, breakfast foods, and lipstick also sold athletes to the public. Behind the sport heroes stood professional pitch men: George "Tex" Rickard, Jack "Doc" Kearns, Charles C. "Cash and Carry" Pyle, and Christy Walsh, to name a few. Then there were the journalists and radio broadcasters prone to hyperbole like Grantland Rice, Arch Ward, Paul Gallico, and Graham McNamee. They created images of athletes which often overwhelmed the athlete's actual achievements. Yet the public idolization of athletes went even deeper than the skillful ballyhooing of the promoters and journalistic flights of fancy. Ultimately, the emergence of a dazzling galaxy of sport idols was a creation of the American public itself. The athletes as public heroes served a compensatory cultural function. They assisted the public in compensating for the

[1]Danzig and Brandwein, eds., *Sports Golden Age: A Close-Up of the Fabulous Twenties* (New York: Harper & Bros., 1948), p. xi. Most efforts to explain the American need for heroes in modern times see the heroes as fulfilling cherished American ideals or myths. Leo Lowenthal in *Literature, Popular Culture and Society* (Englewood Cliffs, N.J.: Prentice-Hall, 1961), pp. 109–40 has interpreted the heroes of the pre-1920 era as "idols of production"—from industry, business, and science—and those of the post-1920 era as "idols of consumption"—from the world of entertainment. For a provocative study that in part confirms Lowenthal see Lary May, *Screening Out the Past: The Birth of Mass Culture and the Motion Picture Industry* (New York: Oxford University Press, 1980). Leverett T. Smith, Jr., *The American Dream and the National Game* (Bowling Green, Ohio: Bowling Green University Press, 1975) sees Ty Cobb as the representative of a community "identified with a democratic capitalistic world," Babe Ruth with an "authoritarian," "paternalistic," and "hierarchical society." In "The Meaning of Lindbergh's flight," in Joseph J. Kwait and Mary C. Turpie, eds. *Studies in American Culture: Dominant Ideas and Images* (Minneapolis: University of Minnesota Press, 1960), John W. Ward finds that in Lindbergh the American people paradoxically celebrated both the self-sufficient individual and the machine. Roderick Nash in the *Nervous Generation: American Thought, 1917–1930* (Chicago: Rand McNally, 1970), pp. 126–37, finds the sport heroes of the 1920s to be surrogate frontiersmen.

passing of the traditional dream of success, the erosion of Victorian values, and feelings of individual powerlessness. As the society became more complicated and systematized and as success had to be won increasingly in bureaucracies, the need for heroes who leaped to fame and fortune outside the rules of the system grew. No longer were the heroes lone businessmen or statesmen, but the "stars" of movies, television, and sports.

Beginning in the 1920s, a popular culture of compensation flourished. The media helped create defense mechanisms for the helpless individual that rested upon a complex set of images, fantasies, and myths. Some were comic: Charlie Chaplin in the movies was the carefree little tramp who eluded cops, bullies, and pompous officials: even the machine could not bring him to heel. Some were dashing and romantic: Douglas Fairbanks slashed his way through hordes of swift-sworded villains. Some were tough: the classic western hero was brave and handsome. He killed bad men and Indians, thus dramatically serving the forces of "good" while saving white America from the "savages." The popular culture of compensation also projected images of heroes vaulting to the top. In nineteenth century drama and fiction, the hero won the hand of the rich man's daughter through his virtuous character; Rudolph Valentino won her through his irresistible physical charm. Even the kings of organized crime, who themselves enjoyed something of a celebrity status in the 1920s, furnished forceful images of power and success.

Above all, fantasies and images of power and instant success flourished in the world of sport. In sport—or so it seemed—one could still catapult to fame and fortune without the benefits of years of arduous training or acquiescence to the demanding requirements of bureaucracies. Unlike most vocations, sheer natural ability coupled with a firm commitment to sport for its own sake could propel the athlete to the top. Determining the level of success of a doctor, lawyer, or business manager might be difficult, but achievement in the world of sport was unambiguous. It could be precisely measured in home runs, knockouts, touchdowns scored, victories, and even in salaries. Those standing on the assembly lines and those sitting at their desks in the bureaucracies found the most satisfaction in the athletic hero who presented an image of all-conquering power. Thus they preferred the towering home runs of Babe Ruth to the "scientific" style of base hits, base stealing, sacrifices, and hit-and-run plays personified by Ty Cobb; they preferred the smashing knockout blows of Jack Dempsey to the "scientific" boxing skills displayed by Gene Tunney. Perhaps it was little wonder that boys now dreamed of becoming athletic heroes rather than captains of industry, and girls dreamed of Hollywood stardom rather than the hearth.

BABE RUTH

No modern athletic hero exceeded Babe Ruth's capacity to project multiple images of brute power, the natural, uninhibited man, and the fulfillment of the American success dream. Ruth was living proof that the lone individual could still rise from mean, vulgar beginnings to fame and fortune, to a position of public recognition equalled by few men in American history. With nothing but his bat, Ruth revolutionized the National Game of baseball. Ruth's mighty home runs represented a dramatic finality, a total clearing of the bases with one mighty swat. Everything about Ruth was extraordinary—his size, strength, coordination, his appetite for the things of the flesh, and even his salary. He transcended the world of ordinary mortals, and yet he was the most mortal of men. He loved playing baseball, swearing, playing practical jokes, eating, drinking, and having sex. Despite his gross crudities, wrote Billy Evans, a big-league umpire, "Ruth is a big, likeable kid. He has been well named, Babe. Ruth has never grown up and probably never will. Success on the ball field has in no way changed him. Everybody likes him. You just can't help it."[2]

Ruth saw himself as a prime example of the classic American success story. "The greatest thing about this country," he wrote in his autobiography, "is the wonderful fact that it doesn't matter which side of the tracks you were born on, or whether you're homeless or homely or friendless. The chance is still there. I know."[3] Ruth encouraged the legend that he had been an orphaned child. While the story had no basis in fact, his early years were indeed grim. He grew up in a tough waterfront neighborhood in Baltimore. His saloon-keeping father and sickly mother had no time for the boy; he received little or no parental affection. By his own admission, he became a "bad kid," who smoked, chewed tobacco, and engaged in petty thievery. At the age of seven, his parents sent him to the St. Mary's Industrial Home for Boys, an institution in Baltimore run by the Xaverian Order for orphans, young indigents, and delinquents. Except for brief interludes at home, Ruth spent the next twelve years at St. Mary's. There, as a teenager, he won a reputation for his baseball prowess and in 1914 signed a professional contract with the Baltimore Orioles of the International League. In the same year the Boston Red Sox purchased him as a left-handed pitcher.[4]

Ruth never had to struggle for success in baseball. For him, both pitching and hitting were natural talents rather than acquired skills. Converted from a top pitching star to an outfielder, Ruth surprised the world of baseball in 1919 by hitting twenty-nine home runs, two more than the existing major-league record which had been set in a crackerbox ball park in 1884. He followed in 1920 as a member of the New York Yankees with a stunning total of fifty-four four baggers, which was a larger number

[2]As quoted in Smith, *The American Dream and the National Game*, p. 207. See also Tristram Potter Coffin,*The Old Ball Game: Baseball in Folklore and Fiction* (New York: Herder and Herder, 1971), Chap. 4.

[3]Babe Ruth and Bob Considine, *The Babe Ruth Story* (New York: Scholastic Books, 1969), p. 9.

[4]There are many biographies of Ruth. Tom Meany, Martin Weldon, Claire Ruth with Bill Slocum, Lee Allen, Daniel M. Daniel, and Waite Hoyt wrote early biographies. Four recent books are superior in most respects to the earlier works: Ken Sobel, *Babe Ruth and the American Dream* (New York: Ballantine, 1974); Kal Wagenheim, *Babe Ruth: His Life and Legend* (New York: Praeger, 1974); Robert W. Creamer, *Babe* (New York: Simon and Schuster, 1974); Marshall Smelser, *The Life that Ruth Built* (New York: Quadrangle/New York Times, 1975).

than any entire team (except the Yankees) in the major leagues compiled. For Ruth, this was only the beginning. From 1918 through 1934 he led the American League in homers twelve times with an average of more than forty a season; from 1926 through 1931 he averaged slightly more than fifty home runs per season. In every 11.7 times at bat he hit a round tripper. In addition, Ruth hit for an exceptionally high average. His lifetime mark of .342 has been equalled by few players in baseball history.

The public responded to Ruth's feats with overwhelming enthusiasm. Before Ruth, the Yankees' best annual attendance had been 600,000, but with him, the team averaged more than a million each year. Everywhere in the league, the fans poured out to the ball parks to see the Yankees play, apparently caring little whether the home team won or lost, only hoping to witness the Babe hammer a pitch out of the park. Even Ruth's mighty swings that failed to connect brought forth a chorus of awed "Ooooooohs," as the audience realized the enormous power that had gone to waste and the narrow escape that the pitcher had temporarily enjoyed. Each day, millions of Americans turned to the sports page of their newspaper to see if Ruth had hit another homer. Indeed, the response may have been unique in the annals of American sport. "In times past," Paul Gallico, a sportswriter reflected, "we had been interested in and excited by prize fighters and baseball players, but we had never been so individually involved or joined in such a mass outpouring of affection as we did for Ruth." To players and fans alike, Ruth was a pioneer exploring "the uncharted wilderness of sport. There was something almost of the supernatural and the miraculous connected with him too," continued Gallico.[5] "I am not so certain now that Ruth is human," added Cleveland catcher, Chet Thomas. "At least he does things you couldn't expect a mere batter with two arms and legs to do. I can't explain him. Nobody can explain him. He just exists."[6]

The Ruthian image of home-run blasts ran counter to the increasingly dominant world of bureaucracies, scientific management, and "organization men." Ruth was the antithesis of science and rationality. Whereas Cobb relied upon "brains rather than brawn," upon, as he put it, the "hit-and-run, the steal and double-steal, the bunt in all its varieties, the squeeze, the ball hit to the opposite field and the ball punched through openings in the defense for a single," Ruth, on the other hand, swung for the fences.[7] Ruth, according to sportswriter F.C. Lane in 1921, "throws science itself to the wind and hews out a rough path for himself by the sheer weight of his own unequalled talents."[8] Ruth seemed to embody the public preference for a compensatory hero with mere brute strength rather than one who exercised intelligence. Ruth played baseball instinctively; he seemed to need no practice or special training. He loved the game for its own sake.

[5]Paul Gallico, *The Golden People* (Garden City, N.Y.: Doubleday, 1965), pp. 36–37.

[6]As quoted in Smith, *The American Dream*, p. 198.

[7]Ty Cobb with Al Stump, *My Life in Baseball—The True Record* (Garden City, N.Y.: Doubleday, 1961), p. 280.

[8]As quoted in Smith, *The American Dream*, p. 190.

"With him the game *is* the thing. He loves baseball; loves just to play it," asserted a sportswriter.[9] No ulterior motives seemed to tarnish his pure love of the game.

The Ruthian image also ran counter to Victorian values. Ruth's appetite for the things of the flesh was legendary. He drank heroic quantities of bootleg liquor; his hotel suite was always well stocked with beer and whiskey. People watched him eat with awe; he sometimes ate as many as eighteen eggs for breakfast and washed them down with seven or eight bottles of soda pop. Ruth was not only the "Sultan of Swat," he was a sultan of the bedroom. In each town on the spring training tours and in each big-league city, Ruth always found a bevy of willing female followers. His escapades were so well known that a sportswriter wrote a parody of them. "I wonder where my Babe Ruth is tonight? He grabbed his hat and coat and ducked from sight. I wonder where he will be at half past three?...I know he's with a dame. I wonder what's her name?"[10] Ruth probably did not know her name, for he had a notorious reputation for being unable to remember the names of even his closest friends. In the 1920s, to those many Americans who were rejecting what they called "Puritanism," Ruth could be identified as a fellow rebel. Marshall Smelser has written that Ruth "met an elemental need of the crowd. Every hero must have his human flaw which he shares with his followers. In Ruth it was hedonism, as exaggerated in folklore and fable."[11]

Ruth's uninhibited behavior often got him into trouble. Several women sued him for paternity and child support costs. For a variety of offenses the Yankee management suspended him five times during the 1922 season. Ban Johnson, president of the American League, wrote him in June 1922: "Your conduct...[is] reprehensible...—shocking to every American mother who permits her boy to go to a game.... It is a leading question as to whether it is permissable to allow a man of your influence and breeding to continue in the game.... The period has arrived when you should allow some intelligence to creep into a mind that has plainly been warped."[12] In 1925, Ruth's excesses caught up with him. On the way north from spring training, Ruth collapsed from what the club called acute indigestion—"the stomach-ache that was heard around the world." (Some of the sportswriters and players thought that Ruth, in reality, was suffering from venereal disease.) Removal of an intestinal abscess temporarily laid him low, but he soon returned to his old ways of staying out all night and drinking heavily. Miller Huggins, the usually tolerant manager of the Yankees, was fed up with Ruth. He slapped him with a $5,000 fine—a major-league record, of course—and suspended Ruth from the club. Ruth was angry, but his appeals went for naught. He had a poor season, but some of his best years still lay ahead.

Ruth's propensity for immediate gratification had its more endearing

[9]Smith, *The American Dream*, p. 205.

[10]Quoted in Harold Seymour, *Baseball: The Golden Age* (New York: Oxford University Press, 1971), p. 431.

[11]Marshal M. Smelser, "The Babe on Balance," *American Scholar*, 44 (Spring 1975), 299.

[12]Seymour, *Baseball*, p. 432.

side. He won a deserved reputation for loving children. Everywhere he went, children flocked to him, simply to see the great Bambino and perhaps to touch his uniform and obtain his autograph. Ruth enthusiastically welcomed their attention. He regularly visited children in hospitals. A legend that has some basis in fact added immeasurably to Ruth's popularity. In its simplest version, Ruth visited a young boy who was dying in a hospital. He promised the lad that he would hit a home run for him that afternoon. He did, which so inspired the boy with the will to live that he miraculously recovered. After that, few writers, when reviewing Ruth's career, failed to mention the home run that saved a boy's life. The public also adored Ruth for his crude egalitarianism. He deferred to no one. Introduced, for instance, to President Calvin Coolidge, he responded: "Hi, Pres. How are you?" According to one story, possibly apocryphal, while Ruth was holding out for a higher salary in 1930, someone pointed out to him that a depression existed and that he was asking for more money than President Herbert Hoover earned. "What the hell has Hoover got to do with it?" Ruth demanded. "Besides, I had a better year than he did."[13]

Ruth's huge earnings added to his heroic stature. From the time Ruth set his first home run record in 1919, he was besieged by commercial opportunities outside of baseball. Since the early days of the game, star players had supplemented their salaries by product endorsements, vaudeville acts, and personal appearances, but no player had the opportunities that became available to Ruth. In the winter of 1921, Christy Walsh, a sports cartoonist turned ghost writer, convinced Ruth to permit him to handle the demand by newspapers for Ruth's "personal analysis" of each home run that he hit. Initially, Walsh served Ruth primarily as a ghost writer; as Ruth's "literary agent" he increased Ruth's writing income from $500 to $15,000 in the first year. For fifteen years Walsh employed a stable of ghost writers, among them Ford Frick, future commissioner of baseball, to write pieces allegedly by Ruth for newspapers and magazines. Ruth "covered" every World Series from 1921 through 1936, earning between $2,000 and $7,000 per series. Eventually Walsh's syndicate provided ghost writing services for a large number of athletes and public celebrities.[14]

Walsh became the first modern athletic business agent. Beginning in 1921, he handled nearly all of Ruth's nonbaseball commercial ventures. In 1921 he signed Ruth to a vaudeville tour, the first of several, which called for Ruth to receive $3,000 per week for twenty weeks, a record-shattering sum for a vaudeville performer. He also managed Ruth's many barnstorming baseball tours in the off-seasons. He assembled a list of all the commercial products with which his client could be associated and set out to convince the manufacturers of the benefits to be gained by Ruth's endorsements. In time, Ruth promoted, among other products, hunting and fishing equipment, modish men's wear, alligator shoes, baseball gear, and sporty automobiles. In Boston he might trumpet the virtues of Packards, in New York Cadillacs, and in St. Louis Reos. He received

[13]Ibid., p. 428.
[14]See Christy Walsh, *Adios to Ghosts!* (New York: n.p., 1937).

between $250 and $10,000 for appearing at banquets, grand openings, smokers, boxing and wrestling matches, and celebrity golf tournaments. When purchasing power and the low income tax of the era are taken into account, Ruth's earnings were phenomenal. His total baseball income ranged between $1.25 million and $1.5 million, his nonbaseball earnings between $1 million and $2 million, for a total in the neighborhood of $3 million. Although Ruth was a hopeless spendthrift, Christy Walsh was able to convince him to put some of his income into untouchable annuities. Thus he survived the stock market crash in 1929 with enough money to retire comfortably in 1935.[15]

Of America's legendary heroes, Ruth is the country's preeminent athletic hero. Even in an age which takes a special delight in smashing false idols, Ruth remains the demigod of sports. His astonishing success reassured those who feared that America had become a society in which the traditional conditions conducive to success no longer existed. He transcended the world of sport to establish an undefinable benchmark for outstanding performances in all fields of human endeavor. The media has heralded Willie Sutton as "the Babe Ruth of bank robbers," Chuck Stearns as "the Babe Ruth of water skiing," Jimmy Connors as "the Babe Ruth of tennis," and Franco Corelli as "the Babe Ruth of operatic tenors." The list could be continued indefinitely. Americans resented anyone who threatened to tarnish Ruth's heroic stature. When Henry Aaron approached Ruth's career record of 714 home runs, he said, "I can't recall a day this year or last when I did not hear the name of Babe Ruth."[16] Roger Maris, when he broke Ruth's mark of sixty home runs in one season in 1961, found himself the victim of a steady stream of abuse from fans, sportswriters, and people in the streets. They repeatedly noted that Ruth had compiled sixty home runs in a 154-game season while Maris had only fifty-nine after 154 games. After the 1961 season, Maris quickly sank into obscurity, but the legend of Babe Ruth lived on. Long after the 1920s, Ruth continued to be a peerless compensatory hero.

A HERO GOES PRO

Pitch-men and journalists also found in the football player Red Grange an almost perfect subject for elevation to the status of a compensatory hero. Like Ruth, Grange projected an image of swift, decisive, all-conquering power. Rather than methodically grinding down the opposition with power plays, Grange's forté was the sudden and total breakthrough, the punt return, the kickoff return, or the long run from scrimmage that climaxed in a touchdown. By exhibiting his phenomenal talent for open field running in a game against Michigan in 1924, Grange stunned the football world. Before the game, Fielding H. Yost, the veteran mentor of many powerful Michigan elevens, assured everyone that the Illinois redhead

[15]Ibid.
[16]Creamer, *Babe*, p. 16.

could be stopped. With 67,000 fans present at the opening of Illinois' new stadium, Grange responded by scoring four touchdowns in the first twelve minutes of the game. He took the opening kickoff for a ninety-five-yard touchdown run; he then had touchdown runs of sixty-seven, fifty-six, and forty-five yards from the line of scrimmage.[17] Modern technology accentuated the dramatic quality of Grange's feats. While few Americans were able to see Grange perform in the flesh, millions saw him in the newsreels of thousands of theatres. The image of Grange, speeded up on the flickering screen, was almost eerie, as it darted, slashed, cut away from would-be tacklers, and crossed the goal line one, two, three, or even five times within a few brief seconds. Little wonder that Grantland Rice hailed Grange as the "Galloping Ghost of the Gridiron."

Grange's career seemed to confirm traditional virtues and the survival of the dream of the self-made man. Like Ruth, he began life under adverse circumstances. One of five children, he was born in the small rustic town of Forksville, Pennsylvania, where his father supported the family by working in local lumber camps. When Grange was but five years old, the family began to break up. His mother died, and his father moved the family to Wheaton, Illinois, a town on the outskirts of Chicago. Shortly thereafter, the elder Grange decided he could not raise his three daughters without a mother and sent them back to Pennsylvania to live with his wife's relatives. As a youth, Red Grange, unlike Babe Ruth, practiced all the Victorian virtues that seemed to be fast disappearing in the United States of the twentieth century. He neither drank nor smoked. He was modest, soft-spoken, and hard-working; in both his high school and college years he toted ice to Wheaton residents. These character traits, according to Grange in his autobiography, paid dividends. Athletics "was my whole life and I put everything I had into it," he wrote. "The future took care of itself. When the breaks came I was ready for them." Confirming the legendary dream of American success, he wrote: "Any boy can realize his dreams if he's willing to work and make sacrifices along the way."[18]

Grange, of course, exaggerated. He owed his success to more than hard work and impeccable personal habits. He enjoyed marvelous natural talents for quickness afoot and the ability to change directions while carrying a football. In high school he was the Illinois sprints and hurdles champion. As a high school football player at Wheaton he created something of a sensation by scoring seventy-two touchdowns in three seasons of play. Contacted by the alumni of several midwestern colleges who wanted to bring his talents to their campuses, Grange finally resolved to attend the University of Illinois. In the fall scrimmages of 1922 he led the freshman team to several victories over the varsity. Robert "Zup" Zuppke, the Illinois head coach, recognized in Grange a potential football immortal. In the spring practice of 1923, he designed a powerful single wing formation with Grange running at tailback. "I got a great break at

---

[17]Allison Danzig and Peter Brandwein, eds., *The Greatest Sports Stories from the New York Times* (New York: A. S. Barnes, 1951), pp. 218–29, offers a convenient source for this game.
[18]Red Grange as told to Ira Morton, *The Red Grange Story* (New York: G. P. Putnam's Sons, 1953), p. 178.

Illinois," Grange later confessed. "...I ended up making most of the team's touchdowns and getting all the publicity, because Coach Bob Zuppke let me carry the ball 90 per cent of the time. In most of the games I carried the ball thirty or forty times."[19]

Bare statistics give only a partial indication of Grange's outstanding collegiate performance. In three seasons he scored thirty-one touchdowns, gained 3,637 yards on the ground (including kickoff and punt returns), and passed for an additional 653 yards. He accounted for an average of 214 yards for each of the college games in which he appeared. By the close of the 1925 season Grange was, according to the *New York Times*, "the most famous, the most talked of, and written about, the most photographed and most picturesque player the game has ever produced."[20]

After the final game of the 1925 season, Grange immediately left the University of Illinois to become a professional football player. Instrumental in his decision was Charles C. "Cash and Carry" or "Cold Cash" Pyle, who was shortly to become a sports impresario with few peers.[21] Without any prior experience in managing athletes or staging sporting spectacles, Pyle approached Red Grange in the fall season of 1925. According to Grange's recollection, Pyle simply said: "How would you like to make one hundred thousand dollars, or maybe even a million?"[22] Without waiting to hear the details, Grange replied in the affirmative. Pyle left Champaign, Illinois the next day for Chicago to confer with George Halas and Ed Sternamen, co-owners of the Chicago Bears, a professional football team in the fledgling National Football League. Secretly the two parties reached a tentative agreement. Grange would join the Bears immediately after the college season to play the remaining league games of the Bears and then he and the team would go on an exhibition tour to be staged by Pyle. Gate receipts for the games would be shared fifty-fifty. Of the Pyle-Grange 50 percent, Grange was to receive 60 percent.[23]

Today we take it for granted that outstanding college athletes will attempt to profit personally from their exploits, but in 1925 Grange's decision touched off a national debate. By abandoning his studies for a blatantly commercial career, he openly flaunted the myth of the college athlete as a gentleman-amateur who played merely for the fun of the game and the glory of his school. Grange's Illinois coach, Zup Zuppke, joined a host of academics in condemning Grange. Not only was professional

---

[19]Ibid., pp. 174–75. See also "Debunking the 'All-American' Football Team Fiction," *Literary Digest*, 91 (November 27, 1926), 60.

[20]*New York Times*, November 22, 1925.

[21]On Pyle see *New York Times*, February 4, 1939; Hugh Leamy, "Net Profits," *Collier's* 78 (October 2, 1926), 9, 32; Myron Cope, "The Game That Was," *Sports Illustrated*, 31 (October 13, 1969), 93–96, 102–3.

[22]Grange, *The Red Grange Story*, p. 91.

[23]Ibid., p. 92; George Halas with Gwen Morgan and Arthur Veysey, *Halas by Halas* (New York: McGraw-Hill, 1979), p. 104. According to George Vass, *George Halas and the Chicago Bears* (Chicago: Henry Regney, 1971), p. 76, Grange and Pyle were to receive a guarantee of $2,000 per game, 10 percent of the first $5,000 of the gate, 20 percent of the next five, and forty cents of every dollar above that. It is unclear whether the agreements described by Grange, Halas, and Vass applied to both tours or only the first one.

football held in low moral esteem, but to them it was unethical for Grange to capitalize upon a reputation that he had acquired in college for direct, personal gain. An idol of the nation's youth and an exemplar of amateur sports simply should not accept "tainted" money.[24] Initially, sympathetic newsmen depicted Grange as an "innocent, decent, trusting chap," who was the "victim of a kind of conspiracy of get-rich-quick promoters who did not care how far they went in prostituting him to their ends."[25] But Grange was hardly an innocent victim. He publicly acknowledged that "I'm out to get the money, and I don't care who knows it." Furthermore, "my advice to everybody is to get to the gate while the getting's good."[26] He did promise his admirers that he would at some future date finish his senior year in college, a promise he never kept.

While the Galloping Ghost was still attracting headlines, Pyle and Grange went all out to maximize their profits. Five days after Grange's final game with Illinois, he played with the Bears at Wrigley Field in Chicago on Thanksgiving Day, 1925. The publicity barrage accompanying Grange's departure from Illinois helped to attract 35,000 fans, to that date the largest crowd ever to attend a professional game. (At the time, the National Football League consisted of eighteen makeshift teams located mostly in smaller cities. The Bears considered 5,000 to be a good draw in Chicago.) The Bears, with Red Grange obliged to play at least half of each game, then played a grueling schedule of ten games in seventeen days.

Everywhere they went—St. Louis, Philadelphia, New York twice, Boston, Providence, Washington, and Pittsburgh—they broke professional football attendance records. In New York 65,000 fans packed the Polo Grounds, and an estimated 20,000 had to be turned away. Until the "Grange Tour" arrived, the New York Giants had been losing money. After taking an eight-day rest in Chicago, Grange and the Bears embarked upon Pyle's 7,000-mile, thirty-five day, fourteen-game barnstorming tour of the South and West. In matches against "pick-up" teams of mostly former collegians, Pyle insisted upon a $25,000 guarantee from local promoters. Newspapers and press syndicates assigned their most distinguished sportswriters to accompany Grange. Westbrook Pegler, Damon Runyan, and Ford Frick, among others, reported daily every facet of Grange's behavior both on and off the field of play. Never had such a tour by an athletic team attracted so much publicity nor been so financially rewarding. Ironically, the Galloping Ghost's performance, perhaps because of a nagging injury, was far less spectacular than it had been as a collegian.

In the meantime, Pyle lined up commercial endorsements for Grange. Within the first ten days after Grange had signed a contract with Pyle, they received 187 phone calls, sixty telegrams, and thirty-nine personal visits from advertising men. Grange endorsed sweaters, shoes, caps, a Red

---

[24]See responses in "Football History as Made by the Illinois Ice Man," *Literary Digest,* 87 (December 26, 1925), 29–34, and Grange, *The Red Grange Story,* pp. 89–90, 92–96.

[25]"Football History as Made by the Illinois Ice Man," 30.

[26]As quoted in John B. Kennedy, "The Saddest Young Man in America," *Collier's,* 77 (January 16, 1926), 15.

Grange football doll, and soft drinks. The "Red Grange Chocolates," according to Pyle, sold six millions bars in thirty days. In New York, Grange signed a movie contract, and Pyle flashed a $300,000 check to amazed reporters. Although the press headlined the event, Grange later admitted that it was "one of Pyle's wild publicity stunts."[27] Grange was actually to receive $5,000 a week while working on the film. But Pyle recognized that large sums of money were important in establishing the heroic status of his clients. Altogether in the first year of their partnership Pyle and Grange split about $250,000 as their share of gate receipts and assorted income from endorsements and promotions.

Emboldened by his spectacular financial success with Grange in the winter of 1925–1926, Pyle expanded his promotional horizons. He first demanded that he and Grange be granted one-third ownership of the Bears. When Halas and Sternamen refused, he attempted to place a second NFL team in New York, only to be blocked by the owner of the New York Giants. He then formed a new professional loop, the American Football League, with Grange and himself as co-owners of the New York Yankees. Because of Grange, the Yankees drew large crowds, but the other teams in the league lost money. After the 1926 season, the new league collapsed. Pyle, with Grange and the financial losses suffered by NFL teams during the 1926 season as leverage, forced the NFL to admit the Yankees as a "road team" for the 1927 season. A permanent knee injury suffered by Grange in the third game of the 1927 season brought financial ruin to the Yankees. Grange and Pyle amicably severed their partnership. Pyle went on to other forms of sport promotion—professional tennis tours and two long-distance walking contests from San Francisco to New York ("Bunion Derbies"). Grange returned to the Bears as a superb defensive back and above-average straight-ahead running back. He played his last game in 1935. In the 1940s and 1950s, he became a successful radio and television sportscaster.

HEROES OF THE RING

The need for compensatory heroes, the ballyhooing of Tex Rickard and Jack Kearns, and the ascension of Jack Dempsey to the heavyweight championship of the world helped make the 1920s the "Golden Age" of American boxing.[28] Never before or since has boxing achieved such a high plateau of popularity. In the prewar years gate receipts from a single bout

[27]"Football History as Made by the Illinois Ice Man," 29–34; Grange, *The Red Grange Story*, p. 102.

[28]On the legalization and financial aspects of prize fighting in the twenties see Jesse Frederick Steiner, *Americans At Play: Recent Trends in Recreation and Leisure Time Activities* (New York: McGraw-Hill, 1933), pp. 94–97. Among the best accounts of boxing in the twenties are James P. Dawson, "Boxing," in Danzig and Brandwein, eds., *Sports Golden Age*, pp. 38–85; Paul Gallico, *Farewell to Sport* (New York: Knopf, 1938), Chaps. 2, 7, 8, 13; Randy Roberts, "Jack Dempsey: An American Hero in the 1920s," *Journal of Popular Culture*, 8 (Fall 1974), 411–26; and Roberts, *Jack Dempsey: the Manassa Mauler* (Baton Rouge: Louisiana State University Press, 1979). Roberts interprets Dempsey as a major symbol of the 1920s.

never exceeded $300,000; in the 1920s, Rickard promoted five consecutive million-dollar gates. Fans paid over $2 million to see the second Dempsey-Tunney fight. In terms of purchasing power, these sums were far larger than any modern gates. Over 100,000 fans personally witnessed each of the Dempsey-Tunney fights—again, figures unequalled in the annals of boxing history. Day after day the major newspapers placed boxing items on the front page. They detailed both the private and public lives of the pugilists.

World War I helped soften the traditional animosity toward prize fighting. During the war, the army used boxing as part of the training of doughboys. After the war, often at the instigation of the American Legion, state after state dropped legal barriers to prize fighting. Boxing acquired a new level of respectability. The old days of clandestine fights on barges, in the backrooms of saloons, or in isolated rural spots gave way to fights held in glittering arenas and in huge stadiums. No longer were fights patronized exclusively by the slummers, roughnecks, ethnic workingmen, and the "sporting set"; even "high society," "proper" women, and middle-income groups went to see the fights. Celebrities from all fields of American life turned the heavyweight championship fights into big "social events." The ordinary people came as much to see the celebrities as they did the fight itself.

No one in the 1920s sensed the possibilities of exploiting the public hunger for heroes better than Tex Rickard. Rickard has been aptly described as the "King of Ballyhoo," "King of Sport Promoters," and the "Phineas T. Barnum" of the twentieth century.[29] To the "insiders" of the fight game, Rickard was always the unsophisticated country "rube," but he won a reputation for square dealing in two professions well-known for their chicanery: gambling and fight promotion. Unlike the insiders of the boxing world, he had the financial backing of wealthy men, which permitted him to outbid others for major fights.

Long before the 1920s, he revealed his willingness to take high risks as well as a talent for promotion. Born in Missouri and raised in Texas, Rickard's early life could have been material for a dime novel or a successful melodrama. Upon the death of his father, when Rickard was but eleven years old, he became a cowhand and participated in several "long drives" to Kansas, Nebraska, and Montana. Elected town marshal of Henrietta, Texas in 1894, he served only one year before departing for Alaska. In the great Yukon-Klondike gold rushes of the late 1890s, he reputedly won and lost several fortunes as a professional gambler, gold speculator, and saloon owner. While in Alaska, he also promoted a few barroom prize fights for small stakes. In 1902 he returned to the States, went to Africa in search of a nonexistent diamond mine, and eventually bought a part interest in a fancy gambling saloon in Goldfield, Nevada.

Rickard first attracted attention on the national sporting scene in 1906.

[29]In addition to the works cited in footnote 28, see Jack Koefoed, "The Master of the Ballyhoo," *North American Review*, 227 (March 1929), 282–86; Joe Humphreys, "The Rickard I Knew," *Collier's*, 84 (November 9, 1929), 28, 59–60; Charles Samuels, *The Magnificant Rube: The Life and Times of Tex Rickard* (New York: McGraw-Hill, 1957); Mrs. "Tex" Rickard with Arch Oboler, *Everything Happened to Him* (New York: Frederick A. Stokes, 1936).

That year he signed Joe Gans and Battling Nelson for a lightweight championship fight to be held in Goldfield, Nevada for the princely purse of $30,000, twice the amount of any previous guarantee in ring history. He also staged the famous James J. Jeffries-Jack Johnson heavyweight championship fight in 1910 at Reno, Nevada. He outfinessed other promoters by approaching Johnson directly and paying him $2,500 cash in advance. He offered the then-astronomical purse of $100,000 and capitalized upon the racial dimensions of the bout. He also invited ex-champions and other popular fighters to attend the bout with their expenses paid, a publicity gimmick that would later become a standard practice for fight promoters. The fight was a financial success, drawing a gate in excess of $200,000, a sum far larger than any previous boxing match.

For the next five years, Rickard continued to pursue multiple careers as a gambling house proprietor, rancher in Paraguay, and fight promoter. In 1916 his name again appeared in the sports headlines. He promoted a "no-decision" bout between the heavyweight champion Jess Willard, who had beaten Jack Johnson in 1915, and Frank Moran in New York. Earning a $30,000 stake from the fight, he promptly doubled it by betting on Woodrow Wilson to win the 1916 presidential election.[30] Having established a tacit priority for the promotion of future Willard fights, he was in a position to launch the Golden Age of American boxing. He needed only a new boxing hero to replace the uncharismatic Willard. Jack Dempsey, an unknown western fighter, soon filled that need.

On the face of it, Dempsey was an unlikely prospect for a popular hero. True, his social origins were modest; he was born into a poor, peripatetic Irish-American family at Manassa, Colorado. But until Jack Kearns became his manager in 1917, Dempsey had been little more than a saloon brawler, fighting in western tank towns for a hundred dollars or less per bout. Dempsey's reputation as a great slugger rested as much on myth as fact. He had been the victim of a knockout in 1917, and he had lost a decision in 1918. His career knockout percentage of .613 was unexceptional, well below that of Floyd Patterson and Primo Carnera, for instance, and only slightly above that of Tommy Burns, who is considered the worst of all heavyweight champions by ring historians. As champion, Dempsey defended his title only six times in seven years and met only two genuinely formidable foes. As a potential hero, Dempsey suffered from an even more serious liability. Having not served in the armed forces in World War I, the federal government in 1920 charged him with being a "slacker." Although acquitted on the grounds that he had provided financial support to his wife and mother, the issue clouded Dempsey's heroic image.[31]

Dempsey acquired the reputation of being "Jack the Giant-Killer" largely through the hokum of Jack Kearns and Tex Rickard. Dempsey had the good fortune of meeting Jess Willard, the "Pottawatomie Giant," in a championship bout staged by Rickard at Toledo, Ohio, in 1919. Willard towered over Dempsey. He stood six feet and six inches tall and weighed

---

[30]Rickard, *Everything Happened to Him*, p. 261.
[31]Roberts, "Jack Dempsey," 413; "War Record of Dempsey," *Literary Digest*, 64 (February 14, 1920), 122–24.

245 pounds, while Dempsey was six feet and one inch tall and weighted 191 pounds. Dempsey floored the massive Willard five times in the first round; at the end of the third round, Willard, his face swollen twice its normal size, bloody and bewildered, conceded defeat. The image of Dempsey as a giant-killer caught on at once. Publicity stunts, such as having Dempsey's sparring partners wear inflated chest protectors and catcher's masks, reinforced the image. The public accepted the mistaken notion that Dempsey was a little man. As Dempsey told it: "Jack Kearns' ballyhoo that made me 'Jack the Giant-Killer' was partially responsible. Various pictures that were published of my different fights, too, added to the misconception. Repeatedly they showed me fighting against men who were inches taller than I and many pounds heavier."[32]

The Dempsey-Willard fight launched Rickard's career as the nation's premier sports impresario. In 1920 the New York legislature legalized prize fighting and set up a state athletic commission to supervise it. Two weeks after the law was passed, Rickard, with the aid of John Ringling of circus fame as a silent partner, obtained the financial backing to lease Madison Square Garden. Under his astute management, the Garden, which had been something of a white elephant to prior managers, became a highly profitable enterprise. Rickard offered a variety of attractions unequalled by any other palace of entertainment in the world. Boxing, wrestling, circuses, horse shows, six-day bicycle races, rodeos, professional hockey—these and many other activities became regular fare on the Garden's schedule.

Rickard juggled conflicting interests with the same skill and daring that he had perfected as a professional gambler. He courted newspaper reporters with frequent "leaks," free cigars, liberal quantities of liquor, and special seating privileges. He always reserved a number of free seats for the minions of the Tammany Hall political machine. Simultaneously, he won the support of New York's superrich. In 1921 at the invitation of Anne Morgan, philanthropic sister of J. Pierpont Morgan, he held a benefit fight in the Garden to kick off a fundraising drive for war-torn France. Such clever gestures assisted Rickard in marshaling the funds for the Carpentier-Dempsey fight in 1921 and for the construction of a new $5 million Madison Square Garden in 1926.[33]

Rickard exhibited the full arsenal of his promotional skills in the Dempsey-Georges Carpentier fight of 1921. Because of political hostility at the State Capitol in Albany, Rickard transferred the fight to Jersey City, where he had a huge stadium built. As Dempsey later confessed, Rickard "dug up" Carpentier, the light heavyweight champion of Europe, and set out to convince the public that the fragile Frenchman was a serious contender for the crown. Rickard explained to Dempsey and Kearns how he planned to ballyhoo the bout. It would be a "foreign foe" versus an American; a war hero—Carpentier had twice been decorated for valor in

[32]Jack Dempsey, *Round by Round: An Autobiography* (New York: McGraw-Hill, 1940), p. 176.
[33]See especially Dawson, "Boxing," pp. 38–85, and Zander Hollander, ed., *Madison Square Garden: A Century of Sport and Spectacle on the World's Most Versatile Stage* (New York: Hawthorn, 1973).

World War I—versus a "slacker," the "rapier" of the skilled fencer versus the "broadsword" of the peasant; the civilized man versus the "abysmal brute." "That's you, Jack," the elated Rickard reputedly exclaimed.[34] The contrast in images was almost perfect. Ike Dorgan, Rickard's assistant, nicknamed Carpentier the "Orchid Man," set up his training camp on Long Island amidst the "social crowd," refused to allow reporters to watch Carpentier spar, and touted the Frenchman's attractions to women. According to Dorgan and the press, Carpentier was handsome, debonair, a "boulevardier," who danced beautifully and sang French chansonnettes.[35]

As Rickard had hoped, the nation took sides. The American Legion passed a resolution condemning Dempsey for his lack of military service in World War I; the Veterans of Foreign Wars retaliated by siding with the champ. In general, the "lowbrows"—workingmen, ethnics, and many from the white-collar class as well—favored Dempsey. The "highbrows," especially the nation's literati, supported Carpentier. Even George Bernard Shaw, the distinguished British playwright, enlisted his vast literary talents in Carpentier's behalf.

The fans at Boyle's Thirty Acres near Jersey City gave Carpentier a larger welcoming applause than Dempsey. As a financial event, the fight was an unprecedented success. Over 80,000 fans paid $1,789,238 to see the fight. Present were the "Who's Who of the social, financial and entertainment world."[36] As an athletic contest, the bout was a farce. Dempsey had little difficulty in knocking Carpentier out in the fourth round. Nonetheless, everyone seemed satisfied. Even the dignified *New York Times* announced the results of the fight in front-page headlines. Few Americans were left untouched by the spectacle at Boyle's Thirty Acres.

Rickard used similar tactics in promoting his next bonanza—Dempsey's fight with Louis Angel Firpo at the Polo Grounds in New York in 1923. Firpo, formerly a bottle washer for a Buenos Aires, Argentina, pharmacy, had come to the United States looking for easy money. Rickard corralled for Firpo a "proper assortment of weak-chinned or canary-hearted boxers. . .to pole-ax into unconsciousness."[37] Firpo, a big, awkward man, soon won appellations by the press as the "Argentine Giant" and the "Wild Bull of the Pampas." Rickard hoped to convince the public that the bout would be "two cave men fightin' with tooth and claw."[38] The actual fight conformed to the ballyhoo much better than anyone expected. In less than four minutes of action, Firpo went down to the canvas ten times, Dempsey twice. After the seventh knockdown of Firpo in the first round, Firpo arose and shot a right to Dempsey's jaw that sent the champion toppling through the ropes. (George Bellows memoralized the event with his renowned painting, *Dempsey - Firpo*.) Reporters hoisted Dempsey back into the ring

[34]Jack Dempsey with Charles J. McGuirk, "The Golden Gates," *Saturday Evening Post*, 207 (October 20, 1934), 11.
[35]See especially Paul Gallico, *A Farewell to Sport*, p. 95.
[36]Jack "Doc" Kearns with Oscar Fraley, *The Million Dollar Gate* (New York: Macmillan, 1966), pp. 147–48; Roberts, "Jack Dempsey," 415–19.
[37]Koefoed, "The Master of the Ballyhoo," 285.
[38]Dempsey, "The Golden Gates," 75.

and the champ finished the round on unsteady legs. But in the next round, Dempsey, swinging both fists wildly, crushed Firpo for a knockout. The exciting battle produced boxing's second million-dollar gate. Most Americans might be the victims of forces beyond their control, wrote Bruce Bliven in the *New Republic*, but within the confines of the boxing ring both Firpo and Dempsey had decided "their own fates."[39] No sport in the 1920s exceeded boxing's capacity to furnish Americans with compensatory heroes.

In the succeeding three years in which Dempsey failed to defend his title, Rickard often stated that a "million-dollar fight" could be staged only once every two years. Rickard himself was busy with the management of the new Garden. Perhaps more importantly, Dempsey enjoyed living the life of a celebrity. Earning perhaps as much as $500,000 annually from endorsements, movie contracts, and vaudeville performances, he was in no hurry to return to the ring. Personal problems also intruded. Dempsey broke with Jack Kearns, his long-time manager, and Kearns proceeded to harass the champion with legal suits. Finally, Dempsey's wife, Estelle, did not want him to return to the ring.

But the primary reason for Dempsey's absence from the ring may have been Harry Wills, the "Brown Panther" from New Orleans, who was clamoring for a crack at the championship. In every respect except race, Wills was a qualified challenger. The story of his inability to get a match with Dempsey is obscured in intrigue and "double talk." On several occasions the New York Athletic Commission, which was appointed by the governor, ordered Dempsey to fight Wills. Apparently these actions were designed to please the black voters of New York City. But according to Rickard, each time he agreed to give Wills a title shot, he received a word from high political figures in Albany that the match would be blocked. Rickard claimed that the politicians in New Jersey likewise opposed the match. Nonetheless, if there is a single culprit in the controversy, it seemed to be Rickard. He showed no interest in staging the fight outside of New York or New Jersey, and he was probably the only person who could have raised a purse adequate for the bout. Apart from possibly being racist himself, Rickard may have feared a loss by Dempsey, a consequent reduction in the gates of future fights, and violent racial incidents similar to the outbreaks that had accompanied Johnson's defeat of Jeffries in 1910.[40]

[39]As quoted in Roberts, *Jack Dempsey*, p. 181.

[40]Dempsey had fought several black boxers on his way to the title, and Kearns had even briefly managed Wills. Rickard had promoted several interracial bouts, including the Jack Johnson-James J. Jeffries match in 1910. The *New York Times* of July 6, 1919, however, quoted Dempsey, after his defeat of Willard, as saying that he would retain the "color line." Nonetheless, Dempsey in his autobiography and in contemporary accounts apart from the statement in the *Times* expressed a desire to fight Wills. James A. Farley, later Postmaster General in the administration of Franklin D. Roosevelt and a member of the New York Athletic Commission in the 1920s, was the most vocal supporter of Wills. The venerable William Muldoon, former Greco-Roman wrestling champion and the chairman of the commission, opposed the proposed fight. See Jack Dempsey, "They Call Me A Bum," in Tom Meany, ed., *Collier's Greatest Sports Stories* (New York: A.S. Barnes, 1955), 95; Nat Fleischer, *Jack Dempsey* (New Rochelle, N.Y.: Arlington House, 1972), pp. 132–35; Roberts, *Jack Dempsey*, pp. 141–48; 213–19.

At any rate, Rickard safely sidetracked Wills and eventually found a new challenger for Dempsey, Gene Tunney, who "was almost universally regarded as a second-rater" by boxing aficionados. The insistence of the New York Athletic Commission upon a Dempsey-Wills match forced Rickard to hold the bout elsewhere. He chose Philadelphia's Susquecentennial Stadium and scheduled the fight for September 23, 1926. The build-up followed Rickard's familiar formula. In the "Battle of the Century" it was the dark, savage-visaged, mauling Dempsey versus the smooth, "scientific" boxer Tunney. To the surprise of nearly all of the 120,757 fans present and several million radio listeners, Tunney defeated Dempsey in the ten-round match on points. While scoring repeatedly on solid but nonlethal blows, Tunney simply avoided Dempsey's famed rushes. The fight was reminiscent of James J. Corbett's upset of John L. Sullivan in 1892. The gate exceeded $1.75 million and Dempsey collected $711,268 for one night's work.

Soon there was a demand for a return bout. Rickard achieved the pinnacle of his promotional career with the second "Fight of the Century" between Tunney and Dempsey in 1927. Over 104,000 customers paid $2,658,660 to witness the event at Soldier Field in Chicago, both records that still stand today. Spectators on the outer perimeter of the stadium sat as far as 200 yards from the ring, making the boxers almost undiscernible. An estimated fifty million Americans heard Graham McNamee's broadcast from one of seventy-three stations connected to the NBC radio network. For the first six rounds, the fight seemed to be a replay of the Philadelphia bout. Then in the seventh round, Dempsey landed a series of blows which crumpled Tunney to the mat. As the referee began to count, he waved Dempsey to a neutral corner of the ring. Dempsey ignored the motion, an action that may have cost him the heavyweight crown. By the time the referee convinced Dempsey to retire to a neutral corner, several seconds had expired. The referee than began the count anew, reaching nine before Tunney came to his feet. Although the referee's action conformed to the Illinois boxing codes, the legendary "long count" furnished a source of endless debate among fight fans. Tunney survived the seventh round and outboxed Dempsey in the final three rounds to win a unanimous decision. In defeat, Dempsey's popularity soared higher than when he had held the championship.

The contrast in the popularity of Dempsey and Tunney reflects the type of hero sought by the American public. The image of Dempsey as the mauler who relied upon quick, physical solutions was far more satisfying to the public than Tunney's exhibition of complex defensive finesse. Millions of Americans who worked in large corporations, bureaucracies, and on assembly lines dreamed of equally direct and decisive answers to their countless frustrations. In addition, Dempsey seemed more human than Tunney. Tunney projected an image of snobbery and intellectuality. He married a socialite, had lectured to a class at Yale on Shakespeare, and was a personal friend of the writer, Thorton Wilder. He remained aloof from the everyday world of ordinary people. He was disdainful of reporters and the camaraderie of the "hangers-on" in the fight game. Americans wanted their heroes to be "average" in all respects except their specialty. Leo Lowenthal has written: "It is some comfort for the little man who has become expelled from the Horatio Alger dream, who despairs of penetrating the thicket of grand strategy in politics and business, to see his heroes as a lot of guys who like or dislike highballs, cigarettes, tomato juice, golf, and social gatherings—just like himself."[41] The "little man" could find confirmation of his own pleasures and discomforts by participating in those of Dempsey.

Dempsey's defeat by Tunney signalled the end of the Golden Age of American boxing. The public did not respond to the new heavyweight king; in 1928 Rickard lost some $400,000 in promoting the Tunney-Tom Henney bout. After the fight, Tunney retired from the ring, leaving the heavyweight scene in chaos. Then, in 1929, Rickard, while launching an elimination series to determine a new champion, suddenly died from an attack of appendicitis. Rickard's funeral revealed that the promoter was in his own right a public celebrity. Over 15,000 persons filed past his ornate, $15,000 bronze casket in the main arena of Madison Square Garden. The next day, 9,000 attended his funeral. No new impresario replaced Rickard, and in the Great Depression of the 1930s, gangsters seized control of boxing. The age of athletic heroes seemed to be over. "After 1930 our stream of super-champions ran dry, replaced by a turgid brook," wrote John R. Tunis in 1934. "The champions were now just ordinary mortals, good players but nothing more."[42] Perhaps super athletic champions simply could not arise in a decade suffering from economic want.

[41]Lowenthal, *Literature, Popular Culture, and Society*, p. 135.
[42]John R. Tunis, "Changing Trends in Sport," *Harper's Monthly Magazine*, 170 (December 1934), 78.

10

Team Sports, 1920-1950

First stages in the construction of a football stadium of steel and concrete, 1921. Courtesy of the University of Nebraska Archives.

In 1928 John R. Tunis, a sportswriter and prolific author of juvenile sport fiction, published a polemical little book entitled *$port$: Heroics and Hysterics*. Tunis used dollar signs in the title to suggest that money had contaminated American sport. To Tunis, the modern boxer was "last of all a fighter"; he was foremost a businessman, a salesman of himself, and a hawker of commercial products. With regard to baseball, Tunis agreed with a remark attributed to Grover Cleveland Alexander, a star pitcher of the St. Louis Cardinals: "Baseball today is 'big business' and most of the fellows going into it are businessmen first and baseball players secondly."[1] To Tunis, prize fighting and baseball could be classified as businesses and perhaps as sciences, "but as sports never." Neither did the great "amateur" associations in golf, tennis, and track, or the high school and college athletic organizations embody "the real spirit of amateur sport." By cataloguing, organizing, documenting, ballyhooing, awarding championships, and permitting charges to spectators, they destroyed the possibility of playing "simply for the love of playing." Tunis was, of course, an incurable romantic and an adherent of the amateur, genteel tradition of Anglo-American sport.

Yet we can detect in his anguished cry a fundamental characteristic of American sport in the post-1920 era, the ascendancy of the spectator. In the Age of the Player, the athletes themselves had generally founded the sport organizations, had written and revised the rules of the games, and had staged athletic contests. Yet in each major sport the emerging power of the fan soon began to be felt. Perhaps it was inevitable. The opportunities for profit and the very human desire to exhibit superior skills to others, whether athletic or otherwise, was difficult to resist.

In the Age of the Spectator, the fans rather than the players ultimately determined the broad contours of American sport. To appeal to the fan, major-league baseball, which had been a spectator-centered sport since its origins, took additional steps in the post-1920 era to improve its moral image and bring more offensive action to the game. Likewise, college football responded with a more wide-open offensive style of play. Many colleges constructed huge concrete stadiums and to aid the fan in his enjoyment of the contest, both baseball and football added numerals to the players' uniforms and installed public address systems in their stadiums. The placement of huge clocks on football scoreboards, which permitted the

[1]For quotations in this paragraph, John R. Tunis, *$port$: Heroics and Hysterics* (New York: John Day, 1928), pp. 4–5, 10.

fans to know the amount of time remaining in the half or the game, added to the dramatic intensity of the contests. Basketball eliminated the center jump after every goal and introduced a fast, running style of play. (Basketball and professional football from 1920 to 1950 will be treated in Chapters Twelve, Thirteen, and Fourteen.) All of the team sports gave more attention to public relations. Even the colleges hired sports information directors to ballyhoo their teams. An old adage was more potent than ever; winning teams attracted more fans than losers. As a consequence, the emphasis upon winning increased and the quality of play improved sharply.

Central to the ascendancy of the spectator in sport was a vastly expanded market for all forms of entertainment. Apart from the growth in population, real income, and leisure time, a concerted attack upon Victorian values created a more favorable climate for the pursuit of commercial amusements. The cornucopia of new consumer delights and the model of the "good life" offered by the media opened new vistas for individual discretion and the immediate gratification of impulses which even the earlier Victorian underworld had only furtively glimpsed. To sell its products, advertisers urged everyone to be youthful, to "have fun," "to live for the moment," and be "carefree." Leisure activity no longer required elaborate moral justification; it was sufficient that leisure served the therapeutic purposes of releasing tensions and refreshing one's self for work. The cultivation of a life-style based upon fun, luxury, and freedom from everyday restraints often replaced a commitment to the work ethic and frugality as badges of personal success. States and municipalities across the nation relaxed their legal restrictions on amusements. Many states repealed or neglected to enforce their Sabbatarian laws and dropped their bans on such underworld sports as prize fighting. But not without conflicts. Especially those who held unskilled and routine jobs and lived in the countryside, small towns, or the ethnic enclaves of the big cities resisted the new values. Even those who embraced the new values most enthusiastically, primarily those with special skills who worked in bureaucracies and lived in the larger cities, frequently experienced agonizing doubts as they rapidly retreated from the age-old values of their forefathers.[2]

In the burgeoning entertainment market, sport enjoyed certain advantages over its rivals. Like sex, drink, or drugs, sport seemed to erase consciousness of everyday reality. But unlike narcotics or alcohol, sport achieved this release by intensifying and concentrating awareness and usually without the harmful side effects of hangovers, withdrawal pains, or

[2]Most general works on the 1920s tend to overstate the shift in values. See for instance Frederick Lewis Allen, *Only Yesterday: An Informal History of the 1920s* (New York: Harper & Bros., 1931), and William E. Leuchtenburg, *The Perils of Prosperity, 1914–1932* (Chicago: University of Chicago, 1958). For attention to those who continue to adhere to traditional values and the ambivalence of those who adopt the new values, see Roderick Nash, *The Nervous Generation: American Thought, 1917–1930* (Chicago: Rand McNally, 1970), and Paul Carter, *The Twenties in America* (New York: Thomas Y. Crowell, 1968). Lary May in *Screening Out the Past: The Birth of Mass Culture and the Motion Picture Industry* (New York: Oxford University Press, 1980), analyzes the subtle shifts in middle class values and behavior as reflected in and caused by the movie industry.

emotional upheavals. Unlike the movies, for instance, sport could satisfy a human need for witnessing live drama that was characterized by both the familiar and the unexpected, by unpredictable reverses and by luck. Sport resolved the drama unambiguously; there were clear-cut winners and losers. Sport could also enhance a sense of individual identity and belonging—to a racial, ethnic, or status group, or, as in the case of international competition, to the nation. Sport might furnish a more satisfactory set of compensatory heroes. Babe Ruth, Red Grange, and Jack Dempsey may have served this function as well as Rudolph Valentino, Douglas Fairbanks, and Charlie Chaplin. In the Age of the Spectator, commercial sport stood somewhere between the movies, with their glamorous stars, and warfare, with its authentic heroes. While sport was staged and ballyhooed like the movies, the outcomes, the climaxes, the risks, and the potential violence in sport were real enough. Thus sport always contained the possibility for genuine drama and genuine heroes.

Standing in this intermediate zone between the glitter of Hollywood and the bravery of the battlefield, commercial sport was the beneficiary of an enormous quantity of free, high-powered publicity. In the 1920s, the magazines, newspapers, and the new medium of the radio all trumpeted the feats of athletes. Radio proved to be a superb medium for the transmission of sport. The fan did not have to wait for his morning newspaper; he immediately shared the drama transpiring on the playing field.

While the radio did not reach its peak as a purveyor of sport until the 1930s, as early as 1923 an estimated two million fans listened to the broadcast of the Louis Firpo-Jess Willard heavyweight fight. The *New York Times* deemed the twenty-three-station network established to carry the 1926 World Series to be such a pioneering venture that it carried the entire narrative of the broadcasts in its sports section. By the end of the decade, Graham McNamee, a former concert singer and the most popular radio announcer of the era, gave play-by-play accounts of all the major baseball, boxing, and football matches over a national hookup. McNamee sensed that an announcer should be more than a disembodied voice objectively describing the action on the field; he should rather be a "personality" in his own right, providing a distinctive point of view and colorful commentary to the audience. McNamee ran "the gamut of emotion, becoming audibly excited at crucial moments, using the popular idiom, putting the spirit of every punch, every pitch, every run into his voice, speeding up his voice with the tensions of the play, letting it subside with the aftermath of calm."[3] After his broadcasts of the 1925 World Series, fans sent him 50,000 letters. By 1930, sport ranked next to popular music in the quantity of time consumed on the air waves.

[3]Alfred N. Goldsmith and Austin C. Lescarboura, *This Thing Called Broadcasting* (New York: Henry Holt, 1930), p. 215. For radio and sport in the 1920s and 1930s, see also Robert West, *The Rape of Radio* (New York: Rodin, 1941), Chap. 11; Red Barber, *The Broadcasters* (New York: Dial, 1970); Jesse Frederick Steiner, *Americans at Play: Recent Trends in Recreation and Leisure Time Activities* (New York: McGraw-Hill, 1933), pp. 97–100; and David Q. Voigt, *America Through Baseball* (Chicago: Nelson-Hall, 1976), pp. 192–96.

But nothing before or since—not even the cool waves of television—created quite the same hot romance between sport and the public as the newspapers did during the 1920s. Torrid journalism was not new to the twenties; in the late 1800s Richard Kyle Fox's *National Police Gazette* had shown that stories of intrigue, violence, and zany behavior sold newspapers. In the 1920s, even the old, respectable newspapers headlined lip-smacking sex scandals, lurid crimes, bizarre fads, and record busting of all sorts. The newspapers eagerly tried to scoop one another in covering such esoteric events as long-distance walking contests, world's champion pie-eating contests, and the world's record for bobbing up and down in a swimming pool. Newspapers might exercise a certain restraint, a degree of objectivity and detachment when reporting political or economic news, but the readers expected hyperbole, editorialization, and legend-building on the sports page. The space devoted to sport increased immensely.[4] Even the *New York Times* gave front-page coverage to major prize fights and the World Series. With the exception of two columns on page one, the *Times* devoted the entire first thirteen pages of its issue of July 3, 1921, to the Dempsey-Carpentier heavyweight championship fight.

The 1920s brought to the fore a marvelous new generation of sportswriters. Self-labeled the "Gee Whizzers," their enthusiasm for sport may have even exceeded that of the fans. Columnists Grantland Rice, Paul Gallico, Damon Runyan, Ring Lardner, Westbrook Pegler, Heywood Broun, Allison Danzig, Arch Ward, and many others wrote daily paeans to the feats of the athletes. Grantland Rice, the "dean" of the sports reporters, had a gift for writing verse a cut above the popular commercial jingles of the day. Youngsters memorized his lines, coaches used them to inspire their teams, and moralists found in them reassurance of the ethical qualities of sport. His most famous: "When the one Great Scorer comes to write against your name he marks—not that you won or lost—but how you played the game." After Knute Rockne's 1924 Notre Dame backfield, assisted by the "seven mules," defeated powerful Army, Rice composed the best-known opening lines in sportswriting history. He wrote: "Outlined against a blue-grey October sky, the Four Horsemen rode again. In dramatic lore they are known as Famine, Pestilence, Destruction, and Death. These are only aliases. Their real names are Stuhldreher, Miller, Crowley, and Layden."[5] Sportswriters frequently dispensed on-the-spot immortality to athletes. Even the race horse, Man O'War, was immortal; he was "the horse of eternity."

Rice and his colleagues released future sportswriters from the obligation to report sports as "hard" news. The sports page itself became a source of entertainment. Thus sportswriters exercised their imaginations freely and

[4]For content analyses that demonstrate the increased coverage of sport compared to other news, see Robert S. Lynd and Helen Merrell Lynd, *Middletown: A Study in Modern American Culture* (New York: Harcourt, Brace & World, 1929), p. 473; Howard J. Savage et al., *American College Athletics* (New York: Carnegie Foundation for the Advancement of Teaching, 1929), pp. 267–72.

[5]New York *Herald Tribune*, October 19, 1924. See Grantland Rice, *The Tumult and the Shouting: My Life in Sport* (New York: A.S. Barnes, 1954).

embellished the games they covered with Biblical and classical allusions. David versus Goliath was a favorite Biblical allusion. They employed endless similes from warfare, natural disasters, and the assembly line. Despite the exaggeration and the looseness of their figures of speech, their style possessed a kind of perverse honesty. For it often subjected sports to subtle mockery and tongue-in-cheek humor.

A Crisis in Baseball

Baseball's first problem in attracting fans was to restore its image of moral incorruptibility. In September of 1920 a shocking revelation rocked the country: the 1919 World Series had been fixed. The worst team scandal in the history of American sport, soon labelled the "Black Sox Scandal," crowded the "Red Scare" and every other major story off the front pages of the nation's newspapers. Amercans were incredulous. According to baseball legend, a small boy approached "Shoeless Joe" Jackson, one of the alleged conspirators and a star outfielder with the Chicago White Sox. "Say it ain't so, Joe," begged the lad as tears welled from his eyes. "I'm afraid it is, son," Jackson responded. The hurt cut deeply. Boston newsboys condemned the "murderous blow" to the national pastime by the "Benedict Arnolds of baseball." In Joliet, Illinois, an angry fan charged Buck Herzog with being "one of those crooked Chicago ball players." A fight erupted, and Herzog was stabbed, even though he was a member of the Chicago Cubs rather than the White Sox. Sensitive Nelson Algren, then a lad on Chicago's South Side, became disillusioned. "Everybody's out for The Buck," he later concluded, "even the big leaguers." A character in F. Scott Fitzgerald's *The Great Gatsby* reflected; "It never occurred to me that one man could start to play with the faith of fifty million people...."[6]

In retrospect, the scandal of 1919 is not so surprising. Wagering on baseball matches had been commonplace since the middle of the nineteenth century. Baseball pools existed nearly everywhere. By purchasing a pool ticket for as little as ten cents, a person could win cash for correctly picking the team that won the most games, scored the most runs, and so forth in a given week. Newspapers cooperated with pool managers by publishing the odds on games and providing weekly totals of wins, hits, and runs. While pools mounted to thousands of dollars weekly, these sums probably paled in comparison to the larger wagering handled by professional gamblers.

Moreover, many baseball owners, managers, and players had rather intimate links with gamblers and other underworld figures. John J. McGraw, the longtime manager of the New York Giants, for instance,

[6]Quotations from Harold Seymour, *Baseball: The Golden Age* (New York: Oxford University Press, 1971), p. 278. For the scandal also see Eliot Asinoff, *Eight Men Out: The Black Sox and the 1919 World Series* (New York: Holt, Rinehart, and Winston, 1963), David Quentin Voigt, *American Baseball: From the Commissioner to Continental Expansion* (Norman: University of Oklahoma Press, 1970); and Lee Lowenfish/Tony Lupien, *The Imperfect Diamond: The Story of Baseball's Reserve System and the Men Who Fought to Change It* (New York: Stein and Day, 1980), Part III.

frequently consorted with known gamblers, owned part interest in two race tracks, and loved to play the horses. Apparently Hal Chase, a star first baseman for several big-league clubs, was a "full-fledged fixer and gambler." Most big-league players, including Ty Cobb, did not hesitate to wager upon themselves or their teams. Yet the ruling body of baseball from 1903 to 1921, the National Commission, probably from fear of libel suits, loss of valuable property, and adverse publicity, attempted to "cover up" all reports connecting baseball with gambling and game "fixing." Had it not been for an enterprising sportswriter, Hugh Fullerton, the 1919 Black Sox scandal would have also remained a mere rumor.

Later evidence revealed that eight Chicago players had taken money from gamblers to fix the 1919 World Series. Apparently to protect his investment in the accused players, Charles A. Comiskey, owner of the White Sox, initially tried to "contain" the rumors of a fix. But eventually seven of the eight admitted to a grand jury they had received sums varying from $5,000 to $10,000—figures that exceeded the annual salaries of most of the accused—to throw the series to Cincinnati. Somehow, however, the grand jury records disappeared before the trial. (Later at a trial in which Joe Jackson sued Comiskey for back pay, the player confessions "mysteriously" reappeared—in the possession of Comiskey's attorney!)

At the trial held in 1921, all of the players repudiated their earlier confessions, leaving the testimony of Bill Maharg, a professional gambler, as the only substantial evidence against them. After a few hours of deliberation, the jury acquitted all the players plus two gamblers. The spectators in the courtroom roared their approval, and the jurymen and players retired to the local restaurant to celebrate. But the joy of the players was short-lived, for Judge Kenesaw Mountain Landis, the newly appointed Commissioner of Baseball, banished them from Organized Baseball for life. The players had become the scapegoats of a big-league effort to project a new moral image.

While the scandal of 1919 was a major reason for the reorganization of major-league baseball, discontent with the National Commission and the power of Ban Johnson, imperious president of the American League, had been building for several years. The Commission had become almost impotent, and Johnson had, over the years, incurred the wrath of several powerful owners. The new National Agreement of 1921 gave sweeping powers to a single man to head all of Organized Baseball. The owners extended to the Commissioner the power to investigate anything "suspected" of being "detrimental to the best interests of the national game." If he determined that leagues, club owners, or players had taken actions harmful to the sport, he was given the authority to suspend, fine, or banish guilty parties. In their eagerness to improve the image of baseball and bring a semblance of order to the game, the owners even agreed to waive their rights to take disputes between themselves or with the Commissioner to the civil courts. The Agreement of 1921 established the model for the governmental structures of professional football and basketball in the post-World War II era. By establishing a "czar" to censor movies in 1922, the movie industry also followed the example of baseball.

In the wake of the Black Sox scandal, "Czar" Landis brought to baseball what Calvin Coolidge would shortly bring to national politics after the revelation of the Teapot Dome scandal. Both men projected an image of staunch integrity, a "puritanism" in the midst of the moral excesses of the 1920s. With a flair for the theatrical that he had revealed as a federal judge, Landis promised an "untiring effort" to rid baseball of gamblers and gambling. "If I catch any crook in baseball," Landis pledged, "the rest of his life is going to be a hot one."[7] His very appearance instilled confidence in his fearless rectitude. Unlike the pudgy, well-fed magnates, Landis was thin, almost emaciated. With a craggy face topped by long, shaggy, unkempt hair, he looked like Andrew Jackson, one of his heroes. Like Jackson, Landis had a gift for using his imposing appearance and his controlled temper to dominate those who confronted him.

Landis wasted little time in trying to alter the image of Organized Baseball. He hired detectives to ferret out alleged wrongdoings and arbitrarily banished more than a dozen players from the game for life. Apparently his campaign was successful, for within a few years, rumors of collusion between gamblers and players almost disappeared. Even the owners did not escape the vigilance of Landis. He ordered Charles A. Stoneham, owner of the New York Giants, and John J. McGraw, Giant manager, to divest themselves of their stock in race tracks located in Cuba and New York. Yet during a reign which lasted until 1944, Landis treated the questionable actions of the owners far more gingerly than those of the players. He rarely interfered with trades between clubs or in their internal affairs. Despite his personal opposition to the "farm system," he took only limited steps to curb its growth. His power over the magnates was far from complete, for if he antagonized enough owners, he jeopardized his position. Nonetheless, upon the death of Landis in 1944, the barons of baseball quickly reduced the power of the commissioner's office. By comparison, Landis' successors were merely "ceremonial" commissioners.

While Landis gave baseball a new image of integrity, the United States Supreme court furnished its legal salvation. All of the Federal League clubs of the 1913–1915 era except Baltimore had dropped their antitrust suits against the major leagues. Having received no remuneration from the 1916 peace settlement, Baltimore continued its court action. Justice Oliver Wendell Holmes, Jr., speaking for a unanimous court in 1922, declared that professional baseball games did not constitute a "trade or commerce in the commonly-accepted use of the words." In a rather tortuous definition of terms, Holmes reasoned that the "personal effort" of ball players was "not related to production" and therefore could not be involved in commerce. Nor was interstate movement essential to their activity, for the movement of ball players across state lines was simply "incidental" to their playing ball.[8] Whatever the merits of the legal justification of professional baseball's exemption from the antitrust laws, the decision provided a legal umbrella for the agreements upon which the professional baseball cartel rested.

[7]Quoted in Seymour, *Baseball*, p. 323.
[8]Federal Base Ball Club of Baltimore, Inc. v. National League of Professional B.B. Clubs and American League of Professional B.B. Clubs, 259 U.S. 200, 42 Supreme Court 465.

At the same time that baseball sought to establish an image of moral purity and received a new legal foundation from the Supreme Court, it took steps to make the game more interesting to the spectator. By introducing the "jack rabbit" baseball, using more balls per game, and outlawing the "spit" ball, the magnates of baseball reduced the effectiveness of the pitchers and enhanced that of the hitters. In 1910, Organized Baseball replaced the rubber-centered ball with a more resilient, cork-centered ball. Gradually, ball manufacturers introduced other modifications to the ball: tighter-wound yarn, reduction of the protrusions of the seams, and thinner leather for the cover. Prior to the 1920s, the umpires, at the directions of the tight-fisted owners, had tried to limit the total number of balls used per game to two or three. Fans had to return balls hit into the stands. After a few innings of play, the balls often became soft, sometimes lopsided, and soiled with dirt, grass stains, tobacco juice, and licorice. Gradually, more balls were used per game, a trend which accelerated when a pitched ball killed a player in 1920. The "spitter," a widely used pitch in the "deadball" era, behaved much like a knuckleball, dipping and breaking sharply in unpredictable ways as it approached the plate. In 1920, the rules committee banned all pitches that involved the application of foreign substances to the ball. However, existing big-league spitball pitchers were exempted from the ban.

These changes produced astonishing results. The "deadball" era ended, and the "live ball" era began. Batting averages, scoring, and home run totals soared. By 1925 the combined batting averages of the major leagues was forty-five points higher than it had been in 1915. Only four hitters in the first two decades of the century had hit .400 or better; eight batters achieved this distinction in the single decade of the twenties. By 1930, major-league teams averaged scoring three and a half more runs per game than in 1915. But the most remarkable development of all was the quantity of home runs. Major-league totals quadrupled, from 384 homers in 1915 to 1,565 in 1930. Once owners became convinced of the popularity of the "Big Bang" style of play, they frequently moved their fences closer to home plate to produce even more four baggers. The players, observing the large salaries of sluggers such as Babe Ruth, began to use lighter bats, grip the bat at the end of the handle, and take a full swing with a complete follow-through. Aficionados of the old style of play, which featured tight pitching duels, bunts, sacrifices, hit-and-run plays, and steals—"scientific" or "inside" baseball—regarded the Big Bang style as a capitulation to new fans ignorant of the finer traditions and nuances of the sport. It probably was, but the owners cared more about attracting fans to the parks than preserving baseball traditions.

DISPARITIES IN COMPETITION

Presumably equalizing the conditions of the competition between teams would also increase fan interest. If more teams had a viable shot at winning the pennant, no single team would dominate the championships over the

Table 10–1 Disparity of competition as shown by pennants won in order of average population rank[a], National League, 1900–1952

New York	Brook.	Chicago	Pitts.	Phila.	Boston	Cinn.	St. Louis
14							
1951							
1937							
1936							
1933		10					9
1924		1945					
1923		1938					1946
1922	7	1935					1944
1921	1952	1932	6				1943
1917	1949	1929	1927				1942
1913	1947	1918	1925				1934
1912	1941	1910	1909			3	1931
1911	1920	1908	1903	2	2	1940	1930
1905	1916	1907	1902	1950	1948	1939	1928
1904	1900	1906	1901	1915	1914	1919	1926

[a]Based on average population during the period, adjusted for number of baseball teams in the metropolitan area.

SOURCE: Adapted from Roger G. Noll, ed., *Government and the Sports Business* (Washington, D.C.: Brookings Institution, 1974), p. 46.

years and pennant races would be closely fought. Overall attendance should also be higher. The major leagues had long argued that the "reserve clause" in player contracts and the "draft" prevented the domination of the pennant races by a few of the wealthier franchises. Without the right to reserve players, professional baseball argued, wealthier clubs could offer higher salaries to players on other teams and eventually corner the market on the best player talent. In theory, the draft gave each club equal access to new player talent; it negated the potential advantages of superior wealth. But the historical record of baseball made a mockery of both of these arguments.[9]

From the beginning of the century, the clubs located in the largest cities enjoyed better records than those in smaller cities (see Table 10–1). From 1900 to 1952 (when the Boston Braves moved to Milwaukee), the New York Giants, Brooklyn Dodgers, and Chicago Cubs, representative of the two largest metropolitan areas in the National League, won thirty of fifty-two pennants. After 1925, the "Rickey effect" (Branch Rickey's farm system at St. Louis) reduced the close correlation between city size and playing strength. Yet Philadelphia, Boston, and Cincinnati, which ranked

[9]For a rather technical discussion of the economics of baseball, see Lance E. Davis, "Self-Regulation in Baseball, 1909–1971," in Roger Noll, ed., *Government and the Sports Business* (Washington, D.C.: Brookings Institution, 1974), pp. 349–86.

Table 10–2 Disparity of competition as shown by pennants won in order of average population rank[a], American League, 1903–1953

New York	Chicago	Detroit	Phila.	Cleve.	Boston	St. Louis	Wash.
20							
1953							
1952							
1951							
1950							
1949							
1947							
1943							
1942							
1941							
1939							
1938							
1937			**8**				
1936		**7**	1931		**7**		
1932		1945	1930		1946		
1928		1940	1929		1918		
1927		1935	1914		1916		
1926	**3**	1934	1913		1915		**3**
1923	1919	1909	1911	**2**	1912		1933
1922	1917	1908	·1910	1948	1904	**1**	1925
1921	1906	1907	1905	1920	1903	1944	1924

[a]Based on average population during the period, adjusted for the number of baseball teams in the metropolitan area.

SOURCE: Adapted from Roger G. Noll, ed., *Government and the Sports Business* (Washington, D.C.: Brookings Institution, 1974), p. 46.

fifth, sixth, and seventh in average population when adjusted to the number of teams in the metropolitan area, won only seven pennants between them. Until the purchase of the New York Yankees by new owners in 1915, the size of the market area bore little relationship to team success in the American League. But after the Yankees acquired Babe Ruth in 1920, they proceeded to win twenty of the next thirty-two flags. During this same era, Chicago won no pennants, and Cleveland, Boston, and St. Louis won only one each. Through 1980, the combined franchises in New York, Chicago, and Los Angeles won over half of the total flags of the two leagues.

The main cause for the predominant success of the teams in the biggest cities was quite simple. The disparities in population between metropolitan areas produced substantial inequalities in attendance and therefore in incomes. Since the nineteenth century, the owners had tried to offset

205

market size by giving 50 percent of the base admission price to visiting teams. But any revenues collected from seats that exceeded the base price, such as box and reserve seats, went to the home club. As more of the higher-priced seats were added to the stadiums in the twentieth century, the percentage of total gate receipts of the visiting teams declined. In 1892 the visiting teams received about 40 percent of the total revenue, by 1929 their share had declined to 21 percent, and by 1950 to only 14 percent. This disparity of incomes benefited those franchises located in large market areas, giving them additional bargaining strength within the major league cartel and additional revenue for the purchase of superior players.

Neither the draft nor the reserve clause prevented the outright purchase of players, either from another big-league club or a minor-league team. In the pre-1945 era, the annual draft allowed the major-league teams to buy players from the minor leagues for a set sum; however, at any time before the draft date a minor-league club could sell a player for a price in excess of the draft price. In exchange for the draft privilege, the majors agreed to respect the territorial rights and player contracts of minor-league clubs. Obviously, richer teams could opt to purchase superior players before the draft date. The prices paid for drafted players (originally $750) were a constant source of friction between the two layers of professional baseball; at times several of the higher minors exempted themselves entirely from the draft, thereby forcing major-league teams to pay open market prices for all their players, in other words, prices usually higher than the draft price. Since wealthier clubs could afford the higher prices, they usually resisted efforts to force the high minors to participate in the draft.

The history of the New York dynasty vividly reveals the importance of the market area served by the club and the advantages of wealthy, free-spending owners. Before Jacob Ruppert, Jr., a rich brewer, and Tillinghast Huston, a prosperous engineer, purchased the Yankees in 1915, the club had had a mediocre record. The club's performance slowly improved as the owners purchased player talent from the minor-league clubs and other big-league clubs. The big Yankee breakthrough came between 1919 and 1923 when the Boston Red Sox virtually became their farm club. Harry Frazee, a Broadway producer and owner of the Red Sox, always seemed short of money. To obtain liquid capital to finance his Broadway shows, he began to dismantle the powerful Red Sox in 1919. (The Red Sox had won pennants in 1915, 1916, and 1918.) That year, he sold star pitcher Carl Mays to the Yankees for $40,000; the next year he unloaded Babe Ruth to the Yankees for $125,000 (plus a $300,000 loan), a sum twice as high as had ever previously been paid for a player. By 1923, eleven of the twenty-four-man Yankee roster had formerly played with Boston. The hapless Red Sox sank to the American League cellar in 1922; they remained there for eight of the next nine seasons.

Superior financial resources permitted the Yankees to dominate the American League championships. Over the next forty-five years, the Yankees lost the flag only fourteen times. A star player was worth more to the owners of the New York franchise than he was to an owner of a club in a smaller city. Consequently, franchises in low-drawing areas typically sold good players to the Yankees. The incentive for selling was often a matter of survival. The Washington Senators, Philadelphia Athletics, and St. Louis Browns repeatedly unloaded star players to the richer clubs. According to economist James Quirk, from 1920 to 1950, while the Yankees spent $1.6 million for talent, the St. Louis Browns sold a platoon of players for some $2.5 million. Had the Browns not sold these players, they would have lost $1.5 million in revenue.[10]

One franchise, the St. Louis Cardinals, under the direction of their brilliant general manager, Branch Rickey, devised an ingenious method of avoiding expensive player purchases and offsetting some of the advantages enjoyed by the clubs in the larger market areas. Rickey's solution was the farm system. When Rickey joined the Cardinals in 1917, the franchise was poverty-stricken and had for several years been the doormat of the National League. Rickey slowly but methodically started purchasing direct ownership of minor-league clubs; by 1940 the Cardinal system contained thirty-two clubs and 700 players. The Rickey system produced remarkable results. The Cardinals won nine league championships between 1926 and 1946 and took second place six times. Despite having lower attendance marks than four other National League franchises in this era, the Cardinals had larger profits than any other league club. Their profits came mostly from player sales. While not purchasing a single player between 1919 and 1945, the Cardinals, in one year alone, had sixty-five players who were products of their farm system on the rosters of other big-league clubs. Owners of the other clubs long resisted the ownership of minor-league clubs, feeling that the costs exceeded the benefits. But as the success of the Rickey system became evident, they too began to emulate St. Louis.

With the growth of the farm system, the major league franchises rather than the minor leagues assumed the burden of scouting new talent. They then found themselves in direct competition with each other for new players. The Depression and the manpower shortages of World War II delayed the appearance of an all-out bonus war until the postwar era. After the war, teams began to pay unprecedented bonuses to outstanding prospects. The baseball cartel took several ineffectual steps—such as subjecting the "bonus baby" to an unrestricted draft at the end of his first year of play if he was not retained on a major-league club roster—to curb the costs of recruitment. In the 1960s baseball finally developed a draft system somewhat similar to professional football. However, unlike football, a player could refuse to sign with the team which had drafted him, wait six months, have his name returned to the draft pool, and hope to get a better offer from another club. Consequently, superior prospects continued to receive substantial bonuses. Such a system benefited the wealthier clubs, for they could afford to pay the larger bonuses.[11]

[10]As reported by Ray Kennedy and Nancy Williamson, "Money: The Monster Threatening Sports," *Sports Illustrated*, 49 (July 1978), 80. George Steinbrenner, the free-spending owner of the Yankees in the 1970s, made the point succinctly. "You measure the value of a ballplayer by how many fannies he puts in the seats. Reggie Jackson is worth 500,000 fannies in New York and 65,000 fannies in Baltimore."

[11]Historically, a few wealthy clubs have been able to block changes in the rules of the baseball cartel that they perceived as against their interests. As of 1978, the American League required a three-fourths and the National League a unanimous vote for substantive rule changes.

Despite the establishment of a commissioner's office, the introduction of the Big Bang style of play, and ostensible efforts to equalize competition on the playing field, evidence suggests that professional baseball declined in popularity in comparison to other forms of leisure activity. True, in the 1920s professional baseball (including the minor leagues) attracted more fans than any other single sport, and millions followed the game in the newspapers and on the radio. But the total attendance failed to keep pace with the growth of the population. In the eleven cities which hosted major-league teams, the population climbed 20.5 percent in the twenties while attendance at ball games grew by only 11.5 percent. The same trend appears to be valid for the minor leagues; the total number of professional leagues remained under the figures attained in the pre-World War I era. By contrast, attendance at motion picture theaters in the 1925-1930 era was 75 percent greater than during the preceding five-year period. While an estimated twenty million fans attended all professional baseball games in 1930, between 100 and 115 million patrons attended the movies each week.[12]

Professional baseball suffered heavily from the Great Depression and World War II. Attendance did not fully recover until 1946; it then enjoyed a temporary boom until 1949 when it entered another "famine era." There were great players aplenty in the thirties and forties—Hank Greenburg, Ted Williams, Joe DiMaggio, and Stan Musial, to name a few— but none had the magic of Babe Ruth. The introduction of night baseball in the late 1930s failed to produce immediate increases in attendance. Only a few clubs prospered. The "have-not" franchises promoted a profit-sharing scheme, but it was voted down by the wealthier clubs. "I found out a long time ago that there is no charity in baseball," Jacob Ruppert, owner of the Yankees, explained, "and that every club owner must make his own fight for existence."[13] The magnates did take effective action in reducing player salaries. Salaries had risen from an average of about $5,000 in 1923 to about $7,000 in 1933; by 1936 the average had fallen to $4,500. Wide disparities existed between franchises. The payroll of the Yankees, for instance, was almost five times that of the lowly St. Louis Browns.

In the face of the great economic crisis of the 1930s, professional baseball experimented with new ways to recoup lost fan support. Beginning in 1933 the major leagues scheduled an annual All-Star game between the best players of each league. Larry MacPhail, general manager of the Cincinnati Reds, daringly departed from some of the staid traditions of baseball. At Cincinnati, MacPhail introduced night baseball (1935), red uniforms, cigarette girls in satin pants, and usherettes. Such innovations led a sportswriter to predict that, when MacPhail arrived in Brooklyn in

---

[12]Steiner, *Americans at Play*, pp. 84, 86, 109–10; John R. Tunis, "Changing Trends in Sport," *Harper's Monthly Magazine*, 70 (December 1934), 80. There is also evidence that participation in amateur and semiprofessional baseball declined in the twenties. See the claim of the National Amateur Athletic Federation in Alexander J. Young, Jr., "The Rejuvenation of Major League Baseball in the Twenties," *Canadian Journal of the History of Sport and Physical Education*, 3 (May 1972), 24.

[13]Voigt, *American Baseball*, p. 251.

1937, fans would be treated to the spectacle of a "merry-go-round in center field of Flatbush." MacPhail's promotional gimmicks, however, paled beside those of Bill Veeck, who, in the post-World War II era, once employed a midget as a pinch hitter.

MacPhail, more than any other single person, broke down big-league resistence to radio broadcasts of games. Although in the 1920s the Chicago Cubs had permitted all of the club's games to be broadcast and the club had experienced a sharp increase in attendance, most clubs feared that radio broadcasts would reduce attendance. In 1934 the Yankees, Giants, and Dodgers, all located in New York, even signed a formal ban on the broadcasts of their games. But as radio stations and networks discovered that they could sell commercials during the broadcasts (and thus pay clubs for broadcast privileges) resistence began to weaken. When MacPhail came to Brooklyn as a general manager he refused to renew the ban on baseball broadcasts in New York; he sold the rights to Dodger games for $70,000. Consequently, the Yankees and Giants felt compelled to permit the broadcasts of their games as well. Increased income from radio, especially in the larger market areas, offset some of the loss in gate receipts. By 1950 each club averaged $210,000 from broadcast rights.[14]

FOOTBALL GOES AFTER THE FANS

Attendance at college football games grew at a much faster pace than the population. Between 1921 and 1930, attendance at all college games doubled and gate receipts tripled. Football's relative popularity shifted decidedly from the East to the Middle and Far West; total receipts increased three and a half times in the Middle and Far West. Most of the crowds flocked to the games of only a few institutions; of the nearly 400 colleges playing football in 1930, forty of them drew about 60 percent of all of the fans. College football also weathered the Great Depression of the 1930s far better than professional baseball. In the early 1930s, attendance fell and several colleges dropped the sport, but estimates in 1937 placed total fandom at twenty million, a figure twice as high as that of 1930. Apparently college football attracted income groups that weathered the Depression more successfully than did baseball fans.[15]

The new popularity of college football stemmed in part from its capacity to generate potent symbols. While retaining the loyalty of a burgeoning alumni, college teams often evoked symbols that transcended the college itself. Intercollegiate games frequently represented to fans symbolic battles for superiority between states and regions, sometimes even ethnic groups,

[14]Richard C. Crepeau, *Baseball: America's Diamond Mind, 1919–1941* (Orlando: University Presses of Florida, 1980), pp. 112–13; Ira Horowitz, "Sports Broadcasting," in Noll, ed., *Government and the Sports Business,* p. 387.

[15]See Steiner, *Americans at Play,* pp. 86–94; "King Football Answers the Depression," *Literary Digest,* 116 (September 16, 1933), 24; John R. Tunis, "The Slump in Football Common," *Atlantic Monthly,* 150 (December 1932), 679–82; "20,000,000 Saw College Games as Football Scaled New Heights," *New York Times,* December 26, 1937.

religions, and ideologies. Citizens in states without a singularly or conspicuously significant history, great civic monuments, or remarkable physical scenery might find in a winning state university football team a source of indisputable state pride. Likewise, contests involving teams from the South versus the West, the Middle East versus the East, and so on, might engender regional pride. World War I supplied new, "built-in" cheering sections for the two service academies. Those who had worn khakis in the war supported Army; bell-bottoms made one a Navy rooter. Thus the annual Army-Navy game became a truly national affair, one that eventually generated more national interest than the classic Yale-Harvard contests.

No team in the 1920s and 1930s exceeded the "Fighting Irish" of Notre Dame in attaining a national following and fierce fan support. The small Catholic boys' school at South Bend, Indiana, first blazed into the sports headlines in 1913 when the passing combination of Gus Dorais and Knute Rockne brought Army to its knees. In the twenties, Catholics everywhere, even those who had never been near a college (the "subway alumni") and regardless of their ethnic origins, became rabid partisans of the Irish. When Notre Dame met Army in their annual tilt in New York, the passions of the city's large ethnic population reached a fever pitch. "New York was never before, or since, so sweetly gay and electric as when Rock brought his boys to town," Paul Gallico wrote, "the city was wild with excitement...."[16] The Notre Dame football team became a symbolic rallying point for the nation's Roman Catholic population. Catholics, a minority within a predominantly Protestant culture, found in the success of the Irish an immensely powerful source of self-pride.

As in the case of professional baseball, college football took steps to increase the interest of spectators in the sport. In the first place, the colleges went on a stadium-building binge. Huge stadiums of concrete and steel reared above the landscape from Columbus, Ohio to Los Angeles, California. Only one college field had a seating capacity of 70,000 in 1920; seven had in excess of that capacity in 1930. (By comparison, only two major-league baseball parks could seat 70,000 fans in 1930.)[17] Then the colleges expanded their ballyhoo; they set up publicity bureaus to hawk the prowess of their teams, potential All-American players, and the wisdom of their head coaches. The colleges also scheduled more intersectional and postseason games with teams they hoped would increase their "drawing power." The 1924 Notre Dame team traveled over 10,500 miles to play teams like Army, Princeton, George Tech, Nebraska, and Stanford. Notre Dame was exceptional for its peripatetic ways, but all major colleges attempted to schedule at least one big intersectional game per season. In the 1930s, annual bowl games became a significant new force in intersectional rivalries. The Tournament of Roses, or Rose Bowl, traces its origins back to 1902 (though with a lapse in play until 1916); in the thirties boosters in Southern cities hoped to attract tourists and outside invest-

---

[16]Paul Gallico, *The Golden People* (Garden City, New York: Doubleday, 1965), p. 142.
[17]Steiner, *Americans at Play*, p. 91.

ments by initiating the Orange Bowl in 1935, the Sun Bowl in 1936, the Sugar Bowl in 1937, and the Cotton Bowl in 1937.

Finally, the colleges tried to offer the fan a more exciting style of play. Like for baseball, the rulemakers attempted to shift the balance of strength from the defense to the offense. In 1927 the colleges moved the goal post ten yards in back of the goal line, thereby reducing the likelihood of field goals and encouraging efforts to score touchdowns. While the forward pass had been legalized in 1906, it had been surrounded by so many restrictions and potential penalties that teams rarely attempted to employ it. Gradually the rules were liberalized, though the last major restriction—the requirement that a forward pass must be made from at least five yards behind the scrimmage line—was not deleted until 1945. In 1912 the rulemakers reduced the circumference of the ball from 27 inches to 23 inches and in 1934 to 21½ inches. Until the 1912 change, passers attempted to throw the ball end-over-end to receivers; the 1912 rule change encouraged the use of the spiral pass which could be thrown more accurately and longer distances.[18] In the twenties the pass-run option helped open up the game for more offensive action; it also enabled coaches to design more effective running formations. Speed, agility, and skill seemed, at least to some degree, to replace sheer brawn as requirements for team success.

For students of the sport, college football offered a fascinating if somewhat bewildering variety of offensive formations and plays. Until 1940 most coaches employed some variation of the single wing, double wing, or Notre Dame box. All of these formations featured direct "hikes" from the center to the ball carrier (or passer) who stood several yards behind the line of scrimmage. The other backs (including the quarterback) blocked for the running back. Unlike the earlier mass formations which concentrated the attack somewhere near the center of the line, these three formations usually involved the ball carrier sweeping outside the tackles or ends. When successful, the plays could result in long gains. "There are no longer any distinctive systems in football," wrote Fielding H. Yost, Michigan Athletic Director and former coach, on the eve of the 1940 season. "Nobody sees a balanced line any more except at Notre Dame, and even some Rockne-trained coaches are getting away from it. There is only one formation that's any good and it's the single wing."[19] That very year, however, Clark Shaughnessey at Stanford introduced the "modern" T formation which rapidly replaced the single wing in popularity. All of the formations since then, be it the split T, pro set, power I, wishbone, or veer, essentially represent variations of the T.[20]

[18]John McCallum and Charles H. Pearson, *College Football U.S.A., 1869–1971* (New York: National Football Foundation, 1971), pp. 246–50.
[19]Quoted in Ron Fimrite, "A Melding of Men All Suited to a T," *Sports Illustrated,* 47 (September 5, 1977), 92.
[20]While most authorities credit Shaughnessey with the "invention" of the modern T, George Halas, longtime owner-coach of the Chicago Bears, claimed Ralph Jones, as Bear coach in 1930, introduced a "man-in-motion" play with a balanced line and backfield. See Halas with Gwen Morgan and Arthur Veysey, *Halas by Halas* (New York: McGraw-Hill, 1979), pp. 136–45, 199–200.

In baseball, heroes usually sprang from the ranks of the players, but in intercollegiate football it was often the head coaches who won public renown. While football coaches like Amos Alonzo Stagg of the University of Chicago created virtual dynasties, players appeared on the field of play only three or four years and then sank into obscurity. In football, perhaps more than any other sport, coaches were the key to success or failure. To win consistently, teams with even superior talent required expert coaching. A slight change in the angle of a block, for instance, might spell the difference between victory or defeat. Under the leadership of a head coach, a staff of experts at the "big-time" football schools instructed linesmen, ends, and backs in the intricacies of their positions. Some colleges used scouts, or "spies," a practice still frowned upon by many observers as being morally suspect, to observe the games of future opponents. On the basis of information gathered by the scouts plus an intimate knowledge of his own personnel, the coach carefully designed a preplanned strategy for accomplishing victory. Coaches tried to field teams that functioned like a precisioned, well-coordinated machine, with interchangeable parts and actions honed to the coach's design. Few private business firms could claim a more rational system for achieving their goals. Paradoxically, while big-time college football achieved a remarkable degree of rationalization in the 1920s and 1930s, curious remnants of the player-centered era remained. For example, coaches could not "legally" transmit signals from the sidelines or send substitutes into the game with plays. Obviously, the custodians of college football were reluctant to drop all pretenses of player-centeredness in the sport.

Coaches who succeeded in winning received handsome rewards. Almost all college head coaches received a higher salary than the professors, and in some cases their salaries equalled or surpassed the college president's. According to a nationwide study made in 1929 by the Carnegie Commission, full professors averaged a salary of $5,158 annually; head football coaches received an average annual salary of $6,107. On the other hand, a losing head coach could expect a short tenure. The median tenure of all head coaches, according to the Carnegie study, was only three years.[21]

In the 1920 to 1950 era, such coaches as Knute Rockne of Notre Dame, Glenn S. "Pop" Warner of Pittsburgh, Stanford, and Temple, Robert Zuppke of Illinois, and Dana X. Bible of Texas A & M, Nebraska, and Texas won popular followings that often exceeded that of their star players. Rockne outdistanced all rivals in capturing the public imagination. Born in Norway, Rockne as a boy had immigrated with his family to Chicago. At the age of twenty-two, he "went down to South Bend with a suitcase and $1,000 feeling the strangeness of being a lone Norse-Protestant invader of a Catholic stronghold."[22] (Later Rockne converted to Catholicism.) At Notre Dame he compiled an outstanding academic record and won certain fame by being the recipient of the passes thrown by Gus

[21]Savage et al., *American College Athletics*, pp. 171–72.
[22]Quoted in Edwin Pope, *Football's Greatest Coaches* (Atlanta, Ga.: Tupper and Love, 1955), p. 195. On Rockne see also Coles Phinizy, "We Know of Knute, Yet Know Him Not," *Sports Illustrated*, 51 (September 10, 1979), 98–112.

Dorais which led to the famous Notre Dame upset of Army in 1913. After graduation, he remained at Notre Dame as a chemistry assistant and assistant football coach. In 1918, at the age of thirty, he landed the head coaching job at Notre Dame.

Rockne's fame stemmed from both his success on the field and his colorful personality. Sending his team against the best elevens from coast to coast, in thirteen years of coaching he compiled an enviable record of 105 victories, twelve defeats, and five ties. His team enjoyed five unbeaten and untied seasons. Rockne was as much a master of psychology as he was of football strategy. Both the players and the press loved him for his quick wit, humor, sarcasm, and ability to evoke pathos. While trailing Army by a touchdown in 1928, Rockne allegedly made the most memorable half-time speech in football history. He told of George Gipp, famed Notre Dame halfback, who had tragically died from pneumonia at the end of the 1920 season. Gipp instructed Rockne on his death bed: "When things are wrong and the breaks are beating the boys, tell them to go in there with all they've got and win one just for the Gipper."[23] In the second half, the Irish responded with two touchdowns, to win 12–6. In 1940 Warner Brothers immortalized the story in the popular film *Knute Rockne—All American,* in which Pat O'Brien played Rockne and Ronald Reagan played the Gipper. Rockne could be caustically hilarious. He reputedly told linemen: "The only qualification for a lineman is to be big and dumb." Then turning to the backs, he said: "To be a back, you only have to be dumb." He was always quotable, gregarious, and willing to hoist a few drinks with the sports scribblers. He won such acclaim that he had to hire a personal agent to answer his mail and handle his commercial endorsements. When Rockne died in a plane crash in 1931 he had just signed as sales promotion manager for Studebaker and had been offered $50,000 to play the coach in RKO's *Good News* movie.

INTERCOLLEGIATE CONTROVERSIES

Regardless of the skills of coaches, fielding winning teams consistently required the recruitment of high-quality athletes. As the decade of the 1920s began, many colleges recruited only in a haphazard fashion if at all. Even at such football powers as Notre Dame, perhaps half or more of the varsity squad obtained their positions simply by trying out for the team. Moreover, the open recruitment of football players violated the amateur code to which, in principle, the colleges universally adhered. Nonetheless, as the pressures to win became more intense, the temptation to recruit and even subsidize players became harder to resist. According to the Carnegie study of 1929, almost every major football power had intensive, highly organized recruiting systems. The colleges sent out thousands of letters to prospective athletes, invited some of them to campus for visits, and

---

[23]Pope, *Football's Greatest Coaches*, pp. 189, 200. There are several versions of the George Gipp story. See esp. "Scorecard," *Sports Illustrated*, 54 (January 12, 1981), 7.

promised the better ones some sort of subsidy. However, unlike the post-1950 era, coaches did not travel about the country visiting high school athletes. To convince the player to attend their school rather than another, they relied mostly upon the college's alumni, the reputation of the college in football, and visits by the athlete to the college campus.

The ingenious and devious methods employed to subsidize athletes were imaginative. Athletes, if they met the scholastic requirements of the college, thus technically qualified for scholarships. Furthermore, the athletic departments offered a wide variety of job opportunities to the "needy" athletes. They might nominally work within the department dispensing towels, giving rubdowns, supervising intramural sports, or pushing a broom. Numerous well-paying jobs, both on and off campus, seemed especially suited for athletes. Colleges in the Southeastern and Southwestern conferences avoided hypocrisy simply by granting direct "athletic scholarships." In a stunning understatement the Carnegie Commission report concluded: "Apparently the ethical bearing of intercollegiate football contests and their scholastic aspects are of secondary importance to the winning of victories and financial success."[24]

The commercialization, professionalization, and hypocrisy endemic to "big-time" college football, all signifying the ascendancy of the fan, evoked a running debate throughout the interwar years. One school of naive critics simply called for the voluntary compliance of the football schools to amateur principles. Consistent with this position, the National Collegiate Athletic Association (NCAA) relied entirely upon moral persuasion to discipline its membership. In contrast to the NCAA, the Western Athletic Conference (Big Ten), known for its self-proclaimed adherence to the amateur code, enjoyed the power to expel offending schools from the Conference. In 1922 the Conference, following the example of major-league baseball, created the position of Commissioner of Athletics, a post held by Major John L. Griffith until 1944. Yet Griffith's powers were mostly nominal, not comparable to those of Landis. Despite patent evidence of repeated violations of conference rules, the Big Ten did not bar a single member school from playing football in the 1920–1950 era.[25] After documenting a convincing case for the impossibility of devising a workable, voluntary system of compliance, the Carnegie Report of 1929 illogically called for college presidents and faculties to lead a crusade for institutional self-restraint.

[24]Savage et al., *American College Athletics*, p. 298. The Carnegie survey which took three and a half years to complete was based on visits to and the accumulation of data from 130 colleges and secondary schools. It aroused a national furor and remains the most thorough inquiry ever conducted of intercollegiate athletics.

[25]In 1929 the conference dropped Iowa for, among other "abuses," the operation of an alumni "slush fund" for athletes. But after minor reforms, the conference readmitted the university. According to the Carnegie Report, at least seven other conference schools were guilty of similar "offenses." See Savage et al., *American College Athletics*, p. 229; Howard Roberts, *The Big Nine: The Story of Football in the Western Conference* (New York: G.P. Putnam's Sons, 1948); Adryn Lowell Sponberg, "The Evolution of Athletic Subsidization in the Intercollegiate Conference of Faculty Representatives (Big Ten)" (unpublished Ph.D. dissertation, University of Michigan, 1968). For the Big Eight Conference see "What Football Players Are Earning This Fall," *Literary Digest*, 107 (Nov. 15, 1930), 28.

College presidents and faculties were in a weak position to obtain compliance with amateurism, even had they desired to do so. To begin with, many of the colleges had a large financial stake in football. They owed huge sums of money for athletic plants, and football generated revenue for other varsity sports. Proponents of "big-time" football often claimed that it supported intramural programs for the students as well, but only meager sums actually went into intramurals. A winning team kept the alumni happy and college authorities believed that it encouraged alumni contributions. In the case of state universities a winning team supposedly assured generous appropriations from the state legislatures. A winning team also assisted in the recruitment of students. Finally, local merchants benefited immensely from the "big game" weekends. Henry S. Pritchett, who wrote the preface to the Carnegie Report of 1929 ought to have remembered what he had written in 1911. "Party politics," he then wrote, "have also played their part in the state institutions in the dismissal of men, notably of presidents who have stood...against the popular cry for...winning athletic teams."[26] The same potential power accrued to those with a stake in the football programs of private colleges. As Blair Cherry, head football coach of the University of Texas, bluntly put it: "In the final analysis the public, not the colleges runs college football."[27]

A second school of critics recognized the power of those who had an enormous emotional or economic investment in intercollegiate football. But to them, football represented a serious misplacement of values and they demanded its complete abolition. Robert Maynard Hutchins, appointed president of the University of Chicago in 1929, led this school of critics. Hutchins rejected two major premises of American educational thought: the notion that education ought to be character-building and the pragmatic notion that truths were proximate and to be found through the interaction of speculation and experience. Instead Hutchins believed in a transcendental world of ultimate truths; the sole function of the university should be the development of the intellect for the perception of these higher truths. He thus rejected one of the principal, time-honored arguments for football, its "character-building" function. To Hutchins, corruption was inevitable and unavoidable in "big-time" football. In 1939 he persuaded the trustees of the University of Chicago to abolish the sport.[28] This dramatic and highly publicized move had, however, little impact on the other colleges. Only those schools suffering from disastrous financial losses from football followed Chicago's example.

[26]Henry S. Pritchett, "Progress of the State Universities," *Annual Report of the Carnegie Foundation for the Advancement of Teaching*, 6 (1911), p. 108.

[27]Blair Cherry, "Why I Quit Coaching," in Harry T. Paxton, ed., *Sport U.S.A.: The Best From the Saturday Evening Post* (New York: Thomas Nelson & Sons, 1961), p. 405.

[28]See Kooman Boycheff, "Intercollegiate Athletics and Physical Education at the University of Chicago, 1892–1952" (unpublished Ph.D. dissertation, University of Michigan, 1954); John M. Hutchins, "Gate Receipts and Glory," *Saturday Evening Post*, 211 (December 3, 1938), 23; Hal A. Lawson and Alan G. Ingham, "Conflicting Ideologies Concerning the University and Intercollegiate Athletics: Harper and Hutchins at Chicago, 1892–1940," *Journal of Sport History*, 7 (Winter 1980), 37–67.

11

The Individual Sports
Go Public, 1920-1950

Walter Hagan, the first professional hero of golf,
sipping from one of the many gold cups he won
during his thirty-year career.

The first United States tennis championship tournament was more of a social event than an athletic contest. Opening on August 31, 1881, at the posh Casino Club in Newport, Rhode Island, it resembled a pleasant, rather casual Sunday afternoon lawn party. A group of less than fifty spectators, representing wealthy vacationers who spent their summers in their magnificent stone "cottages," milled around the court. The gentlemen stood while the ladies sat on folding chairs or camp stools. The ladies wore ankle-length petticoats and carried parasols to protect their delicate skin from the sun; the gentlemen wore white flannels, striped jackets, and straw bowlers. The players likewise sported white flannels, long-sleeved shirts, and neckties. They played by the rules established by the All-England Croquet and Lawn Tennis Club, Wimbledon, in 1877. Richard D. Sears, a slight, bespectacled lad of nineteen, conquered a field of twenty-two players, all of whom were from the eastern coast of the United States. Except as a minor social occasion of the Newport "summer crowd," the press ignored the tournament.

Forty-five years later, on September 16, 1926, the domination of William T. "Big Bill" Tilden over the world of tennis came to an end. During the quarterfinals of the national championships at the West Side Tennis Club, Forest Hills, New York, Tilden's six-year reign crumpled before the attack of a Frenchman, Henri Cochet, in five sets at 6–8, 6–1, 6–3, 1–6, 8–6. The spectators repeatedly broke into wild cheers in the final set. Trailing at 1–4, Tilden appeared to be on the verge of one of his "patented" comebacks. Serving with smashing force and volleying crisply at the net, the crowd roared with applause at each of Tilden's winning shots. He pulled even at 4–4. "The champion, it was agreed, was still the champion of old, capable of lifting his game in an emergency to unassailable heights," according to one reporter. Both men held service for three games to give Tilden a 6–5 lead. Then the debacle came. Tilden won only four points in the last three games, conceding the final set 8–6. "Tilden, the invincible, whose magic with a racquet confounded the greatest players of the world and made America supreme in tennis, at last...relinquished his scepter."[1]

In the forty-five years separating the victory of Sears at Newport and Cochet's dramatic upset of Tilden, tennis experienced a remarkable transformation. In the first instance, a small cadre of wealthy summer vacationers had casually followed the action on the court. By 1926, over

[1] For the quotations see Allison Danzig and Peter Brandwein, eds., *The Greatest Sport Stories from The New York Times* (New York: A. S. Barnes, 1951), pp. 256, 255.

9,000 spectators were seated in a steel and concrete stadium, avidly watching each stroke. All over the world the metropolitan daily newspapers reported the upset in blazing headlines. The quality of play had improved sharply. The players at Newport had relied upon soft, looping shots; the serve had functioned merely to put the ball into play. Both Tilden and Cochet could hit a variety of bewildering serves; they could impart spins causing the ball to break to the right or left or hit flat, straight serves at over ninety miles an hour. From either the forehand or backhand side, they could hit deep, hard drives or they might hit deft chops or drop shots. Tilden usually preferred to play from the baseline, but during his futile effort to make a comeback against Cochet, he repeatedly went to the net, catching the ball in the air for "put-aways." For Sears tennis had been an avocation, but for Tilden and Cochet (though both were technically amateurs) tennis was a full-time endeavor. They played or practiced nearly every day. Tennis was an international sport that featured both men and women's competition. Top-flight players might travel to Italy, France, Germany, England, the United States, and Australia to play in tournaments. In short, tennis, like amateur track and field and golf, "went public." And, like professional baseball and college football, the spectator increasingly became the ultimate determinant of the character of the sport.

TENNIS GOES PUBLIC

Before 1920, tennis showed little sign of going public. Even as a game of the super-rich played on estates and in exclusive clubs, the sport made little headway. Tennis projected a delicate and an effeminate image. The term "lawn tennis" raised visions of prissy dudes in white flannels, pitter-pattering a ball across a net at Newport, Bar Harbor, or Seabright with lady friends. When several Harvard men "deserted" rowing for tennis in 1878, a *Harvard Crimson* editorial writer heaped scorn upon them. "Is it not a pity that serious athletes should be set aside by able-bodied men for a game that is at best intended for a seaside pastime?" he asked. "The game is well enough for lazy or *weak* men, but men who have rowed or taken part in a nobler sport should blush to be seen playing Lawn Tennis."[2] Paul Gallico recalled that during his childhood in New York in the early twentieth century "it was worth your life to be caught anywhere east of Lexington Avenue carrying a tennis racquet under your arm." Invariably a player would be greeted by boys who hooted in falsetto voices: "Deuce, darling," or "Forty–love, dear."[3] Despite such verbal abuse, a few brave men continued to play the sport, perhaps partly because of its popularity among the upper classes of England. By 1895, 106 clubs belonged to the national tennis association. Then, primarily because of the sudden popularity of

---

[2]Quoted in United States Lawn Tennis Association, *Official Encyclopedia of Tennis* (New York: Harper & Row, 1972), p. 10.

[3]Paul Gallico, *The Golden People* (Garden City, N.Y.: Doubleday, 1965), p. 64.

golf in the elite clubs, membership in the association fell sharply, not returning to the 1895 level until ten years later.

Nonetheless, the early twentieth century witnessed harbingers of a new era of tennis. One was an increase in international competition. As early as the 1880s, Englishmen had invaded the Newport tournament and Americans had reciprocated by competing at Wimbledon; such visits became common in the first two decades of the twentieth century. In 1900, a wealthy Harvard player, Dwight F. Davis, encouraged national rivalries by establishing the International Lawn Tennis Challenge Cup (Davis Cup). In the pre-World War I era, teams from the United States, England, and later Australia and New Zealand competed annually for the cup. Until the 1960s, the Davis Cup was one of the most coveted prizes in international competition. In 1909, Maurice McLaughlin, a flashing redhead from San Francisco, brought a new brand of tennis to Newport. His power and speed, learned on the fast, hard-surfaced courts of California, excited an interest never before felt in the East.[4] Finally, the transfer of the national championships in 1915 from Newport to the West Side Tennis Club at Forest Hills, a section of Queens in New York City, reflected the determination of the United States Lawn Tennis Association (USLTA) to attract a larger audience for tennis. In 1923 the West Side Tennis Club built the first modern tennis facility in the United States, which seated 14,000 spectators.

The turning point for tennis as a public spectacle came in the 1920s with the appearance of two outstanding players: Big Bill Tilden and Suzanne Lenglen. The victory of Lenglen in the women's singles at Wimbledon in 1919 and Tilden's triumph in men's singles at Forest Hills in 1920 marked the end of the conservative, casual, and social age of tennis and the beginning of an age in which tennis players became public celebrities. Both Lenglen and Tilden combined superb athletic performances with colorful personalities. Between 1919 and 1926, Lenglen took six titles at Wimbledon, while Tilden won the same number at Forest Hills. Tilden, a tall, gaunt egotist, shared the limelight of men's tennis with no one. Lenglen, glamorous and equally controversial, held sway just as imperiously over women's tennis. Both repeatedly filled stadiums with spectators and captured the headlines of both the front pages and sports pages of the world's newspapers. They were for tennis the equivalent of baseball's Babe Ruth or football's Red Grange.

For Lenglen, tennis had never been a dainty, social sport played for the sheer fun of the game. She was probably the first player in tennis history to be systematically groomed for championship play. Her parents, "well-to-do folk" from France, went south every winter to the Riviera where her father played a bit of social tennis. Her father quickly recognized his daughter's potential for the game and determined to make her a champion. By the age of twelve she had begun to play against adults in local Riviera tournaments and at the age of fourteen won the French Hard Courts championship.

[4]See Lewis R. Freeman, "Why California Tennis Players Win," *Outing*, 65 (October 1914), 22–31.

World War I interrupted her tournament career, but she continued to refine her game through long hours of practice. In 1919 she made her debut at Wimbledon, the center of world tennis. By the time she reached the challenge round against Dorthea Lambert Chambers, the reigning Wimbledon champion, she had completely captivated English fans, including King George V, Queen Mary, and Princess Mary. For the first time in Wimbledon history, fans had to be turned away from Centre Court. Lenglen won in three hard-fought sets.[5]

Everything Lenglen did, said, or wore contributed to her status as an international celebrity. She was tempestuous, a prima donna who haughtily dispatched opponents, quarreled with officials, once snubbed British royalty, and frequently bickered with her domineering parents. No previous woman player had been so uninhibited. "I just throw dignity to the winds," she reportedly said, "and think of nothing but the game."[6] She had sex appeal. Though lacking in facial beauty, she had a figure that could have adorned the stage. She wore daring, low-cut, one-piece dresses that, by 1925, had hemlines slightly below the knees, permitting spectators an occasional glimpse of her mid-thighs. To tennis fans, accustomed to seeing the women players cavort about the courts in corseted waists, long-sleeved blouses, and skirts padded with petticoats, Lenglen's attire was delightfully risqué.

She was controversial. Her first and only appearance at Forest Hills in 1921 evoked an international argument. After losing the first set 2–6 and double-faulting in the opening game of the second set to Molla Mallery, the American champion, Lenglen informed the umpire that she was too ill to continue and stalked off to the dressing room in tears. The American press accused her of "quitting" to avoid further embarrassment; they proclaimed Mallery the world's premier woman tennis player. European newspapers sided with Lenglen. The next summer, Lenglen resolved the dispute by crushing Mallery 6–2, 6–0 in the finals at Wimbledon and 6–0, 6–0 in a tournament at Nice, France.

Lenglen's most famous and most publicized match was her meeting with Helen Wills at Cannes in 1926. In the finals at Forest Hills in 1923, the sixteen-year-old Wills had routed Molla Mallery. "Little Miss Poker Face," as Wills was dubbed by the sportswriters, went on to win six more singles titles at Forest Hills and eight British championships at Wimbledon. Americans rallied behind her as the new women's champion of the world. Although no title of consequence was at stake at Cannes, the match created more excitement than any tennis contest until Billie Jean King played Bobby Riggs in 1973. Seats for the contest sold out far in advance; from all over France and England enthusiasts came to see the "women's tennis

[5]For Lenglen and Tilden see especially Allison Danzig, "Tennis," in Allison Danzig and Peter Brandwein, eds., *Sport's Golden Age: A Close-up of the Fabulous Twenties* (New York: Harper & Bros., 1948), 208–27; Frank Deford, *Big Bill Tilden: The Triumphs and the Tragedy* (New York: Simon and Schuster, 1975); Will Grimsley, *Tennis: Its History, People and Events* (Englewood Cliffs, N.J.: Prentice-Hall, 1971), pp. 41–52, 131–40, 293–96.

[6]Quoted in "Decidedly Unconquerable Is Mlle. Lenglen, Tennis Champion," *Literary Digest*, 62 (September 13, 1919), 80.

match of the century." Hundreds perched on neighboring house tops and in the trees near the court. The atmosphere resembled that of a heavyweight championship fight more than the finals of a staid tennis tournament. Lenglen won in a close, rugged contest 6–3, 8–6, and the French hailed her as the "Jeanne d'Arc of tennis." That was the only match in which the two queens of tennis met. Lenglen left the amateur ranks in 1926 to become a professional player, and Wills continued to dominate amateur play into the early 1930s.[7]

Unlike Lenglen, Bill Tilden was slow to develop into a championship player. From a once socially prominent Philadelphia family whose status was in the process of skidding downward, Tilden learned his tennis at the Germantown Cricket Club. It is remarkable, even for his day, that he did not become a master of the sport until he was twenty-seven years old. After defeat in the finals of the national championships in 1919, he spent the next winter correcting a weak backhand. The next year he stormed back to win the first of seven national championships; he shared the doubles title five times at Forest Hills, won Wimbledon singles crowns three times, and won seventeen Davis Cup matches while losing only five.

Sportswriters did not have to resort to hyperbole to make Tilden an interesting personality. To Tilden, the tennis court was a dramatic stage and he was the leading actor. He loved the theatre and performed the lead in several shows including one Broadway production. If attention at a tournament wandered from him, he brought it back by subtly allowing himself to teeter on the brink of defeat. He then made what appeared to be an incredible comeback. On the court he could be arrogant and irritating. Linesmen who made "bad" calls received menacing glares, and Tilden might deliberately "throw" the next point to show his utter contempt. To the American public, Tilden was the colossal, all-male American giant, who single-handedly held off the tennis invaders from Europe.

Throughout his career, Tilden feuded with the Amerian tennis authorities. While promoting tennis as a spectator sport, the United States Lawn Tennis Association (USLTA) persisted in trying to preserve a player-centered ethos; consistent with this purpose, it adamantly refused to permit the players to profit directly from tennis. The players could not endorse equipment, teach, or write about the sport for pay. Tilden's troubles arose mostly from his tennis journalism. In the twenties, he apparently received as much as $25,000 annually for writing books, syndicated newspaper pieces, and articles for magazines. In 1924 the USLTA informed him that he was violating the amateur code by writing for remuneration. Tilden responded that he had been a professional writer long before he had become an eminent tennis player. After a cursory hearing, the association reaffirmed its position and announced that, unless Tilden ceased, he would be suspended from tournament play. Tilden ignored the threat. Since the USLTA needed Tilden to draw spectators to tournaments and play on the American Davis Cup team, the association compromised. It decided that players could write about tennis as long as

---

[7]See especially Danzig, "Tennis," pp. 225–27.

they did not "cover" the tournaments in which they were currently playing. Tilden evaded the ruling. He continued to write his general column and then produce a paid "interview"—written by himself—of the events in which he played. As long as the USLTA needed Tilden more than Tilden needed the association, there was little it could do. Finally, in 1928, when Tilden was in Europe and past his prime as a player, the USLTA suspended him from the Davis Cup team and further tournament competition.[8]

The USLTA decision touched off an international furor. The news of Tilden's banishment and the reactions to it drove the 1928 presidential election news, the assassination of Mexico's president-elect, and a search for lost aviators in the Arctic off of the front pages of the nation's newspapers. Even the phlegmatic president, Calvin Coolidge, demanded an explanation. French star René Lacoste, winner of the past two American championships, announced that he would not defend his Forest Hills title. French tennis authorities were furious. They had just completed the erection of magnificent Roland Garros Stadium for the challenge round of the Davis Cup with the expectation that Tilden would play for the American team. French tennis officials turned to their government which in turn requested assistance from the American government. Faced with stiff diplomatic pressure, the USLTA backed down. Tilden would be allowed to play in the Davis Cup challenge round in Paris, but he would be suspended when he returned home. Although reinstated by the USLTA in 1929, Tilden turned professional the following year.

Tilden's conflicts with the USLTA reflected the dilemmas confronting a socially exclusive, amateur sport that had "gone public." In its early days, tennis had flourished among the wealthy, those who could afford to own courts or belong to the expensive clubs around the social centers of Boston, Newport, New York, and Philadelphia. Nearly all the tournament players were also people of wealth and position as was the bulk of the small audiences who attended championship matches. But even before the 1920s, upwardly mobile men of new wealth, the "social climbers," had turned to tennis as a vehicle for entering the upper echelons of elite social circles. By the 1920s, when tennis began to attract big box office receipts, these men controlled the USLTA, the regional associations, and many of the tennis clubs. To retain the image of tennis as a high-status sport, the social climbers were adamant in defending a rigorous definition of amateurism.[9]

Yet, for tennis to be successful as a spectator sport, the athletes had to reach professional standards of play. They had to become full-time athletes devoting themselves to long hours of practice and frequent play in tournaments. Thus, unless the players were wealthy, they were forced to circumvent the amateur rules. Moreover, local clubs and their members could gain prestige by sponsoring the development of star players.

[8]See Deford, *Big Bill Tilden*, pp. 108–24.
[9]See Gallico, *The Golden People*, pp. 124–27; Paul Gallico, *Farewell to Sport* (New York: Knopf, 1938), pp. 145–50; John R. Tunis, *$port$: Heroics and Hysterics* (New York: John Day, 1928), pp. 44–75.

Consequently, a promising boy or girl, even if from a family of modest financial circumstances, could find themselves sponsored by a club or a patron. The player's expenses for instruction and appearance in tournaments would be paid fully by someone else. Such a system, according to Sumner Hardy, president of the California Lawn Tennis Association, "made bums out of the boys."[10] At a tender age their lives centered around little else but tennis. Hypocrisy was another inevitable byproduct. While tournament authorities paid the traveling expenses of players (the more prominent the player, the higher the allowance granted), they refused to offer cash prizes or schedule open tournaments in which both amateurs and professionals could compete. To have done so would have jeopardized the social functions performed by the sport for the social climbers.

Because powerful amateur associations controlled the major tournaments of the world and the press generally took a dim view of professional tennis, only a few players could equal their earnings as amateurs. In 1926 Charles C. "Cash and Carry" Pyle, Red Grange's business manager, attempted to eliminate "shamateurism" in tennis by organizing a pro tour. He hoped to force the amateur associations to open their tournaments to pros and award cash prizes. He signed Suzanne Lenglen, Mary K. Browne, and Vincent Richards (but not Tilden) to a tour of the United States and Canada.[11] Apparently Pyle profited from the venture, but when Lenglen demanded a larger share of future gates, he abandoned the promotion of professional tennis. In the early 1930s only Tilden, though in his forties and no longer the world's premier player, could command a large enough audience to make pro exhibitions profitable. For pro tours to succeed, they required continual infusions of new talent, in other words, recent winners of major amateur tournaments who had received large quantities of free publicity. Such a system meant that only a few professional players could earn a decent living from tennis. Pro tennis had to wait for the advent of television and open tournaments in the 1960s before it became a success.

GOLF GOES PUBLIC

The history of golf going public both paralleled and departed from that of tennis. Both sports had their origins in socially exclusive clubs; status-conscious clubs continued to be the major promoters of tennis and golf in the Age of the Spectator. Before 1920 the majority of Americans scorned or simply ignored both sports. Popular hostility to tennis and golf impelled Theodore Roosevelt to warn William Howard Taft of the political dangers in playing them: "It would seem incredible that anyone would care one way or the other about your playing golf, but I have received literally hundreds of letters from the West protesting it." He further cautioned: "I myself play

---

[10]Quoted in Tunis, *$port$*, p. 165.
[11]See Hugh Leamy, "Net Profits," *Collier's,* 78 (October 2, 1926), 9, 32; "Girding for the War Against Professional Tennis," *Literary Digest,* 92 (March 19, 1927), 72–78; "Amateur Players Ask for Open Tennis," *Literary Digest,* 117 (February 17, 1934), 34–35.

tennis, but that game is a little more familiar; besides you never saw a photograph of me playing tennis, I am careful about that; photographs on horseback, yes; tennis no. And golf is fatal."[12] When Taft became President, he ignored Roosevelt's warnings; he thus became the nation's first "golfing" Chief Executive.

Golf, like tennis, developed lively international competition. Long before 1920 golfers participated on both sides of the Atlantic. In 1922 George H. Walker, a former president of the United States Golf Association (USGA), presented a cup for biennial competition between amateur teams representing the United States and Great Britain. In 1927 Samuel Ryder, a British seed merchant whose company had British and American courses as patrons, established a competitive cup for professional teams. Like tennis, both sexes competed in golf, though the best-known women golfers, Alexa Stirling and Glenna Collett, never achieved the celebrity status of a Suzanne Lenglen or a Helen Wills nor the public recognition of such male golfers as Walter Hagen, Gene Sarazan, or Bobby Jones. Yet while the two sports had these important similarities, they evolved in significantly different ways.

Golf "went public" without the controversy that characterized the emergence of tennis as a public spectacle. Unlike tennis, which had developed almost simultaneously in both Great Britain and the United States in the late nineteenth century, golf was already a well-established sport in Scotland when it invaded American shores. Thus the American clubs tended to imitate Scottish customs. In the British Isles the unoccupied links of land (hence the term "links" to describe golf courses) that bordered or stretched into the sea furnished natural hazards. Having no equivalent physical features along the Atlantic seaboard, American clubs had to build inland courses. To approximate the hazards found in the British Isles, they constructed artificial bunkers, sandtraps, small lakes, and planted trees along the fairways. From the earliest days of the sport in the United States, the clubs hired professional Scottish or English golfers to teach their members the finer arts of the game and followed the British custom of holding open tournaments. Both amateur and professional golfers could compete in open tournaments. Finally, the absence of gate receipts at golf tournaments until the 1920s discouraged the adoption of the tennis practice of extending traveling expenses to amateur players.

Golf enjoyed a much larger "built-in" fan constituency than tennis. In the 1920s the country club came of age in the United States. Membership in a country club was a salient badge of distinction, almost obligatory for anyone striving for status in communities both large and small. Golf courses invariably accompanied the growth of country clubs. From seacoast

---

[12]As quoted in Harold Seymour, *Baseball: The Golden Age* (New York: Oxford University Press, 1971), pp. 45–46. Useful general treatments of the history of golf are H. B. Martin, *Fifty Years of American Golf* (New York: Dodd, Mead, 1936); Will Grimsley, *Golf: Its History, People, and Events* (Englewood Cliffs, N.J.: Prentice-Hall, 1966); Herbert Warren Wind, *The Story of American Golf: Its Champions and Championships,* 3rd rev. ed. (New York: Knopf, 1975); and Herb Graffis, *The PGA: The Official History of The Professional Golfer's Association of America* (New York: Thomas Y. Crowell, 1975).

to seacoast, country clubs scooped out kidney-shaped sand traps, felled trees, cleared fairways, leveled greens, and planted new grass. Wealthy courses sported elaborate, fake Mediterranean clubhouses, sometimes valued at more than a million dollars; other clubs had plain wooden shacks of unornamented pine valued at no more than a few hundred dollars. The country club golf fever even swept into the small towns. For instance, in the 1920s almost a hundred small Kansas towns built courses. The town of Gaylord, with a population of 356, claimed the best nine-hole course in north-central Kansas. In 1913 there were 742 links in the entire nation; by 1930 the number had leaped to 5,586, an eight-fold increase.[13]

Golf, in the early days, had been the exclusive sport of the upper "Four Hundred," but in the 1920s it became the sport of the upper "Four Million." Thousands of Americans who had never seen a goosenecked putter or a dog-leg hole before 1920 began to spend many hours every summer trying conscientiously to keep their heads down, hold their arms in, and follow through. In some social circles the ritual of the Sunday morning foursome became as rigid as church attendance was in others. Gambling was often an integral part of the golfing ritual. "Friendly" games nearly always involved wagers; on occasion, wealthier players reportedly bet up to $10,000 a side and $1,000 per hole. Men reassured their anxious wives and their bosses that they got as much business done in the locker room and on the course as they did in their offices. Golf allowed the city dweller "to play the pioneer again," but without the rigors of being physically struck by another person as in football or striking a moving ball as in baseball or tennis. The frontiersman-golfer advanced through rolling country, from one "ambushed outpost" to another (sometimes through hills marked only by a "direction flag"), forded streams, hacked through forests, and found himself snared in traps, until he finally reached his destination, a conquerer of all that was before him. He sought a guide, the golfing pro, to teach him the intricacies of mastering the "frontier" and found inspiration in the golfing champion, the symbolic equivalent of the frontier hero.[14]

As early as 1913 golf exhibited its potential as a public spectacle. Prior to that date a gallery of 200 was considered unusual for a national tournament. In 1913 a crowd of more than 3,000 watched Francis Ouimet, a twenty-year-old amateur golfer, upset Britain's two leading professional golfers in a playoff in the United States Open tournament. Earlier, whenever overseas stars had consented to play in American meets, they had nearly always emerged victorious. Only one American, Walter J. Travis, had ever won a major European championship. In 1913 Harry

---

[13]Wind, *The Story of American Golf*, pp. 165–66; Charles Merz, *The Great American Band-Wagon* (New York: John Day, 1928), pp. 92–93; Jesse Frederick Steiner, *Americans at Play: Recent Trends in Recreation and Leisure Time Activities* (New York: McGraw-Hill, 1933), pp. 70–71.

[14]O. B. Keeler, "Golf," in Danzig and Brandwein, eds., *Sport's Golden Age*, p. 87; "Is Golf Gambling Killing a 'Gentleman's Game?'" *Literary Digest*, 87 (October 31, 1925), 53–55; Merz, *The Great American Band-Wagon*, pp. 94–100. A pastoral interpretation appears to be equally appropriate, for the golf course can be viewed as a "middle landscape" between the savage wilderness and the urban jungle.

Vardon, winner of six British open titles and often hailed as the world's greatest golfer, and Edward "Ted" Ray, reigning British Open crown holder, embarked upon an exhibition tour of the United States. Attracting record crowds wherever they went, they interrupted their tour in mid-September to play in the American Open at The Country Club in Brookline, Massachusetts.

An almost unknown golfer, Francis Ouimet, a former caddy at The Country Club and the son of a French-Canadian immigrant who worked as a local gardener, surprised everyone by tying the British aces at the end of regulation play. The next day, on a rain-soaked course, Ouimet won the playoffs, trouncing Vardon by five strokes and Ray by seven strokes. Newspapers across the country gave Ouimet's victory headline coverage. Overnight, Ouimet was an American hero. "Here was a person all of America, not just golfing America, could understand—the boy from 'the wrong side' of the street, the ex-caddie, the kind who worked during his summer vacations from high school—America's idea of the American hero."[15] Ouimet was golf's version of the Horatio Alger success story.

While Ouimet never again captured an American Open title, one participant in the Brookline tournament, Walter C. Hagen, was to become the world's top professional golfer. The 1913 Open was the first major tournament for the twenty-one-year-old assistant club professional at the Rochester, New York Country Club. Hagen was in no way awed by the British champions. Before the tournament was to begin Hagen supposedly introduced himself to the reigning titleholder of the Open, John McDermott, by saying that he had "come down to help you fellows stop Vardon and Ray."[16] Such youthful bravado stunned McDermott, and the nearby players snickered, but Hagen was absolutely serious. While Hagen failed to "stop Vardon and Ray"—Ouimet did that—he finished only three strokes behind the leaders. The Open began a long career for Hagen that ricocheted back and forth between a series of peaks punctuated by sizable slumps. He won the United States Open in 1914 and 1919, the British Open in 1922, 1924, 1928, and 1929, the Professional Golf Association (PGA) title four years in a row, and overwhelmed Bobby Jones in their only "private" match in 1926.

Hagen was a revolutionary figure in the history of American golf. He, more than any other single individual, was responsible for making professional golf a socially respectable occupation. The first golf "pros," mostly transplanted Scotsmen and Englishmen, had been jacks-of-all-trades. They designed the early courses, kept the grounds, made and repaired the hickory-shafted golf clubs, trained and managed caddies, and gave instructions to novices. Little or none of their earnings came from tournament winnings, product endorsements, or paid exhibitions. While wealthy club members sometimes joined the club pro in friendly games, they viewed him as simply another employee and therefore as a social inferior. In open tournaments the clubs barred the pros from the locker rooms and other clubhouse amenities. As late as 1930, the official

---

[15]Wind, *The Story of American Golf*, p. 85.
[16]Quoted in ibid., p. 120.

programs of the United States Open prefixed the names of amateurs with "Mr." while deleting this distinction from the names of golf professionals.[17]

Hagen helped erase social discrimination in golf. Being a former caddy from a family of modest means did not deter the irrepressible Hagen. He treated kings, industrial tycoons, and caddies all alike. Because of his prowess as a golfer, his pleasing personality, his sartorial elegance, and his impeccable manners, he succeeded in breaking down social barriers in both the United States and Europe. Apparently Hagen unintentionally touched off the "Midlothian Incident" of 1914 at the United States Open held at the Midlothian Country Club in suburban Chicago. Hagen, then a brash, young, but personable professional who appeared to be ignorant of clubhouse social conventions, simply made himself at home in the Midlothian locker room and clubhouse. While no one knows whether words were exchanged or threats were issued, the country club finally acquiesced, constituting what has been described as a "social revolution in American golf." When Hagen arrived at Deal to play in the 1920 British Open, he learned that the clubhouse was off limits to pros—again because they were not regarded as gentlemen. Much to the chagrin of the stuffy British golf officials, Hagen ordered his big, black limousine parked at the front door of the clubhouse and proceeded to use it as a dressing room. The same year, Hagen and the British Open champion, George Duncan, threatened to boycott the French Open unless the social restrictions against the pros were removed. The French, confronted with the possible collapse of their tournament, yielded. The British soon followed the American and French custom of extending equal amenities to both professionals and amateurs.[18]

PUTTING FOR PROFIT

Hagen was the first golfer to make the full-time playing of golf a profitable enterprise. Before the late 1930s, professionals could earn only a few dollars in prize money; they earned their living by serving as club pros. Yet the prize money gradually increased. In 1916 Tom McNamara, a salesman in the golf department of Wanamaker's, sold the idea of the Professional Golfer's Association (PGA) to millionaire Rodman Wanamaker. Wanamaker initially donated a total prize of $2,500; the winner of the annual PGA tournament received $500. During World War I, the American Red Cross sponsored a benefit tour to which it charged admissions to spectators. In 1921 the United States Open copied this practice and soon other golf meets followed suit. Swelling gate receipts permitted the major tournaments to increase their meager purses. In the early 1920s a professional tour of sorts developed in the South. Wealthy golf enthusiasts, often with real estate promotion as a primary motive,

[17]"What a 'Czar' Means to Golf Pros," *Literary Digest*, 105 (May 10, 1930), 68,
[18]Graffis, *The PGA*, p. 59; Grimsley, *Golf*, p. 59.

began to sponsor professional tournaments in resort areas. Yet no golfer could earn a decent living on tournament winnings alone.[19]

Hagen relied upon tours and product endorsements rather than tournaments to earn "big money" from golf. Combining a colorful personality with the fact that for nearly fifteen years he seldom was without a national title made Hagen the most sought-after exhibition golfer in the country. Hagen employed Robert "Bob" Harlow, a veteran Associated Press correspondent, as his business manager. (Harlow, hailed as the "founder of professional golf as it is today," later served many years as the tournament manager of the PGA.) Harlow was to Hagen what Christy Walsh was to Babe Ruth, Jack Kearns to Jack Dempsey, and C.C. Pyle to Red Grange. He capitalized upon Hagen's popularity by lining up endorsements for golf equipment and arranging elaborate tours that took Hagen from the largest cities to golf's remotest outposts. Except for tournament interruptions, from late spring to early fall Hagen gave exhibitions five days a week and during the winter months he played on the "winter circuit" from Florida to California. Harlow "ticketed" the galleries at one dollar a person for weekdays and two dollars for weekends. During the twenties Hagen probably earned between $30,000 and $50,000 annually.[20]

Hagen's personality contributed as much as his magnificent victories to his success as a full-time pro player. Hagen, like Babe Ruth, embodied the new consumer ethic of the twenties. While he outstripped his fellow pros in earnings, he spent his money just as lavishly. He loved good food, drink, all-night parties, and chauffeured limousines. On the golf links, his sartorial splendor had no equal; he was a fashion pace-setter. In his very first major tournament at Brookline in 1913 he surprised the staid galleries by sporting a striped shirt, red bandana, checkered Scottish cap, white flannel trousers, and white buck shoes. He was the first golfer to live like a merry millionaire. His dress, manners, and pleasant personality earned him the affectionate sobriquets of "Sir Walter" and "The Haig." He was the source of a host of amazing legends. One of the best of these stories had him arriving so late for a tournament that he was about to be disqualified. At the last moment he drove up to the first tee in a chauffeured limousine. The Haig, regal in his tuxedo, got out of the car, waved to his mink-wrapped lovely in the tonneau, and proceeded to play the first round in his tuxedo and patent leather shoes. And, of course, he won.

While Hagen wooed thousands of golfers to his exhibitions, only the amateur Bobby Jones became a truly national, even international, golfing celebrity. Jones was born into a wealthy Atlanta, Georgia family. At the age of nine he won the junior golf championship of the Atlanta Athletic Club, defeating a boy seven years older than himself in the final. In 1916, when Jones was but fourteen, he competed in the United States Amateur at the Merion Cricket Club in Philadelphia. He managed to qualify and swept

[19]Graffis, *The PGA*, pp. 78–82; Wind, *The Story of American Golf*, p. 172.

[20]"Is Golf Threatening the Future of Baseball?" *Literary Digest*, 74 (August 5, 1922), 58–9; Alex Pirie, "The Business of the Golf Game," *Saturday Evening Post*, 203 (July 26, 1930), 36, 87–88; Martin, *Fifty Years of American Gold*, pp. 329–30.

through his first two challengers before succumbing to the defending champion in the third round. Despite defeat, Jones was the sensation of the tournament, hailed by sportswriters as the "kid wonder" and the "child prodigy" of golf. But Jones also exhibited an ungovernable temper; after making a bad shot, he threw his clubs and swore with an abandon that belied his age. For several years, the high expectations generated at Merion went unfulfilled. Jones won regional titles with regularity, but national crowns somehow eluded him. Gradually, he eliminated his bad habits. In 1923, when he was apparently on the verge of retiring from competitive golf, he won his first major tournament, the U.S. Open at Inwood on Long Island. From 1923 to 1930, he was the king of world golfers, both professional and amateur. He collected thirteen national titles—five United States amateurs, four United States Opens, three British Opens, and one British Amateur. In the last nine years of his career he competed in twelve national championships and finished first or second in eleven of them, a feat Jones considered to be greater than his winning of the Grand Slam in 1930. He climaxed his short golfing career with the Grand Slam— the American Open and Amateur and the British Open and Amateur, a feat not duplicated since. After the Grand Slam in 1930, when he was at the very peak of his game at the age of twenty-eight, Jones announced his retirement.

The American public adored Bobby Jones. Each time he returned from victories in Europe, he received the welcome of a conquering hero—a ticker-tape parade down Broadway to New York's City Hall to receive the keys of the city from Mayor Jimmy Walker. Public excitement knew no bounds when Jones won the last leg of his Grand Slam, the American Amateur at the Merion Cricket Club in 1930. A vast throng, estimated at 18,000, made a great human fringe around the greens and packed the fairways, following Jones from hole to hole. "Today's match was far more of a spectacle than it was a contest," declared William D. Richardson of the *New York Times*. "It was merely an exhibition on Jones' part, a parade to victory."[21] Women reached out to touch him and little boys sat on their fathers' shoulders to catch a glimpse of their fabulous hero.

The conservative image of Jones stood in sharp contrast to that of the hedonistic Hagen. Golfing commentators referred repeatedly to Jones' game as "mechanical" while Hagen played with an unorthodox flair. Jones seemed to embody the traditional Victorian virtues. At the same time that he competed in golf tournaments, he attended college, obtained a law degree, was admitted to the bar, and began the practice of law. Modest, clean-cut, though noticeably chunky, Jones had a boyish appearance. Paul Gallico, after reviewing all of the major sports heroes of the 1920s, asserted that Jones was "the greatest gentleman of them all."[22] Above all, the public loved the fact that Jones, as an amateur, had defeated the best of the

[21]Danzig and Brandwein, eds., *The Greatest Sports Stories from the New York Times*, p. 342.

[22]Gallico, *The Golden People*, p. 268. Jones and his constant companion, O.B. Keeler, appear to have consciously cultivated this image. See Robert T. Jones, Jr. and O.B. Keeler, *Down the Fairway: The Golf, Life, and Play of Robert T. Jones, Jr.* (New York: Minton, Balch, 1927).

professional golfers and taken the measure of the European champions. By a large strain on the imagination, weekend "duffers" could identify Jones as one of their own crowd. He, like they, held down a regular job and presumably played the sport for the sheer fun of the game.

That the image of Jones sometimes failed to correspond with the facts did not bother his admirers. Upon retirement from tournament competition, Jones, like the professional golfers, attempted to capitalize upon his reputation. With his "Boswell" and longtime traveling companion, O.B. Keeler, Jones did a weekly half-hour radio show recreating the highlights of his career. He made two series of instructional films for Warner Brothers, reputedly for a profit of $180,000, and lent his name to a Spalding line of golfing equipment. He furnished the initiative and much of the design for a magnificent new golf course at Augusta, Georgia, the Augusta National, which featured broad fairways, few traps, and large greens. In 1934 the Augusta National became the home of the Masters tournament, an invitation-only affair consisting of the world's top golfers. In due time, the Masters became one of four major recognized tournaments in the world. As a leisure-time golfer, Jones occasionally played in the Masters (even as late as 1948) and other meets, but never again won a major tournament.

The retirement of Jones, the Great Depression of the 1930s, and World War II set back the American enthusiasm for golf. Without Jones as a drawing card or the emergence of a new golfing celebrity of equal stature, major amateur tournaments were fortunate if gate receipts equalled expenses. Almost a third of the country clubs folded; several became privately owned, daily fee or municipally owned courses. The Public Works Administration and the Works Progress Administration of the New Deal built about 200 courses. Of about 5,200 courses in 1941, some 2,000 were either municipal or privately owned, daily fee courses.

In the 1930s, the "Age of the Amateur" passed. After the victory of Jones in 1930, only one amateur (in 1933) ever again won the U.S. Open. In 1936 the PGA hired a professional promoter, Fred Corcoran, as tournament director. By stressing the advertising value of tournaments to cities and sometimes corporations, Corcoran expanded the size of the pro tour and the prize money. In 1935 the pros had a total of $135,000 available in prize money and the leading money winner earned $9,543. Ten years later, the total prize money had jumped to more than three-quarters of a million dollars, and Byron Nelson won $52,511, to lead all money winners.

The 1930s also introduced the "Age of Steel" and concerted assaults on pars. The average winning score for the U.S. Open in the 1930s dropped six strokes below that of the 1920s. Experts attributed the better scores to high-pressured balls, replacement of hickory shafts with steel, the use of more specialized and more perfectly matched clubs, and the "New Look" of the nation's golf courses. In the 1930s, many clubs filled in traps, thinned the roughs, cropped the grass shorter on the fairways, and softened the greens by watering them more copiously.[23] The 1940s

[23]Keeler, "Golf," pp. 188–89; Wind, *The Story of American Golf*, pp. 268–70.

brought forward a new breed of professional precisionists—Ben Hogan, Byron Nelson, and Sam Snead, for instance—but not until the advent of television and Arnold Palmer in the 1960s did golf again achieve the public attention it had received in 1930.

THE OLYMPIC GAMES

Long before 1920 the fan had been a potent force in track and field. As early as the 1840s and 1850s, professional pedestrianism had gained a considerable following, and it continued to enjoy some support in the early years of the twentieth century. The Scottish Caledonian clubs had also welcomed fans to their meets; they had charged admissions to spectators and awarded cash prizes to winning athletes. Initially, spectatorship was an issue that divided the sporting world of the social elites. The fashionable clubs had sought to use a sport as an agency for building status communities. Status ascription might be strengthened by restricting competition to amateur athletes and spectators to club members and invited guests. On the other hand, the clubs might enhance their status by building a reputation for holding outstanding meets and fielding superior athletes. Eventually this view prevailed. The clubs "went public;" they opened their gates to the public at large and became the nation's premier promoters of track and field. In the twentieth century, the athletic clubs and their parent body, the Amateur Athletic Union (AAU), continued to stage some of the most eminent meets in the nation.

In the Age of the Spectator, elite athletic clubs encountered increasing competition from other organizations in the nurture of superior athletes and the sponsorship of track and field meets. Foremost of these competitors were the high schools and colleges. Northeastern colleges organized the Intercollegiate Association of Amateur Athletes of America (commonly known as the IC4A) in 1876 to supervise running events that had been held at Saratoga, New York since 1873. In 1876, the IC4A began to conduct annual, full-scale track meets. Until the National Collegiate Athletic Association staged its first championships in 1921, the IC4A was the nation's most prestigious collegiate track meet. After 1921 it remained an important event for eastern schools.

The University of Pennsylvania Relays, which began in 1895, introduced a colorful athletic carnival that combined intercollegiate and interscholastic track. At the Penn Relays of 1925 more than 3,000 athletes representing more than 500 colleges and secondary schools competed before 70,000 fans in the finals. The Penn Relays spawned imitators across the country, perhaps the most notable being the Drake University Relays at Des Moines, Iowa. Early in the twentieth century, several other groups joined the athletic clubs, the AAU, and the colleges in the promotion of track and field. In New York City the Millrose Games, the Knights of Columbus Games, and the Wanamaker Mile, among others, added to the opportunities available to spectator and athlete alike.

The existence of competing promotional groups and the absence of a single regulatory body engendered a series of controversies within the world of track and field. The fundamental power struggle between the NCAA and the AAU for hegemony over track and field, which had begun in the early years of the twentieth century, continued unabated. The NCAA, which furnished an ever larger share of the top-flight athletes, resented the AAU's efforts to determine the eligibility of all "amateur" athletes, the AAU's collection of fees for meets which it did not sponsor, the control which the AAU attempted to exercise over international competition, and the AAU's domination of the American Olympic Committee (AOC). Neither the AAU nor the NCAA ever won a complete victory. Sometimes only ad hoc compromises allowed the United States to field a team for the Olympic Games.[24] All too often the athletes themselves appeared to be the innocent victims of the power struggle.

From the perspective of the athletes, they were also the victims of a hypocritical amateur code. While in principle amateur athletes could receive no financial remuneration from their feats, promoters could win both glory and profits from staging meets. Anxious to attract star athletes to their meets, unscrupulous promoters secretly "overpaid" expense allowances and apparently sometimes made direct payments to the athletes. As in the case of tennis and golf, to be a champion in track and field required full-time training and frequent competition. Unless the athlete was independently wealthy, he had to supplement his income in some fashion. The temptation to benefit financially from one's athletic skills was difficult to resist. Furthermore, according to world champion sprinter, Charles W. Paddock, who repeatedly warred with the AAU, the promoters often placed the athletes in an impossible position. On the one hand, they would extend to the young, inexperienced athletes "extra expenses." On the other, whenever the athlete protested any matter, he then could be threatened with exposure and suspension.[25] "Shamateurism" continued to plague the world of track and field after World War II.

In the Age of the Spectator the Olympic Games became the premier track and field spectacle.[26] The 1920 games, awarded to Antwerp in recognition of the horrendous sacrifices made by the Belgians during World War I, was a modest affair. But each of the following Games—Paris in 1924, Amsterdam in 1928, Los Angeles in 1932, and Berlin in 1936—was more extravagant than its predecessor. Despite a worldwide depression, the Los Angeles promoters in 1932 established the pattern for the

[24]See Arnold William Flath, *A History of Relations Between the National Collegiate Athletic Association and the Amateur Athletic Union of the United States, (1905–1963)* (Champaign, Ill.: Stipes, 1964).

[25]Charles W. Paddock, *"The Fastest Human"* (New York: Thomas Nelson, 1932), pp. 48–49, 158. See also the case of Raymond Barbuti, winner of the 400-meter race at the 1928 Olympics. The controversy can be followed in the *New York Times*, March 2, 1929 and April 4, 1929.

[26]For general accounts of the Games see John Kiernan et al., *The Story of the Olympic Games, 776 B.C. to 1976*, rev. ed. (Philadelphia: Lippincott, 1977); William O. Johnson, Jr., *All That Glitters Is Not Gold: The Olympic Games* (New York: Putnam's, 1972).

expensive and ornate facilities that would become characteristic of the modern games. The local organizing committee determined to make the 1932 spectacle a showcase for the city of Los Angeles and the state of California. To finance the spectacle, the City of Los Angeles floated a $1.5 million bond issue, and the voters of California, in a special referendum, approved the expenditure of $1 million in state funds. At Los Angeles the athletes found magnificent facilities: an 105,000-seat stadium, an indoor auditorium with seats for 10,000 a swimming structure with a seating capacity of 12,000 and the first specially constructed Olympic Village. The Olympic Village provided housing in prefabricated cottages, feeding, and recreational facilities for all of the male athletes at a single location.

Not to be outdone by the Los Angeles buccaneers, the Nazis put on an even bigger show at Berlin in 1936. They built a new 100,000-seat track and field stadium, six gymnasiums, and many smaller arenas. They installed a closed-circuit television system, a radio network that reached forty-one nations, photo-finish equipment, and electronic timing devices. In contrast to Los Angeles, they built sturdy brick and stucco cottages to house the male athletes. The Nazis commissioned Leni Riefenstahl, a brilliant producer, to make a $7 million film of the event. Her film, *Olympia,* subsequently became a classic in cinematography. Altogether the Nazis spent an estimated $30 million, far more than the total costs of all the preceding Games. Obviously, competition was no longer restricted to the athletic field, for the staging of ever more spectacular Olympiads had become a contest as well.

The building of elaborate facilities was an integral part of the increased politicization of the Olympic Games. Politicization had begun well before the 1920s and 1930s. Pierre de Coubertin, the founder of the modern Games, had promoted the Games as a means of inspiring the youth of France to greater physical prowess and courage and at the same time as a means of encouraging international ideals. The decision to have the athletes compete as national teams rather than as individuals inevitably gave rise to international rivalries. On the eve of the 1908 Games, James E. Sullivan, leader of the American Olympic delegation, bluntly declared: "We have come here to win the championship in field sports, and we are going to do it, despite the handicap from which we are suffering."[27] For the 1908 Games the American press devised an unofficial point system so that national achievements could be easily compared. And the national organizing committees soon found that by appealing to patriotic sentiments they could raise more money to send athletes to the Games.

Political animosities arising from World War I drove the International Olympic Committee to exclude the losers in the war—the Central Powers of Germany, Austria, Hungary, and Turkey—from the Games of 1920 and 1924. Neither did the IOC extend an invitation to the newly established communist regime in Russia to compete in the postwar Games. (Soviet Russia did not participate in the Games until 1952.) Such actions revealed

[27]As quoted in Robert M Goodhue, "The Development of Olympism, 1900–1932: Technical Success Within a Threatening Political Reality," in Peter J. Graham and Horst Ueberhorst, *The Modern Olympics* (Cornwall, N.Y.: Leisure, n.d.), p. 32.

clearly that the Olympic movement was not immune to the exigencies of international politics.

The politicization of the Olympics reached a climax with the 1936 Games. Nazi Germany's blatant anti-Semitism sparked a movement in the United States to boycott the 1936 Olympics. As early as 1933, shortly after Adolf Hitler had taken command in Germany, Americans serving on the International Olympic Committee had protested Nazi discrimination against Jews and the AAU had voted to boycott the games unless Germany's policy regarding Jewish athletes be "changed in fact as well as in theory."[28] While the German Olympic Committee took nominal steps to reassure the Americans, Hitler, in 1935, proclaimed the "Nuremberg Laws" which deprived German Jews of their citizenship and legalized social practices designed to preserve the integrity of the "Aryan race."

The issue of boycotting the Games divided American athletic officials into two bitter camps. Avery Brundage, the self-made millionaire president of the American Olympic Committee (AOC), led the advocates of participation in the games while the president of the AAU, Judge Jeremiah T. Mahoney, a Catholic who was deeply disturbed by Nazi paganism and anti-Semitism, led the boycott movement. Both sides published pamphlets, issued press releases, and gave radio interviews. A Gallup poll revealed that 57 percent of the American people favored a boycott. Brundage, in a private letter to a Nazi friend, interpreted the boycott movement as a Jewish-Communist conspiracy. "Jews and Communists," he wrote, "threatened to spend a million dollars to keep the United States out of Germany...by use of bribery, corruption and political trickery, and other contemptible tactics."[29] A showdown came at the AAU convention in 1935. Brundage, in a bit of overt skullduggery, was able to muster enough votes to defeat the boycott resolution by two and one-half votes. Mahoney resigned as president of the AAU and was replaced by Brundage, who now headed both the AAU and the AOC.

Controversy continued at the Games in Berlin. The German newspapers contemptuously referred to the ten blacks on the American track and field team as the "Black auxiliary." When Cornelius Johnson, a black, won the high jump with a record leap, Hitler, who had personally congratulated the first two winners in track and field, suddenly left his stadium box. On the following days Hitler carefully avoided public congratulations of any winners. Bitterness flared up within the American ranks. At the last moment the American track and field coach, Dean Cromwell, dropped two Jewish athletes—the only Jews on the American track and field team—from the 400 meter relay team. The coach insisted that the threat of a surprise German victory caused the substitutions. The argument seemed lame, for at least one of the Jewish athletes had times equal to that of one of the substitutes. Regardless, the decision suggested a gross insensitivity to the feelings of the athletes and a further erosion of traditional standards of

[28]Richard Mandell, *The Nazi Olympics* (New York: Macmillan, 1971), p. 71. See also Arnd Kruger, "The 1936 Olympic Games—Berlin," in Graham and Ueberhorst, *The Modern Olympics*, pp. 168–82.
[29]As quoted in Kruger, "The 1936 Olympic Games—Berlin," p. 171.

sportsmanship. Winning and record breaking, it appeared, took precedence over all other considerations.

The 1936 Games revealed that, more than ever before, nations perceived their athletes as their representatives in a struggle for international power and glory. Athletes were national assets, procurable like ballistic missiles, submarines, or bombs. After 1936 many of the nations who sent their athletes to the Nazi Games began to prepare for both war and the 1940 Olympics. It was ironic that the 1940 Games were scheduled for Tokyo just as the 1916 Games had been set for Berlin. In 1938 the Japanese withdrew their invitation to host the 1940 Games and World War II caused the cancellation of the 1944 Olympics.

Minority Olympians

In the interwar era women finally began to break down the Olympic barrier. Pierre de Coubertin had consistently opposed the participation of women in the Games. Nonetheless, while excluded from track and field, women had been permitted to enter golf and tennis competition in the Games of 1900 and a few events in the Games of 1912. European rather than American women led the crusade for female participation in track and field. Coubertin successfully staved off a female invasion of the 1920 Games, but the newly organized Fédération Sportive Féminine Internationale (FSFI) responded by sponsoring the First Women's Olympic Games in Paris in 1922. The competition furnished by the new Women's Olympic Games convinced the IOC to override Coubertin's objections. They adopted a five-event track and field program for the 1928 Olympics. As part of the compromise, the FSFI then changed the title of its meets to the International Ladies' Games, which continued to be held until 1934.[30]

American women wishing to participate in international competition faced the almost unanimous opposition of women physical educators. A small contingent of American females, organized by a male physician, competed in the Paris Games in 1922. The Paris Games touched off a complex debate in the United States about the desirability of women competing in highly competitive sports and an equally complex struggle for power between the AAU and various organizations of women physical educators for control of women's athletics. In 1924 the AAU staged the first national indoor and outdoor championships in track and field for women.[31] The 1928 Games had mixed results for the supporters of women's sports. Of the eleven women entering the 800 meter race, five

[30]Betty Spears, "Women in the Olympics: An Unresolved Problem," in Graham and Ueberhorst, *The Modern Olympics*, pp. 62–83; Mary Leigh, "The Evolution of Women's Participation in the Summer Olympic Games, 1900–1948" (unpublished Ph.D. dissertation, Ohio State University, 1947); Mary H. Leigh and Thérése M. Bonin, "The Pioneering Role of Madame Alice Millait and the FSI in Establishing International Track and Field Competition for Women," *Journal of Sport History*, 4 (Spring 1977), 72–83.

[31]George H. Vreeland, "Track and Field Women Champions," *National Athlete*, 5 (June 1924), 7–8.

dropped out before the race was completed, five collapsed after reaching the finishing line, and the remaining finisher fainted in the dressing room. The incident fueled the belief that women were incapable of coping with such vigorous, sustained physical activity and the IOC dropped the 800 meter race from future programs.

Nonetheless, two female Olympic competitors, Gertrude Ederle and Mildred "Babe" Didrickson, achieved the status of public celebrities. Ederle, who won a gold and two bronze medals in swimming in the 1924 Games, won renown for swimming the English Channel in 1926. She was not only the first woman to swim from France to England—a distance of thirty-three miles—but she accomplished the feat in fourteen hours and twenty-three minutes, smashing the men's record by more than two hours. She became an instant celebrity; the newspapers heralded her as "The Grease Smeared Venus," "Queen of the Waves," and as "America's Best Girl." Though only nineteen years old, the newspapers serialized her biography in microscopic detail. Upon her return to the United States, New York gave her a reception that dwarfed the greeting extended to Sergeant Alvin York upon his return from World War I. Only the return of Charles Lindbergh after his solo flight across the Atlantic a year later surpassed the welcome given to Ederle. Movie, stage, and commercial offers poured in, totalling an estimated $200,000. A pair of songwriters composed a quick tribute: "You're such a cutie, you're just as sweet as tutti-frutti, Trudy, who'll be the lucky fellow."[32] Exhibiting her talents in a huge collapsible swimming tank, Ederle toured American and European vaudeville houses. Then in 1928 she suffered a nervous breakdown. Although she soon recovered from the tragedy, the fickle public forgot her just as quickly as they had made her a public hero.

Though never quite soaring to the heights of public acclaim reached by Ederle in 1926, Babe Didrickson remained in the public limelight for many more years. Six times—in 1932, 1945, 1946, 1947, 1950, and 1954—the Associated Press named her as the Woman Athlete of the Year; in 1950 they picked her as the Woman Athlete of the Half Century. (Jim Thorpe received the honor as the top male athlete of the half century.) Between 1930 and 1932 she held American, Olympic, or world records in five separate track and field events. In 1930, 1931, and 1932 she was an "All-American" girls basketball player and led her team, the Golden Cyclones, to the AAU women's national championship in 1931. As a golfer, both professional and amateur, she had no equal; she won thirty-four of the eighty-eight tournaments she entered. Reportedly, she bowled a 170 average, could punt a football seventy-five yards, and for short distances could swim close to world record times.[33]

Didrickson amply fulfilled the American dream of success. One of seven children from a lower income, Norwegian immigrant family in Galveston, Texas, she joined the local boys in their games. She received her nickname,

---

[32]*New York Times*, August 7, 1926.

[33]See Babe Didrickson Zaharis, *This Life I've Led* (New York: A. S. Barnes, 1955); William Oscar Johnson and Nancy P. Williamson, *"Whatta-Gal": The Babe Didrickson Story* (Boston: Little, Brown, 1977).

"Babe," for her ability to hit home runs on the local sandlots. At Beaumont High School, she participated in all sports available to girls—volleyball, tennis, golf, basketball, and swimming. She excelled in basketball; her team never lost a game when she played. In 1930 the Employers Casualty Company of Dallas offered her a job—ostensibly as a stenographer—to play for the Golden Cyclones. The Golden Cyclones was essentially an arm of the firm's advertising division. The Company also sponsored her as the only member of the squad at the women's AAU track and field championships in 1932. In the space of three hours in a single afternoon, she won six gold medals and broke four world records—in the baseball throw, javelin, eighty-meter hurdles, and high jump. At the 1932 Olympics, she lived up to her legend. She broke the world records in the javelin, the eighty-meter hurdles, and the high jump, though the Olympic officials disqualified her high jump because she had "dived" over the bar. Had women been permitted to enter more than three events in the Olympics, Didrickson would undoubtedly have won even more gold medals.

After her success in the 1932 Olympics, Didrickson attempted to "cash in" on her popularity. She did a stint for the RKO vaudeville circuit, but hated it. She wanted to be outdoors. Opportunities for women in professional sport were virtually nonexistent. Didrickson's only recourse was to become an exhibitionist, to display her athletic prowess on the road, usually as a sideshow to the main attraction. In the fall of 1933 she toured the country with a basketball squad called Babe Didrickson's All Americans. The team consisted of four men and two or three women, including Didrickson. It toured the tank towns, playing against local men's basketball teams. In 1934, as a promotional gimmick, she pitched in spring training games for several major league teams and that summer she toured with the bearded House of David baseball team. Despite the Great Depression, it is estimated that she earned more than $40,000 from product endorsements and barnstorming tours in the first three and a half years of her career as a professional athlete.[34] But she disliked the life of an itinerant athlete and determined to master the game of golf. Her success in golf was as legendary as her feats in track and by 1956, when she died from cancer, she had won nearly every title available to women.

Didrickson's larger significance to women's sports is difficult to assess. She demonstrated dramatically that women could achieve excellence in sport and even earn a large amount of money from it. She was in that sense an inspiration to aspiring female athletes. On the other hand, her personality and associations with vagabond ball players did nothing to advance her as a model for the young women of the day. Her rough social demeanor, especially in her early days, combined with unmitigated arrogance to accentuate the stereotype of female athletes as "muscle molls" who resembled men more than women. Her biographers report that "she was used as a kind of bogeywoman by mothers who wished to prevent their budding tomboy daughters from pursuing sports."[35] In 1938 she married

[34]Johnson and Williamson, "*Whatta-Gal,*" p. 132.
[35]Ibid.

George Zaharias, a professional wrestler, and began to cultivate a more feminine image. As a professional golfer in the 1940s and 1950s she won a certain degree of social respectability, even in the most straight-laced of social circles. Although Didrickson campaigned for bigger purses in women's golf, she was not a crusader for women's equality in sport; she initiated no revolution in women's sport. This revolution awaited the 1960s and 1970s.

Neither did sprinter James Cleveland "Jesse" Owens, the American hero of the 1936 Olympics, spark a revolution in the status of blacks in sport.[36] Like Didrickson, Owens was from a poor family. The son of Alabama sharecroppers, he migrated with his family to Cleveland, Ohio. In both high school and college he won a wide reputation as a track star. (In most cases even Northern colleges excluded blacks from their team sports but welcomed them in the individual sports). As a sophomore at Ohio State University in 1935 he broke four world records at the annual Big Ten meet. In the 1936 Olympics he competed in twelve events, including preliminary heats, and set or equalled world marks nine times. In 1950 the sports reporters selected him as the best track athlete of the first fifty years of the twentieth century; he received twice as many votes as runner-up Jim Thorpe.

Owen's remarkable victories symbolized a kind of savage irony. On the one hand, he gave the lie—at least in the case of sport—to the Nazi argument for "Aryan" supremacy and he was a hero to white and black Americans alike. Yet in 1935 and 1936, twenty-six blacks lost their lives in the United States from lynchings. In 1936 the walls of racial segregation in the United States seemed as unbreachable as ever; no blacks played in major league baseball or professional football and few played on integrated college teams. Owens himself preferred the role of the symbol of what a black man could accomplish in sport rather than that of a crusader for black rights.

[36]See Mandell, *The Nazi Olympics.*

12

Television and Professional Football

In the three decades following 1950 the American sporting scene underwent startling changes. In 1950 millions of Americans had never seen a live big-league baseball, football, basketball, or hockey match. Only forty-two major-league franchises existed, and these were located mostly in the tier of industrial cities of the Northeast and upper Midwest. In 1980 the figure had swollen to 101; by then, big-league franchises had been planted in every section of the nation. In 1950 less than 10 percent of the households owned television sets for watching big-time sport; by the 1960s, 94 percent of American families owned one or more television sets. In 1950 pro football lagged far behind baseball and college football in generating excitement among fans; by the 1960s it had pushed well ahead of its major rivals. In 1950 the reserve clause in player contracts stood inviolate; it prevented the players from using the free market to maximize their salaries. Thirty years later the reserve clause was in legal shambles, the players had formed unions, and players' salaries had soared to undreamed-of heights. In 1950 major-league baseball rosters included nine blacks, the National Basketball Association one, and the National Football League five. Thirty years later some 75 percent of the NBA players were black, as were 50 percent of the NFL and 20 percent of the big-league baseball players. In 1950 intercollegiate sport for women hardly existed; in 1980 some 916 colleges offered fourteen varsity sports for women.

Why the startling changes? To be sure, Americans had more money and leisure time, though the upward spiral in real incomes began to level off sharply in the 1970s. The weakening of individual inner restraints, a process which had been well underway in the 1920s, continued apace. By 1951 psychiatrist Martha Wolfenstein identified the widespread acceptance of what she called a "fun morality." Instead of being suspect and a source of possible shame as it once had been, "having fun" for many Americans had become obligatory.[1] Furthermore, as society became more complicated and as success had to be won increasingly through the acquisition of expertise or the development of a "bureaucratic personality," Americans continued, as they had done as early as the 1920s, to seek compensatory heroes. The "stars" of the world of entertainment—rock music, movies, radio, television, and sport—rather than the worlds of business, science, or politics continued to furnish them with heroes, or perhaps more precisely

---

[1]Martha Wolfenstein, "The Emergence of Fun Morality," *Journal of Social Issues*, 7 (1951), 15–29.

celebrities, who leapt to fame and fortune outside of bureaucratic structures. The world of entertainment also provided a source of excitement for many who otherwise led dull, unexciting lives. Yet a single technological marvel had a more direct and ultimately a more profound impact upon the history of modern spectator sports. That marvel was television.[2]

TELEVISED SPORTS

With the advent of television the fans at home rather than those in the stadium or the arena came to be the ultimate arbiters of American sport. Before the 1950s, newspapers, magazines, and radio had stimulated interest in sport, but television permitted millions who had never seen a major league baseball game, a pro football game, or the Olympic Games to hear and see the spectacles in the comfort of their homes. In 1967, for instance, an average of 575,091 fans attended all National Football League games on a given weekend but some 11.4 million households watched NFL games on television. Ten years later the number of households with television sets tuned into pro football on a typical weekend had jumped to nearly 20 million. In 1970 the three major networks combined telecast about fifteen hours a week of sport; by 1980 the coverage had increased to twenty-five hours.[3]

After 1950 the television moguls and sport magnates increasingly "marketed" sporting spectacles for potential television audiences rather than those who attended the live games. They reshaped sport and the sporting experience to attract television viewers and meet the demands of commercial sponsors. The networks had once considered Saturday and Sunday afternoons to be "slow times" when audience ratings fell far below week nights. Consequently, they often turned the medium over to a "cultural ghetto" of concerts, serious drama, and special news programs. But the potentialities of televised sport changed all of that. Finding that sport could swell the size of an audience in an otherwise low viewing time, the networks added more and more sports programming. Partly after careful scrutiny of A. C. Nielsen ratings and partly on impulse, advertisers decided which contests, if any, they would sponsor on television. More than

[2]For general treatments of television and sports, see William O. Johnson, Jr., *Super Spectator and the Electric Lilliputians* (Boston: Little, Brown, 1971); Donald Edwin Parente, "A History of Television and Sports" (unpublished Ph.D. dissertation, University of Illinois, 1974); Parente, "The Interdependence of Sports and Television," *Journal of Communication,* 27 (September 1977), 128–32; Martin Mayer, *About Television* (New York: Harper & Row, 1972), Chap. 7; Ira Horowitz, "Sports Broadcasting," in Roger C. Noll, ed., *Government and the Sports Business* (Washington, D.C.: Brookings Institution, 1974), 275–324; Bert Randolph Sugar, *"The Thrill of Victory": The Inside Story of ABC Sports* (New York: Hawthorne, 1978).

[3]*New York Times,* December 30, 1979, S7. While television became an ever more important ingredient in the economics of sports, sports also grew in importance for the economics of television. For instance, in 1970, sports accounted for $46 million of NBC's $536 million gross billings to advertisers, or 8.5 percent; five years later the figure had risen to $104 million, or 14 percent.

ever before television wedded spectator sport to the nation's vast entertainment and advertising industries.

Almost single-handedly the new electronic medium revolutionized the economics of big-time sport. No sporting entrepreneur, no matter how rich or imaginative, dared buy a team, stage a sporting spectacle, build a stadium, or even set a date or starting time for a game without first consulting the moguls of television. Television poured millions of new dollars into big league professional and "big-time" intercollegiate sports. Soaring television revenues helped induce numerous franchise shifts and a rapid increase in the number of professional sport franchises. Real and potential television income plus favorable federal income tax laws ignited spiraling increases in the market value of major-league sport franchises. Television revenue plus the assistance of the federal courts and the player associations encouraged a players' revolt among professional athletes. Many of them secured multiyear, six-digit contracts and made as much money from lucrative television commercials and other endorsements as they did from playing their games.

But television could also be harmful to sport. For instance, in the late 1940s and early 1950s television lifted boxing to a new "Golden Era" only to deal it a blow from which it never recovered. In 1944 the Gillette Safety Razor Company signed a pact with Madison Square Garden to sponsor weekly telecasts of fights. Soon other sponsors followed and the weekly Gillette fights became something of a Friday night institution. Millions of Americans who had never seen a prize fight before became devotees of the sport. Fascinated fans even loved the Golden Glove bouts which usually featured the flailings of inept amateurs. The pay days for boxers soared; at the peak of the televised era of boxing, each fighter received about $4,000 per bout.

Then in the 1950s the happy union of television and boxing came apart. To continue programming such a busy schedule of bouts required an endless supply of winning fighters. "The big thing you were up against is that there had to be a loser, you know? And you couldn't bring a loser back on TV," explained Chris Dundee, a prominent fight promoter from Miami Beach, Florida. "The sponsors didn't want losers, just winners. And let's face it, the sponsors called the shots during the TV age of boxing."[4] Moreover, the sponsors wanted sluggers. Television fight fans had little patience for exhibitions of boxing skills; they wanted heavy hitters and frequent knockouts. Consequently, television drove down live attendance and destroyed dozens of once-prospering small fight clubs which were responsible for the nurture of future fighters. (While television was primarily responsible for the decline of boxing, fight corruption, which was highly publicized in congressional hearings in the 1950s, also contributed to the problems of the sport.) By 1960 only the Gillette Friday night bouts (cancelled in 1964) appeared regularly on network television. Never again

[4]Johnson, *Super Spectator*, p. 92. See also Arthur Daley, "Is Boxing on the Ropes?" *New York Times Magazine* (January 31, 1954), 19, 22; Charles Einstein, "TV Slugs the Boxers," *Harper's Magazine*, 213 (August 1956), 65–68; and Barney Nagler, *James Norris and the Decline of Boxing* (Indianapolis, Ind.: Bobbs Merrill, 1964).

would boxing recover its glory days of the late 1940s and early 1950s.

Television compelled the professional sports tycoons and college authorities to alter the nature of their games. Meeting the needs of television sometimes required only slight modifications in the rules and traditions of the sport; in other instances age-old practices had to be abandoned. In football, television forced changes in the rhythm and time sequence of the sport. The National Football League reduced half-time intermissions from 20 to 15 minutes, thereby permitting the networks to fit games conveniently into two-and-a-half hour time segments without interrupting their regular programming. So that the requisite number of commercials could be shown, referees received signals from the television crew to call arbitrary time-outs. By the mid-1970s, the networks called fourteen timeouts while the game was in progress. Consequently, to include the increased time committed to commercials, the networks had to lengthen the schedule for each game from two-and-a-half hours to three hours.

To speed up play and to increase chances of having a "big name" player in the final rounds, golf abandoned match for medal play and introduced the "sudden-death" tie-breaker when two or more players were tied for the lead at the end of regulation play. Tennis likewise began to use a tie-breaker system when sets reached six games for each contestant. Television alone did not appear to be responsible for any major rule changes in baseball, but to attract a larger television audience, the major leagues did agree to switch the World Series from its traditional daytime hours to nighttime. Television induced directly or indirectly many other smaller, subtle changes in the nation's sports.

Some sports were intrinsically better suited to the requirements of the medium than others. Baseball, for instance, fared poorly in competition with football. Unlike football, in which much of the action of the game could be distilled to a small part of the field, the essence of baseball included an acute awareness of the entire playing area. The baseball fan not only enjoyed the isolated instances of action—the pitch, hit, catch, or put-out—but he also wanted to see the runner leading off base, the signals of the third base coach, and the positions taken by the fielders. The relationship of the hit ball to the playing area was a vital part of observing a baseball game. Only the fan in the stands, not the television viewer, could command all these perspectives. Unlike football fans, few lovers of baseball claimed that watching a televised game was superior to being physically present at the game.

Football, on the other hand, was an ideal sport for telecasting. The central requirement of the game—that the offense must move the ball ten yards in four plays or give it up to the opposing team—set up recurring crisis points that kept the viewer's attention riveted to the little silver screen. The twenty-second intermission between plays permitted the viewer to savor the drama. If the situation were third down and long yardage, would the linebackers blitz? Would the quarterback throw or call a draw play? Viewers could second-guess the coach or the quarterback. Moreover, instant replays and slow motion shots allowed the fans to experience an entirely different game from that of the spectator in the stands. While the fans' attention might be diffused or centered on extraneous action during the original play, the replay and slow motion shots could pinpoint the receiver running his pattern, the vicious blocking of interior linemen, or the balletlike steps of running backs eluding would-be tacklers. In short, television altered the characteristic space and rhythm of football. More than one viewer shared the judgment of Richard Kostelanetz who declared that, compared to telecast games, "live games now seem peculiarly inept, lethargic, and pedestrian."[5]

Suspecting that the presentation of sport alone would not hold the viewer's attention, producers of sport telecasts experimented with ways of making the contests more interesting. From the earliest days of the medium they supplemented the visual images with interviews, graphics, catchy music, and the words of play-by-play announcers. As announcers, they initially employed mostly former radio broadcasters who were known for their "golden throats" and abilities to describe in abundant and vivid detail the course of a game. Television presented special problems for radio men who had been converted into television announcers. They tended to talk too much, to fill vacuums in the action with repetitive small talk about matters already familiar to the fans. Apparently television producers feared that any gap in talking would cause fickle fans to turn off their sets.

The play-by-play men confronted other problems. Despite risking ridicule for engaging in hyperbole and over-dramatization (when the fans could see the game themselves) garrulous announcers rarely curbed a propensity for exaggeration and endless truisms. Since nearly all announcers were either employed by the local team, or at least dependent upon the team's or league's approval, they rarely criticized the home team, the players, umpires, or the commissioners of professional sports leagues. In most cases they acted as the salesman for the sports which they covered. Those few announcers who did take a more critical stance found their jobs jeopardized.[6]

The telecast producers replaced many of the former radio play-by-play men with "expert" analysts or celebrities. By the 1960s, dozens of athletes, ex-athletes, and even referees began to invade the broadcast booths. While the diction of athletes-as-announcers sometimes bordered on incomprehensibility, the producers believed that the athlete's "inside" knowledge added to the fan's enjoyment. Producers also chose announcers for their personal popularity with the fans. In 1948 *Newsweek* declared that Dennis James, who would later become a popular television game host, had "become a minor celebrity" in New York for his role as a commentator on television wrestling matches and a daily five-minute sports highlights show.[7]

---

[5]Richard Kostelanetz, "Fanfare for TV Football," *Intellectual Digest*, 3 (August 1973), 54. See also Joan M. Chandler, "TV & Sports: Wedded with a Golden Hoop," *Psychology Today*, 10 (April 1977), 64–76.

[6]See Jerry Kirshenbaum, "And Here, to Bring You the Play by Play...," *Sports Illustrated*, 35 (September 13, 1971), 33–43; and "FCC Investigates NFL Control over TV Announcers," *Audible* (November 1973), 4.

[7]"James of the Tele-Waves," *Newsweek*, 31 (April 26, 1948), 56–57.

In the 1950s, following the path of Dennis James, Jay Hanna "Dizzy" Dean took the center stage, leaving the game as background images for the spell of his personality. Dean, a former pitching star for the St. Louis Cardinals in the 1930s, began his broadcasting career in 1940 as a radio commentator for the St. Louis Browns. In 1950 he moved to New York to describe the Yankee games for WBAD, the flag station of the DuMont radio and television network. He was an "instant success" in New York and in 1955 joined Buddy Blattner, another ex-major-league ball player, to do CBS's national "Game of the Week." Dean, who claimed to have attended a one-room school in Chickalah, Oklahoma only long enough to get into the "Second Reader," enthralled viewers with his country drawl, unusual verbal conjugations, uninhibited anecdotes, and "corn pone idiom." He mixed descriptions of the game with lengthy discourses on the marvels of eating black-eyed peas and hunting "possums" in persimmon trees. When the game was unusually slow or boring, he might bawl out an impromptu version of the "Wabash Cannonball." Yet Dean remained something of an exception. By and large, announcers belonged to what one critic called the "colorless, odorless, bloodless, hapless school of commentary."[8]

In the 1960s and 1970s Roone P. Arledge of the sports division of ABC revolutionized the sportscasting industry. After winning a television Emmy for producing the best children's program—"Hi, Mom"—in 1959 on NBC, Arledge joined ABC in 1960 to direct and produce the network's football games. Arledge was determined, as he put it, "to get the audience involved emotionally. If they didn't give a damn about the game, they still might enjoy the program."[9] To obtain more audience involvement, Arledge attempted to capture the full ambience of the game setting. He used cranes, blimps, and helicopters to furnish better views of the stadium, the campus, and the town; hand-held cameras for close-up shots of cheerleaders, pretty coeds, band members, eccentric spectators, and nervous coaches; and rifle-type microphones to pick up the roar of the crowd, the thud of a punt, or the crunch of a hard tackle. Arledge made the crowd itself part of the performance. Once the fans perceived themselves as potential performers, they began to carry banners, run onto the playing field, and engage in unseemly antics to grab the attention of the television cameras. In the early 1970s shots in the stands of scantily clad women—usually local strippers seeking free publicity—aroused so much protest that ABC cut back its coverage of some of the more bizarre forms of off-the-field behavior.

Arledge also brought his talents to "The Wide World of Sports" and the Olympic Games. In 1961 Arledge began production of "The Wide World of Sports," which soon became a weekend institution. Winner of four Emmys—more than any other sport telecast—the first sport program to use satellites, the first to beam a sport program directly from the Soviet Union, and a pioneer in stop-action filming, Wide World consisted of a

[8]"Swing, Swanged, and Swunged," *Time,* 55 (April 24, 1950), 59–60; Frank X. Tolbert, "Dizzy Dean—He's Not So Dumb," *Saturday Evening Post,* 224 (July 4, 1951), 25, 102–4; P. W. Reese, "Old Diz Wasn't Just A-Woofin," *Reader's Digest,* 107 (October 1975), 167–68; Curt Smith, *America's Dizzy Dean* (St. Louis: Bethany, 1978), pp. 141–74.

[9]Quoted in Johnson, *Super Spectator,* p. 161. See also Roone Arledge with Gilbert Rogin, "It's Sport...It's Money...It's TV," *Sports Illustrated,* 24 (April 25, 1966), 92–106.

potpourri of feats and games, including, among others, boxing matches, track meets, ski races, surfing, cliff diving, barrel jumping, wrist wrestling, and demolition derbies. The program was especially effective in stimulating public interest in winter sports. Although normally effusive in its enthusiasm for all sports, no matter how trivial, Wide World's occasional interviews by Howard Cosell of Muhammad Ali, Joe Namath, and other more or less controversial sports figures added spice to the telecasts. The program spawned several imitations by the other networks, none of which quite equalled the technical finesse and lively pace of Wide World. Finally, Arledge turned the 1968, 1972, and 1976 Olympic Games into marvelous television extravaganzas. So successful were Arledge's productions that Pete Axthelm suggested, perhaps with tongue in cheek, that Arledge ought to be put in charge of the entire management of the Games. The ABC sports department helped to push the network from a weak third place in ratings in the 1960s to the top in the mid-1970s.[10]

One of Arledge's productions, "Monday Night Football," outstripped all other regular sportcasts in popularity. Initiated in 1970, this prime-time sports show altered the Monday-night habits of a large portion of the American people. Movie attendance reportedly nose-dived, restaurants closed, and bowlers rescheduled their leagues. Much of the success of Monday Night Football stemmed from Arledge's decision to hire Howard Cosell, already the most controversial sportscaster in the country, as a commentator. (At Arledge's insistence, ABC refused to sign the traditional contracts providing for "announcer-approvals" by the sports leagues.) From the first telecast, Cosell, who had championed Muhammad Ali's resistance to the Vietnam draft and right to retain the heavyweight crown, sparked controversy. Analysts concluded that Cosell was a man the audience "loved to hate." While Cosell often sounded like any other announcer of the "great play" tradition, he also proudly claimed to "tell it like it is." Caustic, unctuous, polysyllabic, given to overblown rhetoric, his comments often offended patrons of a mythic sports world. Yet the very same patrons found him irresistible. Unlike any other broadcaster, Cosell was able simultaneously to promote, report, and criticize an event packaged and merchandised by his own network. With characteristic bluntness, Cosell summarized his own role as a performer and television's effort to enhance the sporting experience with extraneous entertainment. "Look there is no damn way you can go up against Liz Taylor and Doris Day in prime-time TV and present sports as just sports or as religion."[11]

[10]"Playboy Interview: Roone Arledge," Playboy, 23 (October 1976), 63–86; "Shooting Craps," Newsweek, 54 (January 1, 1962), 52; "Programming: A Locker in the Living Room," Time, 90 (October 20, 1967), 73; Frank Deford, "TV Talk," Sports Illustrated, 34 (April 16, 1971), 7; Leonard Schecter, "Why It's Better to Watch on TV," New York Times Magazine (March 3, 1968), 32–38; Pete Axthelm, "Let Roone Do It," Newsweek, 88 (August 9, 1976), 51.

[11]Quoted in Randall Poe, "The Angry Fan," Harper's, 251 (November 1975), 86. On Cosell and Monday-night football, see "This is Howard Cosell," Newsweek, 80 (October 2, 1972), 54–56, 61–62; Robert Daley, "The Man They Love to Hate," New York Times Magazine (September 1, 1974), 10–11, 27; Robert H. Boyle, "TV Wins on Points," Sports Illustrated, 33 (November 2, 1970), 14–17; and, above all, Howard Cosell, Cosell (New York: Pocket Books, 1973).

As Cosell hinted, television made it increasingly difficult for the fans to distinguish between the real and the unreal in sports. One of the principal attractions of sport, unlike other forms of entertainment, was its "spontaneous reality," or absence of contrivance. Even on television, sports often seemed to be a "lush island of the authentic" surrounded by a "sea of the synthetic."[12] Yet television's power to project and magnify competing images tended to obliterate a sharp division between the real and the pseudoevent. For instance, the image of O. J. Simpson, star running back of the Buffalo Bills, barreling down the sidelines competed with the images of Simpson furiously pedaling a bicycle on "Superstars," futilely trying to hit a backhand on "Celebrity Tennis," and gracefully leaping through airports for Hertz Corporation advertisements.

[12]Poe, "The Angry Fan," 86–95; Herbert I. London, "TV Sports: Real Life's Last Stand," *Television Quarterly*, 13 (May-July 1976), 57–60.

Which of Simpson's feats was the "real" sporting event? Which represented Simpson as the "real" athletic hero? As athletes assumed multiple media roles and the networks introduced more activities extraneous to the sporting event to the airwaves, the line between the sports hero and the mere celebrity tended to vanish. Frequently the fans in cities where the Monday Night Football games were telecast appeared to be more interested in the announcers and the accompanying fanfare than the game itself. Who could tell whether the heroes were broadcasters Frank Gifford, Don Meredith, and Howard Cosell or the athletes on the field? In short, contrivances external to sports as well as the power of television to magnify images tended to interfere with or overwhelm the fan's capacity to distinguish between the genuine and the artificial in sports.

Nonetheless, the networks began to add more "trashsports" to regular sports programming. ABC initiated the proliferation of trashsports with "The Superstars" in 1973. "Superstars" featured the nation's top athletes competing against one another in events outside of their specialties. At ABC "The Superstars" begat "The Women Superstars," "The World Superstars," "The Super-Teams," and "Battle of the Network Stars." CBS responded with "Challenge of the Sexes" and "Celebrity Challenge of the Sexes." NBC entered the competition with "Dynamic Duos" and "US Against the World," a celebrity Olympics. "The way we are going," asserted Curt Gowdy, a spokesman of the old school of sportscasting, "we'll see Secretariat racing a Wyoming antelope." There seemed to be no end for the potential of trashsports. "I've got ideas for telecasts in envelopes piled as high as this building," declared Bob Wussler, the president of CBS Sports in 1978. "I'll bet 25 percent of those ideas are good ones."[13] Trashsports were troubling enough to sports purists, but the networks also began to produce their own tennis and boxing matches, putting up the prize money and handpicking the participants. Critics could envision a new era of sport completely managed by television.

In 1979 "sports junkies" rejoiced when a new corporation, the Entertainment Sports Programming Network (ESPN), launched the nation's first round-the-clock sports telecasts. Using 625 television cable systems and a satellite for transmission, ESPN could reach 20 percent of the nation's television viewers. The network encountered no difficulties in recruiting sponsors. In its first year, it concentrated upon the telecast of regional college sports. Under its contract with the NCAA, ESPN could telecast hundreds of NCAA events in some eighteen sports. To protect ABC's exclusive rights to carry live intercollegiate football games, ESPN had to restrict its telecasts of football games on a tape-delayed basis. The network also initiated negotiations with the major professional leagues in football, baseball, hockey, and basketball to telecast games not under contract by the major networks. While skeptics wondered whether there were enough

---

[13]Both statements quoted in Poe, "The Angry Fan," 95. For trashsports also see, "See Willie Mays Bowl," *Newsweek,* 91 (March 6, 1978), 101–2; Dan Levin, "You Got to Have a Gimmick," *Sports Illustrated,* 38 (March 5, 1973), 24–25; Curry Kirkpatrick, "There Is Nothing Like a Dame," *Sports Illustrated,* 42 (January 6, 1975), 22–24.

sports addicts to keep the network afloat, a founder of ESPN declared that "We believe that the appetite for sports in this country is insatiable."[14] The major networks worried lest ESPN gain the financial clout to snare the telecast rights of such major sporting events as the Olympic Games, the Super Bowl, or the World Series.

THE EARLY DAYS OF PRO FOOTBALL

By far the biggest beneficiary of television was professional football. The pro version of the game had modest origins. The tough mine and mill towns in western Pennsylvania and Ohio furnished the cradle for the infant sport that was to become modern professional football. As early as the 1890s, local athletic clubs, YMCAs, or employees of a particular business concern organized football teams and bolstered their playing strength by hiring an outside player or two, usually for sums of less than $100 per game. In the first two decades of the twentieth century, intense rivalries between teams from Massillon, Canton, Dayton, and Youngstown, Ohio, led to the practice of paying a fee or part of the gate receipts to all the players. For most of the players, football was simply a weekend activity. No one could make enough money from football alone to survive. The Panhandlers, a team representing the Panhandle Shops of the Pennsylvania Railroad in Columbus, Ohio, may have been typical of the pre-1920 teams. "The boys worked in the shop until four Saturday afternoon, got their suppers at home, grabbed the rattlers to any point within twelve hours' ride of Columbus, played the Sunday game, took another train to Columbus and punched the time clock at seven Monday morning."[15] No leagues existed in the pre-1920 era and each team scheduled its own matches.

Unlike the college game with its aura of respectability arising from its origins among the upper-status, old-stock Americans, pro football's early ambience was ethnic, Catholic, and working class. Team rosters included a broad spectrum of racial and ethnic groups: Irish, East Europeans, native Americans, and blacks were especially conspicuous. For almost a decade Jim Thorpe, the hero of the 1912 Olympics and Carlisle Indian School football great, was the game's premier attraction. Collegians and ex-collegians, especially from Notre Dame, often played under aliases and would "jump" from one team to another, playing where they could earn the most money on a given Sunday. Knute Rockne and Gus Dorais, for

[14]Quoted in William Oscar Johnson, "Sports Junkies of the U.S., Rejoice!" *Sports Illustrated*, 51 (July 23, 1979), 43. See also Harry F. Waters, "An All-Sports TV Network," *Newsweek*, 94 (November 12, 1979), 124; Lorenzo Middleton, "The Cable Connection," *Chronicle of Higher Education*, 19 (December 3, 1979), 6–7; Brooks Clark, "ESPN: It's Not for Everybody," *Television Quarterly*, 16 (Winter 1979–80), 53–60.

[15]Harry A. March, *Pro Football: Its Ups and Downs*, 2nd ed. (New York: J. B. Lyon, 1934), p. 65. For pro football see also Tom Bennett et al., *The NFL's Official Encyclopedic History of Professional Football* (New York: Macmillan, 1977); and George Halas with Gwen Morgan and Arthur Veysey, *Halas by Halas* (New York: McGraw-Hill, 1979).

example, played for six different teams in a single season. The playing of collegians and sometimes high school athletes under assumed names, the wagering of the players on the contests, and charges of game fixing damaged the public image of the sport. In response to these conditions and in hope of improving the profitability of pro football, Joseph F. Carr, a sportswriter, minor-league baseball executive, and manager of the Columbus football team, suggested that pro teams form an alliance. Of the indeterminate number of teams that joined the American Professional Football Association in 1920—renamed the National Football League (NFL) in 1922—most were located in Ohio, and none represented a major metropolitan area.* Carr served as president of the league from 1921 to his death in 1939.

In the 1920s and 1930s the NFL teams rarely enjoyed success at the box office. In the twenties the entire attendance of the NFL for a given Sunday seldom exceeded 75,000; by 1930 several colleges could draw that many fans to a single contest. In the thirties, big games between winning teams and play-off games might attract 30,000 to 40,000 fans, but an attendance of 4,000 to 5,000 was more typical. Unlike the colleges, the pros suffered from the absence of a built-in constituency. Among many college men, especially the nonethnics, play for pay continued to carry the stigma of ungentlemanly behavior. They frowned upon former collegians who joined the pro ranks or became fans of the pro game. Thus in the early days pro football had to appeal largely to a noncollege audience which was unfamiliar with the delights of football. Moreover, the newspapers all but ignored the pro game. Even in the daily papers located in cities with pro franchises, the reader could often find pages of speculation and reports on college games, but no mention at all of pro games.[16]

The NFL suffered from other problems. The low costs of obtaining a franchise and fielding a team—salaries, the major team expense, seldom averaged more than $100 per player for each game—encouraged the entry of franchises from small market areas. In the twenties, more than thirty cities dropped in and out of the league. Gradually the NFL shed its "small-town" character. In 1921 George Halas transferred the Decatur, Illinois, franchise to Chicago, in 1922 the Chicago Cardinals joined the loop, and in 1925 Timothy Mara, a bookmaker, and Billy Gibson, the manager of Gene Tunney, planted a franchise in New York. The Great Depression of the 1930s wiped out the franchises in the smaller cities; by 1934 Green Bay, Wisconsin, was the sole survivor of the small-town era. Despite its size, the Packers, under the leadership of Curly Lambeau, fielded one of the strongest teams of the decade. The league also suffered from an inability to attract a large number of top college players to the game. Even though the NFL signed some of the college heroes of the twenties, such as Red Grange, Ernie Nevers, and Bronco Nagurski, most college graduates could make

*Several teams that joined the loop played no games against league opponents. In 1921 the playing teams in the league consisted of the Chicago Staleys, Buffalo, Akron, Green Bay, Canton, Dayton, Rock Island, Chicago Cardinals, Cleveland, Rochester, Detroit, Columbus, and Cincinnati.

[16]"Poor Professional Football," *Outlook*, 144 (October 1926), 262.

more money in business or the professions than in playing the pro game.

Despite the grimness of the depression, omens of a better future for the NFL appeared in the 1930s. Pro rulemakers boldly departed from the collegians. They moved the hashmarks ten yards inside the sidelines (1933), permitted forward passes from any spot behind the line of scrimmage (1933), and allowed free substitutions (1943). In 1934 renowned humorist Will Rogers warned the colleges: "Now, as football is not only the backbone but the very gravy of college existence, you fellows better open up your game for this pro game was just made for an audience."[17] The adoption of two divisions in 1933 with a championship game between the winners at the end of the season also enhanced interest in the sport. In 1936, at the instigation of Bert Bell of the Philadelphia Eagles, the NFL adopted the "draft" which allowed teams the exclusive right to contract for the services of college players in reverse order of their league standing for the previous season. Ostensibly, the draft was designed to equalize competition between clubs, but it also strengthened the owner's bargaining position with potential players.

In the 1930s the professionals began to dispel the common idea among fans that the quality of their play was inferior to that of the collegians. In a 1930 charity game between the New York Giants and a Notre Dame all-star alumni team coached by Knute Rockne, the Four Horsemen failed to get untracked; the former Irish gained only one first down the entire game, and the Giants won 21–0. In 1934 Arch Ward, sportswriter for the *Chicago Tribune,* invented the College All-Star Game which pitted the NFL champion of the previous year against recently graduated college seniors. Although in the first decade of the series the champions failed to overwhelm the collegians, the series attracted large gates, added to the respectability of pro football, and gained the attention of the nation's press. By 1939 league attendance reached a new high, averaging nearly 20,000 fans per game.

The NFL encountered a new set of problems in the 1940s. World War II ravaged rosters and staffs of the teams. At the conclusion of the war, attendance again spurted upward, almost doubling the 1939 average. However, the NFL now confronted an expensive war with the All-America Conference, organized in 1946. The competition for player talent drove up salaries, costing the combined leagues an estimated $6 million. In 1949 the All-America Conference finally surrendered to the NFL, though the Cleveland, San Francisco, and Baltimore franchises were allowed to enter the NFL on favorable terms. Three other developments boded well for the NFL's future. In 1946 the Cleveland franchise transferred to Los Angeles and promptly led league attendance with an average of 38,700 fans per game. Increasingly, the NFL was also able to sign most of the college stars to contracts. Finally, television, which had been experimentally used to telecast pro games as early as 1939, promised not only to provide a new source of lucrative income for pro teams, but it also created a new body of fans for the sport.

[17]Quoted in March, *Pro Football,* p. 122.

From the earliest days of television, professional football was more successful in managing the electronic medium than were other sports. Unlike the savagely independent barons of baseball, the owners of football franchises were willing to delegate much of their authority to the office of the commissioner. Their willingness to relinquish power stemmed in large part from their common ethno-religious origins and the long history of financial tribulations that had beset the sport. Through the many years of shoestring operations, team owners George Halas, Arthur Rooney, Jr., Timothy Mara, DeBenneville "Bert" Bell, and George Preston Marshall had worked together closely. Thus the NFL owners, unlike the more prosperous baseball owners had developed a "clubby" relationship, or, to use Robert Lipsyte's terms, they had come to constitute an "Irish Catholic clan."[18] Unlike the barons of baseball, they chose as commissioners men who had experience in the business side of the game.

Much of the success of the NFL in the era of televised sport was attributable to the astute leadership of commissioners Bert Bell and Alvin "Pete" Rozelle. Bell, a former owner-coach of the Philadelphia Eagles, had been appointed commissioner in 1946 and had proceeded to guide the NFL through a costly but successful four-year war (1946–1950) with the rival All-America Conference. Bell established the framework for the powerful NFL of the 1960s and 1970s headed by Rozelle. Unlike the timid, largely impotent commissioners of pro baseball and pro basketball, Bell used his authority to promote the welfare of the entire NFL. He was able to unite the faction-prone owners into what was essentially a single economic cartel, one far stronger than existed in any other professional sport.[19] After the death of Bell in 1959, the owners appointed Rozelle, formerly public relations director of the Los Angeles Rams, as commissioner in 1960. Rozelle was to become the most remarkable "czar" in the history of professional sport. The owners eventually delegated to him nearly complete authority to handle television negotiations, relations with the Federal Government, and controversies among themselves.

As early as 1952 Bell began to form the foundations for the NFL's successful marriage to television. The marriage, finally consummated with the passage of the Sports Broadcasting Act in 1961, rested on the blackout of home games, the blackout of telecasts of outside games in a team's home territory, and the league negotiating a network "package" contract rather than each franchise negotiating separate television contracts. The experience of the Los Angeles Rams convinced Bell of the need for restricted telecasts. In 1949 the Rams drew 205,109 fans to their home games. In 1950, when for the first time the club telecast each of its home games,

---

[18]Robert Lipsyte, *Sportsworld: An American Dreamland* (New York: Quadrangle/New York Times, 1975), p. 60.

[19]Benjamin G. Rader, "DeBenneville 'Bert' Bell," *Dictionary of American Biography, Supplement Six* (New York: Charles Scribner's Sons, 1980), 47–48. On Rozelle, see Frank Deford, "Long Live the King," *Sports Illustrated*, 52 (Jan. 21, 1980), 100–119.

attendance fell to 110,162. In 1951 the Rams again blacked out home games, and attendance promptly doubled.[20] Bell concluded that, when dealing with the new medium, the league has to act as a single unit. Despite the formidable opposition of several owners who wanted to retain individual control over all broadcast rights, Bell rammed through the 1952 owners' meeting amendments to the NFL bylaws. The new bylaws would make Bell the dictator of NFL television.

But then the Department of Justice intervened; the Department insisted that the revised NFL bylaws constituted a restraint of trade and thus violated the Sherman Anti-Trust Act. Bell rallied the owners to fight the order in the federal courts. In 1953, Judge Alan K. Grim of the Federal District Court for Eastern Pennsylvania ruled that professional football was indeed a "unique kind of business" in which the classic forms of economic competition could lead to disaster for the entire league. Although Grim rejected the commissioner's sweeping power to control the telecasts of member franchises, he implicitly upheld the home-game blackouts and the prohibition of the telecast of outside games when the home team was playing.[21] Bert Bell was elated.

With telecast rights partially restricted, the electronic medium proved to be an immense stimulus to the popularity of pro football. Television helped the novice fan to understand and appreciate the intricacies of the sport. As one fan put it: "You watched a game on television and, suddenly, the wool was stripped from your eyes. What had appeared to be an incomprehensible tangle of milling bodies from the grandstand, made sense. [Television] created a nation of instant experts in no time."[22] One game, the 1958 championship tilt between the Baltimore Colts and the New York Giants, seemed to trigger the national mania for pro football, which would reach unprecedented proportions in the next decade. With only seven seconds left in the game, Steve Myhra of the Colts calmy kicked a twenty-yard field goal to tie the game at 17–17. For the first time in NFL history, the championship game went into a "sudden death" overtime. Some thirty million fans watched their screens intently as John Unitas, the Baltimore quarterback, took "the Thirteen Steps to Glory," marching the Colts down the field for the winning touchdown. Television had enabled millions to share the excitement of a classic sporting contest.

Television also played a key role in the eventual success of the American Football League. In 1959 Lamar Hunt of Dallas and K. S. "Bud" Adams of Houston, two millionaire Texans who had been rebuffed in their efforts to obtain franchises in the NFL, announced the formation of the rival AFL. The AFL began to play in 1960 with eight teams: Boston, Buffalo, Dallas, Denver, Houston, Los Angeles, New York, and Oakland. The NFL retaliated by placing competing franchises in Dallas and preempting

[20]Ira Horowitz, "Sports Broadcasting," in Robert G. Noll, ed., *Government and the Sports Business* (Washington, D.C.: Brookings Institution, 1974), pp. 285–86, offers factors other than television that account for the ricocheting attendance at the Rams' games.

[21]US v. National Football League, 116 F. Supp. 319 (1953).

[22]Quoted in Associated Press, *A Century of Major American Sports* (Maplewood, N.J.: Hamond, 1975), pp. 17–18.

Minnesota. The AFL nearly lost the struggle for survival at the outset; it lost an estimated $3 million the first year and the undercapitalized New York franchise, the key to the AFL's potential success, threatened to drive the entire league into bankruptcy. In 1960 Harry Wismer, former sportscaster and eccentric owner of the New York team, persuaded the AFL owners to sell the league's national television rights to ABC. (Previously each pro sport franchise had sold their television rights separately.) Although the contract with ABC was not a lucrative one, it reduced AFL losses and apparently induced the NFL to sign a similar pact with CBS in 1961.

The contract which gave CBS exclusive national telecast rights of NFL games resulted in an immediate suit by the Justice Department. Judge Grim concluded in 1961 that the pooled telecast contract eliminated competition between franchises, in other words, the right of each franchise to negotiate separate contracts with the networks, and thus was an "undue restraint" upon trade. After this adverse decision, the professional leagues (including major-league baseball) turned to Congress for remedial action. In the congressional hearings, the sports magnates argued that package contracts were essential for preserving the existence of the leagues. Pooled television contracts tended to equalize revenues among franchises. Moreover, NFL Commissioner Pete Rozelle testified that the absence of pooled contracts would "seriously impede the league's effort to maintain a balanced league."[23] None of the witnesses noted the increased profits for all franchises that would likely result from this monopolistic practice. Congress quickly passed and President John F. Kennedy signed the Sports Broadcasting Act of 1961 which permitted the professional clubs to negotiate as a single economic unit the sale of national broadcast rights. The act clearly exhibited the clout of professional sport on Capitol Hill.

The Sports Broadcasting Act of 1961 and the mounting enthusiasm for pro football opened the door to skyrocketing television contracts. Rozelle initiated the spiraling inflation in TV revenues by negotiating an annual $4.5 million contract with CBS in 1962, but the turning point came in 1964. That year both ABC and NBC determined to try to land the NFL telecasts, making the NFL the object of an all-out bidding war. By paying $14 million annually, nearly three times the previous contract, CBS won the contract. Little wonder that Arthur J. Rooney, Jr., veteran owner of the Pittsburgh Steelers exclaimed: "Pete Rozelle is a gift from the hand of Providence." With the 1964 contract, each NFL franchise received over $1 million annually. "What Rozelle did with television receipts probably saved football at Green Bay," commented Vince Lombardi, the head coach of the Packers, whom many thought had saved football at Green Bay himself.[24]

[23]*Telecasting Professional Sports Contests,* Hearings before the Antitrust Subcommittee of the Committee of the Judiciary, 87th Cong., 1st Sess. (Washington, D.C.: GPO, 1961), p. 4. The Department of Justice, in a letter to the subcommittee (p. 69), pointed out the monopolistic character of the package contracts. In 1960 CBS paid $1.5 million for the rights to televise the games of 80 percent of the NFL franchises. By contrast, the NFL received $4.65 million from the 1961 contract, a 200 percent increase.

[24]The Rooney-Lombardi statements are in Joseph Durso, *The All-American Dollar: The Big Business of Sports* (Boston: Houghton-Mifflin, 1971), pp. 58–59. For details of the television negotiations, see Johnson, *Super Spectator,* Chaps. 6–8.

NBC, a loser in the 1964 bidding war for the NFL telecasts, decided to retaliate by gambling on the AFL. To provide enough funds for the AFL franchises to compete for player talent, NBC agreed to pay the fledgling league $42 million over five years, five times what ABC had been paying to telecast AFL games. With the new contract signed in 1964, each AFL franchise received about $850,000 annually from television rights. The new contract permitted the AFL to engage in an all-out "battle of the paychecks" with the NFL for college football stars. In 1965 the AFL landed the biggest prize of all, a slope-shouldered quarterback from the University of Alabama, Joe Willie Namath. The hierarchy of the New York Jets, now headed by Sonny Werblen, recognized that the salary of a player ought to encompass both talent and charisma. Namath had both. The Jets offered Namath $420,000 for three years, a figure far in excess of any contract ever granted to an athlete in either pro football or baseball. Soon other players received even larger contracts so that Namath's salary proved to be one of the best bargains in pro sports.

The "battle of the paychecks" between the two leagues, of which Namath was a conspicuous beneficiary, led to an NFL-AFL peace settlement in 1966. Under the terms of the agreement, Rozelle became the sole commissioner, the leagues established a common player draft to end the bidding war for player talent, and the two leagues (or conferences, as they were to be called after 1969) agreed to a championship game to begin in 1967. Despite the requirement that the AFL pay the NFL $18 million for their territorial "invasions" of the New York and San Francisco areas, "the two things we wanted we got—the championship game and the pre-season games," declared Lamar Hunt of the AFL. To prevent prosecution in the federal courts, Congress quickly passed the Football Merger Act (1966) exempting the leagues from antitrust action. Senate Whip Russell Long and House Whip Hale Boggs, both from Louisiana, were chiefly responsible for guiding the legislation through Congress. Perhaps not coincidentally, shortly thereafter the NFL awarded New Orleans an expansion franchise. One thorny problem remained—the disparity between the television market areas of the two leagues. To reduce the differences, in 1970 Cleveland, Baltimore, and Pittsburgh switched from the National Football Conference (old NFL) to the American Football Conference (the old AFL). The realignment reduced the NFC's 2–1 television market advantage to 7–5.[25]

Initially, the AFL fared poorly in the championship games. Vince Lombardi's Green Bay Packers whipped the Kansas City Chiefs 35–10 in 1967 and the Oakland Raiders 38–10 in 1968. But Super Bowl III in 1969 symbolically established the AFL's parity with the NFL on the playing field. That year, Joe Namath, leading the champion New York Jets of the AFL against the Baltimore Colts, confidently predicted: "We'll win. I guarantee it." And the Jets did, 16–7. In the 1970s, AFC teams dominated NFC rivals in inter-league competition.

The 1964 television bonanza was the beginning of pro football's successful relationship with the electronic medium. By 1970, the merged NFL received nearly $50 million from television, nearly two and a half times the 1964 figure. By signing a Monday-night telecast with ABC in 1970, pro football even invaded prime-time television. In 1977, "Pete the Shark," as one network negotiator dubbed Rozelle, engineered a whopping $656 million, four-year package with the three major networks. From the new package, each pro franchise received nearly $6 million annually, six times the revenue they had gotten from the 1964 contract. For the first time in NFL history, television income exceeded gate receipts as a source of team income. Perhaps it was little wonder that some observers conjured up visions of pro football becoming solely a "studio sport."[26]

[25]See Tex Maule, "They'd Rather Switch Than Fight," Sports Illustrated, 30 (May 26, 1969), 20–23; Gwilyn S. Brown, "Owners Can Be Tackled, Too," ibid., 34 (March 22, 1971), 19; Johnson, Super Spectator, pp. 138–39. Johnson claims that Rozelle virtually bribed the NFC owners by promising them he could deliver $1.5 million per team in television revenues if they approved the franchise realignment.

[26]Ray Kennedy and Nancy Williamson, "Money in Sports: Part I," Sports Illustrated, 49 (July 1978), 75–78. According to the New York Times, December 30, 1979, S7, each team received about $5 million annually. See also "NFL Negotiates for $575 Million," Audible (October 1977), 1.

By any measure, pro football in the 1960s and 1970s was a staggering success. Although the owners were reluctant to open their finances for public perusal, apparently few teams lost money. "Any dummy can make money operating a pro football club," declared Al Davis, managing partner of the Oakland Raiders.[27] Average game attendance leaped from 30,257 in 1960 to 52,381 in 1970. In the 1970s, each pro stadium regularly exceeded 90 percent of its capacity, even for preseason training games. The average audience for televised games increased from about 11½ million households in 1967 to nearly 20 million in 1977. (By contrast, the average audience for televised baseball games was slightly over 10 million in 1977). Two league policies almost guaranteed a team against failure. By giving visiting teams 40 percent of the gate receipts, the NFL avoided the gross disparities in revenues between franchises that were characteristic of pro baseball and pro basketball. Furthermore, the NFL split television revenues equally among the franchises. As Art Modell, Cleveland Browns owner, quipped: "We're 28 Republicans who vote socialist."[28]

Nonetheless, these measures failed to prevent certain teams from dominating the field of play. From 1966–1980, four teams repeatedly participated in the conference championship games (see Table 12–1). Dallas played in ten and Los Angeles in five of the fourteen NFC championship tilts. In the AFC, Oakland played in ten and Pittsburgh in six conference title games. On the other hand, seven teams never reached the finals, and seven more got into the championship game only once. In theory, the draft eventually permitted weaker teams to catch up with stronger ones. But practice departed from theory. While the team with the poorest record drafted first, its next pick came only after all other teams had chosen a player. In other words, the only significant advantage the last-place team had over the first-place team was one man, the first pick. Unlike baseball, the population of the city served by the franchise was not an important variable in accounting for the disparities in performance. Given the gate and television sharing policies of the NFL, the gross revenues of all teams were approximately equal. Apparently the key to success on the field of play was simply better long-term management and more skillful coaching.

Television alone did not account for pro football's dazzling success. Pro football produced its own set of heroes. The first of these in the 1960s was Vince Lombardi, head coach of the Green Bay Packers. Not since Knute Rockne's reign at Notre Dame was a coach as idolized as Lombardi. Like Rockne, tragedy cut short Lombardi's career and added to its mythic dimensions; Lombardi died from cancer in 1969 at the age of fifty-seven. Like Rockne, Lombardi was a winner. The Green Bay Packers, representatives of the smallest city in the NFL and winner of only one game in 1958,

[27]Quoted in Kennedy and Williamson, "Money in Sports," 56.
[28]Quoted in "Scorecard," *Sports Illustrated*, 51 (October 15, 1979), 24. For comparative television ratings over time see Kennedy and Williamson, "Money in Sports, Part 3," *Sports Illustrated*, 49 (July 31, 1978), 39.

appointed Lombardi, a former assistant coach with the Giants, to the position of head coach and general manager in 1959. Over the next nine years he led the team to ninety-nine victories, six conference titles, and five championships.

Lombardi's Packers were the epitome of a paramilitary organization. "He's the general and we're the privates," one of his players aptly said. He insisted upon iron-clad discipline, perfection in technique, and professional pride. Yet he was an emotional man; he often resorted to old-fashioned rhetoric and saw his team as members of one "big family." He implicitly condemned the counterculture movement of the 1960s. "Everywhere you look," he said, "there is a call for freedom, independence, or whatever you wish to call it . . . [but] we must learn again to respect authority, because to disavow it is contrary to our individual natures."[29] Lombardi and the success of the Packers seemed to reassure those who were troubled by the cultural unrest of the 1960s.

"Broadway" Joe Namath, a celebrity idolized both on and off the field of play, seemed to be the perfect contrast to the NFL's Vince Lombardi. If Lombardi represented a father figure, then Namath symbolized the rebellious youth of the 1960s. Johnny Sample, a teammate of Namath's, wrote: "Our heroes were a new breed of players. Men like Joe Namath who wore their hair long and bragged about how good they were had replaced the men like Johnny Unitas, the clean-cut All-American-kid type."[30] Namath projected multiple, sometimes contradictory images. He was handsome and personable, an ideal subject for television. He was an ethnic in a decade of rising ethnic consciousness. He had a mythic wound—a damaged knee. He was iconoclastic, projecting an image of the "hippie" of the sports world who could not abide schedules, discipline, authority, restraint, or Commissioner Rozelle.[31] He was also Hugh Hefner's ultimate playboy, the quintessential bachelor. Perhaps Namath's heroism was simply that of being "mod," of being at the vanguard of an age perpetually seeking to identify with the latest fad or novelty.

While pro football produced its share of heroes, it also took concrete steps in the 1970s to increase the fan's interest in the sport. Critics frequently charged that the pro game lacked the excitement and glamour

---

[29]Quoted in Leonard Schecter, "The Toughest Man in Pro Football," *Esquire,* (January 1968), 140. Howard Cosell helped build the Lombardi legend with a documentary television production "Run for Daylight," shown in 1970. Like all heroes, Lombardi has inspired a vast literature. Unanalytical, but perhaps the most perceptive, is Jerry Kramer and Dick Schaap, *Instant Replay* (Cleveland: World, 1968), and *Farewell to Football* (Cleveland: World, 1969). But also see Kramer, ed., *Lombardi: Winning is the Only Thing* (Cleveland: World, 1970); Vince Lombardi and W. D. Heinz, *Run for Daylight* (New York: Dunlap, 1967); Leverett T. Smith, Jr., *The American Dream and the National Game* (Bowling Green, Ohio: Bowling Green University Popular Press, 1975), pp. 209–56; Paul Hornung and Al Silverman, *Football and the Single Man* (New York: Doubleday, 1965).

[30]Quoted in Gerard O'Connor, "Where Have You Gone, Joe DiMaggio?" in Ray B. Brown et al., eds., *Heroes of Popular Culture* (Bowling Green, Ohio: Bowling Green University,1972), p. 95.

[31]By selling his Bachelor III nightclub-restaurant in New York, Namath did in fact capitulate to Rozelle. See Gary Ronberg, "To Be a Good Joe, It Takes a Hard Sell," *Sports Illustrated,* 31 (July 28, 1969), 12–13.

Table 12–1 Disparities in competition as reflected by the years that teams participated in conference championship games, 1966–1980

Dallas	Oakland	Pitts.	Los Angeles	Miami	Minn.	Balt.	Houston
1980	1980						
1978	1977						
1977	1976						
1975	1975						
1973	1974	1979					
1972	1973	1978	1979				
1971	1970	1976	1978	1977	1976		
1970	1969	1975	1976	1973	1974	1971	1979
1967	1968	1974	1975	1972	1973	1970	1978
1966	1967	1972	1974	1971	1969	1968	1967

Kansas City (1966, 1969), Green Bay (1966, 1967). Cleveland (1968, 1969), and San Francisco (1970, 1971) participated in two while Buffalo (1966), New York Jets (1968), Washington (1972), Denver (1977), Tampa Bay (1979), Philadelphia (1980), and San Diego (1980) participated in only one conference championship game. St. Louis, New York Giants, Chicago, Detroit, Atlanta, New Orleans, Cincinnati and Seattle did not play in a conference championship during the entire 1966–1980 era.

of the college game. The pro game was too dull and predictable; coaches seemed determined, above all else, to avoid costly mistakes. They seemed willing to settle for field goals rather than to mount daring offensive drives that might culminate in touchdowns. The coaches seemed to be especially conservative in the games that should have been the most exciting of all: the playoffs and the Super Bowl. Much of the problem apparently stemmed from more rapid improvements in defense than in offense. Since a football field consists of a rigidly defined and limited amount of space, the appearance of ever larger, speedier, and better-trained defensive players reduced offensive capabilities. Moreover, defensive coaches designed shifting "zone" and "prevent" defenses that were more effective than traditional "man-to-man" pass coverages.

To restore more offensive action to the game, the NFL adopted major rule changes in 1972, 1974, and 1978. In 1972 the rule makers moved the hashmarks, or inbound lines, closer to the center of the field and narrowed the distance between the goal post crossbars. Partly in response to the challenge of the short-lived World Football League, the NFL in 1974 moved the goal posts back to the endline, changed kickoffs from the forty- to the thirty-five-yard line, and reduced the offensive holding penalty from fifteen to ten yards. The combined rule changes immediately reduced reliance upon the field goal, increased the number of touchdowns, and helped introduce the "era of the running back." In 1972 a record-breaking ten players rushed for 1,000 yards or more; the following year O. J. Simpson of the Buffalo Bills broke the single season rushing record with 2,003 yards. But the offense enjoyed only a temporary revival. By 1977 offensive statistics had again fallen. For the 1978 season the NFL took even more drastic action. The rulemakers permitted pass defenders to "chuck," or bump a potential receiver only once and then only within five yards of the line of scrimmage, allowed offensive linemen to extend their arms and open their hands to protect the passer, and adopted additional measures to protect the quarterback from "unnecessary roughness." The changes appeared to introduce a passing revolution. Terry Bradshaw of the Pittsburgh Steelers initiated the passing barrage in the 1979 Super Bowl when he passed for a personal career high of 318 yards against the Dallas Cowboys. In 1979, *Sports Illustrated* reported that "the offenses are going wild."[32] On the weekend of November 9, 1980, the NFL broke all previous records for total points. Football purists were horrified. Whatever the merits of the rule changes, one effect was positive: the injury rate, especially for quarterbacks, fell sharply.

The NFL did not rely upon rule changes alone to retain or spark interest among the fans. The league took steps to get more teams involved in the playoffs for the championship. Beginning in 1970, eight teams rather than four participated in the playoffs. The "wild-card" berth in the playoffs added excitement. Under this system one wild-card team from each conference, the team with the best won-loss record apart from divisional champions, joined divisional winners in the playoffs. In 1977 Rozelle introduced a controversial "parity" or "position" scheduling which had the effect of pitting more of the weaker teams (according to their records in the previous season) against each other and consequently more of the stronger teams against each other for regular season play. "Position scheduling is just another attempt to placate the television moguls...," declared Jim Finks, general manager of the Chicago Bears.[33] The new scheduling system seemed to assure that a majority of the teams had a crack at the playoffs up to the final few weeks of the season. Finally, NFL teams attempted to attract fans by adding a dash of sauciness to the sport. In the late 1970s, most of the clubs hired scantily-clad cheerleaders to prance along the sidelines.

The growing popularity of football in the 1960s and 1970s evoked an unusual amount of social commentary. Many observers saw football as related to the larger social upheavals of the era. To right-wing political leaders, football was a miniature school for testing and nurturing physical and moral vigor. Analogies between the battlefield and the football field abounded in the public utterances of President Richard M. Nixon and Vice President Spiro T. Agnew. They saw football as a healthy antidote to the breakdown of law and order, to excessive individual freedom, in short, to the "youth revolt." Nixon even proudly displayed upon his desk an autographed football given to him following the 1969 Pro Bowl game. From the White House he regularly placed long-distance telephone calls to

[32]Paul Zimmerman, "The Name of the Game Is Now Armball," *Sports Illustrated,* 51 (November 19, 1979), 36–43.

[33]Quoted in Anson Mount, "Playboy's Pro Football Preview," *Playboy,* 28 (Aug. 1981), 146.

stadium locker rooms to congratulate winning college teams. On occasion he personally presented the annual award to the number-one-ranked college team in the nation. The strategy and tactics of football intrigued Nixon. He even gave unsolicited suggestions, including diagrams, to George Allen, coach of the Washington Redskins, and Don Shula, coach of the Miami Dolphins, on pass plays for big games. He repeatedly used the term "game-plan" to describe his proposals for ending the Vietnam war and for dealing with the nation's economic problems. Proponents of the counterculture, on the other hand, connected the popularity of football to the war in Vietnam. Only a nation addicted to the violence of a sport like football, they said, could pursue such an immoral and brutal war.[34]

Several observers linked the popularity of football to the growing size of the white-collar and professional classes in the United States. According to national public opinion polls, football appealed most to the "successful," to those who had the benefit of a college education, lived in the suburbs, held jobs in the professions, and enjoyed higher incomes than the national average. Football, more than baseball, seemed to echo their work experiences. Football was a corporate or bureaucratic sport; eleven men acted in unison against eleven opponents. Football was time-bound; the ever-present clock dictated the pace and intensity of the game. Teams "worked" with or against the clock. Football embodied rationality and coordination; a game of staggering complexity, football required careful planning and preparation. Since its strategic requirements resembled those of warfare, the game invited the fans to become generals, plotting and second-guessing the warriors on the field. Yet football suggested that committees, systems, bureaucracies, and technologies were still just the tools of men, not their masters. The long completed pass and the breakaway run reflected not only careful planning and long hours of practice, but human potency, natural skill, and "grace under pressure." And like all sports, fate or luck could be decisive. Even the best of well-made plans and human performance might fall victim to an unpredictable bounce of the oblong ball. At a more primitive level, the violence so central to football may have attracted those who led lives of rigid self-control.[35]

[34]For a convenient summary of the views of right-wing political leaders and the leaders of the counterculture, see Paul Gardner, *Nice Guys Finish Last: Sport and American Life* (New York: Universe Books, 1975), pp. 118–25.

[35]The social composition of those who were asked to name their favorite sport in 1960 can be found in George H. Gallup, *The Gallup Poll*, 3 vols. (New York: Random House, 1972), 3, 1699–1700, and for each year from 1974 through 1977 in *Lincoln* (Neb.) *Star*, September 1, 1977. For the social composition of football television audiences, see A. C. Nielsen, *Televised Sport*, published annually after 1972. For the argument that football reflected the work experiences of the "successful," in a somewhat different form than mine, see Murray Ross, "Football and Baseball in America," in John T. Talamini and Charles H. Page, eds., *Sports and Society: An Anthology* (Boston: Little, Brown, 1973), 102–12, and Michael Novak, *The Joy of Sports: End Zones, Bases, Baskets, Balls, and the Consecration of the American Spirit* (New York: Basic Books, 1976), Chap. 5. On the "catharsis" effect of football, see Allen Guttmann, *From Ritual to Record: The Nature of Modern Sports* (New York: Columbia University, 1978), Chap. 5.

13

College Sports

University of Nebraska football players taking oxygen at Boulder, Colorado game.
Courtesy of Journal Star Printing Company.

In the three decades after 1950, the colleges, while continuing to pay lip service to the time-worn principles of player-centered sport, began to frankly acknowledge their stake in sport as a commercial endeavor. College football, as Frank Broyles, the dapper and articulate athletic director of the University of Arkansas, explained, "is in competition for the entertainment dollar and [teams have]. . . to put on a good performance if they want their share."[1] A good performance entailed far more than it had in the past. A team not only needed to defeat traditional rivals and emerge at the end of the season with a winning record, it needed to obtain a high ranking in the national wire-service polls. Only those teams at the top of the polls filled stadiums, received bowl invitations, appeared regularly on network television, and generated adequate revenues to finance their expensive athletic programs.

The pressures to obtain a high national ranking pushed college football and basketball closer to a completely spectator-centered orientation. Skillful management of a large, complex bureaucracy became essential to a successful college sports program. To play a single, big-time football game in the 1980s required some 250 players, coaches, and officials plus some 2,000 other people "to get the spectators in the stadium, to keep them safe and orderly, informed, reasonably comfortable and content while there, and to get them out of the place afterward."[2] Handling the traffic on the highways and streets around the stadium and controlling the crowds within might require more than 500 municipal police and state troopers. It was not surprising that athletic directors in a 1976 poll rated administrative problems as their major concern; player and participatory problems

[1]Quoted in J. Robert Evans, *Blowing the Whistle on Intercollegiate Athletics* (Chicago: Nelson-Hall, 1974), p. 36. For intercollegiate sport also see James V. Koch, "The Economics of Big-Time Intercollegiate Athletics," *Social Science Quarterly*, 52 (September 1971), 248–60; George H. Hanford, *A Report to the American Council of Education on an Inquiry into the Need for and the Feasibility of a National Study of Intercollegiate Athletics* (Washington: American Council on Education, 1974); Joseph Durso, *The Sports Factory: An Investigation into College Sports* (New York: Quadrangle/New York Times, 1975); Jim Benagh, *Making It to #1: How College Football and Basketball Teams Get There* (New York: Dodd, Mead, 1976). The focus of this chapter is on the 263 NCAA Division I institutions (as of 1978) which sponsored what might be described as "semiprofessional" sports programs. As many as 900 colleges probably did not expect their athletic programs to generate substantial revenues. See the typology of different kinds of programs in Robert N. Atwell et al., *The Money Game: Financing Collegiate Athletics* (Washington, D.C.: American Council on Education, 1980).

[2]Bil Gilbert, "Hold That Tiger—Big Game at Mizzou!" *Sports Illustrated*, 53 (September 1, 1980), 78.

ranked sixth and seventh in the poll.[3] Neither did the college athletes themselves place concern for their academic careers or play for its own sake on par with, or ahead of, the advancement of their athletic careers.

Spectator-centeredness encouraged the increased specialization and bureaucratization of college sports. While the number of male players in varsity sports rose by 11.8 percent between 1966 and 1972, the number of full-time personnel involved in administration climbed 35.9 percent. The number of part-time administrative employees jumped 52.7 percent. In 1966 the ratio of players to coaches in college football stood at thirty to one; seven years later it was eight to one. Similar ratio changes occurred in other varsity sports.[4] Athletic directors who once performed multiple roles as business managers, sport information directors, fund-raisers, and coaches, all but disappeared from the college scene. Fewer coaches (and players) applied their skills to more than one sport.

THE NCAA BECOMES A CARTEL

In managing college sport as a spectator-centered enterprise, the colleges confronted a unique problem, one not shared by professional sports leagues. The problem was that of recruiting athletes. Without a draft system, some 120 colleges might compete for the same blue-chip football or basketball player. With the stakes so high, the temptation to cheat in the recruitment and retention of top-flight athletes intensified. To equalize and regularize the conditions of competition for athletes and to improve potential revenues from television, the colleges turned to the NCAA. Consequently, by the 1960s, the formerly impotent NCAA had become a large, yet somewhat unwieldy and ineffectual economic cartel.

The years between 1941 and 1953 constituted a watershed in the evolution of the NCAA into an economic cartel. Prior to 1941 the colleges had limited the NCAA's authority to the making of rules for various sports and the supervision of certain national tournaments. While frequently issuing statements condemning athletic subsidies and unseemly recruiting, the NCAA could only resort to moral suasion to enforce its principles. Traditionally, colleges had accepted the basic premise that, being honorable institutions, they should police themselves. Yet the great football debates in the 1920s and 1930s had revealed the utter inadequacy of self-imposed restraints. In 1941 the colleges finally departed in principle from the policy of self-discipline; they ratified a new NCAA constitution that provided for the expulsion of members who failed to abide by association rules.

[3]J. Frank Broyles and Robert D. Hay, "Survey: Key Troubles Facing Today's Collegiate Administrators," *Athletic Administration,* 11 (Winter 1976), 8–9.

[4]James H. Frey, "The Organization of Amateur Sport: Efficiency and Entropy," *American Behavioral Scientist,* 21 (January/February 1978), 367–68; *The Final Report of the President's Commission on Olympic Sports,* 1975–1977, 2 vols. (Washington, D.C.: GPO, 1977), II, 345, 354.

The new constitution had no immediate impact. World War II interrupted intercollegiate sport and the colleges failed to expel a single
institution. In fact, with a resurgence of public enthusiasm for college
football and basketball after World War II, the competition among colleges
to field winning teams reached heights undreamed of in the interwar years.
Many of the colleges blatantly violated NCAA rules on recruiting and
subsidies. To curb the worst abuses and to regulate and equalize the
conditions of competition between colleges, the colleges decided to break
with a fundamental principle of amateur athletics—the ideal that no athlete should receive monetary rewards simply for play. The so-called "sanity
code" adopted in 1948 permitted the extensions of scholarships and jobs to
athletes. But the sanity code did provide one major restriction. The grants
or jobs had to be awarded solely on the basis of the athlete's demonstrated
financial "need."

Soon after the adoption of the sanity code, the colleges confronted a
series of shocking revelations that forced them to reconsider all aspects of
intercollegiate sports. In 1950 the United States Military Academy acknowledged that all but two members of its varsity football team had been
dismissed for cheating on examinations. The guilty cadets had stained the
image of the great Army teams that had dominated college football for a
decade. The next year, in 1951, the public learned that college basketball
was the victim of the biggest scandal in the history of American sport, one
of even larger dimensions than the Black Sox World Series in 1919. The
New York District Attorney's office accused thirty-three players from seven
colleges of "point-shaving"—keeping the margin of points between teams
within a range called for by gamblers from whom the players received cash
payments. Widespread revelations of illegal recruiting and under-the-table
payoffs to football and basketball players by alumni, booster groups, and
the colleges themselves soon followed. In 1953 the NCAA reported that
Michigan State, which had fielded the nation's top football team in 1952,
operated a huge "slush fund" from which football players were paid
handsomely. A highly publicized educational survey in 1952 suggested that
the University of Maryland had become a "football factory." According to
the survey, 54 percent of Maryland's total scholarship funds went to
football players.[5]

The apparent failure of the sanity code, the absence of strictures on
postseason bowls, and the negative effect of unrestricted television upon
attendance induced the colleges to extend additional powers to the NCAA.
Many colleges, especially those in the Southwestern and Southeastern
conferences, defied the NCAA by continuing to offer "full-ride" athletic
scholarships regardless of the athlete's need or academic promise. A
showdown vote came in the 1950 NCAA convention when a motion to
suspend seven colleges cited for noncompliance fell short of the necessary
two-thirds vote. With this setback, the NCAA repealed the sanity code and,
in 1952, decided to permit the awards of full scholarships based only upon

[5]Benagh, *Making It to #1*, pp. 192–95; Charles Rosen, *The Scandals of '51: How the Gamblers
Almost Killed College Basketball* (New York: Holt, Rinehart and Winston, 1978).

athletic ability. At the 1952 convention, the colleges also extended to the NCAA the power to impose sanctions upon those colleges which violated the association's legislation. For the 1952–1953 seasons, the NCAA for the first time placed two colleges, Kentucky and Bradley, on probation. Finally, the convention adopted legislation governing postseason bowls, named a full-time executive director (Walter Byers), and established a national headquarters in Kansas City, Missouri (later moved to a suburb of Kansas City, Shawnee Mission, Kansas). With the 1952 actions, the colleges had taken the first steps toward converting the NCAA into a major athletic regulatory body.

Television eventually provided perhaps the most important lever for enhancing the authority of the NCAA. The colleges were eager for the additional revenues offered by television as well as the publicity attendant to having their contests televised. Consequently, they at first laid down no restrictions on telecasts. Each college negotiated its own contracts with television stations or networks. By the fall of 1950, football telecasts virtually flooded the country. In September of 1950 the *New York Times* reported: "TV football coverage will offer New York fans a choice of five different games every Saturday afternoon during most of the season and three nighttime games in addition."[6] Apparently many fans decided to stay at home and watch the games. Attendance at college games plummeted; in 1950 it fell 1,403,000 below 1948 totals.

Alarmed college officials responded by forming a television committee within the NCAA. The committee immediately recommended a moratorium on the wholesale telecasts of football games. In 1951 the NCAA authorized the telecast of only seven regular season games in each region and negotiated a national network football package with the Westinghouse Broadcasting Company. Although reports of possible Justice Department action against the NCAA for violation of the federal antitrust laws appeared in the press, the Department took no action to prevent this form of economic collusion. Several colleges also threatened to ignore the NCAA. Notre Dame suffered the most from the restrictions of the NCAA. If Notre Dame had been able to sign a separate television contract with a national network, given its large national following, it could have earned much more than through the NCAA package. In the end, all of the colleges decided that it was in their best interests to cooperate.[7] Despite the NCAA "blackout" policy, overall college football attendance continued to lag behind 1948 figures for a decade and until the 1960s, the colleges received extremely modest revenues from telecasts. Nonetheless, the decision of the colleges to turn over the control of their television rights to the NCAA gave the organization additional power and eventually a weapon with which to discipline member schools.

[6]Quoted in William O. Johnson, Jr., *Super Spectator and the Electric Lilliputians* (Boston: Little, Brown, 1971), p. 90.

[7]See "Sports Vs. TV," *Newsweek*, 37 (June 25, 1951), 52; "Football Heretics," *Time*, 57 (June 18, 1951), 69. In 1955 the Big Ten and Pacific Athletic conferences threatened to sign a separate television package. See "Football: Calling a 'Bluff,'" *Newsweek*, 45 (January 17, 1955), 79.

In the 1960s, television, an exciting style of football, and the weekly press polls all contributed to a resurgence of interest in college football. Annual attendance jumped from twenty to thirty million, and television ratings almost equalled that of the professionals. Fans loved the wide-open offensive style of the college game. Due to clock-stopping rule changes, the colleges averaged twenty-seven more plays per game in 1968 than in 1964. The full adoption of two-platoon football in 1965 allowed the coaches to perfect more complicated offensive systems. Two platoon football also resulted in the disappearance of one of the last remnants of the player-centered era, namely the players rather than the coaches calling nearly all offensive and defensive plays. The 1960s produced record highs in scoring, passing, rushing, receiving, and kicking. Coaches with fleet split ends or flankers frequently went for the "bomb." Quarterbacks sometimes filled the air with fifty or more passes per game, figures that would have astonished football fans of the 1920s and 1930s. The "I formation," a popular offensive system developed by Tom Nugent at Maryland in the 1950s, permitted a team to combine both a potent running and passing attack. Even more remarkable were the triple-option formations which featured the quarterbacks as an integral part of the running attack. Oklahoma's wishbone (invented by a Texas high school coach and adopted first at the college level by Darrell Royal at Texas) and Bill Yeoman's veer at Houston regularly produced more than 400 yards rushing per game. Many fans found the college game, with its explosive action, more exciting than the pros.

The weekly press polls for determining the top teams in the nation furnished an additional source of excitement to the fans. Individual journalists had named national champions since the 1890s, but it was not until 1936 that the Associated Press invented the weekly press poll. To name the top twenty teams, the Associated Press polled about fifty writers and broadcasters nationwide. By establishing a board of college coaches to name the top teams in 1950, the United Press International joined the polling game. The absence of a system for determining the relative strength of teams or a national champion made the polls a powerful symbolic substitute. Many fans echoed the feelings of Dan Jenkins: "I . . . will assure anyone who is uncertain about it that there is no drama, suspense, excitement, thrill or feeling of necessity in sport that can equal the countdown to an opening kickoff between two great teams or contenders for that elusive, cantankerous, agonizing, dreadful and wonderful thing called No. 1."[8] By the 1960s, a college's standing in the weekly press polls was often more important to fans, players, and coaches alike than the defeat of a traditional rival or a conference championship.

Other "pseudoevents"—events created largely or solely by the media—stimulated interest in college football. Walter Camp had named mythical

[8]Dan Jenkins, *Saturday's America* (Boston: Little, Brown, 1970), pp. 45–46.

270

Former President Richard M. Nixon awarding the National College Football Championship to University of Nebraska team, 1971. Courtesy of the Journal Star Printing Company.

"All-America" teams as early as the 1890s, but in the 1960s, the selection of all-star teams of college football players became something of a national ritual. The press services, magazines, broadcasters, and organizations of football fans chose not only all-American teams and all-conference teams, but participants for East-West, North-South, Blue-Grey, and other all-star bowl games. The biggest individual prize became the Heisman Trophy, which had been awarded each year since 1936 by the Downtown Athletic Club of New York City in honor of a former coach and athletic director. A group of sportswriters and sportcasters chose for the award the "outstanding" intercollegiate football player of the year. That the winner of the award was nearly always an offensive back, played on a nationally ranked team, had appeared in nationally televised games, and was the beneficiary of an intensive selling campaign led by the sports information director of his college did not seem to tarnish the glamour of the award. And the recipient welcomed the publicity, the potential commercial endorsements, and the likelihood of a better pro contract that accompanied the award.[9]

The soaring popularity of college football in the 1960s strengthened the NCAA's bargaining position with the television networks. ABC, which held the regular season package after 1964, increased its payments to the colleges from $3 million annually to $6 million in 1969, $16 million in 1976, and $29 million in 1979. The combined ABC-CBS contract of 1982 called for $65.7 million annually. The participating schools, their conferences (providing that the schools belonged to a conference), and the member schools of the NCAA shared the telecast receipts. The "big-time"

[9]See especially Neil D. Amdur, *The Fifth Down: Democracy and the Football Revolution* (New York: Delta Book, 1971), Chap. 5.

football schools received about two-thirds of the receipts from the total package; the remainder went to the schools that played football at a lower level of competition. For colleges playing big-time football, television revenue became essential to their economic survival.

Given the stakes involved in fielding top-rated teams the temptations for colleges to seek advantages, both fairly and unfairly, over their competitors were difficult to resist. The head coaches were especially vulnerable. If they failed to produce winning teams, they could expect short tenures. Essential to fielding a strong team was the recruitment of a stable of blue-chip athletes. Since the colleges had no draft system for recruitment and the NCAA imposed a maximum grant-in-aid that could be offered to a prospective athlete, recruiters had to resort to other means to induce a promising athlete to attend their college rather than another. Athletes from families with modest financial means were especially susceptible to illegal inducements.

Recruiters relied heavily upon personal contacts. Coaches spent thousands of hours poring over data on high school athletes, watching films of high school games, telephoning, and driving and jetting about the country to talk to prospective players. To recruit highly touted running back Elvis Peacock in 1973, Oklahoma coaches allegedly flew ten times from Norman, Oklahoma, to Miami, Florida, Peacock's home, spending over $10,000 in air fare and telephone calls. Coaches encouraged local alumni, especially if the alumnus happened to be a celebrity, to assist in recruiting. Joseph Durso, in a survey of college sports in 1975, found that state governors, astronauts, singers, actors, big-league baseball players, and professional football players had lent their assistance in recruiting efforts. Increasingly, colleges appealed to rising racial, ethnic, and regional consciousness. Big-time football powers usually hired at least one black, an Irish-American or a representative of another Catholic ethnic group, and several coaches who had strong identification with regions outside the state in which the college was located. Once the prospective athlete arrived on campus, he might be greeted by a member of the "Gibson Girls," "Husker Honies," or "Gater Getters," organizations of comely coeds recruited by the athletic departments to act as official "hostesses."[10]

To convince a callow high school athlete to attend their college rather than another, the recruiters might promise legal "fringe" benefits or illegal ones. Without violating NCAA rules, the recruiter might emphasize to the potential recruit the likelihood of a good job after graduation, the quality of the coaching staff, the seating capacity of the stadium, the number of past telecasts and bowl appearances, enhanced opportunities of joining the pro ranks after graduation, or, a less likely possibility, the quality of education offered by his college. Illegal inducements could extend as far as the imagination of the coaches, alumni, or booster groups making them.

---

[10]John Underwood, *The Death of An American Game: The Crisis in Football* (Boston: Little, Brown, 1979), p. 188; Durso, *The Sports Factory*, pp. 57–63. See also John J. Rooney, Jr., *The Recruiting Game: Toward a New System of Intercollegiate Sports* (Lincoln: University of Nebraska, 1980), esp. Chaps. 3 and 4. For a colorful account of the recruitment of a blue-chipper, Jack Mildren, see Jenkins, *Saturday's America*, Chap. 10.

Alumni and booster groups, usually with the tacit approval or at least the knowledge of the coaches, might grant free cash, new cars, new clothes, rent-free apartments, unlimited use of charge accounts, or high-paying summer jobs. One of the most common abuses was the sale by athletes of complimentary season tickets. If the tickets were issued by a school where games were regularly sold out, such tickets could generate several thousand dollars of extra income for the athlete. To obtain the admission of an athlete with a poor high school or junior college record, coaches might also "tamper" with transcripts. To make up deficiencies in hours of college credits or grades, coaches might arrange for "snap" correspondence or extension division courses.

Given the intensity of competition among the colleges for top-flight athletes, the NCAA faced an almost insuperable enforcement problem. A thin line sometimes separated legal from illegal practices. The NCAA bylaws of 1975 contained a 4,500-word section on recruiting "dos" and "don'ts." Coaches often complained that minor infractions were nearly impossible to avoid. Nonetheless, instances of infractions were difficult to prove. Until 1966, the NCAA had only one full-time investigator; in 1975 the staff increased to ten. These ten had the awesome responsibility of policing over 600 colleges. Although the NCAA acted as policeman, prosecutor, and judge, it had no subpoena powers. The organization necessarily relied mostly upon reports of its members of alleged violations. Apparently most coaches had a tacit understanding to ignore all but the most blatant forms of cheating. Consequently, close observers of the college athletic scene, including coaches and athletes, estimated that only a small fraction of the total violations resulted in punishment by the NCAA.[11]

Despite the efforts of the NCAA to equalize the conditions of competition, glaring disparities in playing strength between teams appeared throughout the era of televised sport. Year after year, the same teams dominated conferences and appeared regularly in postseason bowls. Altogether, between 1952 and 1980, fifty-seven colleges appeared in the "top ten" of the United Press International coach's poll. But of these, nine colleges repeatedly won a spot in the top ten. Oklahoma led the parade by being chosen in the top ten for twenty of the twenty-seven years, followed by Alabama (19), Notre Dame (17), Ohio State (16), Michigan (14), Nebraska (14), Texas (13), Southern California (13), and Arkansas (12). Oklahoma was the most remarkable team of the era. In the late 1940s and the 1950s, Charles "Bud" Wilkinson led the Sooners to thirty-one- and forty-seven-game winning streaks. In the 1960s and the 1970s, Oklahoma, led first by Charles "Chuck" Fairbanks and then by Barry Switzer, continued to be the winningest team among big-time schools. In 1981 Paul

[11]See Larry Van Dyne, "College Sports' Enforcement Squad," *Chronicle of Higher Education,* 14 (March 7, 1977), 1, 14; Ray Kennedy, "427: Parts I & II," *Sports Illustrated,* 40 (June 10–17, 1974), 87–100, 24–30; John Underwood, "The NCAA Goes on the Defense," ibid., 45 (February 27, 1978), 20–22, 24, 29; Hanford, *A Report to the American Council of Education,* pp. 88–9. Between 1952 and 1976 the NCAA placed a total of sixty-four college football and sixty-one college basketball schools on probation.

"Bear" Bryant, long-time mentor of the second most successful team (Alabama), broke Amos Alonzo Stagg's career record of 314 wins.

Disparities in competition arose from a host of tangible and intangible variables. A few conferences imposed tougher standards than the NCAA. By refusing to grant any athletic scholarships, the Ivy League schools, for instance, dropped all pretenses to big-time football. The Big Ten schools, which until 1973 disallowed redshirting and permitted only one team to appear in a postseason bowl, fared poorly against foes outside of the conference. Winning traditions and skilled coaching also played an important part in the disparities, but recruitment was the single most important key in the establishment of winning programs. "Recruiting, not coaching, is the name of the game," explained Barry Switzer, the nation's most successful coach in the 1970s. Oklahoma has "built its tradition with Texas high school players—and I'm proud of it. We've got to go where the players are. Texas has 1,400 high schools playing football. There are just 200 in the entire state of Oklahoma."[12]

Despite mounting television revenues, a jump in annual football attendance from twenty to nearly thirty million for the decade of the 1960s, and a modest increase to thirty-five million in the 1970s, most college athletic programs faced recurring financial difficulties. In the 1960s and early 1970s, forty-two colleges dropped football. In 1975 Durso estimated that nine of every ten college athletic programs operated at a deficit. In the 1970s, the costs of a large program often exceeded $3 million. General inflation, nationwide recruiting (costly jet travel was necessary for major recruiting efforts), lavish athletic facilities (typically more extravagant than the pros), large coaching staffs (again, larger than the pro teams), two-platoon football, stadium expansion, installation of artificial turf in stadiums, the growth of minor sports programs, and the expansion of women's athletics as a consequence of Title IX—all of these contributed to the spiraling costs. Grants-in-aid constituted the single largest increase in costs. Between 1965 and 1975 the general price index increased 30 percent while the costs of full-ride scholarships leaped over 100 percent. As the decade of the 1970s closed, the financial crisis in college sports continued unabated. Only around forty schools managed to earn profits from football.[13]

The colleges responded to the financial squeeze by trying to increase revenues and cut costs. To generate more revenue, they raised ticket prices, increased student athletic fees (not all big-time programs assessed the general student body for fees to support varsity sport), and in 1970 added an eleventh game to the regular season football schedule. In exchange for private "gifts" the colleges extended such "perks" as membership in booster clubs, special parking places, good seats, and public

[12]Quoted in *Lincoln* (Neb.) *Star,* August 30, 1979. For a pointed discussion of the "plight" of the Big Ten see Benagh, *Making It to #1,* Chap. 14.

[13]Durso, *The Sports Factory,* pp. 87–95; Pat Ryan, "A Grim Run to Fiscal Daylight," *Sports Illustrated,* 34 (February 1, 1971), 18–32; Lorenzo Middleton, "Sports Programs' Costs Lead Colleges to 'Financial Disaster,' Report Charges," *Chronicle of Higher Education,* 20 (July 16, 1980), Atwell et al., *The Money Game,* p. 31.

recognition. To reduce costs, the NCAA in the 1970s made freshmen eligible for varsity competition, cut back on the number of grants-in-aid, reduced the number of assistant football coaches, and limited the campus visits by athletes as well as the visits by coaches to potential recruits. In the late 1970s the reduction in the number of scholarships appeared to encourage more equal performances among Division I teams. The big-time schools also cut back expenses on the relatively inexpensive minor sports. Ironically, big-time schools usually had a smaller percentage of the student body participating in varsity athletics than their small college counterparts.

Nonetheless, the strictures, pushed through the NCAA primarily by the smaller football colleges, encountered the stiff resistance of the colleges with successful, big-time athletic programs. The big-time schools found themselves locked in a vicious circle. To obtain the needed revenue, they had to produce winners. To win—especially at those colleges in areas of low density population—they had to offer large numbers of "full-ride" grants-in-aid. In 1976 about sixty of the major football schools formed the College Football Association. The association threatened to secede from the NCAA, debated the establishment of a super football conference, and considered the possibility of selling a separate television package. By giving the big-time schools a larger share of the television package negotiated in 1981, the NCAA may have staved off a complete rupture with the CFA.

COLLEGE BASKETBALL BECOMES A SPECTATOR SPORT

Until the mid-1930s, basketball had been primarily a player-centered rather than a spectator-centered sport. From the time of its invention in the 1890s it had attracted participants from diverse social groups. Members of both sexes had played the game. They played on organized teams in YMCAs, churches, city recreation programs, high schools, colleges, and industrial leagues; many more played informally in driveways, playgrounds, school yards, and gymnasiums. Even in the 1890s a few teams could be classified as professional: they charged admission and, after paying expenses, split the remaining receipts among the players. In the pre-World War I era, several pro leagues along the East Coast appeared and soon collapsed. In a few places—notably in Kentucky, Indiana, and Illinois—high school and college basketball caught on as a popular spectator sport. Yet in most places, football was the king of campus sports; football fans often looked upon basketball as a "sissy" game—it was played in short pants, indoors, and by girls—and sneeringly referred to it as "round ball." College gymnasiums usually held only a few thousand spectators, the colleges scheduled few if any intersectional games, and coaching turnovers were frequent. On most campuses, even track and field generated more excitement than basketball.[14]

[14]For general treatments of college basketball see Alexander Weyand, *The Cavalcade of Basketball* (New York: Macmillan, 1960); Neil D Isaacs, *All the Moves: A History of College Basketball* (Philadelphia: J. B. Lippincott, 1975); Zander Hollander, ed., *The Modern Encyclopedia of Basketball* (New York: Four Winds, 1969).

Perhaps architecture more than anything else converted college basketball into a spectator-centered sport. To capitalize upon the boxing craze of the 1920s, entrepreneurs in about a dozen cities built large arenas seating several thousand spectators. With the Great Depression and the decline in the popularity of boxing in the 1930s, the owners desperately sought other ways to make their arenas profitable. Intersectional college basketball games displayed potential in 1931 when Major Jimmy Walker of New York asked a group of sportswriters to organize tripleheaders in Madison Square Garden for the benefit of the city's relief fund. Despite the Depression, the "Relief Games" of 1931, 1932, and 1933 drew full houses. One of the sportswriters who had organized the relief games, Edward S. "Ned" Irish, decided in 1934 to stage his own college games. He rented the Garden, which held over 16,000 fans, paid the fees to visiting teams, and kept whatever was left over as a profit. To maximize interest among New York residents, Irish usually pitted strong local colleges against the most powerful rivals he could attract from other parts of the nation. The Garden games promoted by Irish served as a catalyst for the transformation of college basketball into a full-fledged spectator sport.

One game promoted by Irish became a legend in basketball history. In 1936 he matched Long Island University, winner of forty-three consecutive games, and Stanford University, led by tall (for that day) Angelo "Hank" Luisetti. Stanford won 45–31, but Luisetti was the bigger story. Luisetti scored fifteen points—all on unorthodox one-handed shots—and became the nation's first basketball hero. His one-handed shots defied years of conventional coaching. "That's not basketball," sneered veteran City College coach Nat Holman. "If my boys ever shot one-handed, I'd quit coaching."[15] Yet the one-handed shot and its derivative, the jump shot, could be shot as accurately, more quickly, and with less danger of being blocked than the standard two-handed set shot. The new shooting styles, along with the elimination of the center jump after each goal in 1937, increased scoring and won the plaudits of fans.

From the late 1930s through the 1940s—World War II notwithstanding—New York was the hub of big-time college basketball. In 1938 the Metropolitan Basketball Writer's Association of New York organized the National Invitational Tournament (NIT), designed to determine the national championship team at the end of each season. The following year, the NCAA founded its own post-season invitational tournament, though until 1951 the NIT remained the premier college tourney. After World War II, Ned Irish extended his promotion beyond the Garden to Philadelphia and Buffalo, thereby offering at least a three-game package to college teams venturing to the East. Irish also increased the number of doubleheaders to twenty-five or more per season. By 1950, the Garden college program drew over 600,000 spectators. It became every schoolboy's dream to play one day in the Garden. For both financial and publicity purposes, appearances at the Garden were obligatory for those college

[15]Quoted in Zander Hollander, ed., *Madison Square Garden: A Century of Sport on the World's Most Versatile Stage* (New York: Hawthorne, 1973), p. 76.

teams striving for big-time basketball status. Never had the promise of basketball as a spectator sport looked more roseate than in 1950.

Then disaster struck. In 1951 New York District Attorney Frank Hogan revealed that thirty-two players from seven colleges, including players from the strongest teams in the nation, had been involved in fixing point spreads. The Garden was not only the mecca of college basketball; it was the "clearinghouse" for New York's sports gambling establishment. With the invention of the point spread by gamblers, basketball had become a hot attraction for betters. Rather than picking a winning team or giving odds on favorites, the better wagered on how many points a particular team would win by. Such a system invited "fixing," for a fixed team did not have to lose the game; they merely had to win by less than the quoted point spread. The revelations of the fixes shocked the entire country. Coinciding in time with the "fall" of China, the commencement of the Korean War, the Soviet detonation of an atomic bomb, and spectacular charges of treason in high governmental places, the basketball scandal contributed to a general climate of suspicion and mistrust.

The scandal had a far-reaching impact upon American sport. Apart from the apparent widespread immorality of college basketball players, the scandal revealed that many colleges, in their mad scramble for opportunities to play in the big city arenas and win national renown, engaged in the "illegal" recruitment and subsidization of players. The Catskill Mountain hotel resort leagues represented the most notorious examples of illicit subsidization. As many as 500 college players "worked" for munificent salaries in the Catskill resorts where they "incidentally" played basketball in organized leagues. College coaches and presidents reacted to the scandals and revelations of athletic subsidies with dignified horror; many colleges announced that they would no longer permit their teams to compete in the big-city arenas. The scandal ended the Garden's pivotal place in the financial structure of big-time college basketball. Irish's famed Garden doubleheaders collapsed. The scandal also wiped out the powerful basketball programs of New York's metropolitan colleges. After the scandal, the local colleges no longer attracted the best talent in the city; most of them went elsewhere. In the 1950s and 1960s, state universities began to fill the vacuum by building large fieldhouses and scheduling intersectional holiday tournaments. Between 1967 and 1977, the colleges built eighty-two new basketball arenas, thirty-nine of which seated in excess of 10,000 people.[16]

Almost simultaneously with the scandal of 1951, basketball entered the televised era of sport. Television, at least until the 1970s, offered little to college basketball. Although production costs were small compared to other sports, the NCAA failed to land a major network contract for regular season games until 1976. Until then, individual teams, conferences, and the NCAA received modest fees for regional and occasional national telecasts. The failure of basketball to command a television audience equal

---

[16]See Benagh, *Making It to #1*, pp. 192–95; Rosen, *The Scandals of '51; NCAA News,* March 1, 1977.

to football or baseball appeared to stem partly from the intrinsic nature of the sport. Basketball, unlike its counterparts, was a game of continuous action with few pauses to allow commentators or the fans to build up dramatic tension. Finally, a key to much of the enjoyment of the sport was a kind of special intimacy between the fans and the athletes, duplicated only by hockey. Being physically present at a basketball game in an enclosed arena, yelling at the "bad" calls of referees, shouting instructions to the coaches or players, and feeling the reciprocal emotions of the crowd and the players was a sharply different experience from watching a game on television.

Despite the scandal of 1951 and basketball's problems with television, when all levels of basketball were combined, the sport apparently outdrew football and baseball in live attendance. Estimates in the 1970s placed total annual attendance at 150 million per season. For sports fans, the basketball season bridged perfectly the gap between football in the fall and baseball in the spring. Unlike baseball, competition from other forms of recreation was less intense in the winter months. Since the season was long, a team could easily play several games per week, the costs of fielding a team were small, and the sheer number of basketball games exceeded those of football and baseball combined. The sport appealed to all sizes and types of communities. In the small towns of mid-America, high school basketball often furnished a source of common pride, identity, and purpose, a shared experience equalled perhaps only when a natural disaster struck the community. At the other end of the spectrum, basketball flourished in the ethnic and racial enclaves of the big cities. In fact, city basketball from the 1930s to the 1970s reflected the ascent of ethnic and racial groups from the ghettos. In the 1930s and 1940s, Irish, Jewish, and Italian athletes dominated the rosters of metropolitan high schools and colleges; in the 1950s, blacks began to replace the earlier ethnic groups. By the 1960s, the position of blacks in college and professional basketball had become so conspicuous that observers wondered if the sport was not especially suited to blacks, either because of physical or cultural reasons.[17]

New modes of play also helped account for the popularity of basketball in the age of televised sport. Player skills improved remarkably. By the 1970s, dozens of players six feet, six inches tall and taller had reached higher levels of coordination and dexterity than most of the shorter men of the pre-1940 era. Prior to the 1940s, few big men had played the game effectively; most of them had been slow and awkward. Coaches had believed that the optimum height for skillful players ranged from five feet, ten inches to six feet, three inches. In the 1940s, Robert Kurland of Oklahoma A & M, a towering defensive specialist, and George Mikan of De Paul, a prolific scorer, initiated the revolution in height. The next decade produced two more outstanding big men. Bill Russell of San Francisco demonstrated that the tall center could be a dominating force as a rebounder and defender, and Wilton Chamberlain, a center with the University of Kansas who stood over seven feet tall, demonstrated that a

[17]See for example Martin Kane, "An Assessment of 'Black is Best'," *Sports Illustrated*, 34 (Jan. 18, 1971), 72–83.

big man could be almost unstoppable as a scorer. Rule changes to restrict the impact of the big men (defensive goal tending in 1944 and widening the free-throw lane in 1955) failed. Moreover, the fans loved the "playground style" of play led by the black players from the big-city ghettos. The playground style featured individual moves and spectacular ball handling. To fans who had observed basketball in the pre-1940 era, the basketball of the 1970s seemed like an entirely different sport.

As an enterprise involved in the business of entertainment, college basketball resembled a scaled-down version of college football. While basketball as a whole did not generate as much revenue from spectators or television as college football, it cost much less to field a team. Since costs were modest, many more colleges tried to play big-time basketball. Like football, a high rating in the national press polls helped insure a team a berth in the NCAA of NIT tourneys, a profitable season, and "free" publicity for the college. In turn, the key to a successful team was the recruitment of blue-chip athletes. Unlike football, however, one or two super athletes might reverse the fortunes of an otherwise mediocre basketball team. Thus each year scores of coaches, many of whom were hired more for their recruiting ability than their coaching skills, sought the services of a dozen or so of the most talented high school seniors. Coaches even subscribed to commercial scouting services to assist them in locating the more promising prospects; many colleges hired a black assistant coach so they could make a special pitch to black athletes. Given the intensity of competition for the more promising prospects, the basketball coaches tended to be even more flagrant in violating or ignoring NCAA rules than their football counterparts.[18]

Basketball could offer a relatively simple and inexpensive means by which an otherwise unknown smaller college could attract national attention. In the post-World War II era, more than a score of smaller Catholic-affiliated colleges decided to drop football and place the major part of their athletic resources into basketball. In some instances, basketball programs of smaller colleges suddenly sprang into national prominence. One example in the 1960s and 1970s was Oral Roberts University, founded by evangelist Oral Roberts in Tulsa, Oklahoma, in 1965. Roberts, who was also the president of the institution, determined from the outset to make the university a "Notre Dame of the Hardcourts." He candidly explained why: "Many people are not as faithful in church attendance on Sunday mornings as they once were. But 40 million men read the sports page on Sunday morning. In my ministry, we try to reach people where they are...."[19] Each year, Oral Roberts upgraded its schedule; the school built a plush, elliptical basketball arena, and in 1969 the university brought in Ken Trickey, a high-powered recruiter from Middle Tennessee State, as head coach. Never did a team rise so fast to national prominence. Under Trickey in the early 1970s the college twice led the nation in scoring, played in both

[18]See Pete Axthelm, "Scandal on the Court," *Newsweek*, 94 (Dec. 24, 1979), 77.

[19]Quoted in Benagh, *Making It to #1*, p. 5. On the phenomenon of Catholic colleges and basketball see James A. Michener, *Sports in America* (New York: Random House, 1976), pp. 231–34.

the NIT and NCAA tourneys, and at one time ranked eleventh in the wire service polls. Although those close to the college basketball scene (especially Trickey's fellow coaches) branded Oral Roberts as an "outlaw school" for its presumed infractions of NCAA rules, the university successfully avoided NCAA sanctions. At the height of the team's success, Trickey, after a controversy with Oral Roberts, left for Iowa State, and Roberts decided to "deemphasize" basketball. But only temporarily. In the late 1970s, Roberts determined again to go "big-time," only to find itself placed upon two-year probation by the NCAA in 1978.

The NCAA found the enforcement of their restraints upon recruiting and subsidization to be extremely difficult. While the organization could penalize a college and the players for misconduct, the coaches, who were usually most directly responsible for the infractions, simply took jobs elsewhere. Jerry "Tark the Shark" Tarkanian, coach at Long Beach State and the University of Nevada at Las Vegas was a notorious example. While at Long Beach from 1968 to 1973, Tarkanian's teams compiled an enviable record of 122 wins and only twenty losses. In 1975, the NCAA placed Long Beach on indefinite suspension (with a minimum of three years) for a long list of violations ("among the most serious which it has ever considered") that spread over nine single-spaced, typed pages. But the NCAA's penalties did not inhibit Tarkanian, for in the meantime he had accepted a lucrative contract to coach at Las Vegas. Apparently Tarkanian resumed the same practices at Las Vegas. Allegedly, some of the Las Vegas players earned $20,000 a year "working" in the local gambling casinos. Again, the NCAA stepped in, placing Las Vegas on probation and insisting that Tarkanian be fired, but the coach brazenly resisted dismissal, sued the university and the NCAA for defamation of character, and claimed that the NCAA was engaging in a personal vendetta against him. In 1978 Tarkanian's case triggered a congressional investigation (led by a Nevada congressman) of the NCAA and a special NBC television news program which sympathetically explored Tarkanian's charges against the NCAA. As the decade closed, it appeared that the NCAA had successfully weathered Tarkanian's counterattack but had failed to set up measures to prevent rampant violations of the organization's rules.[20]

The primary intent of NCAA regulations in basketball, like football, was to equalize the conditions of competition among college teams. Unlike football, smaller colleges with modest enrollments and endowments sometimes cracked the top ten in the media polls. LaSalle, San Francisco, Cincinnati, Loyola (Ill.), and Texas Western all won NCAA national titles. Nonetheless, certain institutions with well-established basketball traditions and well-known coaches tended to dominate conference championships and the top ten in the national polls.[21]

[20]Ray Kennedy, "427: Parts I & II," *Sports Illustrated,* 40 (June 10, 17, 1974), 87–100, 24–30; John Underwood, "The NCAA Goes on the Defense," ibid., 48 (Feb. 27, 1978), 20–29.

[21]Michael E. Canes, "The Social Benefits of Restrictions on Team Quality," in Roger G. Noll, ed., *Government and the Sports Business,* (Washington, D.C.: Brookings Institution, 1974); pp. 89–90. Canes's data (p. 90) indicated that between 1950 and 1965 basketball teams in the major conferences tended to win successive championships more often than football teams.

In fact, between 1964 and 1975, the dominance of the University of California at Los Angeles in college basketball far exceeded the feats of any college football team of the era. In that time John Wooden's UCLA team won nine NCAA championships in ten years, including seven titles in a row. Inasmuch as the NCAA tourney format (where a single defeat eliminated a team) and the limit on the eligibility of a player to three years (after 1972 to four years) made such a feat appear to be virtually impossible, UCLA's success may have represented the most remarkable achievement in sport history. Wooden's first two championships seemed to be simply the products of astute coaching combined with superior athletes. But after 1965, UCLA was the beneficiary of several of the most promising players in the country. Two of the most spectacular big men to ever play the game—Lew Alcindor (1967–1969) and Bill Walton (1971–1974)—contributed directly to five of UCLA's ten championships.

As the 1970s closed, the prospects of college basketball as a spectator sport appeared to be good. The NCAA national tournament had become one of the premier events of the sporting year, ranking only behind the pro football playoffs, the World Series, and college football bowl games in generating fan interest. Television ratings for the tourney even exceeded that of the professional basketball playoffs. In the 1979–80 season, in head-to-head competition with the telecasts of regular season pro games on Sunday afternoons, the colleges also drew a large audience.[22] To increase the size of the television audience, the NCAA spread out the tournament over several weeks and expanded the number of participating teams. By 1980 roughly one-fifth of the 257 schools in Division I basketball competed in the tourney. To televise the expanded playoff system and regular season games, NBC paid the colleges $18.5 million, nearly twice as much as the former contract had provided.

In 1981 CBS wrested the NCAA tournament from NBC and established a separate regular season schedule of telecasts. Apart from numerous games that had recently become available on cable television, fans could now watch college basketball for two days on each weekend on two separate networks. Each team in the final four of the NCAA tournament received nearly one-half million dollars from television rights, a sum as lucrative as most college football bowl games.[23]

COLLEGE SPORTS IN CRISIS

Despite rising attendance and television ratings, college sports entered the 1980s in a state of crisis which bordered on panic. In 1980 a string of ugly stories leaped to the headlines of the nation's press. In the Southwest reports indicated that Arizona State football players received credits for unattended, off-campus "extension courses." A sordid story of forgery and fakery wrecked the University of New Mexico basketball team. Then came

[22]"Scorecard," *Sports Illustrated,* 51 (Aug. 27, 1979), 6; "E Pluribis Unum Time in the NCAAs," ibid., 54 (Feb. 12, 1981), 94.

[23]Curry Kirkpatrick, "And So, On with the Show," ibid., 55 (Nov. 30, 1981), 37–38.

even more startling revelations. Half of the Pacific-10 Conference schools admitted that they had "laundered' academic transcripts and granted false course credits to athletes. The culprits included UCLA, for many years the premier team in college basketball, and the University of Southern California, a perennial contender for the national football crown. Given the nature of big-time college sports, there seemed to be no easy way of avoiding corruption. Doug Barfield, head coach of Auburn University, put the choices confronted by college coaches succinctly: "Go on as you have been and eventually get fired. Cheat more and survive. Or quit."[24] Below the surface of the sensational reports of gross corruption simmered such equally intractible problems as the declining profitability of football and the rising costs of financing women's sports.

Proposals for the reform of college athletics came from many quarters. James Michener, popular novelist and author of a study of sports, recommended the colleges adopt a draft system similar to professional teams; geographer John F. Rooney, Jr., suggested that the big-time colleges simply form professional teams. Others proposed less drastic solutions. The NCAA at its 1981 convention adopted regulations (1) requiring that athletes complete twelve credit hours per semester to remain eligible, (2) prohibiting athletes from using for credit extension courses from other institutions, and (3) tightening the responsibilities of presidents and chancellors for certifying that the athletes were academically eligible. These reforms appeared to be largely cosmetic, for the same convention rejected proposals for granting scholarships only upon the basis of economic "need" and efforts to raise the high school, grade-point-average requirements of athletes entering the colleges.[25]

[24]"The Shame of College Sports," Newsweek, 96 (Sept. 22, 1980), 54. See also John Underwood, "The Writing Is On the Wall," Sports Illustrated, 52 (May 19, 1980), 36–72; and Lorenzo Middleton, "Colleges Check Athletes' Academic Records as Scandal over Unearned Credits Spreads," Chronicle of Higher Education, 19 (January 7, 1980), 1, 14.
[25]Michener, Sports in America; Rooney, The Recruiting Game; Underwood, "The Writing is On the Wall;" Lorenzo Middleton, "NCAA Toughens Rules," Chronicle of Higher Education, 21 (January 19, 1981), 1, 6.

14

Big-League Baseball and Professional Basketball

While football's corporatism, rationalization, and time-consciousness reflected modern America, baseball echoed an older America, a leisurely-paced past of farms and small towns. Baseball's spatial organization, as Murray Ross has so imaginatively argued, suggested an "artificial environment, one removed from the toil of urban life, which spectators could be admitted to and temporarily breathe in."[1] Most of the action revolved around the hitter and the pitcher in one corner of the playing field. From this "urban corner," the field opened up to less busy, rural-like vistas. Compared to football, baseball was an individualistic team sport; the batter confronted the pitcher in utter solitude. Baseball was also bound by its own sense of time. Released from the tempo of the clock, each team had equal opportunities (innings) to score. Finally, baseball seemed to elicit the slow rhythms of the seasons. "Is there anything that can evoke spring...better than the sound of the bat as it hits the horsehide...," asked novelist Thomas Wolfe?[2] Given these characteristics, perhaps baseball appealed most to those who yearned for a return to nature, to a simpler past, to a retreat from the insistent present.

Few observers attempted to saddle basketball with a comparable social meaning. Perhaps this was because no one could be sure that basketball reflected the lives or needs of any particular social group. One observation did seem to be self-evident: basketball in the 1960s and 1970s increasingly appeared to be a "big city" or "black sport." Perhaps basketball echoed the close proximity of people, fluidity, deception, and improvisation characteristic of life in the inner city. The "one-on-one" challenge, the essence of the new playground style of basketball, argued Pete Axthelm, "takes on a wider meaning, defining identity and manhood in an urban society that breeds invisibility."[3] This may have been so, but basketball continued to flourish in

[1]Murray Ross, "Football and Baseball in America," in John T. Talamini and Charles H. Page, eds., *Sport and Society: An Anthology* (Boston: Little, Brown, 1973), p. 102. For the social composition of baseball television audiences, see A. C. Nielson, *Televised Sport*, published annually after 1972. See also Gordon L. Wise and Myron K. Cox, "Public Policy Questions Loom on the Horizon as the Consumer Confronts Selected Aspects of Major League Baseball," *American Behavioral Scientist*, 21 (Jan./Feb. 1978), 451–64.

[2]As quoted in Paul Gardiner, *Nice Guys Finish Last: Sport and American Life* (New York: Universe Books, 1975), p. 64. Allen Guttmann has suggested that baseball has a dual appeal to modern Americans: "The place of baseball in the cycle of the seasons and the tendency of baseball toward extremes of quantification." *From Ritual to Record: The Nature of Modern Sports* (New York: Columbia University Press, 1978), p. 100.

[3]Pete Axthelm, *The City Game: Basketball in New York from the World Champion Knicks to the World of Playgrounds* (New York: Harper & Row, 1970), p. xiv. See also Michael Novak, *The Joy of Sports: End Zones, Bases, Baskets, Balls and the Consecration of the American Spirit* (New York: Basic Books, 1975), Chap. 6.

"Middle America" as well as the big cities. In the 1970s per capita production of college players from the states of Indiana, Illinois, and Kentucky actually exceeded that of the metropolitan areas, though this was probably not the case with professional players.[4] Perhaps basketball appealed most to those who, regardless of their social characteristics, yearned for freedom from constraints, for individual virtuousity, and a fluid, free-flowing life style.

THE WOES OF THE BIG LEAGUES

Regardless of the larger social meanings of baseball and basketball, in the era of televised sport neither one equalled the spectacular success of football. Both sports suffered from slower growth in attendance and lower television ratings (and thus less lucrative television contracts). While big-league baseball's total attendance crept upward in the era of televised sport, the gains lagged far behind the population growth of the metropolitan areas served by major league franchises. Moreover, average game attendance between 1953 and 1978 remained below the marks achieved in the 1948–1952 seasons. And in the 1960s and 1970s the audience for regular season baseball telecasts was usually only half as large as that for regular season professional football telecasts. Furthermore, television was largely responsible for the near-destruction of the once-thriving system of minor league baseball. To add to the woes of the sport, the owners of big league franchises failed to devise successful policies for reducing the disparities between team performances and they permitted the continuation of gross inequalities between the incomes of professional franchises.

Baseball's relative loss of fan support appeared to spring from several sources. By evoking the past, baseball failed to attract a proportionate share of the nation's youth. In the 1970s men fifty years old and over constituted the largest television audience for baseball games. Critics often complained that the sport was too slow, too dignified, too out-of-touch with modern life. But baseball suffered from more tangible problems as well. Beginning in the 1950s summer vacations, shorter working hours, and widespread affluence triggered virtual manias in touring, camping, going to the beach, water sports, drive-in movies, and auto-racing. Mini-booms in summer sports like golf and tennis also absorbed some of the interest of potential baseball fans. Apart from the intrinsic difficulties that television had in capturing all of the fascinating dimensions of baseball, the sport's long season and many games (compared to football or basketball) meant that only a few games seemed crucial enough in determining league or divisional championships to attract large television audiences. To the horror of both baseball traditionalists and the team owners, Thomas W.

[4]See John J. Rooney, Jr., *Geography of American Sport* (Reading, Mass.: Addison Wesley, 1974), Chap. 7; and Rooney, *The Recruiting Game: Toward a New System of Intercollegiate Athletics* (Lincoln: University of Nebraska Press, 1980), Chap. 8. Rooney did not locate the origins of pro players. As a televised sport, blacks on the whole preferred baseball and football to basketball. See Donald E. Parente, "A History of Television and Sports" (unpublished Ph.D. dissertation, University of Illinois, 1974), pp. 164–65.

Moore of the ABC television network proposed in 1964 that the major leagues reduce their schedules from 162 to sixty games.[5]

For all three of the decades following 1950 the problem of devising a satisfactory television policy plagued Organized Baseball. The magnates of baseball, long known for their factionalism and inability to function as a close-knit economic cartel, were unable or unwilling to formulate and implement a television policy that benefitted all franchises equally or protected the interests of the minor leagues. The return of general prosperity in the 1940s had stimulated a new boom in minor league ball, one that exceeded the pre-World War I era. Annual attendance between 1939 and 1949 increased nearly three-fold, from fifteen million to forty-two million. Then came the invasion of commercial television. Alone, the minor leagues could do nothing to stem the intrusion of big-league telecasts into their home territories. In 1940 the major leagues had adopted a rule which essentially "blacked out" radio broadcasts and telecasts of its games in the home territories of minor league clubs. But threatened with antitrust action by the Justice Department and greedily seeking to maximize their own broadcast revenues, the major league owners repealed the rule in 1951.[6]

For the minor leagues, the repeal of the blackout rule was disastrous. After 1950 nearly everyone who owned a television set could see the big leaguers play for free. The local minor league heroes seemed to pale before such big league superstars as Henry Aaron, Stan Musial, Willie Mays, Warren Spahn, Ted Williams, Bob Feller, and Mickey Mantle. The crowds at minor league games fell from forty-two million in 1949 (before the advent of nationally televised major league games) to fifteen million in 1957 and ten million in 1969. In 1949 there had been fifty-one minor leagues; that number fell to thirty-six in 1954 and, by 1970, to only twenty. In the 1970s, in order to survive, almost all minor league clubs had to receive substantial subsidies from major league affiliates. By then college baseball teams began to replace the minor league franchises as a major source of big-league recruits.[7]

Unrestricted telecasts initially dealt almost equal damage to major-league attendance. The television history of the Braves (Boston, Milwaukee, and Atlanta) dramatically illustrated the impact of the cool medium. In 1948 the Boston Braves won the National League pennant and drew nearly 1½ million fans to their home games. For the paltry sum of $40,000 the management then sold the rights to telecast all Braves games for the 1951 and 1952 seasons as well as most of the 1953 and 1954 seasons.

[5]See Jack R. Griffin, "TV Kidnaps Sports," *Nation*, 200 (May 29, 1965), 336–38; Wise and Cox, "Public Policy Question . . ."; Ralph Andreano, *No Joy In Mudville: The Dilemma of Major League Baseball* (Cambridge, Mass.: Schenkman, 1965).
[6]See Parente, "A History of Television and Sports," pp. 62–64.
[7]See ibid., pp. 65–66; *Organized Professional Team Sports,* Hearings before the Subcommittee on Antitrust and Monopoly of the Senate Committee of the Judiciary, 85th Cong., 2nd sess. (Washington: GPO, 1958), p. 687; Lance E. Davis, "Self-Regulation in Baseball, 1909–1971," in Roger G. Noll, ed., *Government and the Sports Business* (Washington, D.C.: Brookings Institution, 1974), pp. 374–75; "Baseball: Major Minor Troubles," *Newsweek*, 51 (Jan. 13, 1958), 53.

Although the Braves finished in the first division of the league in three of these four years, their home attendance fell to an abysmal 281,278 in 1952, a loss of 81 percent. Faced with financial disaster, the Braves owner, Lou Perini, moved his club to Milwaukee in 1953. At first he allowed no telecasts of Braves games; he relented only when Milwaukee played in the 1957 and 1958 World Series. Then, beginning in 1962, he permitted limited telecasts of road games.

Although attendance at Milwaukee was consistently above the major league median for all franchises—the Braves drew nearly a million fans during their last season at Milwaukee—a new set of owners transferred the franchise to Atlanta in 1964. Television and radio revenues rather than attendance dictated the move. Milwaukee, the new owners reasoned, had a media market circumscribed by Chicago to the south, Lake Michigan to the east, Canada to the north, and Minneapolis-St. Paul to the west. While the Braves had garnered $525,000 from broadcasts at Milwaukee, Atlanta offered them $1.5 million for their television-radio rights. "We moved south in the first place because of TV," explained Thomas Bennett of the Braves public relations office. "We filled that gap in eight states which had been without a big league team."[8] In the 1960s and 1970s potential broadcast revenues rather than population concentrations often determined the location of major league baseball franchises.

Until 1961 major league baseball was unable to negotiate a national television package that included all the franchises. In 1954 the majors submitted to the Department of Justice a plan for a "Game of the Week" in which the Commissioner of Baseball would negotiate with the networks for the sale of the national telecast rights of the member franchises. The Justice Department advised that the proposal was in conflict with federal antitrust laws and Organized Baseball again acquiesced without taking the issue to the federal courts. A Congressional investigation in 1951 of baseball's exemption from the antitrust laws plus a pending suit in the federal courts challenging the legality of the reserve clause may explain the timidity of the owners in challenging the Justice Department. In short, the owners may have feared the possible loss of baseball's unique legal status. At any rate, the networks negotiated packages with individual clubs for national telecasts. Under such circumstances the fans enjoyed a bonanza of televised baseball in the late 1950s, but those clubs which could not land network telecasts (usually those located in smaller population areas) suffered from both declining attendance and a reduction in potential broadcast revenues.[9]

After the passage of the Sports Broadcasting Act of 1961 the major leagues negotiated package contracts with the television networks in which all clubs shared equally in the revenues. Yet the revenues of baseball's contracts fell far behind that of pro football. In 1980 baseball's television contracts with NBC and ABC grossed $47.5 million while pro football

---

[8]Quoted in William O. Johnson, Jr. *Super Spectator and the Electronic Lilliputians* (Boston: Little, Brown, 1971), p. 102.

[9]See Ira Horowitz, "Sports Broadcasting," in Noll, ed., *Government and the Sports Business*, pp. 303–4.

received $164 million for its regular season telecasts. But, unlike pro football, the majors continued to permit the individual franchises to retain the rights to sell local telecasts. Some clubs such as the Chicago Cubs televised nearly all of their games while others televised as few as twenty games. Local telecasts, especially when combined with radio broadcasts, resulted in wide disparities between clubs in revenues. In 1978 the Kansas City Royals, for example, received a mere $350,000 from local broadcast rights while the Yankees garnered $1.3 million. In the National League the Los Angeles Dodgers got $1.8 million while the San Diego Padres obtained only $710,000. Differences between clubs in broadcast receipts contributed almost as much as differences in attendance to the disparities between clubs in gross revenues.[10]

THE RESPONSE OF THE BIG LEAGUES

Several owners of big-league clubs hoped to solve these media and attendance problems by shifting the location of their franchises to other cities. The astonishing success of the transfer of the Braves to Milwaukee in 1953 touched off a mini-stampede by club owners seeking more lucrative markets. The St. Louis Browns, which perennially lost money in competition with the Cardinals, moved to Baltimore in 1954 and the Philadelphia Athletics transferred to Kansas City in 1955. After the euphoria of the first year of major league baseball had worn off, both clubs suffered from a combined 28 percent loss in attendance. The willingness of Arnold Johnson, the owner of the Kansas City team, to trade or sell some of his best players (including Roger Maris, who was to break Babe Ruth's single season home run record) to the powerful Yankees did nothing to encourage the success of major league baseball in Kansas City. Yet the apparent failures of big league baseball in Baltimore and Kansas City did not deter the transfer of franchises.

The decisions of Walter O'Malley, owner of the Brooklyn Dodgers, and Horace Stoneham, owner of the New York Giants, to abandon New York for the West Coast in 1958 revealed the complex dynamics of franchise hopping. In the previous five years Brooklyn had been the most prosperous franchise in the major leagues, but O'Malley claimed that Ebbetts Field, the home of the "Bums," was beyond repair. It seated only 35,000 spectators, had parking spaces for only 700 cars, and was located in a decaying neighborhood. The Polo Grounds of the Giants suffered from similar liabilities. To both O'Malley and Stoneham the future of baseball in New York depended upon the construction of new parks in good locations with adequate parking facilities. By the 1950s cars had begun to replace trolleys and subways as the primary means of transporting fans to games.

[10]Jim Kaplan, "Is There a Ceiling?" *Sports Illustrated,* 54 (Jan. 5, 1981), 35; Ray Kennedy and Nancy Williamson, "Money in Sports, Part I," ibid., 49 (July 17, 1978), 75–76; Oscar Kahan, "TV—Radio Revenue Important to Major Leagues," *Sporting News,* (April 9, 1977), 13, 38. In 1977 local television and radio rights amounted to about $43 million.

If Milwaukee takes in twice as many dollars as Brooklyn, O'Malley said, "they'll eventually be able to buy talent" and dominate league play.[11] Unable to reach an agreement with New York authorities upon a satisfactory site for a new stadium in Brooklyn, O'Malley turned to Los Angeles.

For O'Malley, Los Angeles proved to be a bonanza. He obtained the exclusive right to move his franchise into the nation's third largest metropolitan area which promised not only an increase in attendance but a large television market uncontested by other big league clubs. The city agreed to provide the Dodgers with an ideal site for a new park, the Chavez Ravine, 300 acres in downtown Los Angeles with easy access to several freeways. Originally the site had been scheduled for a public housing project for the poor. A 1958 referendum to block the use of the land by the Dodgers narrowly failed. While the Dodgers bore the costs of the actual stadium building, the city and county of Los Angeles spent some $5 million preparing the site for construction. The new stadium, completed in 1962, held 53,000 spectators and had parking spaces for 24,000 cars. In the meantime, Stoneham, who had been persuaded to move to San Francisco by O'Malley in order to reduce traveling costs and resume the popular "subway series" between the two clubs, was not so fortunate. Candlestick Park, built by the city, was poorly located for the use of cars and was buffeted regularly by high bay winds which sometimes turned baseball games into survival contests.

The construction of Candlestick Park and Dodger Stadium initiated a wave of stadium building for both professional baseball and football teams. Just as the cathedral represented the spirit of the Middle Ages and the great railroad terminals the nineteenth century, the sports stadium seemed to express the civic pride of urban America in the 1960s and 1970s. Of the twenty-eight teams in the National Football League, for example, twenty-six played in city, county, or state facilities. Never before had local governments furnished such massive subsidies to professional sports teams. A study completed in 1972 found that each resident in twenty-five localities paid an average of sixty-five cents in taxes each year to finance the new stadiums. The stadiums carried high price tags. A modest stadium cost about $30 million, but Houston's Astrodome, the first stadium with a roof for all-season play, cost $45 million to complete in 1965. The cost of the Astrodome paled before that of the New Orleans Superdome which mounted to at least $300 million before it was finished in 1975.[12]

In many communities stadium building generated public controversy. Stadium promoters saw the structures not simply as homes for football and

---

[11]Quoted in Elihu Lowenfish, "A Tale of Many Cities: The Westward Expansion of Major League Baseball in the 1950's," *Journal of the West,* 18 (July 1978), 77.

[12]Jerry Kirschenbaum, "Let Me Make One Thing Clear," *Sports Illustrated,* 34 (June 7, 1971), 34–39; Charles G. Burck, "It's Promoters vs. Taxpayers in the Superstadium Game," *Fortune,* 87 (March 1973), 104–7, 178–82; Steve Cady, "Sports 'Marriage' with Cities Often Ends in Divorce," *Lincoln* (Neb.) *Star,* April 21, 1977; Benjamin A. Okner, "Subsidies of Stadiums and Arenas," in Noll, ed., *Government and the Sports Business,* pp. 325–47; *New York Times,* July 17, 1975.

baseball teams, but as great cultural monuments, sources of community pride, stimuli to the revitalization of the city, and an important means of luring tourist and investment dollars to the city. They attempted to convince reluctant taxpayers that new stadiums would be self-financing (which in fact was never the case). Sometimes team owners presented cities with an ultimatum: either the municipality built a new stadium or the franchise would move elsewhere. Critics responded that 1) the cities should use the revenue for the resolution of more pressing problems, 2) building the stadiums in the suburbs (nearly 20 percent of the new parks were in the suburbs rather than the inner cities) simply encouraged the further deterioration of downtown areas, 3) corruption in financing and construction resulted in costs far exceeding original estimates, and 4) in effect, all residents subsidized the entertainment of the "advantaged."[13] In the 1960s and 1970s most voters rejected the arguments of the critics, but as the nation faced a new era of austerity it appeared that the "age of the superstadium" had passed.

Increasing the number of big-league franchises seemed to offer yet another possible solution to the problems of professional baseball. In 1960 a congressional investigation that threatened to result in a reversal of baseball's exemption from the antitrust laws, the formation of a proposed third major league (the Continental League headed by Branch Rickey), and the willingness of investors to pay $1.8 million (plus several million dollars for the purchase of players from other clubs) for a new franchise, led both leagues to announce plans to expand from eight to ten teams each. By 1977 the American League consisted of fourteen franchises and the National League twelve. Each loop set up divisional play. Divisional winners then competed for league championships and the league pennant winners played in the World Series. The expansion and juggling of franchises sometimes confused and angered fans. Much of the appeal of baseball, critics of expansion and franchise-hopping argued, stemmed from hometown loyalties. Baseball, more than football, declared veteran sportswriter Dick Young, helped satisfy a human need for rootedness in a society characterized by rampant geographic mobility.[14] Yet expansion made big league baseball available to many more fans and divisional play seemed to promise increased interest in regular season play.

While owners worried about declining attendance and meager television revenues, baseball aficionados began to ask: "Whatever became of the .300 hitter, or, where did the runs go?" In the 1920s rule changes and the "live" ball had produced higher batting averages, soaring home-run totals, and record highs for runs scored. In 1930 the entire National League had hit for an average of .303. Gradually batting averages (but not home run totals) had slipped downward. Then came a precipitous drop. Between the

[13]See Kennedy and Williamson, "Money in Sports, Part I," 72; Mark S. Rosentraub and Samuel R. Nunn, "Suburban City Investment in Professional Sports: Estimating the Fiscal Returns of the Dallas Cowboys and Texas Rangers to Investor Communities," *American Behavioral Scientist*, 21 (Jan./Feb. 1978), 393–414.

[14]Dick Young, "It's a Religion, Baby—Not Show Biz," *Sports Illustrated*, 38 (April 9, 1973), 54–56.

1962 and 1963 seasons major league run totals fell by 1,681, home runs by 297, batting averages by twelve points, and bases on balls 1,345. Pitchers recorded 1,206 more strikeouts. The 1963 totals became the standard for the next five years. Carl Yastrzemski won the American League batting crown in 1968 with an average of .301, the lowest in major-league history.[15]

Baseball experts offered a large number of reasons for the decline in hitting. Among those that appeared to have some merit: (1) better pitching, especially the increased use of relief specialists; (2) efforts of more players to hit home runs rather than singles—"Home run hitters drive Cadillacs; singles hitters don't," explained Pittsburgh slugger, Ralph Kiner—; (3) bigger and better constructed fielders' gloves; (4) more night games; (5) coast-to-coast air travel; and (6) larger, more symmetrical ball parks. However, one special circumstance largely accounted for the sudden drop in 1963. Sensitive to the charge that baseball was losing patrons to football because of its slower pace, the major leagues had instructed the umpires to enlarge the strike zone.

In 1969 the major leagues began to take steps to counter the decline in offense. The rulemakers lowered the pitching mound from fifteen to ten inches and ordered umpires to reduce the size of the strike zone. Charlie Finley, the controversial owner of the Oakland Athletics, suggested the use of orange baseballs for better visibility, three balls for a free base, the use of designated hitters to replace the pitchers in the batting order, and the free substitution of base runners. The American League adopted the designated hitter rule in 1973, but rejected Finley's other recommendations. In the 1970s batting averages, runs, and home runs again increased. But the improvement in offensive output may have been due as much to the widespread use of artificial playing surfaces as to the rule changes, for artificial turfs did not retard the speed of ground balls as much as natural grass.

DISPARITIES IN COMPETITION

While the major leagues enjoyed some success in restoring more offense to the game, glaring disparities in competition continued to plague the sport. (See Figures 14-1 and 14-2.) In the 1950s and early 1960s the New York Yankees completely dominated the American League pennant races; in a fifteen-year span, they won thirteen flags while losing only two. Superior resources arising from larger attendance, more broadcast revenues, and skilled management accounted for the continuation of the Yankee dynasty. Casey Stengel, the erstwhile field manager of the Yankees from 1949 to 1960, had at his disposal so many good players that he platooned nearly all of the hitters, using left-handed hitters against right-handed pitchers and vice versa. Under new management and ownership in the late 1960s and

[15]See William Leggett, "The Season of the Zero Hitter," *Sports Illustrated* 28 (June 17, 1968), 20–23; Leonard Koppett, *All About Baseball* (New York: Quadrangle/New York Times, 1974), pp. 324–34.

Figure 14–1 Disparity in competition, Major League Baseball 1950–1980 as reflected in American League Pennants*

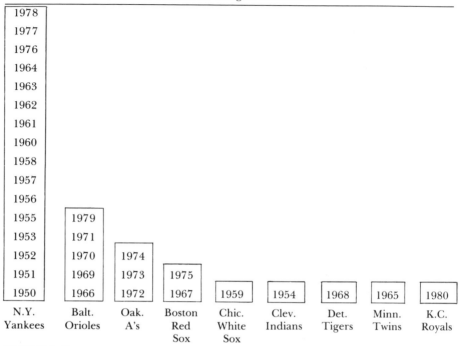

1978								
1977								
1976								
1964								
1963								
1962								
1961								
1960								
1958								
1957								
1956								
1955	1979							
1953	1971							
1952	1970	1974						
1951	1969	1973	1975					
1950	1966	1972	1967	1959	1954	1968	1965	1980
N.Y. Yankees	Balt. Orioles	Oak. A's	Boston Red Sox	Chic. White Sox	Clev. Indians	Det. Tigers	Minn. Twins	K.C. Royals

*The Milwaukee Brewers, Toronto Blue Jays, California Angels, Seattle Mariners, and Texas Rangers did not win a single flag.

early 1970s the Yankee dynasty suffered a temporary eclipse. But when George Steinbrenner, a free-spending construction magnate, gained control of the club in 1973 the Yankees returned to their winning ways. For similar reasons the Brooklyn-Los Angeles Dodger franchise enjoyed almost equal success in the National League; the Dodgers won eleven flags. Except for the two pennants of the New York Mets and one pennant by the Kansas City Royals, no expansion team managed to win a flag.

Efforts by the major leagues to equalize competition proved to be futile. Gate receipts continued to be highly unequal with visiting teams receiving only some 20 percent.** Visiting teams shared none of the local broadcast revenues. NFL football, on the other hand, had a 60-40 split in attendance revenues and equally divided national television rights. In 1965 baseball instituted two changes designed ostensibly to equalize competition.

**Since baseball has a complicated formula for determining the visiting team's share of the gate receipts, estimates vary. Roger Noll estimates that the home team keeps about 80 percent in the American League and 90 percent in the National League. See Noll, "Attendance and Price Setting," in Noll, ed., *Government and the Sports Business* (Washington, D.C.: Brookings Institution, 1974), p. 131.

Figure 14–2 Disparity in competition, Major League Baseball 1950–1980 as reflected in National League Pennants*

Brook/LA Dodgers	Cin. Reds	St. L. Cards	NY/SF Giants	Pitt. Pirates	Mil/Atl Braves	NY Mets	Phila. Phillies
1978							
1977							
1974							
1966							
1965							
1963							
1959	1976						
1956	1975						
1955	1972	1968	1962	1979			
1953	1970	1967	1954	1971	1958	1973	1980
1952	1961	1964	1951	1960	1957	1969	1950

*The Chicago Cubs, Montreal Expos, Houston Astros, and San Diego Padres did not win a single flag.

First, the major leagues exempted only forty-one men on the roster of the parent club from the annual draft; this presumably kept a club from "stocking up" on extra major league talent. Secondly, baseball implemented a "free agent" draft of unsigned high school and college players similar to that of pro football. Yet both measures had a minimal effect on improving the playing strength of the "have not" clubs. The freedom gained by the veteran players to "play out" their options in the mid-1970s appeared to leave the wealthier owners in a position to sign a galaxy of superstars. George Steinbrenner was especially successful in wooing established players to the Yankees without having to pay an equivalent compensation to the team that lost the player. Yet for the 1979 and 1980 seasons, the maximum of eight different teams won divisional titles, suggesting that free agentry might actually promote competitive parity.

Despite baseball's tribulations, the sport continued to be able to generate an intense excitement among urban residents. No other professional sport quite "got to" a city the way major-league baseball did during a tight pennant race. Perhaps the most striking instance was the "amazin'" New York Mets, an expansion team which lost 100 or more games for five of their first six seasons in the National League. In 1968 they finished ninth in the ten-team league. Then in 1969 the Mets surprised everyone by winning the pennant and then the World Series from the powerful Baltimore Orioles. Blasé New Yorkers gave the team a celebration unequalled in the Big Apple since the armistice ending World War II. Similar outbursts of civic pride erupted in St. Louis in 1967 and Detroit in 1968, two cities that may have escaped massive racial riots because of the pennant drives of their respective ball teams. In 1979 the Pirates and the entire city of

Pittsburgh rallied behind their aging superstar, Willie Stargell, to chant repeatedly a hit song, "We Are a Family." Baseball, it seemed, exceeded any other sport in evoking a sense of community and rootedness in a "rootless society."

As the decade of the 1970s closed, Organized Baseball was in an anomalous position. On the one hand, the sport had lost substantial ground in the popularity contest with football. Yet, there were portents of the sport regaining some of its earlier ascendancy. The freedom of players—more than in any other pro sport—to play out their options and sign contracts with clubs that could pay the highest salaries led to an annual "flesh market" for the services of superstars. Those teams in the larger cities and with bigger media markets appeared to be in a stronger financial position to "buy" pennants. Yet free agentry may have encouraged competitive parity, most big-league franchises made a profit, and the value of franchises continued to spiral upward. For instance, the Payson family bought the New York Mets in 1962 for $1.8 million and sold them in 1980 for $21.2 million. As in the case of all professional sport franchises, the appreciation in the value of franchises flowed from more than simply profit potential. Until 1976, the federal government gave new team owners a spectacular tax break. The owners could count as a tax deduction the value of their players as a large part of the purchase price of the franchise. They could then depreciate the value of players over a number of years and thereby reduce their income tax liabilities. (The Tax Reform Act of 1976 reduced the loopholes. Prior to 1976 some owners had depreciated up to 90 percent of their costs.)[16] Also, the ownership of a pro sports franchise assured one of an immediate celebrity status. A surprising number of the new owners in the era of televised sport were men of a "new wealth" who apparently purchased teams as a way of gaining public recognition and prestige.

Basketball Keeps Pace

For many years professional basketball as a big-time spectator sport languished behind the college game.[17] In the 1920s and 1930s only a few barnstorming pro teams enjoyed more than short-term success. The New York Original Celtics, the most prosperous team in the 1920s, sometimes drew over 10,000 fans for big games at Madison Square Garden. In the 1930s the New York Rens, an all-black five, and the Philadelphia Sphas, an all-Jewish quintet, fielded the strongest professional teams. One national

---

[16]For a discussion of the complex tax laws of professional sports see Benjamin A. Okner, "Taxation and Sports Enterprises," in Noll, ed., *Government and the Sports Business*, pp. 159–84; Arthur T. Johnson, "Congress and Professional Sports, 1951–1978," *Annals of the American Academy of Political and Social Science*, 445 (Sept. 1979), 109.

[17]For general treatments of the history of pro basketball see Leonard Koppett, *24 Seconds to Shoot: An Informal History of the National Basketball Association* (New York: Macmillan, 1968) and David S. Neft et al., *The Sports Encyclopedia: Pro Basketball* (New York: Grosset & Dunlap, 1975).

pro loop, the American Basketball League organized in 1926, struggled along until the Great Depression brought about its demise in 1931. In 1937 commercial concerns located in medium-sized towns in the Midwest organized the National Basketball League (NBL). The NBL remained a regional loop until 1949 when its surviving members joined the Basketball Association of America (BAA) to form the National Basketball Association (NBA).

The turning point for the pro game came in 1946 when a group of big city arena owners decided to form the Basketball Association of America.* Although the BAA brought pro basketball into the big city arenas, the founders had a limited vision of the profit potential of the sport. The arena owners' primary interest was in the promotion of pro ice hockey and college basketball. They saw pro basketball simply as a sport that could fill vacancies in their winter schedules. Consequently, when pro basketball games conflicted with potentially more profitable uses of the arenas, the teams had to play elsewhere. In the first season of 1946, for example, the New York Knickerbockers played only six of their thirty home games in Madison Square Garden. Until 1951, the Knicks typically played less than half of their home games in the Garden.

Neither did the BAA initially attempt to compete seriously for the best college talent. Although the BAA set up a draft system copied after pro hockey, many of the best players opted to play in the National Basketball League, on Amateur Athletic Union teams, or, if black, with the Harlem Globetrotters. Since the 1920s companies in towns where basketball enthusiasm ran high had formed powerful AAU teams composed mostly of college stars. Inasmuch as the players ostensibly worked at regular jobs for the companies, they were technically amateur rather than professional athletes. Yet they could make more money playing AAU ball than they could by joining the pro ranks. Until 1950, when Boston drafted Charles Cooper of Duquesne, no black played in the BAA. Racial prejudice was one factor. The arena owners of BAA franchises also did not want to offend Abe Saperstein, the owner of the Globetrotters, by raiding his near-monopoly of the top black talent, for the arena owners enjoyed a profitable relationship with Saperstein. The Globetrotters were a big draw for the arenas; until the 1950s the Trotter games drew larger crowds than BAA games.

In the 1950s pro basketball began to emerge from the long shadows cast by the colleges, the AAU teams, and the Globetrotters. Gradually the BAA absorbed, wiped out, or reduced the public following of its major rivals. In 1949 the surviving teams of the National Basketball League joined the BAA to form the National Basketball Association, an unwieldly seventeen team loop. After one season six teams dropped out of the new association and the NBA adopted a two-division playoff system. The emergence of the powerful Minneapolis Lakers, led by towering George Mikan, strengthened the NBA's claim that the league featured the "best of

---

*Charter franchises were located in Boston, New York, Philadelphia, Providence, Toronto, Washington, Chicago, St. Louis, Cleveland, Detroit, and Pittsburgh.

basketball." While the Globetrotters had been able to battle NBA teams on equal terms in exhibition games in the late 1940s, in the 1950s the NBA began to recruit the top black players. Consequently, to draw crowds, the Globetrotters resorted increasingly to showmanship rather than serious basketball. Likewise, in the 1950s fewer of the college stars joined the AAU teams. Ironically, the college basketball scandal of 1951 also assisted the fledgling NBA. In the wake of the scandal most of the colleges cancelled their games in the big-city arenas and the arena owners replaced the college games with NBA games. Thus most metropolitan fans either had to forgo satisfying their hunger for watching basketball or attend pro games instead.

Yet the NBA continued to have problems. Early television contracts, first with the DuMont network (1952–1953) and then NBC (1953–1962), produced only modest revenues. The failure of the NBA to land a lucrative television deal highlighted a persistent financial weakness of the league—its failure to field a strong team in New York. Ned Irish, who controlled the Knickerbockers, was primarily responsible. Irish repeatedly made ill-advised trades and drafted players for their immediate publicity value rather than their future potential for the team. His abrasive personality irritated the other franchise-holders. As something of a league outcast, Irish was unable to obtain their assistance in building a strong New York franchise. A winning Knickerbocker team would have increased the league's overall attendance and its capacity to negotiate more favorable contracts.

The NBA also had a problem in coping with low scoring and a rough-and-tumble style of play. Excessive fouling and low scoring annoyed fans. Until 1954, once a team had obtained the lead in a game, it could resort to stalling tactics. Both in order to stall effectively and prevent stalling, the players engaged in more physical contact. Pressure from the fans and NBC television induced the NBA in 1954 to adopt a twenty-four second rule; each team had to take a shot at the basket within twenty-four seconds or lose possession of the ball. The time limit on shooting "literally" saved the NBA, concluded the leading historian of the league.[18] Yet experience disclosed that the time limit rule produced subtle, unforeseen difficulties. With the new rule, it was hard for fans to get excited about the game until the middle of the last quarter of the game. Since it was difficult for a team to build up a lead and "sit" on it, to the fans it appeared that the players did not exert themselves fully until the last quarter. On the one hand, if a team did have a large lead in the final quarter of the game, then the last portion of the game was likely to be unexciting. On the other hand, if the score was close in the middle of the last quarter, then what transpired earlier seemed to be insignificant.

Fan interest in the 1960s centered largely around the epic playoff duels between Bill Russell and Wilt Chamberlain. Chamberlain, while playing for Philadelphia, San Francisco, Philadelphia again, and finally Los Angeles, confronted Russell and the Celtics eight times in NBA playoff competition. The playoffs generated two sharply contrasting images of the giant centers.

[18]Koppett, *24 Seconds to Shoot,* p. 86.

Because of the success of Boston, Chamberlain gained the reputation of being a "loser." He was bigger and stronger than Russell, a far better shooter in his prime, yet only once did his team defeat the Celtics in the playoffs. Fans tended to blame Chamberlain. They believed his selfishness, uncooperativeness with teammates and coaches, and obsession with his salary accounted for the failure of his teams to win the big games. Russell, on the other hand, fit perfectly the public mood of the 1960s. He projected an image of unselfishness, cooperation, and of being "modern." He was the first black head coach in the NBA and would eventually identify closely with black rights. Yet more sophisticated basketball observers could argue that Chamberlain was the victim of forces beyond his control. Boston seemed consistently to field a stronger cast of supporting players and was the beneficiary of superior front office management.

In the meantime the style of NBA play changed sharply. Apart from the jump shot which became part of the standard repertoire of most of the players, Bob Cousy of the Boston Celtics introduced a razzle-dazzle style of guard play that featured pinpoint passing (even behind the back) and expert dribbling that foreshadowed the black playground style of the 1960s and 1970s. Bill Russell, also of the Celtics, initiated a revolutionary style of play for the big center. Russell, who enjoyed exceptional quickness and agility, not only reduced the effectiveness of the opposing center, but by playing in effect a one-man zone (zone defenses were technically illegal in the NBA) he clogged up driving lanes and prevented easy lay-ins by the guards. With Russell in the middle Boston's other four players could gamble by pressing the ball everywhere, causing numerous turnovers without fear of becoming victims of "chip" shots. Russell's rebounding and precise outlet passes also ignited Boston's fastbreak offense. With Russell leading the way, Arnold "Red" Auerbach's Celtics captured nine NBA championships between 1957 and 1966. Before retirement in 1969, Russell, as coach of the Celtics, led the team to two additional championships.

Pro basketball shared in the largesse of the sports boom of the 1960s, though not as spectacularly as pro football. Fans seemed to like the general improvement in the quality of play, Boston's exciting ball-hawking defense and fast-breaking offense, and the titanic duels between Russell and Chamberlain. NBA attendance leaped from slightly less than two million in 1960 to over five million in 1970 and it exceeded ten million each season in the late 1970s. Yet the NBA was not so successful in landing lucrative television contracts. NBC even dropped its telecasts of regular season games in 1962; the network claimed that pro basketball games bored the audience. In 1964 the NBA signed a contract with ABC for $650,000 for regular season Sunday afternoon telecasts. The NBA-ABC marriage, despite its modest beginnings, proved to be a happy one. By 1972 each franchise received about $325,000 annually. In 1974 a new contract with CBS increased the earnings of each team to $535,000 annually.[19]

The prosperity of the NBA in the late 1960s induced a group of wealthy

[19]See Bureau of the Census, *Statistical Abstract of the United States, 1978* (Washington: GPO, 1978), p. 246; and Parente, "A History of Television and Sports," pp. 89–91.

young men to form a rival loop, the American Basketball Association (ABA) in 1967. The ABA owners, using the pro football merger of 1966 as their model, hoped to attract a national television contract and force a merger with the NBA. The subsequent war between the two leagues dramatically increased player salaries by an average of five times. By 1969 the ABA believed that its hopes for success rested upon the signing of Lew Alcindor (who changed his name to Kareem Abdul-Jabbar in 1971). Alcindor had just completed a spectacularly successful career with UCLA. Since Bill Russell had retired and Wilt Chamberlain was nearing the end of his career, all observers agreed that Alcindor would be pro basketball's next superstar. Although the ABA pooled its financial resources and offered Alcindor a million dollars, Milwaukee of the NBA signed him for $1.4 million.

While the loss of Alcindor was a major setback for the ABA, the leagues sought to curb the escalating salary war by reaching a merger agreement in 1970. However, unlike the football players in 1966, the basketball players went to court to block the merger and lobbied against a bill in Congress that would have exempted the merger from the antitrust laws. The players recognized that the merger would weaken their bargaining power for higher salaries. Complex legal issues ensued, but the upshot of the conflict was clear enough. Four ABA teams obtained admission into the NBA in 1976, each paying the NBA astronomical sums for the privilege, the reserve clause had been destroyed in the federal courts, and the players won major concessions from the owners.[20]

Paradoxically, in the 1970s the NBA enjoyed the most competitive balance of the three major professional team sports. Indeed, no team won successive championships and seven different teams took titles. The success of the NBA in promoting competitive balance was not due to its financial structure. The market areas of franchises ranged from Portland, Oregon (398,000) to New York (7,895,000). The gate-sharing arrangements favored the large market areas. Unlike any other professional sports league, the NBA allowed the home team to retain all gate receipts. "We go into the Garden to play the Knicks," groused one owner, "and they rake in more in one night than we make in two weeks at home."[21] The New York Knickerbockers typically took in twice as much in gate receipts as the clubs from the smaller cities. Yet television revenues by 1980—from a package contract with CBS worth $880,000 annually to each team—helped equalize revenues. Furthermore, it seemed that a club composed of superstars was not the key to success in the NBA. Coaches who could mold five good players into playing a "team" game had more success than teams composed of several superstars.

As pro basketball entered the 1980s, its future remained uncertain. A schedule of 82 regular-season games, unparalleled in its physical demands by any other team sport, seemed to guarantee that the players would

[20]For a summary of the war see Lewis Cole, *A Loose Game: The Sport and Business of Basketball* (Indianapolis/New York: Bobbs Merrill, 1978), Chap. 3.
[21]Quoted in Kennedy and Williamson, "Money in Sports; Part I," 82. See also *New York Times*, Dec. 30, 1979, S7.

experience endless fatigue and numerous injuries, both minor and major. The schedule combined with long-term, no-cut contracts led the players to approach regular-season games with increasing lethargy and indifference. To many whites, the declining intensity in play confirmed their suspicions of innate black laziness. With some three-fourths of the players black, but with the sport largely dependent upon white fans, the perception that black players were not "putting out" and the inability of whites to identify with black players threatened to reduce fan support for the sport.

15

The Olympic Games, Golf, and Tennis

Golfers at Lincoln, Nebraska Country Club, early 1975. Courtesy of the Journal Star Printing Company.

By the 1980s player-centeredness was no longer characteristic of sports performed at the championship levels. Of course, at the lower levels of performance millions of Americans played softball, tennis, golf, ran, and bowled largely as player-centered enterprises. The professional versions of baseball, football, basketball, and boxing had always been spectator-centered. Money from gate receipts and, later, radio and television had shaped the destinies of these sports. In the so-called "amateur" sports an uneasy amalgam of the player and spectator ethos often existed together. As early as the 1890s college football and by the mid-1930s college basketball, while continuing to espouse the ideals of a player-centered sport, had become commercial spectacles. "Amateur" track and field, golf, and tennis, all individual sports with origins among the elite athletic clubs of the late nineteenth century, were the last sports to succumb completely to the ascendancy of the fans. Player-centeredness had begun to erode in track and field as early as the 1870s, yet the sport clung tenaciously in principle to a player-centered ethos as late as the 1970s. Both golf and tennis at highest levels of performance "went public" in the 1920s and in the 1960s and 1970s television, more than any other single force, completed the transformation of these games plus the Olympic Games into full-fledged spectator sports.

THE POLITICS OF THE GAMES

In the post-World War II era, Olympic officials continued to adhere to a notion repeatedly expressed by Avery Brundage, the Chicago construction magnate and president of the International Olympic Committee (IOC) from 1952 to 1972. "Sport...like music and the other fine arts, transcends politics...," declared Brundage. "We are concerned with sports, not politics and business"[1] Yet this nineteenth century athlete-centered ideal of the Olympics had never fully corresponded with reality. The Games had always been managed and staged by nonathletes. Pierre de Coubertin, the

---

[1] International Olympic Committee, ed., *The Speeches of President Avery Brundage* (Lausanne: IOC, 1968), p. 67. For a general analytical account of the external and internal forces shaping the Games in the postwar years see Richard Espy, *Politics of the Olympic Games* (Berkeley: University of California Press, 1979). See also David B. Kanin, "Superpower Sport in Cold War and Detente," in Benjamin Lowe et al., eds., *Sport and International Relations* (Champaign, Ill.: Stipes, 1978), 249–63.

founder of the modern Olympics, had established the IOC as a self-perpetuating body, in theory independent from control by athletes, politicians, or businessmen. But in the postwar years the gap between official Olympic ideology and practice widened further. The Olympic Games increasingly served as vehicles for promoting the interests of nation-states, business concerns, and sports bureaucracies rather than the athletes themselves or athlete-centered ideals.

The very structure of the Olympics militated against an athlete-centered orientation. By requiring that athletes compete as representatives of nations rather than as individuals, the Games inevitably became forums for international politics. In the postwar era the combatants in the Cold War and the new nations of the Third World were especially prone to use the Olympics to further their own international political goals. As the Games grew in size, cost, and the power to generate international attention, commercial considerations also shifted the focus away from the individual athletes. Financing the expanded games required ever larger sums from television, corporations, and governments. Moreover, business interests seized upon the Olympics to sell products. Finally, nation-state pressures, pressures from local organizing committees, and the vast sums of money required to finance the Games forced the Olympic movement to place its emphasis upon the success of its organizations rather than the interests of the athletes. Consequently, the Olympic movement tended to define its goals in terms of its size and growth rather than in terms of its athlete-centered ideals.

The importance of forces external to the interests of the athletes and sport for its own sake first became manifest in the postwar era at the 1952 Games held in Helsinki, Finland. The 1948 Olympics, scheduled in war-ravished London, had occurred with a minimum of commercialization and political friction. Yet American Olympic and political officials did worry about the Soviet Union. While the Soviets did not enter the 1948 Games, they did send a battery of observers. When the Soviets announced that they would send a team to the 1952 Games and a Soviet delegate was appointed to the IOC, American worries turned into alarm. To raise funds to counteract the "Red Menace" in 1952, the United States Olympic Committee (USOC) arranged for an Olympic Telethon starring Bing Crosby and Bob Hope. Hope set the tone for the American effort when he cracked: "I guess Joe Stalin thinks he is going to show up our soft capitalistic Americans. We've got to cut him down to size."[2]

Athletic rivalry between the two superpowers dominated the 1952 Helsinki Games. To the chagrin of the IOC, both countries devised ingenious self-serving scoring systems which allegedly demonstrated the athletic superiority of their respective social and political systems. Athletic success, the Americans and Soviets believed, would bolster national self-

---

[2]Quoted in William O. Johnson, Jr., *All That Glitters Is Not Gold: The Olympic Games* (New York: G.P. Putnam's Sons, 1972), p. 223. For expression of concern by U.S. Government officials see Richard B. Walsh, "The Soviet Athlete in International Competition," *Department of State Bulletin*, 25 (Dec. 24, 1951), 1007–10.

confidence, enhance the respect of allies and nonaligned nations, and demoralize the opposition. Little wonder that the athletes began to conceive of themselves as surrogate warriors in the Soviet-American battle for prestige and influence. Bob Mathias, the Olympic decathlon champion, captured the mood of the American team: "There were many more pressures on the American athletes [in 1952] because of the Russians than in 1948. They were in a sense the real enemies. You just loved to beat 'em. You just had to beat 'em. It wasn't like beating some friendly country like Australia."[3]

The 1952 Games also raised the issue of "state amateurism" which served as a recurring source of Cold War polemics. The West, particularly the United States, regularly protested that the Soviet bloc athletes enjoyed an unfair advantage in Olympic competition. While Americans were unable to enter their professional athletes, the communist countries, the Americans charged, fully subsidized their athletes, thus violating the amateur code. The Soviets responded that their athletes held state jobs—in the military, academia, or civil service—and received no remuneration from sport. The IOC refused officially to take sides. Avery Brundage, president of the IOC, in effect condemned both sides for violating the amateur spirit. He pointed out that American Olympic athletes usually received indirect subsidies from athletic scholarships granted by colleges.

In reality, the high level of success enjoyed by the Soviet bloc nations in the postwar Olympics was due to more than simply "state amateurism." While the Western nations—at least the United States—continued to insist upon the strict separation of the central government from sports, the communist countries made sport an integral part of state policy. The Soviets, who dominated the Olympic Games after 1952 (except for 1968), used the state to develop highly centralized, systematic programs for identifying and nurturing world-class athletes (see Figure. 15–1).* The Soviet bloc nations invested millions of dollars in sports centers, facilities, training programs, medical and drug research, and competitions. Such investments plus state control paid dividends. East Germany, a nation of only seventeen million people, won more gold medals in the 1976 Olympics than the United States, a nation of over 200 million people.[4]

---

*Rather than state control alone, part of the Soviet success can be accounted for by their emphasis upon women's athletics and the more obscure, less popular forms of sport found in the Olympic Games.

[3]Quoted in Espy, *The Politics of the Olympic Games,* p. 38. For the 1952 Games see also Maxine L. and Reet Howell, "The 1952 Helsinki Olympic Games: Another Turning Point?" in Peter J. Graham and Horst Ueberhorst, eds., *The Modern Olympics* (Cornwall, N.Y.: Leisure Press, n.d.), 182–93.

[4]See Andrew Strenk, "What Price Victory? The World of International Sports and Politics," *Annals of the American Academy of Political and Social Science,* 445 (Sept. 1979), 128–40; James Riordan, "Soviet Sport and Soviet Foreign Policy," and Andrew Strenk, "Diplomats in Track Suits," in Lowe et al., eds., *Sport and International Relations,* pp. 316–68; G. Carr, "The Use of Sport in the German Democratic Republic for the Promotion of National Consciousness and International Prestige," *Journal of Sport History,* I (Fall 1974), 123–36.

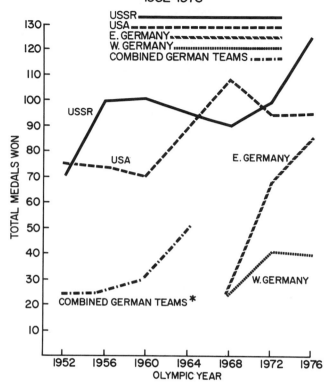

FIGURE 15-1

LEADING OLYMPIC MEDAL WINNERS, SUMMER GAMES,
1952-1976

SOURCE: ADAPTED FROM CHRONICLE OF HIGHER EDUCATION, JAN. 17, 1977

*GERMANY HAD COMBINED TEAMS AT THE 1952, 1956, 1960, AND 1964 GAMES

The United States, on the other hand, had no coordinated program for the identification of potential Olympians, their training, nor their final selection for the Olympic team. Control of American "amateur" sport remained deeply divided. On one side stood the high schools and colleges which conducted the preponderance of athletic programs. On the other side was the Amateur Athletic Union and other athletic organizations recognized by the international sports governing bodies as having the power to select national teams and certify them for international competition. The result was periodic conflict between organizations with the athletes serving as pawns. After numerous efforts to negotiate a truce between the warring factions, Congress finally stepped in. The Amateur Sports Act of 1978 empowered the United States Olympic Committee to be a coordinating authority for Olympic sports and granted the USOC $16 million for the development of minor sports and sports medicine. Whether the enforced truce and federal appropriations would produce more success in future Olympics remained to be seen.[5]

The degree to which the rivalry between the United States and the Soviet Union impinged upon the Olympics usually depended upon the intensity of the Cold War. The Games of 1956 at Melbourne, Australia, and 1960 at Rome reflected a new phase in the Cold War. Repercussions from the Soviet invasion of Hungary and the joint British, French, and Israeli seizure of the Suez Canal from Egypt in 1956 inevitably spilled over into the Melbourne Olympics. The Netherlands, Spain, and Switzerland withdrew from the Games to protest the Soviet action; Egypt, Lebanon, and Iraq pulled out because of the Suez invasion; and refugee Hungarians used the Games to stage several anti-Soviet demonstrations. Yet the IOC determined to remain aloof from the international turmoil. Avery Brundage asserted that "every civilized person recoils in horror at the savage slaughter in Hungary but that is no reason for destroying the nucleus of international cooperation...." He repeated the myth that "the Olympic Games are contests between individuals and not between nations."[6] Neither did the United States use the games to condemn Soviet aggression against Hungary. By the mid-1950s the classic phase of the Cold War had passed.

In the new phase of the Cold War, Soviet-American athletic relations assumed a somewhat less belligerent character. At Melbourne the United States and Soviet Union track officials announced a tentative agreement for an exchange of track meets to begin in Moscow in 1957. At the Rome Games of 1960 East-West goodwill abounded; Soviet and American athletes openly fraternized. The chairman of the Soviet Olympic Committee, Constantin Andrianov, was even moved to say "Politics is one thing, sport another. We are sportsmen."[7] (Yet apparently the poor showing of the highly touted American track and field team at Rome led President John F. Kennedy to enlarge the program of the President's Council on Physical Fitness.) In the 1960s and 1970s regularly scheduled athletic competition between the Soviet Union and the United States constituted part of a wide-ranging program of cultural exchange between the two nations.

In the 1960s the apartheid of South Africa replaced the Soviet-

---

[5]See Kenny Moore, "The Campaign for Athletes' Rights," *Annals of the American Academy of Political and Social Science*, 445 (Sept. 1979), 59–65. Congress rejected the President's Commission on Olympic Sports' (1977) call for unified control of Olympic sports in the form of a new organization, the Central Sports Organization. For a review of the complex network of amateur sports' bodies in the late 1970s see James H. Frey, "The Organization of American Amateur Sport: Efficiency to Entrophy," *American Behavioral Scientist*, 21 (Jan./Feb., 1978), 361–78. Frey argued that increased centralization would decrease the quantity of total athletic participation in the United States. Few Americans, when debating the proper means of administering "amateur" sport, argued that winning medals at the Olympic Games was a questionable national goal.

[6]Quoted in Espy, *Politics of the Olympic Games*, p. 40.
[7]Quoted in Johnson, *All That Glitters*, p. 236.

American conflict as the focus of Olympic politics.[8] Apparently in an effort to gain influence with the new African states, the Soviet delegate to the International Olympic Committee first raised the issue of racial discrimination by South Africa in 1959. (Until the 1960s there were no black African delegates on the IOC.) Accepting the assurances of compliance with the IOC principle of nondiscrimination by the South African delegate to the IOC, the committee permitted South Africa to participate in the 1960 Games at Rome. But the IOC soon discovered that regardless of the position of the South African National Olympic Committee, the South African government had no intention of permitting fully integrated sports. Consequently the IOC barred South Africa from the 1964 Games at Tokyo.

The IOC action failed to still the South African issue. After 1964 the black African states mounted a concerted drive to isolate South Africa from the world community. Sport was one of their most potent weapons. In the meantime, South Africa, a nation whose white minority was intensely sportsminded, promised to eliminate manifest racism from its Olympic program. The promises of reform reassured Brundage. To him, the sole concern of the IOC should be racism in Olympic sports, not the general apartheid policy of the South African government. In January of 1968 a three-man commission, one of whom was a black African, reported that after having visited South Africa, sportsmen, both white and black, were satisfied with the reforms. With the favorable commission report in hand, the members of the IOC voted by postcard to readmit South Africa to the 1968 Mexico City Games.

Apparently Brundage and the majority of the IOC seriously misjudged the consequences of their actions. To the black African nations, the central issue was not racism in sport but general apartheid. Within thirteen days after the announcement of South Africa's return to the Olympic fold, almost all of the African nations and several sympathizing Third World countries withdrew from the Games. The Soviet Union threatened to boycott and American black athletes, led by San Jose State sociology instructor Harry Edwards, announced a probable boycott. (Later at the Games, Tommie Smith and John Carlos, black American sprinters, stood on the victory platform during the playing of the national anthem with black-gloved fists raised defiantly in the air and heads bowed to protest racism in the United States). With the 1968 Games seriously jeopardized, Brundage hastily called a meeting of the IOC executive committee. To save face for both the IOC and South Africa, the IOC declared that the international climate of "violence" made it necessary to bar South Africa from the Games. In fact, the executive committee had capitulated to

[8]For the South African issue in addition to Espy, *Politics of the Olympic Games*, see Richard Edward Lapchick, *The Politics of Race and International Sport* (Westport, Conn.: Greenwood, 1972); Lapchick, "South Africa: Sport and Apartheid Politics," *Annals of the American Academy of Political and Social Science*, 445 (Sept. 1979), 155–65.

political pressure. In 1970 the IOC officially expelled South Africa from the Olympic movement.

Despite the expulsion of South Africa, the black Africans continued to use the games as a political weapon. In May of 1976 New Zealand scheduled a rugby tour in South Africa. The Organization of African Unity announced that its member states would boycott the 1976 Games unless New Zealand were barred. Only forty-eight hours before the opening ceremonies at Montreal, fifteen African nations sent the IOC an ultimatum: either send New Zealand home or they would boycott. The IOC responded that rugby was not an Olympic sport and New Zealand did not practice apartheid. In this instance, the IOC refused to accede to African demands and thirty countries pulled out of the Montreal Games. No action indicated so clearly the absence of concern for the individual athletes. Track and field fans were especially angry because the boycott prevented a classic confrontation between the two top milers of the world—Tanzania's Filbert Bayi and New Zealand's John Walker. Several African athletes paid their own expenses to Montreal and tried to compete under the Olympic flag, but Olympic officials, apparently hoping to woo the African countries back into the Olympic fold, refused to allow them to participate.

The political use of the Games reached grotesque proportions in the 1972 Munich Olympics when a group of Arab terrorists seized the Israeli compound and eventually killed nine Israeli athletes. The tragedy dripped with irony, for the West Germans had hoped to erase the ugly memories of Nazism only to have Jewish blood once again spilled on German soil. But this time the Germans were the would-be rescuers. After having scaled an eight-feet-high fence and capturing the Israeli compound, the terrorists made five demands for the release of the nine hostages, including the freeing of some 200 Arab guerillas in Israel and elsewhere. The West German negotiators, guided by top Israeli government officials, refused to make any major concessions. In the meantime the terrorists postponed deadlines for the execution of the hostages. Television cameras positioned near the compound zoomed in on the hangmanlike-visage of a terrorist in a stocking cap who seemed to symbolize the total prostitution of the Games to nonsports-centered goals. West German and Israeli officials finally settled upon a desperate plan which was to culminate in an ambush of the terrorists at an airport near Munich. The plan failed. The terrorists killed all of the Israeli hostages, though German authorities captured three of the Arab guerillas and killed the others. Despite the massacre, Olympic officials decided that the Games ought to continue.[9] As a consequence of the Munich tragedy, fears of terrorist attacks also clouded the 1976 Games in Montreal and the 1980 Games in Moscow.

Scheduling the 1980 Games in Moscow once again brought the Soviet-American rivalry to the forefront of Olympic politics. Both Moscow and Los Angeles submitted bids for the 1976 summer Games; both cities

[9]See Jerry Kirshenbaum, "A Sanctuary Violated," *Sports Illustrated*, 37 (Sept. 18, 1972), 24–26.

offered attractive inducements to the IOC, but a "swing bloc" on the committee chose Montreal on the second ballot to host the 1976 Games. The Soviets angrily charged that the two North American cities had colluded to deny Moscow the Games. Mayor Sam Yorty of Los Angeles, while expressing regret that his city did not win the bid, was pleased that the Games would remain in the "free world." Only Los Angeles and Moscow submitted bids for the 1980 Games. Harassment by Russians of Israeli athletes at the World University Games held in Moscow in 1973 unleashed a torrent of criticism from various quarters against Moscow as the site for the 1980 Games. Israel protested that the exhibitions of "racism and anti-Semitism" at the University Games made the Soviet Union an inappropriate host; in the United States, forty congressmen and the USOC publicly condemned the Moscow site, although the American protest seemed to be somewhat self-serving inasmuch as the Americans had an interest in promoting the candidacy of Los Angeles. Regardless, the IOC, impressed by Soviet promises of efficient management and a desire to expand the influence of the Olympic movement, awarded the Games to Moscow. Most Americans, basking in a new detente between the superpowers, acquiesced to the decision without noticeable concern.

The invasion of Afghanistan by the Soviet Union in 1979 suddenly reawakened the latent antagonism between East and West. Although the United States had not withdrawn from the earlier Games to protest Soviet invasions of Hungary and Czechoslovakia, President Jimmy Carter quickly called for a world-wide boycott of the 1980 Games. Fearing Soviet expansion into the Persian Gulf region, American officials apparently believed that a boycott would serve as a moral condemnation of the Soviets, perhaps induce them to withdraw from Afghanistan, and deal a severe blow to Soviet prestige. Although only Canada, West Germany, and Japan, of the industrial states, cooperated fully with the American boycott, it was the first instance of one of the superpowers withdrawing from the Games. Furthermore, the boycott denied the Soviets access to the immense American television audience.

MONEY AND THE GAMES

Commercial considerations, though perhaps not as spectacular as political intrusions, likewise undermined the Olympics as an athlete-centered event. Brundage visualized the Games as "a revolt against Twentieth Century materialism...[as] a devotion to a cause and not the reward."[10] But such noble sentiments ignored the realities of the Olympic movement in the postwar era. As was the case with sports in general, television was the single most important force in altering the commercial and financial structure of the Games. Television enormously increased the size of the audience for the Games, played upon national rivalries, became a favorite medium for using the Olympics to sell commercial products, and was eventually

[10]Quoted in Johnson, *All That Glitters,* p. 24.

essential to the financial solvency of the Games. The contracts between American television networks and the Olympics grew slowly until the 1970s when they soared to astronomical heights (see Figure 15–2). ABC's coverage of the 1968, 1972, and 1976 Games contributed immensely to the transformation of the Olympics into a television extravaganza. ABC brought to the Games the technical innovations and experience it had gained from producing "Wide World of Sports" and college football. Apart from good Nielsen ratings, which perhaps resulted in part from the expression of patriotic sentiments that had been stilled by the Vietnam war, the networks believed that televising the Games enhanced their image and provided valuable "lead-ins" to their fall programming. To the surprise of many veterans of the television industry, the networks had little difficulty in selling enough commercials to cover costs.

Television helped provide the host cities with the opportunity to present themselves as glittering showcases of modernity. Host cities hoped the Games would attract tourists, improve the image of the city, and promote trade. The 1964 Winter Games at Innsbruck, Austria, and Summer Games in Tokyo were the first since the Berlin Games in 1936 to exploit fully the opportunities presented by the Olympics. The Austrians used the Winter Games to promote the sale of their ski equipment and to transform Innsbruck into a major sports center and tourist attraction. While the Tokyo Games served as a stimulus for badly needed urban renewal and the construction of new housing projects, the Games also served as a vehicle for launching Japan as one of the world's top trading nations. "Without the Olympics," declared Ryotaro Azuma, the mayor of Tokyo, "Japan would not have risen to its high position in world trade so fast. Our national prestige depended on the Tokyo Games being a success...."[11] Nonetheless, the costs of hosting the Games mounted to staggering heights. Montreal budgeted $310 million for the 1976 Games, but final costs exceeded $1.5 billion. To bail out the city, Montreal had to call upon the provincial government of Quebec. Observers began to wonder if the benefits equalled the costs of hosting the Games. Excessive costs seemed to require either the radical reform or the demise of the Games.

Business firms found in the Olympic Games a wonderful opportunity to advertise their products. They spent large sums of money to get athletic equipment or clothing identified with the Games. Traditionally, American athletes had not worn coordinated apparel; but in 1964 textile firms began providing free, coordinated outfits for the entire team. In exchange the industry received tax deductions, exhibited their product to the world, and received the good will arising from having contributed to the Olympic team. The manufacturers believed that the clothes of the Olympic team exerted a strong influence upon the purchases of youth, especially in the fall market following the Games. The local organizing committees, national committees, and IOC increasingly relied upon money received from "official" suppliers as well as television. By the time of the 1976 Games, sport fans could use official "Olympic" butter, beer, sugar, petrol, cameras,

[11]Quoted in ibid., p. 25.

Figure 15–2 Television contracts with American networks for the summer Olympic Games in millions of dollars

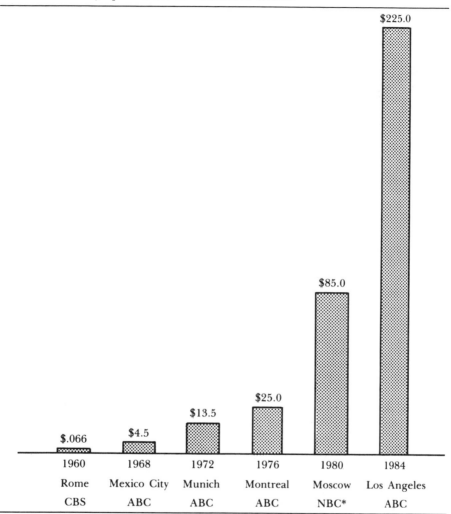

	1960	1968	1972	1976	1980	1984
	$.066	$4.5	$13.5	$25.0	$85.0	$225.0
	Rome	Mexico City	Munich	Montreal	Moscow	Los Angeles
	CBS	ABC	ABC	ABC	NBC*	ABC

*Cancelled after partial payment because of United States' withdrawal from the Games.

watches, and a host of other products. At Montreal, Coca Cola alone paid $1.3 million to supply the athletes with free Olympic-endorsed soda. With the costs of the Games skyrocketing and financial considerations daily becoming more complex, Olympic organizations found that business matters absorbed far more of their time and attention than sport itself.

Financial considerations impinged directly upon the athletes, at least those athletes from the West. In order to preserve the athlete as the focus of the Games, Coubertin had insisted that only pristine amateurs could compete. Such an ideal sprang from the nineteenth-century world of elite sports in which wealthy "gentlemen" had adequate means to finance their own athletic endeavors. Gentlemen athletes presumably shared a constellation of values and behavior traits which included "fair play," self-restraint, and the pursuit of sport simply for the pleasure that it afforded. Consequently, winning, training, and specialization should be subordinated to the end of immediate pleasure, not wealth or recognition. Yet with increasing world attention focused upon the Games and potentially lucrative endorsements stemming from successful athletic performance, winning superseded all other goals. To compete successfully in the Games, the athlete had to engage in full-time training and compete frequently. Unless the athlete were wealthy, he had to receive financial support from external sources. Such support violated the spirit if not the letter of the Olympic creed.

Subsidization came in several forms. In Soviet bloc nations and many Third World countries the states fully financed their Olympic teams. In the United States, college athletic scholarships, generous traveling allowances, and sometimes "under-the-table" payments or gratuities permitted athletes to engage in the full-time training necessary to compete successfully in the Games. In the 1960s the endorsements of sporting equipment by athletes, either directly or indirectly, became something of a world-wide scandal. European skiers represented the most notorious example. To display prominently the trademarks of their equipment, many skiers received cash payments from manufacturers. After the 1968 Summer Games, it was revealed that two manufacturers—Adidas and Puma—had apparently paid track and field athletes to wear their shoes. Further inquiry disclosed that many manufacturers regularly paid athletes to use their equipment and that such payments constituted a major source of income for athletes.[12] "Most of us are aware," declared Jack Kelly, president of the Amateur Athletic Union, "that as many as two-thirds of the athletes signing the Olympic oath are committing perjury."[13] The rampant hypocrisy finally induced the IOC in 1974 to modify its strict rules; it permitted "amateur" athletes to receive their regular salaries when in training for international competition and not actually working. Furthermore, athletes could openly endorse products so long as the fee from such an endorsement was paid to the national sport organization to which the athlete belonged. In turn, the sport body could pay the athlete expense money or what in effect constituted a salary.[14]

Many potential gold medal winners appeared to be driven more by the hopes of future commercial payoffs than by love of sports. Mark Spitz, winner of seven gold medals in swimming at Munich in 1972, reputedly received $5 million to endorse a wide array of products. Bruce Jenner, winner of the decathlon at Montreal in 1976, frankly confessed that he

---

[12]See John Underwood, "No Good Two-Shoes," *Sports Illustrated,* 30 (March 10, 1969), 14, 23. Allegedly the two shoe manufacturers distributed $100,000 at the 1968 Games. Individual athletes received as much as $10,000 each.

[13]Quoted in Johnson, *All That Glitters,* p. 38.

[14]"Scorecard," *Sports Illustrated,* 50 (April 23, 1979), 24; *The Final Report of the President's Commission on Olympic Sports,* 2 vols. (Washington, D.C.: GPO, 1977), II, 343.

Members of Soviet Junior Olympics Team examining sale items at K-Mart, Lincoln, Nebraska. Courtesy of the Journal Star Printing Company.

engaged in the arduous training required to win only for the sake of future monetary returns. After his victory at Montreal, Jenner and his wife became "commercial billboards" huckstering everything from breakfast foods to cameras. The motives that impelled Spitz and Jenner to participate in the Games were obviously far removed from those that Coubertin and Brundage had hoped to encourage.[15]

By the 1980s the IOC, the international bodies that supervised competition at the Games, and the national Olympic committees became increasingly absorbed in the tasks of maintaining their own existences. (In most cases—at least in the West—the sport bodies were self-perpetuating, responsible to no one but themselves.) The Olympic movement had become a huge unwieldly network of bureaucracies. The IOC itself reflected the trend toward bureaucratization. Until 1964 the permanent staff of the IOC consisted of only the president and two part-time assistants in Chicago (Brundage's residence) and a chancellor and two part-time assistants in Lausanne, the headquarters of the organization. Until 1960 the entire expenses of the IOC had been less than $10,000 per year. In the

[15]On Spitz, see Jerry Kirshenbaum, "On Your Mark, Get Set, Sell," *Sports Illustrated*, 38 (May 14, 1973), 36–46.

1960s and 1970s the staff and expenses of the IOC soared; in 1980 the administrative head of the IOC, Monique Berlioux, alone, received an annual salary of $100,000, and the Lausanne office included more than thirty-five full-time employees. A similar bureaucratization occurred in the United States where the USOC spent over half of its budget on administration.[16] In sum, the exigencies of finance, politics, and self-preservation forced the Olympic movement to define its goals and concerns in terms of the growth and size of its organizations rather than in terms of athlete-centered ideals.

TELEVISION AND THE ASCENT OF GOLF

In the era of televised sport, golf entered a new "golden era," or as some golfing commentators described it, "The Age of Arnold Palmer." In the 1950s the ambience of golf continued to be that of the country club, lavish resorts, and wealthy old men, but in the 1960s golf rather suddenly joined the mainstream of spectator sport. The number of active players and courses doubled. The professional tour achieved unprecedented popularity and prosperity. In 1956 all the television networks carried only five and a half hours of golf for the entire year; by 1970 viewers could see nearly that much golf each week. By then television poured about $4 million annually into the sport and more than 10 million people watched the major tournaments. Earnings on the pro tour soared from about $1.5 million in 1958 to $5.5 million in 1968 and to $10 million in 1978. Golf furnished the Associated Press "Athlete of the Decade" for the 1960s—Arnold Palmer. In terms of all-time total income (through 1977), including nonsports income, Palmer, according to *Sports Illustrated,* outdistanced runner-up Muhammad Ali by $55 million to $5.75 million. In the 1960s and 1970s, golf had become a big-time spectator-centered sport.[17]

Signs of the new golden era of golf were apparent in the 1950s. Although the total number of courses was even less in 1957 than in 1945, interest in golf had grown steadily. Ardent golf fans admired the "precisionist" play of Ben Hogan and Sammy Snead, perennial winners of major championships in the late 1940s and the 1950s. In the nation's capital, the new President, Dwight D. Eisenhower, loved to play the game and, unlike two of his golf-playing predecessors—William Howard Taft and Warren G. Harding—made no secret of his addiction to the game. At every opportunity the President played with golfing pros, business tycoons, or entertainment celebrities, either in the Washington, D.C. area or at the Augusta, Georgia, National Course where anonymous club members built

[16]See Espy, *Politics of the Olympic Games,* pp. 163–71; *Final Report of the President's Commission on Olympic Sports,* II, 422, 442; Anita Verschoth, "Carrying the Torch," *Sports Illustrated,* 54 (April 13, 1981), 70.

[17]See Ray Kennedy and Nancy Williamson, "Money in Sports: Part 2," *Sports Illustrated,* 49 (July 24, 1978), 43; "The £2 Billion Golf Business," *Economist,* 236 (July 11, 1970), 50–51; Herbert Warren Wind, *The Story of American Golf,* 3rd rev. ed. (New York: Knopf, 1975), Part Seven.

him a vacation cottage in 1952. At the other end of the continent Hollywood celebrities took up golf with a new enthusiasm. Bing Crosby, Bob Hope, Perry Como, Danny Thomas, Andy Williams, and Jackie Gleason, among others, joined such commercial concerns as Buick, Firestone, and Dow Jones in sponsoring new professional tourneys. (Each year the Crosby Pro-Am enjoyed a television rating equal to the major championship tournaments.) The association of golf with a popular President and a host of celebrities lent to the sport a glamour perhaps unequalled by any other sport.

Then in the 1960s came the potent combination of television and Arnold Palmer. Palmer brought to golf high drama and a charismatic personality. The son of a club pro from the Latrobe, Pennsylvania, Country Club, Palmer's first major victory came in the 1954 National Amateur; four years later he attained some national prominence by winning the Masters, the first of four triumphs on Bobby Jones's home course at Augusta. Then came the U.S. Open at Denver in 1960. Before a nationwide television audience on a searingly hot afternoon, he established his reputation for the Palmer "charge," "a heart-attack approach to golf that demanded the situation look hopeless before one really begins to play."[18] Entering the last round of the tourney while trailing by seven strokes and fourteen players, Palmer exploded, scoring one birdie after another to finish with an epic 65, a score low enough to take the title. Golf fans never forgot the 1960 Open, but Palmer added to his own legend by fashioning an incredible string of come-from-behind victories. He won at Palm Springs with a final round of 65, at Pensacola with a 67, at Hartford with a 67 that got him to the playoff which he won, and at Mobile with a 67. Few experiences in sport equalled the sheer drama of the Palmer charge.

Not since the historic feats of Bobby Jones in 1930 had a golfer created so much national excitement. Golf fans loved Palmer and he reciprocated their affection. He acted and looked like a "regular guy" who needed the help of the fans. Unlike the typical stony-faced pros, Palmer's face registered his emotions. He celebrated his good shots with a wide, disarming grin and by raising his club high in the air as if to say "We did it"; bad shots produced painful grimaces. Long after Palmer stopped winning many championships "Arnie's Army," as the immense throngs who accompanied him were dubbed, continued to be larger than any group following a pro golfer. Even Palmer's capitalization of his popularity seemed to enhance his heroic stature. His manager, Mark McCormack, a Cleveland lawyer who was to become the most successful of all sports managers, made Palmer into a one-man conglomerate, a corporation that produced and endorsed a galaxy of products many of which were unconnected with golf. Palmer helped wash away the image of golf as a snobbish and exclusive sport. "The game had often been maligned as a pastime for rich old men (the more captious critics refused to acknowledge that it was even a sport)," wrote Frank Deford in 1979, "but Palmer, the

[18]Joseph Durso, *The All-American Dollar: The Big Business of Sports* (Boston: Houghton Mifflin, 1971), p. 185. See also Mark H. McCormack, *Arnie: The Evolution of a Legend* (New York: Simon and Schuster, 1977).

handsome charger, [gave]. . .the game glamour, expanded its horizons. *He made people proud to be golfers.*"[19]

In the mid-1960s Jack Nicklaus challenged Palmer's supremacy. Although he never won the public affection that accrued to Palmer, Nicklaus proceeded to become the winningest and perhaps the greatest golfer of all time. Between 1959 and 1980 he won the U.S. Amateur twice, the Masters five times, the U.S. Open three times, the British Open three times, and the PGA four times. By 1980 he had won seventeen major titles plus fifty-four tour tourneys for total winnings from golf of nearly $3.5 million, almost twice as much as his nearest rival. His style of play amazed the world of golf. No one had ever been so consistent in driving the ball down the fairway for distance, height, and accuracy. His ball soared over natural obstacles and he rarely had to use a fairway wood club. A stunned Bobby Jones acknowledged: "Jack Nicklaus plays a game with which I am not familiar."[20] Several major tournaments even felt compelled to redesign their courses to present Nicklaus with a more formidable challenge. Nicklaus could justifiably be described as the Babe Ruth of golf.

Television was the other key to golf's golden era. Like football, the marriage of the electronic medium to golf was essentially an idyllic one. Although golf matches were expensive to telecast—typically double that of a NFL telecast—the cameras could easily capture the bucolic scenery and the excitement of a tournament. The drama of thousands of dollars hanging on the success of a single putt could hardly be matched by any other sport. Gaps in play permitted analysis by commentators and the build-up of dramatic tension. Sponsors thought that golf telecasts reached an especially affluent, male clientele. Unlike fans of most professional sports, the average golfer could easily identify his own play with that of the tournament professional whom he saw on television. During a lifetime of playing golf, the weekend golfer sometimes duplicated the feats of the pros; he or she occasionally sank a thirty-foot putt, chipped a shot hard against the flag, or blasted a 250-yard drive straight down the fairway. Thus television produced a closer emotional bond between the amateur and professional athlete than existed in most sports.

Television, more than any other single factor, altered the economics and the governing structure of pro golf. The number of tournaments on the pro tour grew from thirty-one in 1947 offering $352,000 in prize money to seventy-six events in 1973 and a total purse of over $8 million. In the 1970s some 250 pros regularly participated in the tour; after 1973 more than fifteen (by 1979 thirty-five) regularly made more than $100,000 annually. Television was also primarily responsible for inducing the touring pros to break away from the PGA, which was controlled by the club pros. In 1968 the touring pros formed the American Professional Golfers and prepared to conduct their own tour in 1969. Finally the warring parties reached a settlement which called for the establishment of a separate division within the PGA, the Tournament Players Division, with its own commissioner.

---

[19]Frank Deford, "Still Glittering After All These Years," *Sports Illustrated*, 49 (Dec. 25, 1978–Jan. 1, 1979), 32.
[20]Ibid., 26.

The TPD appointed Joseph C. Dey, Jr., who for thirty-five years had been an executive with the USGA, as its commissioner. Unlike the chaotic world of professional tennis, the TPD brought a large measure of order and stability to professional golf.[21]

Until the 1970s the prize money and public exposure of women's professional golf lagged far behind that of the men's game. In 1946 a handful of women had formed the Women's PGA (changed to Ladies Professional Golf Association in 1948). The LPGA sponsored the U.S. Women's Open from 1948 to 1953 when the USGA took charge of the tourney. Even with Fred Corcoran, a veteran promoter of men's golf in charge of the tour, the prize money remained pitifully meager. In 1948, for example, the ladies' tour consisted of only nine tournaments and Babe Zaharias, the leading money-winner, garnered only $3,400. As late as 1970 the women's tour offered only $345,000, divided among twenty-one events. Then, in apparently belated recognition of the purchasing power of the nation's females, television and large corporations suddenly took an interest in the women's game. By 1980 the number of tourneys had grown to thirty-nine, offering a total prize money of $5.1 million with an average of 100 competitors in each event. During the decade of the 1970s the average purse grew from $20,000 to $127,500 and television coverage from two to fourteen events. The prosperity of women's pro golf seemed to be assured.[22]

The same could not be said for golf at the grass-roots level. Although the number of active amateur players continued to grow in the 1970s, the rate of increase was much slower than in the 1960s. Some analysts blamed the "curse of slow play," claiming that the amateurs tried to imitate the slow, deliberate style of the pros who they watched on television. Regardless of the cause, on weekends at most courses playing eighteen holes required five or more hours. Some golfers shifted to tennis where a brisk three-set match could be played in an hour and a half. Other analysts blamed the slow growth of golf on the spiraling costs of playing the game. Chronic inflation in the late 1960s and the 1970s drove some private clubs out of existence and forced others to raise fees or embark upon expanded membership drives. While the costs of maintaining a club increased sharply, profits from restaurants and bars, traditionally major sources of income for clubs, declined. As the 1970s closed, the success of golf at the grass-roots level seemed to depend less upon the private clubs and more upon courses built by municipalities, resorts, and real estate developers.[23]

Neither did the prosperity of the men's professional game appear to be assured. The composite television ratings on all three networks fell from 7.4 in 1975 to 5.4 in 1979 and several large corporate sponsors began to withdraw their financial support. In 1980 Chevrolet, the single largest television sponsor, reduced its golf advertising by some $12 million and

[21]See Herb Graffis, *The PGA: The Official History of the Professional Golfers' Association of America* (New York: Thomas Y. Crowell, 1975), Chap. 26.

[22]*New York Times*, Dec. 30, 1979, S7.

[23]See "Country Clubs Fall Short of the Green," *Business Week* (March 6, 1971), 77–78; Wind, *The Story of American Golf*, pp. 517–18.

CBS announced plans to slash its golf coverage from twenty to fourteen tournaments per season. In a rather desperate effort to capture higher television ratings, both golf officials and the television networks introduced innovations. Deane Beman, the PGA tour commissioner, decided to add myriad statistics to the golfer's performance, hoping to make the tour a more "viable force in the sports marketplace." For the 1980 tour, golf fans learned each week—down to several decimal points—driving accuracy, driving distance, birdie percentages, along with five other indices. Both NBC and CBS renovated their telecasts; the networks added a third camera to bolster close-up coverage and featured new player profiles.[24] No one could forecast whether these changes would recapture lost fans, but what the men's tour appeared to need most was a new hero to replace the aging Palmer and Nicklaus.

TENNIS—OPEN TO ALL

Patterns of competition in tennis, one of the last bastions of the player-centered era and one of the most conservative of sports, changed little from the 1930s to the mid-1960s.[25] "Social climbers," more interested in using tennis as a means of earning a social reputation than in promoting tennis as a spectator sport, continued to dominate the management of the game. Consequently, the ambience of tennis remained stuffy, formal, and pompous. The tennis establishment permitted and encouraged "shamateurism," usually in the form of paying amateurs liberal "expense" allowances for appearing in tournaments. Most players could make more money by remaining nominal amateurs than they could by becoming avowed professionals. Professional tennis could support only two or three players in a decent fashion. Beginning with the formula established by Bill Tilden in the 1930s, a handful of pro players embarked each year upon international tours, but these itinerant pros played in relative obscurity—in matches that the public often perceived as mere exhibitions. On the other hand, the absence of the best known players in the great amateur tournaments at Forest Hills and Wimbledon robbed the tourneys of potential excitement. To be successful as a spectator sport, tennis needed to shed its "country club" image and develop a format which would feature classic confrontations between the world's greatest players, regardless of whether the players were professional or amateur.

"Open" tennis seemed to be a solution. In the 1950s Jack Kramer, winner at Forest Hills in 1946 and 1947 and Wimbledon in 1947 and the best known figure in American tennis, launched an intensely personal campaign for the open game. Tournaments open to both pro and amateur

---

[24]See Dan Jenkins, "Now You Can Look It Up," and Stan Isaacs, "The Shot Heard Round the Links," *Sports Illustrated,* 52 (Jan. 21, 1980), 84–86, 88; "Scorecard," ibid., 53 (Nov. 17, 1980), 26.

[25]For a general survey of recent tennis history from the perspective of the United States Lawn Tennis Association see their *Official Encyclopedia of Tennis* (New York: Harper & Row, 1972), pp. 50–67.

players, with prize money, Kramer reasoned, would not only erase the blatant hypocrisy endemic to big-time amateur tennis but would generate a renewed public interest in the sport. At the same time, tennis officials within the United States Lawn Tennis Association (USLTA) worried about falling tournament receipts and the drastic decline in the performance of American amateur players. Between 1953 and 1968 American men failed to capture a singles title at Forest Hills; a series of great Australian players (Australia had a population approximately equal to New York City) dominated the sport.

The decision of an Australian, Rod Laver, winner of the Triple Slam—British, American, and Australian championships—to turn pro in 1963, when the game most needed a star gate attraction, and the establishment of a small but successful pro circuit in 1964 were important turning points in the movement for open tennis. While the USLTA wavered in its support for the open game, the British, French, and Australian associations joined the movement. Only the International Lawn Tennis Federation (ILTF), controlled by the national associations of the smaller nations, resisted the open game. By announcing that Wimbledon would be an open event in 1968, the British unilaterally defied the ILTF and thereby inaugurated a new era of tennis. The next year the United States championships at Forest Hills also opened its gates to the pros. Faced with a virtually united front of the largest tennis playing nations, the ILTF finally capitulated.

Open tennis, television coverage of the big tournaments, the emergence of a new set of American stars such as Stan Smith, Arthur Ashe, Jimmy Connors, Billie Jean King and Chris Evert, and bourgeoning purses all contributed to a heightened public interest in tennis. "The big purses," said Smith, "made people watch who didn't know a lob from a volley, and suddenly a lot of people realized tennis was good for spectators, and good to play."[26] Although television ratings remained below that of the team sports and golf, production costs were far less than the other sports and advertisers suspected that televised tennis matches reached an exceptionally affluent market. Between 1970 and 1973 the networks tripled the amount of time devoted to the sport and NBC paid a record $100,000 for the rights to televise each of eight World Championship Tennis tournaments. Televised tennis reached a peak in 1975. That year the networks telecast fifty matches and CBS paid $600,000—a sum exceeding an NFL telecast—to cover a match between Jimmy Connors and John Newcombe.[27]

Yet televised tennis suffered from a major handicap; it did not fit neatly into a predetermined time slot. Television producers frequently responded by using delayed videotapes with parts of the matches sliced out and urged the tournaments to adopt the "sudden death" tie-breaker when a match reached six games for each player. Television also encouraged the abandonment of all white tennis wear and white tennis balls. None of these changes completely solved the problems of televised tennis. Fans complained that delayed telecasts destroyed the inherent drama of the contests;

[26]Quoted in Judson Gooding, "The Tennis Industry," *Fortune*, 87 (June 1973), 126.
[27]See William Leggett, "Serving Up Tennis to a Fault," *Sports Illustrated*, 42 (March 24, 1975), 54.

often they already knew who had won the match. And sometimes fans were treated to the spectacle of the same player simultaneously playing a different opponent on separate networks.

Promoters also experimented with alterations in the playing surface. Traditionally, tennis courts had been made of grass or clay, but in the twentieth century concrete and asphalt became popular for all-weather play, especially in the United States. In the early 1970s promoters decided that the "serve-and-volley game" characteristic of the American players failed to excite the maximum potential interest of fans so they installed slower surfaces. "It was for television. TV was going to drop tennis if we didn't do something to get away from the serve-and-volley game," declared Edward Brodeur, inventor of the most popular of the slower surfaces.[28] But the slow surfaces gave foreign players an advantage over the Americans. While most foreign players learned their games on clay, American players generally nurtured their games on fast asphalt surfaces. As a compromise, by the late 1970s most major tournaments installed "happy-medium" speed surfaces.

Open tournaments with larger purses marked a decline in the monopolies of the national associations and the ILTF and the rise of a new set of promoters.[29] The promoters engaged in a vicious, cutthroat competition for profits. In 1970 Lamar Hunt, Texas millionaire and owner of the Kansas City Chiefs football team, bankrolled World Championship Tennis, which, for a guarantee, would provide pro tours anywhere in the world with a tournament of competing stars. The same year Jack Kramer established the Grand Prix, nominally under the jurisdiction of the ILTF, which awarded points to players for high finishes in major tournaments and prize money to top winners at the conclusion of the season. The top winners then played in a Masters tournament for bonus money. Bill Riordan, the maverick manager of Jimmy Connors, operated yet a third circuit. In addition, in 1975 and 1976, Riordan promoted three successful television extravaganzas in Las Vegas pitting Connors against various opponents in what were billed as the "Heavyweight Championship of Tennis." Later CBS television network confessed that it had falsely advertised the matches as "winner-take-alls." In reality the players received large guarantees—win or lose—to appear in the matches. Largely because of the international nature of the sport, tennis was unable to establish a single economic cartel to govern itself and maximize profits for promoters.

Several observers forecast that tennis would replace football and golf as the major "growth" sport of the 1970s. The early years of the decade seemed to confirm their prediction. Apart from the professional game which was suddenly the beneficiary of unprecedented purses for tournaments, rich endorsement contracts, millionaire stars, and an abundance of

[28]Quoted in Ray Kennedy, "The Way the Ball Bounces," *Sports Illustrated*, 52 (April 21, 1980), 45. Simply by knowing the kind of surface a match was to be played upon, according to Brodeur, he could predict "exactly what will happen."

[29]On the politics and economics of tennis see especially Rich Coster, *The Tennis Bubble: Big Money Tennis—How It Grew and Where It's Going* (New York: Quadrangle/New York Times, 1976).

television coverage, tennis became the "in" sport of upper middle income groups. According to a Nielsen survey, 34 million people played the game in 1975 compared to 10.6 million in 1970. In the first three years of the decade sporting goods companies tripled, then quadrupled their sales of tennis gear; in 1973 the manufacturers, unprepared for the sudden boom, even ran short of balls. The demand for tennis instruction, especially in more or less exclusive social circumstances, reached new heights. John Gardiner, who started the country's first tennis ranch in 1957, pioneered in intensive instruction in a resort setting. Gardiner's program included professional instruction in basic strokes and tactics, the use of videotape replays, and rapid-firing, ball-throwing machines. Hundreds of indoor tennis centers sprang up across the country. In 1961 only one indoor facility operated in the Chicago area; by 1974 there were forty-three centers.[30]

But in the late 1970s the tennis boom apparently began to fizzle. The construction of new resort and indoor facilities tapered off, the sale of tennis equipment slumped, and, except for Wimbledon and the U.S. Open, the networks cut back sharply on television coverage. "Unless there's better organization and focus," predicted NBC's Don Ohlmeyer, "[tennis is]...going to die on television in the 80's. There's eight million tournaments and only two that mean anything—Wimbledon and the U.S. Open."[31] The rampant inflation and modest increases, if any, in real income by many of those in the middle and upper middle income brackets in the late 1970s may have stalled the growth of both tennis and golf as participant sports. Apparently in the mid-1970s both sports had passed the peaks of their popularity.

[30]Gooding, "The Tennis Industry," 124–33.
[31]Quoted in New York Times, December 30, 1979, S7. Racket sales tumbled from a high of $184 million in 1976 to $138 million four years later. See Ray Kennedy, "Howard Head Says: I'm Giving Up the Thing World," Sports Illustrated, 53 (Sept. 29, 1980), 64.

16

Blacks and Women
Demand Equal Opportunity

Jackie Robinson signs contract offered by Branch Rickey of the Brooklyn Dodgers.
Courtesy of the Jackie Robinson Foundation.

By and large the players welcomed the ascendancy of the spectators. Few players called for an end to spectator-centered sports. Only a brief, largely ineffectual, "countercultural" athletic revolt in the late 1960s and early 1970s demanded the abolition of sports bureaucracies, athletic specialization, the obsession with records, and the relentless demands for achievement intrinsic to modern sports. While the players sometimes nostalgically recalled childhood games or an earlier era of American sports in which the athletes presumably played for sheer fun, rarely did such sentiment result in the athlete becoming a "jock hippie." For, above all, most of the players wanted to exploit the benefits made possible by the spectacular growth of spectator sports. And two groups traditionally discriminated against in American sports—blacks and women—struggled for additional opportunities to display and profit from their athletic skills, not for the right to play for its own sake.

THE SLOW PROCESS OF DESEGREGATION

"Brooklyn announces the purchase of the contract of Jack Roosevelt Robinson from Montreal," read a terse press statement released by Branch Rickey on April 9, 1947.

The announcement revealed nothing of the larger significance of the event. It did not mention that Robinson was black, that he would be the first black to play in the major leagues since the 1880s, or that breaking the "color ban" in the "National Game" might be of incalculable symbolic importance. No one knew that the racial integration of Organized Baseball would herald the beginning of a black breakthrough in many other sports. The previous fall, two blacks, Kenny Washington and Woody Strode, had played with the Los Angeles Rams of the NFL. In 1949 the American Bowling Congress opened its lanes to blacks. The next year Chuck Cooper and Nat "Sweetwater" Clifton joined the National Basketball League and Althea Gibson played at Forest Hills. The Professional Golfers Association finally admitted the first black golfers in 1961, but then only as a consequence of a California court order. While a few blacks had played in northern colleges throughout the twentieth century, by the 1970s thousands played on college teams in both the North and the South. By then blacks, in terms of their percentage of the total American population, made up a disproportionate share of the athletes in the major team sports (excluding hockey).

The desegregation of these sports arose from a combination of pressures: pressures by blacks from outside the world of sports, assertions of black political power, international circumstances, shifting attitudes by whites toward blacks, and quests for additional profits by sports entrepreneurs. Outside the sports world, resistance to the segregation of blacks had begun to mount since the 1920s. The massive movement of blacks from the South to northern cities—about two million in the 1910s, a million in the 1920s, 400,000 in the 1930s and another million in the early 1940s—encouraged black assertiveness. Urban blacks manifested a stronger racial consciousness than their rural counterparts. Early in the 1920s millions of city blacks found inspiration in the black nationalism of Marcus Garvey, who promised salvation in an Empire of Africa. The "Harlem Renaissance" of the 1920s, an outpouring of eloquent black literature from New York City, stimulated black pride and sympathy for the plight of blacks among white intellectuals. Finally, in the 1930s the National Association for the Advancement of Colored People, with its main strength located in northern cities, embarked upon a vigorous campaign for black rights.

Although blacks made little headway against discrimination in the 1930s, they did win additional white supporters and began in the 1940s to develop more effective strategies for battling segregation. The war against Nazi racism offered blacks new opportunities to combat American racism. Early in 1941, as the nation mobilized for an anticipated war with Germany, A. Philip Randolph, president of the Brotherhood of Sleeping Car Porters, threatened to hold a mass rally in Washington to demand an end to discrimination in defense industries and the armed services. Although irritated, President Franklin D. Roosevelt did not want to alienate black voters nor have American racial discrimination publicized when the country was about to engage in war with a racist Nazi Germany. Roosevelt issued an executive order banning discrimination in hiring "because of race, creed, color, or national origins" by the federal government and its war-related contractors. But severe labor shortage in World War II did even more than the poorly enforced executive order to expand opportunities for blacks and weaken Jim Crow rules.

Blacks also learned that trading black votes for black rights could be a highly effective tactic. Since the northern cities lay in highly competitive, two-party states with large electoral votes, a solid black vote could tip the balance in elections. In the same years—1946 and 1947—that blacks joined major league baseball and football teams, several northern states and cities passed anti-Jim Crow laws or ordinances. In New York Governor Thomas E. Dewey sponsored an antidiscrimination law and in New York City Mayor Fiorello La Guardia established a Committee on Unity to study the problems of race relationships, including the apparent discrimination against blacks in baseball. Branch Rickey was a subcommittee member of La Guardia's Committee on Unity. Thus political circumstances in New York City, with its large black vote, were highly favorable to Rickey's assault on the walls of segregation in baseball. In fact, pressure from La Guardia may have induced Rickey to sign a black player more quickly than he intended.[1]

Inside the world of sports two black athletes—Jesse Owens and Joe Louis—both of whom had moved from the South to northern cities as youths, enhanced black pride and won the admiration of many whites. The success of Owens, the hero of the 1936 Berlin Olympics, seemed to be the perfect answer to Nazi racism, but it also highlighted the existence of racial discrimination in the United States. The discrepancy between racial practice at home and propaganda against Nazi racism abroad was not lost upon American blacks nor their white sympathizers. The career of Joe Louis, the victor in 1938 over the darling of the Nazis, Max Schmeling, revealed a similar discrepancy.[2]

The sharp decline in public interest in boxing after the retirement of Gene Tunney in 1928, the nonthreatening image of Louis, and international tensions all contributed to the circumstances that gave Louis a shot at the title and won him a large following among both whites and blacks. Five different men had held the championship between 1928 and 1937. Heavyweight boxing needed a new hero and Louis, with his superb boxing skills and powerful knockout punches, was, except for his race, the most likely candidate to fill the need. The promoters of Louis consciously determined to avoid the image problems that had beset Jack Johnson: they successfully imposed upon Louis a rigid code of personal conduct. "The colored boy is clean, fine and superb, as modest and unassuming as a chauffeur or as the man who cuts and rakes the lawn once a week," declared a sportswriter.[3] Unlike Johnson, Louis inspired little racial fear among whites.

Louis also benefitted immensely from the international climate of the 1930s. By defeating ex-champ Primo Carnera of Italy in 1935, at the very time that the Italian Fascist dictator Mussolini was blatantly overrunning defenseless Ethiopia, Louis won the plaudits of both white and black America. In 1936 Louis lost by way of a knockout to Max Schmeling, who had briefly held the crown after Tunney's retirement. One year after his humiliating defeat, Louis defeated James J. Braddock for the championship. In 1938 he fought Schmeling again in a fight freighted with international tension. Only two months before the fight Hitler had annexed Austria. Approximately two-thirds of the people in the United States heard the fight on the radio. Louis knocked out Schmeling in the first round. Americans everywhere rejoiced. Louis further improved his standing among whites by voluntarily joining the Army in World War II. When he announced his retirement in 1949 he had held the heavyweight

---

[1]See Milton J. Shapiro, *Jackie Robinson of the Brooklyn Dodgers* (New York: Julian Messner, 1957), pp. 61–66.

[2]On Louis see Barney Nagler, *Brown Bomber* (New York: World, 1972); Anthony O. Edmonds, *Joe Louis* (Grand Rapids, Mich.: William B. Eerdmans, 1973); Gerald Aston, *"And a Credit to His Race"* (New York: Saturday Review, 1974); Alexander T. Young, Jr., "Joe Louis: Symbol, 1933–1949," (unpublished Ph.D. dissertation, University of Maryland, 1968).

[3]Quoted in Edmonds, *Joe Louis*, p. 64.

crown for nearly twelve years and twenty-five defenses—both records for any weight divisions.

In view of the establishment of the principle of nondiscriminatory hiring in World War II, the passage of several state nondiscrimination laws, American condemnation of Nazi racism, and the heroics of Jesse Owens and Joe Louis, the continuation of racial segregation in baseball appeared to be at odds with a new phase in the history of white-black relations. During the 1930s urban black newspapers and a few influential white sportswriters began to attack the ban. Not only would integration assist the "Negro cause," they claimed, but it would open an enormous new pool of talent to big league clubs. The spokesmen for baseball issued contradictory responses. One was simply a denial that the color ban existed. Another was a suggestion that integration would decimate the Negro leagues and therefore harm blacks. In the 1930s and 1940s both a Negro National and American League existed. Since the teams in these leagues often played in major league parks, the big league owners had a vested interest in their survival. The shortage of players in the major leagues in World War II led to several attempts to arrange tryouts for black players; finally in 1945 a few blacks did "try out" for the Dodgers, Boston Red Sox, and Boston Braves. But none of the black players received a contract.[4]

In 1945, unknown to the public, Branch Rickey quietly prepared to integrate Organized Baseball. Apart from his apparently genuine sympathy for blacks, Rickey probably responded to political pressure in New York, saw the move as a way of strengthening his team, and hoped to appeal to black fans. So that he could scout black players without his plans being detected, Rickey announced the formation of a new all-black league, he carefully "sounded out" the stockholders of the Dodgers, and he sought a black athlete who could be assured of making the club and would wear a "cloak of humility" in the face of the expected abuse from white players and fans. Jackie Robinson perfectly fitted Rickey's requirements. As one of Robinson's biographers put it:

> Robinson had a good American-boy background—poor parents, working his way through school, tremendous athletic achievement, college experience at UCLA, army service with an honorable discharge as a lieutenant in the cavalry...track and field achievements, and a record as one of the great basketball stars on the Pacific Coast.[5]

He was then playing on the Kansas City Monarchs baseball team in the Negro National League. In October of 1945 Rickey extended to Robinson a contract to play at Montreal, a Dodger farm team, in 1946.

Despite the dire prophecies of bloodshed and violence when Robinson

[4]See Gerald W. Scully, "Discrimination: The Case of Baseball," in Roger G. Noll, ed., *Government and the Sports Business* (Washington: Brookings Institution, 1974), pp. 226–28.

[5]Arthur Mann as quoted in Leonard Broom and Philip Selznick, "The Jackie Robinson Case," in John T. Talamini and Charles H. Page, eds., *Sport and Society: An Anthology* (Boston: Little, Brown, 1973), p. 237.

arrived in the big leagues in 1947, none came to pass. Sportswriters almost unanimously applauded the end of the color ban and gave Robinson favorable coverage, but both Rickey and Robinson bore the brunt of a barrage of criticism and insults from other quarters. W. B. Bramham, the commissioner of the minor leagues, accused Rickey of selfish motives. "We can expect Rickey Temple to be in the course of construction in Harlem soon," he allegedly said. "It is those of the carpetbagger stripe of the white race, who, under the guise of helping, but in truth using the Negro for their own selfish interest, retard the race...."[6] Robinson often faced torrents of verbal abuse from fans and opposing players, but his magnificent performance on the field of play and his courteous behavior dampened the ardor of many would-be critics.

Performance and profits eased the way for Robinson. In 1946 he led the International League in batting while playing for the Montreal Royals, and the next year with the Dodgers he won the "Rookie of the Year" award. While Robinson's teammates had been initially cool toward him, they eventually began to give him tips on how to improve his game. Robinson was probably correct when he wrote: "They hadn't changed because they liked me any better; they had changed because I could help fill their wallets."[7] (Robinson assisted the Dodgers in winning six National League flags during his ten year career). Monetary motives also enhanced his acceptability among the owners of other teams. The first road game of the Dodgers in St. Louis brought out so many black fans to the park that they could not be seated in the segregated section that had been traditionally reserved for them. The St. Louis management, aware that their discrimination against black fans was costing them money, quickly eliminated the prejudicial seating system. Black fans poured out in other National League cities as well to see Robinson play.

The Cold War between the Soviet Union and the United States also helped solidify the racial integration of the "National Game." A superb opportunity for Branch Rickey to link symbolically the racial integration of baseball to American patriotism arose in 1950 when the House Un-American Activities Committee called upon witnesses to denounce Paul Robeson, a black ex-college football hero and popular singer, who had defended the Soviet Union and denounced American racism. It was unthinkable, Robeson had asserted in 1949, "that American Negroes would go to war on behalf of those who had oppressed us for generations" against the Soviet Union, which "has raised our people to full human dignity." Of the witnesses called upon by HUAC to repudiate Robeson, Jackie Robinson was by far the most famous. With the assistance of Rickey, Robinson drafted a statement declaring that blacks could win the struggle against segregation without the aid of Communists. "We don't need their help," Robinson said. The next day a newspaper headline announced:

[6]Quoted in Shapiro, *Jackie Robinson*, p. 167.
[7]Jackie Robinson, *I Never Had It Made* (New York: Putnam's, 1972), p. 10. See also Jay J. Coakley, *Sport in Society: Issues and Controversies* (St. Louis: C.V. Mosby, 1978), p. 279.

"JACKIE HITS ROBESON'S RED PITCH," a sentiment undoubtedly shared by millions of Americans.[8]

Nonetheless, Robinson's success did not result in full-scale integration nor the end of racial discrimination in baseball. A few weeks after Robinson joined the Dodger organization, Rickey signed four more black players, but no other team followed his example. The pace with which blacks joined major league clubs was agonizingly slow. By the 1957–1958 seasons, ten years after Robinson had entered baseball, blacks finally achieved a percentage in the big leagues commensurate with their proportion of the total population. Yet even then entry barriers for blacks continued to exist. Club owners set informal quotas. Driven ultimately by the profit motive, franchise owners tried to calculate whether increasing the number of black players on their teams would result in more wins and thereby increase attendance or whether it would adversely affect the identification of whites with the team and thereby reduce attendance and revenues. The net effect of such a consideration was that blacks had to outperform whites in order to make team rosters. Blacks, for example, batted an average of 20.8 points higher than whites from 1966–1970.[9]

The integration of professional football and college team sports also proceeded at a slow pace. From the earliest days of pro football in the 1890s, a few blacks had played on biracial teams. But in 1933 the NFL imposed an informal "color line" which continued until 1946. Gradually, as more blacks played on college teams, the percentage of blacks in the pro game increased. In the 1940s and 1950s several ugly racial incidents marred relations between colleges—usually between northern and southern schools. The Supreme Court decision of 1954, outlawing segregation in the public schools, stimulated the racial integration of college teams in both North and South. Nonetheless, the process was painstakingly slow. The University of Kentucky, for instance, did not integrate its basketball team until 1968. By 1970, however, a disproportionate number of blacks (compared to their percentage of the total population) played on racially integrated teams.

THE BLACK ATHLETIC REVOLT

Partly because of continued racial discrimination, black athletes, somewhat tardily, joined the larger civil rights movement. While Robinson had breached the color ban in the "National Game" well before the momentous Supreme Court decision of 1954 (which with one stroke undercut the entire structure of Jim Crow laws), black athletes had been conspicuously absent from the "sit-ins" of the early 1960s, the Freedom Riders, and the March on Washington in 1963. By conforming to white expectations and

---

[8]Quotations from Richard Polenberg, *One Nation Divisible: Class, Race and Ethnicity in the United States Since 1938* (New York: Viking, 1980), pp. 112, 113. See also Ronald A. Smith, "The Paul Robeson-Jackie Robinson Saga and a Political Collision," *Journal of Sport History*, 6 (Summer 1979) 5–27.

[9]Scully, "Discrimination," pp. 233–36.

the authoritarian structure of spectator-centered sports, black athletes had clawed their way to fame and fortune. To protest racism in sport or elsewhere might have jeopardized their newly won status. Consequently few athletes lent their names or financial support to the larger civil rights struggle. Nonetheless, a new stage of militancy in the civil rights movement in the mid-1960s, rising black expectations, and the controversy swirling around Muhammad Ali finally spawned a black "athletic revolt."

Initially, Ali's career furnished few indications that he would become a focal point of the massive social and cultural unrest of the 1960s. He seemed to fit the mold established by other black athletes. As Cassius Clay, he had won the light-heavyweight gold medal at the 1960 Olympic Games in Rome by defeating a more experienced Russian boxer. Asked by a Soviet reporter about racial prejudice in the United States, he responded with a statement that could have been written by the press secretary of the State Department. "Tell your readers we got qualified people working on that, and I'm not worried about the outcome," he said. "To me, the U.S.A. is still the best country in the world, counting yours." After the triumph at Rome, he began a rapid climb to the heavyweight championship. His good looks, exuberance, and locquacity attracted more than the usual attention given to aspiring heavyweight boxers. Ali himself exhibited a penchant for self-promotion. Soon known as the "Louisville Lip," he asserted in 1961, "Boxing is dying because everybody's so quiet." In 1964, in a revealing self-description, he told a reporter: "Cassius Clay is a boxer who can throw the jive better than anybody you will probably meet anywhere." Prior to the fight with Sonny Liston for the heavyweight title in 1964, he proclaimed, "I am the greatest."[10] At the time few boxing aficionados found his braggadocio offensive. The promoters in 1964 sold Ali as the underdog hero and Liston as the villain. Liston, depicted as a glowering, evil man, had served several prison sentences for a variety of crimes.

After his defeat of Liston, Ali shocked boxing fans by renouncing his "slave name" of Clay in favor of Ali and proclaiming his conversion to the Black Muslim faith. The world of boxing, with its reputation for shady connections, had always tried to cloak its athletes in the mantle of orthodox religion, conventional morality, and patriotism. By rejecting Christianity and joining a militant black religious sect that opposed racial integration, Ali defied these conventions. Most white Americans feared the Black Muslims: the sect had a reputation for self-discipline, extreme piety, the use of violence, and a belief in black racial superiority. Ironically, the fact that Ali, consistent with his new faith, renounced coffee, pork, liquor, and drugs, did nothing to allay white fears. It only intensified them.

Moreover, Ali's announcement coincided with mounting social conflict. In the summer of 1964 riots broke out in Harlem, three white civil rights activists were murdered in Mississippi, and the Senate adopted the Gulf of Tonkin Resolution which opened the way for a large American troop buildup in Vietnam. Ali himself became increasingly iconoclastic; he expressed his utter contempt for past boxing heroes, declaring them to be

[10]For Ali quotations in this paragraph see "Through the Years with Ali," *Sports Illustrated*, 45 (Dec. 20–27, 1976), 111, 113.

ugly, slow, and inept. His outrageous doggerel often satirized American ideals. Consequently, Ali's fight in 1965 with Floyd Patterson, a former heavyweight crown holder, took on the character of a "Holy War," of Christian versus Moslem. Patterson, a recent convert to Roman Catholicism, determined "to give the title back to America." "The image of a Black Muslim as the world heavyweight champion disgraces the sport and the nation. Cassius Clay must be beaten and the Black Muslims' scourge removed from Boxing."[11] In the ring Ali dashed such hopes. He totally outclassed Patterson, mocking and humiliating him before the referee finally called a halt to the mismatch in the twelfth round.

Apparently against his will, Ali then plunged himself into the midst of the heated Vietnam controversy. In 1964 Ali had failed the intelligence portion of the Army's induction test, but two years later, when the standards had been lowered, his draft board reclassified him 1A. Responding to reporters' questions about his reactions to the new classification, Ali blurted out, "I ain't got no quarrels with them Viet Congs," a memorable remark that soon furnished a rallying cry for youthful opponents of the war. Called for induction, Ali claimed exemption as a conscientious objector. The Federal Government rejected his claim and eventually indicted him for draft evasion. Minutes after he refused to step forward for induction, but before he had been arrested or charged, much less convicted, the New York Athletic Commission suspended his boxing license. Four hours later the World Boxing Association took away his title. Stripped of his livelihood and facing a possible prison term, Ali became a powerful cultural symbol. On the one side, the supporters of the war and traditional values found in Ali a highly visible target for their anger and frustration. On the other side, opponents of the war, participants in the youth revolt of the decade, and civil libertarians found in Ali a noble martyr.

Ali's actions as the best known black in the United States and the world placed other black athletes in an uncomfortable position. As a measure of the degree of their militancy, coaches and reporters repeatedly asked black athletes what they thought about Ali. Often the black athletes tried to weasel. Ali's aggressive anti-Christianity, his opposition to the war, his pronouncements against liquor, drugs, "race-mixing," and sex genuinely bothered many black athletes. Yet his bravery infused many others with additional courage. They began to ask: Had Ali been a white and a Christian, would his title have been taken from him? Would he have been indicted? Were black athletes as free as whites to develop their skills and fulfill their ambitions? Were they the victims of racism and exploitation? Ali's actions helped trigger a larger black athletic revolt.

The most dramatic phase of the black athletic revolt arose in the "amateur" sports, especially track and field. In 1967, the year after Ali had been stripped of his title, Harry Edwards, a black sociology professor at San Jose State College, inspired and organized a movement to boycott the 1968 Olympic Games. As a condition for their participation, the boycotters

[11]Robert Lipsyte, *SportsWorld: An American Dreamland* (New York: Quadrangle/New York Times, 1975), p. 110.

demanded that Ali's crown be reinstated, Avery Brundage be ousted as president of the International Olympic Committee, South Africa and Rhodesia be barred from the Games, black coaches be added to the American team, and that the New York Athletic Club be desegregated. The protestors first aroused national attention by boycotting the 100th Anniversary Track and Field Games of NYAC held at Madison Square Garden in 1968. For many years the annual meet had been a showcase for black athletes who later starred on the U.S. Olympic team. The NYAC, now, according to one reporter, a "crusty old Irish-dominated club," refused to admit blacks and had only a few Jewish members. Surrounding the Garden, the demonstrators chanted "Muhammad Ali is our champ!" The boycott was a success. The Soviets pulled out and most black and many white athletes refused to compete in the event.[12]

Edwards had less success in organizing a boycott of the 1968 Olympics. While he obtained the support of prominent black civil rights leaders and broadened the purpose of the boycott to include a dramatization of the general plight of American blacks to the rest of the world, he could not generate universal support among the black athletes themselves. Apparently less than half of the black athletes likely to make the Olympic team favored the boycott. Consequently, Edwards made the boycott voluntary and recommended that those who did decide to compete should protest in their own fashion. Lew Alcindor, the hero of ULCA's championship basketball team, did pass up the games, but most athletes opted for participation. At the Games sprinters Tommie Smith, a gold medalist, and John Carlos, a bronze medalist, mounted the victory stand and, while the National Anthem played, bowed their heads and raised their gloved fists in the air in a Black Power salute. The United States Olympic Committee quickly suspended Smith and Carlos from the team; the committee then gave them only forty-eight hours to leave Mexico.

While the Mexico City boycott fizzled, the success of the NYAC boycott, Ali's disbarment from the ring, and the Smith-Carlos demonstration helped mobilize an increasing militancy among black athletes on campuses across the country. Between 1967 and 1971 revolts occurred on at least thrity-seven campuses. Since black athletes were especially conspicuous symbols on many campuses, they often experienced pressure from radical student groups—both black and white—to join various "liberation" movements. Often specific complaints touched off the revolts. To protest the Morman Church's views toward blacks, black athletes at the University of Wyoming asked coaches to permit them to wear black armbands in a game against Brigham Young University. The head coach dismissed all the blacks from the team. When head football coach Ben Schwartzwalder (a pioneer in actively recruiting black athletes) of Syracuse University refused to hire a black assistant coach, the black players walked out of spring practice. Schwartzwalder suspended them but eventually lost his job. In the

---

[12]Pete Axthelm, "Boycott Now—Boycott Later," *Sports Illustrated*, 28 (Feb. 26, 1968), 24–26; "The Angry Black Athlete," *Newsweek*, 72 (July 15, 1968), 56–60; Harry Edwards, *The Revolt of the Black Athlete* (New York: Free Press, 1969), pp. 64–70.

course of the revolt, black athletes formulated a long list of more general grievances. Among them were "stacking," absence of black coaches, concern by the white coaches only for athletic performances and eligibility of black athletes (not their educations), expressions of racial prejudice by coaches and white teammates, and restrictions on personal freedom.[13]

The sudden militancy of black athletes along with a few white athletes shocked coaches everywhere. During the campus unrest of the 1960s, athletes had generally been the most conventional and conservative of all students; on several campuses they had taken leading roles in physically beating radical demonstrators. To many coaches, the black protest exhibited a lack of gratitude for the opportunities offered by sports for blacks to escape the nation's ghettos. Moreover, coaches had traditionally exercised an unbridled authority over the public and personal lives of their charges. Any relinquishment of their authority, they believed, would reduce the likelihood of the team winning. They were especially sensitive to what they interpreted as symbolic challenges to their authority. Many coaches thought that beards, Afro hair styles, and interracial dating symbolized personal license and a rebellion against authority. On the other hand, the athletes themselves tended to confuse the discipline necessary to build winning teams with excessive authority. By placing a higher priority on player concerns, the athletes did, in fact, challenge the entire structure of spectator-centered sports.

Yet the net effect of the revolt was minimal. Reforms more often took the form of gestures rather than substance. Athletic departments hired black coaches, both to placate and recruit black athletes. As the popular culture as a whole adopted fashionably long hair and more liberal dress styles, most coaches compromised their codes of dress and appearance. The traditional crew cut of the athletes suddenly disappeared. The image of Ali changed. By the mid-1970s Wilfrid Sheed argued that even "the squares love him now. He has become their kind of nigger: self-reliant, keeps to his own kind, harmlessly entertaining.... His naughtiness seems almost old-fashioned by now and ready for the nostalgia bank."[14] The token reforms, the rapid decline in general student and black unrest in the early 1970s, the built-in turnover of student athletes, and changed cultural climate brought a quick end to the black athletic revolt.

Rather than a matter of active protest, the position of blacks in sport in the 1970s became the subject of lively speculation and debate. Scholars and others asked why there was a disproportionately large number of blacks in the big-time team sports. Martin Kane, a senior editor of *Sports Illustrated*, inaugurated a running debate by asserting that blacks had distinctive physical features that gave them decided advantages over whites in certain

---

[13]See John Underwood, "The Desperate Coach," *Sports Illustrated*, 30 (Aug. 25, 1969), 70; Pat Putnam, "End of a Season at Syracuse," ibid., 33 (Sept. 28, 1970), 22–23; Pat Putnam, "No Defeats, Loads of Trouble," ibid., 31 (Nov. 3, 1969), 26–27; Edwards, *Revolt of the Black Athlete*, Appendix B; Neil Amdur, *The Fifth Down: Democracy and the Football Revolution* (New York: Delta, 1971).

[14]Wilfrid Sheed, "Muhammad Ali—King of the Picture Gods," in Tom Dodge, ed., *A Literature of Sports* (Lexington, Mass.: Heath, 1980), p. 296.

sports. Harry Edwards promptly challenged this genetic explanation; he insisted that the differences in black-white numbers in certain sports and in their performances was culturally induced. Blacks believed that sport offered an unusual opportunity for upward social mobility. Thus black youth on the whole spent more time in preparation for sports than their white counterparts.[15]

Several sport sociologists attempted to determine if sports indeed furnished an unusually good social escalator for blacks. Sport was considered by many one area of American life where blacks could succeed purely by merits. The sociologists found that discrimination continued to exist. In 1975–76, there were 888 blacks in professional team sports; there were over twenty-four million blacks in the United States. Thus professional sport provided an opportunity for less than one black out of every 18,000 black people. Of course, opportunities for whites in sports were likewise circumscribed. Moreover, the playing careers of athletes, white or black, was short. In football the average playing career was four and a half years for positions played by most blacks. Obviously sport did not provide opportunities for large numbers of blacks to move upward socially or economically. Finally, in trying to become pro athletes, many blacks may have been diverted from other pursuits in which the chances of success might have been greater.

Racial discrimination took other forms. Blacks tended to be relegated to certain playing positions and excluded from others, a phenomenon known as "stacking." In 1976, for instance, 52 percent of the major-league outfielders were black, 4 percent of pitchers, 4 percent of catchers, none of the shortstops, 17 percent of the third basemen, 39 percent of the second basemen, and 50 percent of the first basemen. Studies made of other seasons revealed a similar pattern. Stacking also existed in professional football. Blacks were more likely to be found playing at a wide receiver or running back position than at quarterback or in the middle of the offensive line. On defense blacks usually constituted a majority of the cornerbacks and safeties, but few of them played linebacker positions. Sport sociologists speculated that white management discriminated in favor of whites when choosing players for "central positions," those positions that required more leadership, cooperation, coordination, and personal interaction between players. Perhaps this pattern was self-perpetuating, for blacks may have concluded that their chances of succeeding would be improved if they prepared themselves for noncentral positions.

Neither did blacks receive equal rewards for equal performance or equal opportunities in sports-related activities. In all professional team sports blacks earned lower salaries than whites for equivalent performances. They also earned less in endorsements and off-season activities. The Equal Opportunity Commission reported that in the fall of 1966 black athletes appeared in only 5 percent of 351 commercials associated with New York

[15]For general summaries of the research on racial discrimination in sports see Coakley, *Sport In Society*, Chap. 11; and "Racism in Sports," *Social Science Quarterly*, 55 (March 1975), 919–66. Baseball appeared to have the most "enduring color line." See "Scorecard," *Sports Illustrated*, 51 (Oct. 8, 1979), 21.

sports events. Impressionistic data suggests that blacks in the 1970s obtained a much higher proportion of endorsement opportunities than in 1966, though probably less than their numbers would warrant. No black owned a professional sport franchise and few of them held positions as game officials, managers, coaches, or executives. As of 1980 only two blacks—Frank Robinson and Larry Doby—had ever served as managers in the major leagues and no black had ever been a head coach in the NFL. Although blacks composed about 75 percent of the NBA rosters, in 1980 only five of seventeen head coaches were black. Only a half dozen big-time colleges had a black head basketball coach; there was no black head football coach.

WOMEN'S SPORTS IN TRANSITION

Like the black players, aspiring women athletes confronted limited opportunities to display and profit from their skills. Before puberty girls might join boys on the playing fields but once they had passed into adolescence girls encountered heavy social pressures to withdraw from the most physically active sports. At puberty and beyond, the public expected girls to retire to the sidelines or the grandstands; there they were to act as cheerleaders or fans of male athletes. For women the public approved only the most physically sedate of sports; they supported only those sports which confined physical contact between players and featured physical grace. Thus such sports as tennis, golf, and swimming won far more approval than track and field, softball, or basketball. Furthermore, from the 1920s to the 1960s the nation's educational institutions, which were major training grounds for male sports, essentially prohibited highly competitive sports for women. Only in the "industrial sports"—sports sponsored by industry or business concerns—did women have opportunities approximating those available to men. Then in the 1960s and 1970s came a sports revolution for women. Spurred on by athletic competition with the Soviet Union and a revived feminist movement, plus legislative and court mandates, the walls of sexual discrimination in sport began to crumble.[16]

Outside of the nation's educational system, the 1920s witnessed a substantial growth in women's sports. In that decade women's tennis and golf "went public." In tennis Suzanne Lenglen and Helen Wills and in golf Glenna Collett, "the female Bobby Jones," shared some of the limelight with the great male athletes of the decade. Neither of the sports, however, won anything approaching a mass following among women. With the high schools and colleges withdrawing sponsorship of varsity sports for women,

[16]For general treatments, see Bil Gilbert and Nancy Williamson, "Sport Is Unfair to Women," *Sports Illustrated*, 38 (May 28, 1973), 88–98; Stephanie L. Twin, ed., *Out of the Bleachers: Writings on Women and Sport* (Old Westbury, N.Y.: Feminist, 1979), Introduction; Ellen Gerber et al., *The American Woman in Sport* (Reading, Mass.: Addison-Wesley, 1974), Part I.

Woman golfer. Courtesy of the Journal Star Printing Company.

the Amateur Athletic Union and its affiliates expanded programs of women's athletics. The AAU sponsored national meets in swimming (1916), track and field (1924), basketball (1926), and gymnastics (1931). The successful debut of American female swimmers in the 1920 Olympic Games, Gertrude Ederle's highly publicized swim of the English Channel in 1926, the introduction of the lighter and more abbreviated Kellerman bathing suit, and a sun-tanning craze contributed to a marked growth in women's swimming, though most of the women swam recreationally rather than competitively.

Participation in AAU women's track and field competition sharply increased in the 1920s, but declined in the 1930s, never to regain its former popularity until the late 1950s. The refusal of the high schools and colleges to encourage highly competitive track and field cut off a major source of potential athletes.[17] In the decades of low involvement, black women, especially from Tuskegee Institute and Tennessee State, dominated national meets and comprised most of the female members of the American Olympic teams. Apparently traditional images of femininity were less pronounced among blacks than whites. From 1956 to 1978

[17]Maria Sexton, "Women in Sport," *Wooster Alumni Magazine* (Aug. 1978), 8.

336

Tennessee State women athletes won twenty gold medals at the Olympic games, thirty AAU titles, and twenty-six events at the Pan-American Games.[18]

Until the 1970s opportunities for women to compete in sports were limited mostly to those sponsored by industrial or commercial concerns. A few employers, especially industrial corporations, began early in the twentieth century to furnish athletic facilities and organize sports for their employees, both men and women. In the 1920s, as part of a larger movement to improve employee morale, specialists in personnel policy prepared chatty newspapers, invited workers to suggest improvements in the firm's operations, and organized company recreation programs. In addition to such sports as baseball, softball, bowling, and basketball for employees, a few companies formed top-flight women's teams as a means of advertising their firms. In these spectator-oriented women's sports, the promoters often combined playing skills with novelty and sex appeal. For example, Marty Fiedler, hailed as the "Flo Ziegfield of sports," gave women's softball teams such alluring names as Slapsie Maxie's Curvacious Cuties and the Balian Ice Cream Beauties. The appearance in the 1920s of beauty queen contests, female movie stars, flappers and the popularity of Ziegfield's Follies all seem to suggest an expanded physical freedom for women, but a freedom that focused on sexual attractiveness rather than athletic skills. Colonel Melvorne McCombs, head of the women's sports program of the Casualty Insurance Company of Dallas, claimed that controversies over the shorts of the women's basketball team raised game attendance from 150 to 5,000.[19] Emphasizing the sexual attractiveness of the female athletes may have posed a less direct threat to traditional sexual stereotypes while evoking yet another stereotype.

Bowling, which was to become the most popular participatory sport among women, illustrated the key role played by industry in the pre-1970s era. In the first decade of the twentieth century, commercial concerns, especially in the Midwest, began to sponsor bowling leagues for women and men. Interest was sufficient in 1907 for the World Bowling Congress to conduct a women's tournament in conjunction with the men's event. In 1916 women, mostly employed in industry, formed the Women's National Bowling Association (later renamed the Women's International Bowling Congress) which scheduled national tournaments and had a membership of almost 5,000 within a decade. World War II touched off a new surge of women's bowling, as employers organized thousands of women's teams and leagues. In the 1950s automatic pin setters initiated yet another wave of growth in women's bowling. Relieved of dependency upon the free time of young boy pinsetters, housewives could now bowl during the day. Women's bowling grew much faster in the Midwest than in the East. Easterners often looked upon bowling as a disreputable sport associated with the lower classes and beer drinking. Consequently, from 1916 to 1961 midwestern women completely dominated bowling at the championship levels. Although by the 1970s the number of women bowlers apparently exceeded

[18]Cheryl Bentsen, "Tigerbelle Tradition," *WomenSports*, 5 (Feb. 1978), 52–53.
[19]Twin, *Out of the Bleachers*, pp. xxix–xxx.

that of men, the prize money available to women remained only a fraction of that which could be won by men.[20]

Industry also played a key role in the growth of softball, the second most popular participatory sport among women. Although softball's origins extended back to 1887, it became a popular sport only in the 1930s. In 1933 the Amateur Softball Association held the first national championship tournaments for both men and women. Business concerns invariably sponsored the teams that played at the championship levels; in fact these semiprofessional teams frequently played games across the nation. World War II furnished an immense stimulus to the growth of women's softball; estimates placed the total number of teams at over 40,000, a figure probably representing about one-fourth of all teams.[21]

The war also witnessed an effort to form a professional baseball-softball league. In 1943 Philip K. Wrigley, chewing gum magnate and owner of the Chicago Cubs, organized the All-American Girl's Baseball League when he became concerned that major league baseball might be disbanded during the war. (Initially the league required underhanded pitching with a standard-sized baseball.) At one time or another the league consisted of ten franchises located in middle-sized cities in the Midwest. The promoters carefully cultivated a feminine player image. Each team hired a chaperone and instructed the girls in proper posture, etiquette, and "how to take a called third strike." In 1948 attendance reached a peak of nearly a million spectators, but competition from minor league baseball and television brought about the demise of the league in 1954.[22]

With the decline in varsity women's high school and college basketball in the 1920s and 1930s, both business concerns and the AAU became involved in the sport. In 1926 the AAU held the first national tournament using boys' rules. Nearly all the teams, which were usually sponsored by business concerns seeking publicity, came from the Midwest and the South. Until 1939 Wichita, Kansas usually hosted the national tournament; after that date St. Joseph, Missouri, was the favorite site for the tourney. A few itinerant women's professional teams appeared as early as the 1920s. The most famous and enduring team was the Red Heads, organized in 1936. Reportedly by 1947, despite a five-year break due to World War II, the Red Heads had played before two million basketball fans in forty-six states. The team, with the players sporting wigs or dyed red hair, combined the display of quality basketball with showmanship in a fashion similar to the Harlem Globetrotters. Playing by men's rules and against local men's teams, the Red Heads won a high percentage of their contests.[23]

The existence of highly competitive sports sponsored by business concerns may suggest an exaggerated picture of the extent of women's sports. Even in the industrial leagues men had far more opportunities to

---

[20]Gerber et al., *The American Woman in Sport*, pp. 95–99.

[21]Ibid., pp. 117–21.

[22]Ibid., pp. 118–19; "Baseball: Babette Ruths," *Newsweek*, 28 (July 1946), 68–69.

[23]William Johnson and Nancy Williamson, "All Red, So Help Them Henna," *Sports Illustrated*, 40 (May 6, 1974), 76–91.

compete in sports than women. Moreover, women who played in industrial leagues risked charges of being unfeminine or on the other hand, of flaunting their sexual attractions. Frequent condemnation for the unlady-like atmosphere, masculine playing strategy, brief wearing apparel, and the use of male coaches beset those women who dared to play in the industrial sports leagues.[24]

WOMEN'S SPORT REVOLUTION

If women were to establish a world of sports equivalent to that of the men, it was essential that they reverse the stance of the nation's educational system. While the majority of women physical educators continued to be opposed to varsity sports for women as late as 1970, a growing minority favored intercollegiate and interscholastic competition. As early as 1941 Gladys Palmer of Ohio State invited fellow physical educators to form a women's intercollegiate athletic association. Palmer wanted to broaden the competitive athletic opportunities of women "who have attained above average to superior skill in certain sports."[25] Almost singlehandedly, Palmer also scheduled the first women's intercollegiate golf tournament at Ohio State the same year. Thirty females participated. But the national body of female physical educators quickly responded with a resolution condemning Palmer's efforts to organize intercollegiate women's competition. According to a survey in 1943, two out of every three women physical educators disapproved of national tourneys. Nevertheless, the number of colleges sponsoring some form of varsity sport increased from 16 percent in 1943 to 26 percent in 1951.

The Cold War between the United States and the Soviet Union furnished a more important impetus for breaking down the resistance to women's varsity sports. The State Department, the United States Olympic Committee, and the AAU became increasingly concerned in the 1950s and 1960s about the poor showing of American female athletes in the Olympic Games. For the 1952 Games the American women's track and field team consisted of only ten athletes and a manager-coach. The team had no high jumpers or discus throwers and only one hurdler, one shot-putter, one broad jumper, and one javelin thrower. To improve the performance of the female contingent of the team, the USOC had to turn to the high schools and colleges. In 1958 the USOC created a Women's Advisory Board, a board composed of representatives from the AAU, former women Olympic athletes, and sympathetic physical educators. Another turning point came in 1960 when Doris Duke Cromwell, heiress of the Duke tobacco fortune, donated a half million dollars to the USOC to promote women's Olympic competitors. With these funds the Women's

[24]See Sexton, "Women in Sport," 9.

[25]Quoted in Virginia Hunt, "Governance of Women's Intercollegiate Athletics" (unpublished Ed.D. dissertation, University of North Carolina at Greensboro, 1976), p. 19.

Board and the Division of Girls and Women's Sports (DGWS) of the
national physical education association set up a series of national institutes
for the training and coaching of women athletes.[26] Nonetheless, most
educators hoped that the female performance on the American Olympic
Team could be improved without the colleges and high schools committing
themselves to varsity track and field programs.

In addition to the experience gained by women in building a stronger
Olympic team, the revival of the feminist movement in the 1960s struck a
responsive chord. In the same years that the civil rights movement
intensified, opposition to the war in Vietnam mounted, and many of the
nation's youth embarked upon experimental life styles, women began to
demand the same opportunities as men to fashion their own destinies.
Emboldened by the new cultural ferment and their involvement in the
Olympics, a small band of women's physical educators inched their way
toward the establishment of full-fledged varsity sports programs for
women. In 1964 the DGWS devoted an entire program at the national
convention of men and women physical educators to "Competition for the
Highly Skilled Girls" and adopted a statement essentially reversing the
famous 1923 position on intercollegiate sports for women. Two years later
a group of women within the DGWS formed the Commission of Intercollegiate Athletics for Women which became the Association of Intercollegiate Athletics for Women (AIAW) in 1971. Threatened by the prospect
of the NCAA entering the arena of women's sports, the Commission
scheduled the first set of national championships for 1969.[27] Only one
thing was missing for women's sports to make major inroads in the schools.
That was funding. Title IX of the Educational Amendments Act of 1972
appeared to offer a partial solution to that problem.

THE RESULTS OF THE REVOLUTION

Title IX, the result of women's lobbying in Congress (but strongly opposed
by the NCAA), in effect simply outlawed any sexual discrimination by
school districts or institutions of higher education which received federal
aid. Its provisions thus applied to nearly every school in the nation. Exactly
how the act was to be applied to sport remained a source of running
controversy in the 1970s. Male athletic directors insisted that equal funding
for women would destroy the major revenue-producing sports of men's
football and basketball. Consequently neither men nor women would have
enough funds to maintain sports programs. In response to cross pressures
from women's groups and the NCAA, the Department of Health,
Education, and Welfare (HEW), which was responsible for administering
Title IX, repeatedly revised its regulations for implementation of the act.
One point did emerge clearly: colleges and high schools would have to
commit much more of their resources to women's sports than they had in

---

[26]Sexton, "Women in Sport," 10: Gerber et al., *The American Woman in Sport,* pp. 162–66.
[27]See especially, Sexton, "Women in Sport," 11–12.

the past. The 1979 HEW interpretation of Title IX required that the total amount of scholarship aid made available to men and women be "substantially proportionate to their participation rate" in intercollegiate sports, but appeared to permit institutions to spend more money per capita on the revenue-producing men's teams.[28]

The newly found riches made available by Title IX to women had far-reaching implications for women's sports. Before Title IX women probably received less than 1 percent of the total national intercollegiate budget; by 1980 the women's percentage may have exceeded 10 percent. Should women push for sexually integrated sports or sexually separate but equal sports programs? In the early 1970s in several places across the country girls tried out for boys' teams; the successful effort to sexually integrate Little League Baseball aroused the most public furor. But given the general physical differences between the sexes (especially beginning at puberty) and the real fear that men might absorb complete control of women's sports, women sport leaders generally chose a separate but equal world of women's sports. To have done otherwise might have sharply reduced the total number of women who would have been able to participate in varsity-level sports and probably would have resulted in the male management of high school and college sports.[29]

Yet those women who pushed for total equality and a more androgynous society noted that separate women's sports programs were reminiscent of the official racial policy of the United States prior to the Supreme Court decision in 1954. In 1954 the Court had concluded that the "separate but equal" doctrine when applied to race was intrinsically unequal. If boys and girls were separated in sport, sport might encourage sexual stereotyping and reinforce distinctive sexual roles rather than provide a training ground for the elimination of sexism. While Title IX did not lead to sexually integrated varsity sports, it did encourage integrated physical education classes and experiments with integrated intramural sports programs.

Circumstances rather than a clearly formulated philosophic stance led to the bulk of the money resulting from Title IX being used for varsity sports rather than athletic programs for all female students. After all, the establishment of varsity sports furnished highly visible, if not conclusive, evidence that an educational institution was attempting to comply with Title IX. Between 1972 and 1977 nearly every high school and college in the country rushed to form varsity teams in a half-dozen or more sports. By 1980 nearly two million girls participated in a varsity sport during their high school years, a jump from 294,000 in 1970–71. Once priority was given to varsity sports, the women confronted an additional issue. Should

[28]Gil Sewall, "The New Sex Rules," *Newsweek,* 94 (Dec. 3, 1979), 84; Cheryl M. Fields, "What Colleges Must Do to Avoid Sex Bias in Sport," *Chronicle of Higher Education,* 19 (Dec. 10, 1979), 1, 14; Patricia Huckle, "Back to the Starting Line: Title IX and Women's Intercollegiate Athletics," *American Behavioral Scientist,* 21 (Jan./Feb. 1978), 379–92.

[29]For this paragraph and the following one see "Comes the Revolution," *Time,* 111 (June 26, 1978), 57; Frank Deford, "New Georgy-Porgy Runs Away," *Sports Illustrated,* 40 (April 22, 1974), 26–37; Judith R. Holland and Carole Oglesby, "Women in Sport: The Synthesis Begins," *Annals of the American Academy of Political and Social Science,* 445 (Sept. 1979), 80–90.

they imitate the spectator-centered character of men's sports or attempt to build a world of player-centered sport for women? The overwhelming majority of women physical educators, including those who were in the inner circle of the AIAW and those who favored varsity sport, hoped to avoid the "evils" of men's sports. Thus they opposed athletic scholarships, recruiting, and the supremacy of a winning-at-all-costs ethos.[30]

Yet inexorably the women's sports programs moved toward a spectator-centered orientation. A 1973 court case in which a woman athlete charged that the prohibition on athletic scholarships by the AIAW discriminated against women forced the AIAW to permit the awards of athletic grants-in-aid. Soon afterwards every major college began awarding athletic scholarships. By the late 1970s the number and money value of women's scholarships (as compared to men) became the principal test for compliance with Title IX. The availability of scholarships firmly launched women's sports into the Age of the Spectator. By the end of the 1970s women's basketball, in particular, began to resemble men's programs, even to the extent of widespread charges of the extension of illegal inducements to star players. By then the influence of women's physical educators on varsity sports had sharply declined. Administratively on most campuses women's sports either constituted a separate department from physical education or a division within the men's athletic programs. And coaches, especially in women's basketball, found their jobs dependent upon the won-lost record of their teams. In 1981 the NCAA decided to compete directly with the AIAW in the sponsorship of women's intercollegiate sports. Consequently the future survival of a separate women's sport organization was also in doubt.[31]

Apart from colleges and high schools, the tennis court furnished the other major battlefield in the struggle to establish a separate-but-equal world of women's sports. Traditionally, tennis had been a bastion of genteel sexism. Women had been permitted to play the sport by the American social elites, but only within the confines of genteel expectations of female behavior. In mixed doubles the male player played the most conspicuous and dominant role. Proper decorum, circumspection, and subordination had been imposed on women players, even though the emphasis placed upon winning by such players as Suzanne Lenglen in the 1920s and Maureen Connolly in the 1940s had threatened to upset the delicate role assigned to women players. In the 1960s and 1970s Billie Jean King, a California player from a lower middle-income family, led the crusade against sexism in tennis. King was not only a superb player, but she was confident, articulate, and assertive. She "gave soul" and "personalized" the "bringing of tennis—classiest of sports—to the people." She, more than any single person, helped erase the stiff formality and pomposity from the sport.[32]

[30]See "Comes the Revolution," 54–60; *New York Times*, December 30, 1979, S7.

[31]See Hannon, "Too Far, Too Fast," *Sports Illustrated*, 48 (March 20, 1978), 34–45; and Cheryl M. Fields, "200 Colleges Expected to Quit Women's Sports Association," *Chronicle of Higher Education*, 22 (June 1, 1981), 2.

[32]See Lipsyte, *SportsWorld*, pp. 222–30; and Billie Jean King with Kim Chapin, *Billie Jean* (New York: Harper & Row, 1974).

King led the women in demanding a separate but equal world of opportunity for women in professional tennis. Although women's matches sometimes attracted audiences as large as those of the men, until the 1970s the prize money available to women was only about 10 percent of the men's purses. With the advent of open tennis several promoters, assuming that women could not draw financially rewarding gates, had dropped women from their tournaments. Neither Lamar Hunt's World Championship Tennis circuit nor Jack Kramer's Grand Prix circuit offered competition for women. In response to their exclusion, King and seven other players collaborated with Gladys Heldman, publisher of *World Tennis* magazine, to form in 1971 the Virginia Slims, a separate circuit for women. At the urging of Heldman, the Philip Morris Tobacco Company decided to underwrite the circuit and promote it as part of the revived feminist movement. The Slims acquired a substantial television contract and by 1975 awarded nearly a million dollars in prize money. By threatening to withdraw from Forest Hills and Wimbledon, the women also obtained far more equitable portions of the purses. As an arena offering opportunities to women in professional sport, tennis was the most lucrative of all sports. In 1971 King became the first woman athlete to earn $100,000 in a single year; four years later Chris Evert won more than $300,000.[33]

King's significance, like that of Muhammad Ali, extended far beyond the world of sport. She became one of the most important symbols of the revived feminist movement of the early 1970s. Harrassed by reporters for her frank pursuit of tennis as a profession and her decision not to have children, she insisted upon her right to be a full-time professional athlete. "Almost every day for the last four years," she told a reporter, "someone comes up to me and says, 'Hey, when are you going to have children?' I say 'I'm not ready yet.' They say, 'Why aren't you at home?' I say, 'Why don't you go ask Rod Laver why he isn't at home?' "[34] To those many Americans who held traditional notions of femininity such remarks seemed revolutionary. For a woman in sports to equate herself with a man inspired feminists and aroused the wrath of many males.

A 1973 tennis match between King and Bobby Riggs became a dramatic focal point for both the women's struggle for greater opportunity in sport and for the feminist movement in general. By 1973 women had made substantial gains in acquiring equal purses in tournaments, but fifty-five year old Bobby Riggs, a former triple-crown winner at Wimbledon (1939) and a long-time sports "hustler," publicly claimed that women players were inferior to men and thus overpaid. He boasted that despite his age he could defeat the best of the women players. He first challenged King, but she refused, arguing that regardless of the outcome such a match could not benefit the cause of women's tennis.[35] Nonetheless, Margaret Court, another top-flight women's player, accepted the challenge of Riggs. On Mother's Day, 1973, a nervous Court, who had recently become a

[33]King, *King*, Chap. 6; Jane Leary, "Daring Decade: How Women Served and Won," *WomenSports*, 5 (Jan. 1978), 22–23.

[34]Quoted in Lipsyte, *SportsWorld*, p. 223.

[35]See Gerber et al., *The American Woman in Sports*, pp. 403–84.

mother—this fact became part of the hype for the match—lost to Riggs, 6–2, 6–1. To the surprise of television producers, the audience rating for the match topped the WCT championship match played the same day.

The victory by Riggs, when reinforced by his flamboyant male chauvinism, appeared to jeopardize the advances made by women's tennis. King, as the militant leader of the women in tennis, now felt compelled to play Riggs. The offer of more than $100,000 in television rights and endorsements plus an additional $100,000 if she won no doubt influenced her decision. In a circuslike atmosphere, she confronted Riggs in Houston's Astrodome before a crowd of 30,472, the largest audience ever to attend a tennis match. Millions more watched on prime time television which, via satellite, extended its coverage to thirty-six nations. Advertised as "The Battle of the Sexes," King routed Riggs, 6–4, 6–3, 6–3.[36]

[36]See Joe Jares, "Riggs to Riches—Take Two," Sports Illustrated, 39 (Sept. 10, 1973) 24–29; Curry Kirkpatrick, "There She Is, Ms. America," ibid., 39 (Oct. 1, 1973), 30–37.

17

The New Status of Professional Athletes

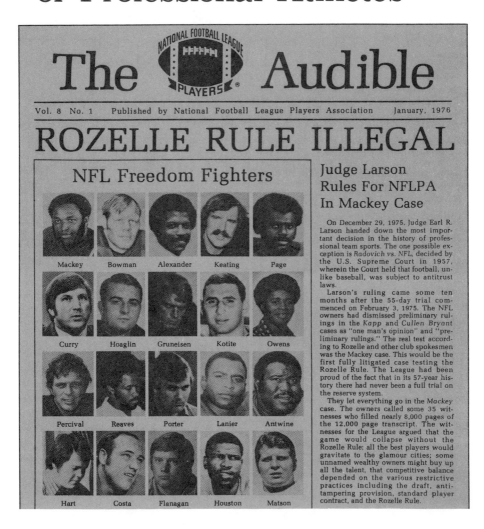

The 🏈 Audible

Vol. 8 No. 1   Published by National Football League Players Association   January, 1976

ROZELLE RULE ILLEGAL

NFL Freedom Fighters

Mackey   Bowman   Alexander   Keating   Page

Curry   Hoaglin   Gruneisen   Kotite   Owens

Percival   Reaves   Porter   Lanier   Antwine

Hart   Costa   Flanagan   Houston   Matson

Judge Larson Rules For NFLPA In Mackey Case

On December 29, 1975, Judge Earl R. Larson handed down the most important decision in the history of professional team sports. The one possible exception is *Radovich vs. NFL*, decided by the U.S. Supreme Court in 1957, wherein the Court held that football, unlike baseball, was subject to antitrust laws.

Larson's ruling came some ten months after the 55-day trial commenced on February 3, 1975. The NFL owners had dismissed preliminary rulings in the *Kapp* and *Cullen Bryant* cases as "one man's opinion" and "preliminary rulings." The real test according to Rozelle and other club spokesmen was the Mackey case. This would be the first fully litigated case testing the Rozelle Rule. The League had been proud of the fact that in its 57-year history there had never been a full trial on the reserve system.

They let everything go in the *Mackey* case. The owners called some 35 witnesses who filled nearly 8,000 pages of the 12,000 page transcript. The witnesses for the League argued that the game would collapse without the Rozelle Rule; all the best players would gravitate to the glamour cities; some unnamed wealthy owners might buy up all the talent, that competitive balance depended on the various restrictive practices including the draft, anti-tampering provision, standard player contract, and the Rozelle Rule.

In the era of televised sports the image and status of professional athletes underwent revolutionary changes. No longer did the public perceive them simply as "dumb jocks"; they seemed to be shrewder, better educated, and more sophisticated than their predecessors. Whereas in the past the public had often looked upon a career in pro sports as being morally suspect and financially risky, in the 1970s the pro athlete held one of the most glamorous positions in the popular culture. In the 1970s nearly all traces of the traditional player-centered ethos disappeared; players frankly admitted that they placed the making of money ahead of play for its own sake. The pro athletes escaped serfdom. By striking down the reserve clause in baseball and similar player reservation systems in the other sports, the federal courts released the players from perpetual bondage. The pro athletes organized labor unions, fomented strikes, and signed collective bargaining agreements. In the 1970s player salaries suddenly soared. By then star players began to receive incomes commensurate with celebrities in popular music, television, and the movies. Two conditions—the increased incidence of genuine competition among franchises for player talent and the demise of traditional player reservation systems—were largely responsible for these radical changes.[1]

PLAYER ASSOCIATIONS AND SOARING SALARIES

In the past, direct competition for the services of players had been rare. Whenever the franchises in team sports could do so, they had resorted to the reserve clause and the draft to avoid the rigors of bidding against one another for talent. Ordinarily this system broke down only when rival leagues formed. If two leagues bid against one another for player services, then salaries and fringe benefits improved. Yet historically such periods of open market competition had been brief, for new leagues usually folded within a few years or merged with an existing league. Without interleague competition the players had a weak position from which to bargain. In fact, nothing guaranteed that big league salaries would even keep up with inflation or owner profits. For example, while the median income of baseball players in 1963 was nearly $13,000, a figure that compared

[1]No satisfactory account of the players in the era of televised sport exists, but see James G. Scoville, "Labor Relations in Sports," in Roger G. Noll, ed., *Government and the Sports Business*, (Washington; Brookings Institution, 1974), 185–219, for a general treatment up to about 1974.

favorably with the incomes of physicians, lawyers, and dentists, the actual purchasing power of the average big league salary appears to have declined between 1946 and 1963. Competition between the NFL and the All-American Football Conference in the late 1940s pushed up the average football salary to about $8,000 in 1949. But in that year, the All-American league collapsed. Subsequently in the 1950s the average NFL salary grew slowly, reaching $9,200 by 1959, again an increase that failed to keep pace with the inflation rate between 1949 and 1959.[2]

The rivalry in the 1960s between the American Football League and the National Football League dramatically revealed the impact on player salaries of franchise competition for player services. When the AFL signed a lucrative television contract with NBC in 1964, it obtained the financial means to launch an all-out bidding war with the NFL for players. The salaries of highly sought veterans and draftees immediately skyrocketed. The moguls of both leagues quickly called a halt to the "Battle of the Paychecks;" they merged the leagues in 1966. The merger reversed the upward spiral in player salaries. Whereas Joe Namath had received $420,000 to sign a three-year contract with the New York Jets in 1964, four years later Kenny Stabler, who had shattered all of Namath's passing records at Alabama, received only a $20,000 bonus and a $25,000 annual salary to sign with Oakland. Overall, despite the fact that football was the most prosperous of professional sports, the merger apparently led to the reduction of the salaries offered to new draftees by one-third to one-half. Furthermore, in the late 1960s the average income of all the players in the newly merged league declined.[3]

In the meantime the general cultural unrest of the 1960s, the awarding of large contracts to televise sports, increasing salary expectations stemming from the general prosperity of professional sports, and the almost simultaneous appointment of a new set of executive directors of the player associations in baseball, basketball, and hockey helped induce a growing player militancy. In the 1960s and 1970s the militancy led in two directions. One path led to the formation of more powerful player associations or unions, while the other led to the federal courts.

The players organized the most effective unions in baseball and basketball. Basketball was especially suited for unionization. The teams played many games and the total number of players barely exceeded 100, making communication among them easier and more intimate than in football and baseball. The high proportion of blacks in the NBA who had been inspired by the civil rights movement and common experiences of racial prejudice, and the selection of Oscar Robertson, a highly respected black superstar, as president of the Players Association created a unity among the basketball players unmatched in baseball, football, or hockey.

[2]Ralph Andreano, *No Joy in Mudville: The Dilemma of Major League Baseball* (Cambridge: Schenkman, 1965), p. 140; "Player Association Testifies on NBA-ABA Merger," *Audible*, 4 (July 1972), 3. Scoville, "Labor Relations in Sports," (200–201), argues, on the other hand, that average NFL salaries in the 1950s increased slightly faster than average family incomes.

[3]"Scorecard," *Sports Illustrated*, 28 (April 8, 1968), 20; "Pro Football's Average Wage Ranks Lowest," *Audible*, 4 (July 1972), 1; "Real Salary Down," ibid., 5 (April 1973), 2.

The players hired Lawrence Fleisher, an experienced labor leader, to revamp the moribund association. Fleisher immediately imposed a trade union type of discipline upon the players. In 1967 the players exhibited their newly acquired muscle; on the eve of the playoffs they threatened to strike. The owners, convinced that the players could successfully strike, capitulated. They awarded the players a munificent contract, though they refused to alter or bargain on basketball's player reservation system.

The NBA Players Association and its membership then benefitted immensely from the formation of the American Basketball Association in 1967 and its subsequent bidding war with the NBA for player talent. Data for an earlier era of no interleague competition for players in the NBA (1952–1957) indicated that the median salary for players rose by 33 percent. In contrast, the median salary in the NBA leaped from $25,000 to $40,000, or 60 percent, from 1967–1971, a period of interleague competition for players.[4] Aware of the effect of the football merger upon player salaries, the NBA and ABA athletes adamantly opposed a basketball merger. They testified before congressional committees against legislation that would have exempted basketball from the antitrust laws, thus permitting a merger. And in 1970 the NBA Players Association filed a class action suit enjoining the merger as well as the application of the draft and the reserve system to the joint leagues. Eventually, in 1975 the players approved a merger, but only upon the condition that the classic forms of the draft and reserve system be abolished.

Organizing a strong union among the baseball players was a somewhat more formidable task. Many more players were involved—some 600—and baseball players had enjoyed for many years the distinction of being the best paid of professional athletes. In the 1950s the Major League Players Association, founded in 1953, had been essentially a "paper" organization, its main activity being to develop a pension plan and certain minor fringe benefits. Then in 1966 the players hired a full-time executive director Marvin J. Miller, an economist by profession who had worked for many years for the United Steelworkers Union. Miller brought to the association organization, discipline, factual knowledge, and a keen, painstaking mind. "To a disinterested observer," reported Robert H. Boyle in 1974, "Miller comes on like a David with an ICBM in his sling while the owners stumble around like so many befuddled Gladiators."[5] Ironically, the adamant opposition of the owners to Miller personally helped unite the players behind the union. In the late 1960s and early 1970s the association won a series of victories: increased minimum salaries, a grievance procedure which led to outside arbitration rather than to the Commissioner of Baseball, the right of counsel in individual contract negotiations, and a larger pension fund.

The conflict between the owners and the players association reached

[4]Scoville, "Labor Relations in Sports," 198.

[5]Robert H. Boyle, "This Miller Admits He's a Grind," *Sports Illustrated*, 40 (March 11, 1974), 23. See also Ron Fimrite, "Whither Opening Day, 1980?" ibid., 52 (March 3, 1980), 56–70.

something of a crossroads in 1972. That year baseball experienced its first real strike, one that delayed the start of the season by almost three weeks. The strike ostensibly resulted from a new pension plan, but hovering in the background was the general agreement that was to be negotiated in 1973. While the strike was in progress, the Curt Flood lawsuit which frontally assaulted the reserve clause was before the Supreme Court. In their defense the owners argued the reserve clause ought to be a matter of labor negotiations—an understandable reversal of their earlier positions— rather than law. The owners decided to make the pension issue a test of strength with the union; in short they hoped to break the players' union. To the surprise of most observers, the players held firm, voting 663–10 to strike. Owner unity, on the other hand, vanished.[6] The 1972 strike not only helped insure the strength of the association but facilitated another player victory in 1973. Although the owners refused to modify the reserve clause—they had won the Curt Flood case—they did agree to submit salary disputes to an outside arbitrator.

The players had the most difficulty in organizing an effective union in the sport that prospered the most—pro football. Several obstacles confronted those seeking to organize the football players. As was the case in baseball and basketball, many players continued to subscribe to what might be described as the "amateur myth." To them, forming unions somehow tarnished the ethos of sport. Second, a football owner could replace, without damaging the team's performance, one or more football players more easily than could a baseball or basketball owner. Third, unlike the owners of baseball teams, the football moguls composed a close-knit, by and large cooperative group headed by a shrewd powerful commissioner, Pete Rozelle. Finally, the players were slower to organize. Because of fewer games and more athletes, communication among NFL players was more difficult. Until 1970 the NFL Players Association had only one permanent staff member and he was an attorney rather than an experienced union man. Little wonder that *Sports Illustrated* described the football union's bargaining with the owners in 1968 as "sandlot labor relations," for the players and their representatives lacked the experience and sophistication of their counterparts in basketball and baseball.[7]

The NFL Players Association had been organized in 1957 but had remained largely dormant until 1966, the year that the NFL and AFL merged. The merger, the subsequent decline in player salaries, the highly publicized television contracts, and talk of an effort by the Teamsters to organize the players put some life into the association. In 1968 John Gordy, a Detroit Lion guard and president of the union, and Dan Shulman, "an obscure Chicago labor lawyer," formulated twenty-one demands, the major ones being higher pensions, permission to have counsel present at individual salary negotiation, and a higher minimum salary. (While baseball contributed about $4.1 million annually to its pension fund, the NFL gave $1.4 million. In 1968 nearly 20 percent of the football players

[6]*Monthly Labor Review*, 95 (June 1972), 62.
[7]"Scorecard," *Sports Illustrated*, 29 (July 15, 1968), 16.

made under $15,000.) The players agreed to "strike" at the NFL summer training camps; the owners retaliated by "locking out" veteran players. Apparently pressured by the television networks, the owners agreed to negotiate. The players nearly doubled their pension benefits and the league agreed to increase the minimum annual salary from $5,000 to $12,000, though the players did not attempt to alter the NFL's player reservation system.[8]

After the strike-lockout of 1968 the owners appear to have engaged in a systematic effort to harrass the players association out of existence. Since the teams retained the power to determine whether a player had the talent to play or not and football players, even the stars, could be more easily replaced without harming the teams performance than their counterparts in basketball and baseball, many teams found it convenient to take punitive action against the player representatives of the union. In 1971 Gwilym S. Brown reported that "a player reps' chance of being traded, waived, or cut is about three times as high as that of a player who minds his own business.... In addition, reps have been demoted to the taxi squad, benched, and pressured."[9] Such union-busting tactics failed. Inspired by the hope of securing a larger chunk of Rozelle's $45 million contract with the three television networks, the players made a new set of demands in 1970. After a month-long lockout strike in the preseason, the owners nearly doubled the player benefits—pensions, disabilities, and the like. The players exhibited remarkable solidarity; only twenty-one of some 1,300 veteran players reported to camp during the strike.[10]

In 1974 the players association decided to tackle the player reservation system of the NFL. Technically, football did not have a career-bound reserve system, for a player could "play out" his option, that is, he could play for one year after his contract had expired and become a free agent. Hypothetically, he could then look forward to bids for his services from all of the other NFL teams. But because of the "Rozelle Rule," which provided that a team that had signed a player who had played out his option had to indemnify the player's former team, the option system was in practice almost as restrictive as the reserve system in baseball. Not knowing how much indemnity they might have to pay, wishing to discourage players from transferring from one team to another, and, above all, hoping to avoid open bidding for player services, the owners rarely signed a player who had played out his option. Until the abolition of the Rozelle Rule in 1976, Rozelle had named compensation only twice in ten years. Rozelle, however, awarded compensation only when the two clubs involved could not reach an agreement.

Overall, the 1974 strike represented a setback for the players association. After walking out for forty-five days in the preseason camps, the

[8]"Scorecard," ibid., 28 (May 6, 1968), 10; Edward Shrake, "Pro Football Forces a Delay Game," ibid., 28 (May 27, 1968), 22–23; Bud Shrake, "Let's Get Back to Playing Football," ibid., 29 (July 22, 1968), 54–55; *Monthly Labor Review*, 91 (Sept. 1968), 68.
[9]Brown, "Owners Can Be Tackled, Too," *Sports Illustrated*, 34 (March 22, 1971), 19.
[10]*Monthly Labor Review*, 93 (Oct. 1970), 56.

association suspended the strike. The NFL had proceeded to play the preseason games without the veterans, using mostly rookies and free agents to fill their rosters. The owners seemed determined to play the entire schedule with strikebreakers, even though attendance at exhibition games dipped to record lows. The owners also threatened retaliation. "I have to think there will be a terribly large turnover on our squad," remarked Wellington Mara of the Giants.[11] With the strike lingering on and no quick settlement anticipated, unity among the veteran players began to weaken. Some of the veterans disliked Ed Garvey, the executive director of the NFLPA whom Mike Curtis, a Baltimore linebacker, called a "left-wing opportunist." In early August, led by Roger Staubach, the veterans, especially the white players, began to cross the picket lines. The players association and the NFL did not reach a new agreement until 1977.

While none of the player associations had been able to modify or nullify the player reservations systems or the player drafts, within the three years from 1975 to 1977, the federal courts undercut the entire structure of strictures on player freedom. The first breakthrough came in basketball.[12] In 1975, in face of a challenge by the players, the NBA sought judicial approval of its draft and reserve system. The following year the court denied approval and strongly hinted that its player control system was illegal. Rather than take the issue to court, the NBA negotiated a contract with the NBA players which called for modified compensation for a team that lost a player to another team. In 1980 all compensation ended for veteran players. The combination of interleague competition between 1967 and 1975 and the new player freedom gained in 1976 spurred the salaries of basketball players to record highs. In 1967, the year the ABA began, NBA salaries averaged slightly over $20,000; eight years later the figure had leaped to $107,000; in 1980 it stood at $185,000.[13]

The venerable reserve system in baseball fell in a more indirect fashion. In 1975 the Major League Players Association filed grievances in behalf of Andy Messersmith and Dave McNally alleging that, since the two players had played the prior season without a written contract, both were free agents. As provided by the bargaining agreement between the owners and players, the issue went to an arbitration panel. By a vote of two to one the panel held that Messersmith and McNally were free agents. The owners promptly appealed the decision to a federal district court and the United States Court of Appeals. In both instances the courts ruled in favor of the

[11]Quoted in "Scorecard," *Sports Illustrated,* 41 (Aug. 12, 1974), 11. See also Ray Kennedy, "Star Struck Canton," ibid., 41 (Aug. 5, 1974), 10–12; *Monthly Labor Review,* 97 (Oct. 1974), 75. For the 1977 agreement see *Audible,* 9 (May 1977), 1, 3.

[12]See Willie Schatz, "Landmark Court Rulings Affecting Major Sports," *Washington Post,* April 13, 1980, for a concise summary of the facts, rulings, and significance of the court decisions. See also Edward R. Garvey, "From Chattel to Employee: The Athletes Quest for Freedom and Dignity," *Annals of the American Academy of Political and Social Science,* 445 (Sept. 1979), 91–101.

[13]For 1967 salary averages see Ray Kennedy and Nancy Williamson, "Money in Sport; Part I," *Sports Illustrated,* 49 (July 17, 1978), 46; for 1975, *Lincoln,* (Neb.) *Star,* May 5, 1976; and for 1980, *Washington Post,* April 13, 1980.

players. Suddenly the reserve clause was extinct. As in the case of basketball, the players union negotiated a modified reservation system.* The contract also included a complex salary arbitration procedure. When a case went to arbitration, both management and the player submitted salary figures. The arbitrator then chose one of the figures as binding. As the owners bid for the services of star players and players took their salary disputes to an independent arbitrator, baseball salaries soared. In 1975, before the Messersmith-McNally decision, the average baseball salary was $46,000; five years later it exceeded $135,000. The jump in salaries resulting from free agency in basketball and baseball exceeded the imagination of even the most optimistic players.

In football the players were not so successful. John Mackey, president of the NFL Players Association, along with several other players, alleged in federal court that the Rozelle Rule violated antitrust laws. In 1975 a federal district court found in favor of Mackey and his fellow players. Two years later the players union and the NFL signed a new contract which provided over $15 million in compensation to the past victims of the Rozelle Rule and established a new formula for payments to teams that lost players via the free agent route.** In practice the 1977 contract offered players only slightly more freedom than they had enjoyed under the old Rozelle Rule. Football teams, unlike baseball and basketball teams, simply did not make lucrative offers to free agents. Of the 295 NFL players who became free agents during the first three years of the new contract, only four signed with new teams.[14]

The refusal of the owners to engage in competitive bidding for free agents apparently arose from a combination of three considerations. The owners maintained that proven veteran players were worth little more than inexperienced draft choices—a proposition that tested the credulity of the most naive observer of the game. Second, to keep salaries down, the owners may have secretly and informally agreed to ignore free agents. Finally, and probably most important, since the owners essentially shared revenues equally, they had little or no economic incentive to build winning programs by signing the more expensive free agents. "I think they'd [the owners] like to win," declared Ed Garvey, head of the NFL Players Association. "But will

---

*The original baseball agreement permitted a player to become a free agent after six seasons. The team losing the player obtained the right to the first or second round draft choices of the team with which the veteran player signed. The baseball owners came to feel that their form of compensation was highly inadequate. "When you get an amateur choice in baseball, you've got zilch," asserted Ray Grebey, Director of the Major League Baseball Owner's Player Relations Committee. *Washington Post*, April 13, 1980. The baseball agreement of 1981, reached after a prolonged strike over free agent compensation, provided that a team could protect twenty-four players from compensation. Their other players went into a "compensation pool." A team losing a player, depending on the player's skills, could select a player from the pool or receive a draft choice from the signing team.

**Under terms of the 1977 football contract a free agent who had received an offer to sign with another club had to give his old team a chance to sign him for the same monetary figure. If the old team failed to exercise this option, the player could sign with the new team. The former team was then entitled to compensation in the form of draft choices; the level of the draft choice depended upon the salary offered.

[14]See Ed Garvey, "Free Agents in Deep Freeze," *Audible* (May 1979), 1, 5; *New York Times*, December 30, 1979, S6.

Table 17–1 Salary averages for selected years, 1967–1980*

	1967	1975	1980
Baseball	$19,133	$ 46,000	$135,000
Basketball	20,000	107,000	185,000
Football	25,000	42,000	69,000

*These figures are conservative, based primarily upon surveys and calculations of the player associations. In each instance team owners would claim that the average salaries were higher than those given here. Part of the discrepancy in the figures of the two groups arises from provisions in player contracts calling for a portion of the salary to be paid on a deferred basis. In some cases contracts made in the 1970s called for payments beyond the year 2000. Given the expected inflation of the last quarter of the twentieth century, deferred payments would have less purchasing power than immediate payments. Thus, in terms of real income, the more conservative estimates of the player associations appear to be more valid.

SOURCE: Year 1967—Ray Kennedy and Nancy Williamson, "Money in Sport," *Sports Illustrated,* 49 (July 17, 1978), 46; Year 1975—*Lincoln* (Ne.) *Star,* May 5, 1976; Year 1980—*Washington Post,* April 13, 1980.

they spend money to win? No!"[15] Given the absence of bidding among the owners for free agents, salaries in the NFL rose more slowly than in basketball or baseball. In 1975 the football players averaged $42,000; in 1980 the figure rose to $69,000. Wide disparities existed according to playing position. While quarterbacks averaged $113,932 in 1980, defensive backs averaged only $58,874. By 1980 the disillusionment of the Players Association with free agentry was so complete that it decided to abandon the system in its negotiations of the 1982 contract. For the new contract the association planned to demand that 55 percent of the gross revenues of the teams go to player salaries.

IMPLICATIONS OF THE NEW STATUS

The salary explosion plus the long-term contracts of pro athletes had significant implications for American sports. First, it focused public attention as never before on the professional athletes rather than athletes in the colleges, high schools, industrial leagues, or on the nation's playgrounds. The astronomical salaries permitted a few of the athletes to compete with popular entertainers for celebrity status. Talk-show hosts invited them to appear on prime-time television shows and the players could command large fees to endorse products or to speak at luncheons or dinners. In the 1970s Andy Warhol, the guru of avant garde art, did silk screens of baseball pitching star Tom Seaver and other athletes. "Sports figures are to the '70s what movie stars were to the '60s," proclaimed Warhol.[16] Often the players seemed to be better known for their salaries or simply for their "well-knownness" than for their athletic feats.

Sport fans worried lest the big salaries, the outside endorsements, and the long-term contracts destroy the player's drive to compete and damage the cooperation essential to success in team sports. "Regardless of what the

[15]Quoted in *Lincoln* (Neb.) *Star,* Jan. 23, 1981.
[16]Quoted in Kennedy and Williamson, "Money in Sports: Part 2," *Sports Illustrated,* 49 (July 24, 1978), 49.

athlete says, if he has total security and is put in a tough spot, he may go through the motions and say, 'The hell with it. I've got mine'," said Thomas Tutko, noted sport psychologist. Players often seemed to put their own welfare ahead of that of the team. "Kids have the wrong idea about basketball," declared Rick Berry, NBA superstar. "They are now all hungry to score points. They read that the high scorers are making the money and it's true. . . . I'll tell you what money has done. It's changed the philosophy of the game. Pro basketball is not played as well today as it was ten years ago. Players don't know the fundamentals."[17] Likewise the authority and prestige of the once-revered "skippers" declined. Coaches and managers often had to defer to their superstars. If clashes developed between a superstar and a coach, the owner usually felt compelled to side with the star.

The quest for greater security and a larger share of the revenue produced by professional sports tended to obliterate all traces of the spirit of play in sports. "I am not happy about that," asserted Julius "The Doctor" Erving, an NBA superstar. "I love basketball. I'd play for free."[18] But Erving, like most pro athletes, found such a stance naive; to maintain the happy innocence of sport for play invited exploitation by the owners. Even in preadolescent boys' sport, player-centeredness was subordinated to spectator or adult-centeredness. The leagues modeled themselves closely after professional leagues. Thus the spirit of work pervaded nearly all levels of sport.

The conspicuous success of pro athletes shaped the dreams of aspiring players of all ages. To make millions as a pro player appeared to require no extensive intellectual training, no effort to solve the riddles of complex bureaucracies, only practice in one's chosen sport. The ladder from the bottom to the top was deceptively simple. "It starts from the day a [well-meaning] Little League coach takes a youngster under his wing and tells the boy he can be a great baseball player," explained Bill Walsh, coach of the San Francisco Forty-Niners. " 'But to do it,' he tells the boy, 'you've got to forgo all other sports—no tennis, no swimming. Never mind the piano, practice your baseball!' "[19] Sport became the boy's ticket to a distinctive educational experience. When he arrived in high school, the coach would arrange the boy's life to maximize the opportunities for the youngster to obtain an athletic scholarship in college. If the boy won a scholarship, he probably lived in a special dormitory, socialized only with fellow athletes, ate special foods, and had his courses carefully chosen for him. If he was one of the lucky few—one of the fortunate 2 percent of the total number of college athletes—he was drafted by a pro team. Then if he became a star he probably earned in excess of $100,000 annually.

The ladder of upward athletic mobility could be a cruel hoax, especially for thousands of black youths. Only a few actually made it to the top. In the 1970s some 700,000 boys played high school basketball and one million played interscholastic football each year. The colleges reduced these

[17]Quoted in ibid., 44.
[18]Quoted in ibid., 41.
[19]Quoted in John Underwood, "Student Athletes: The Sham, The Shame," *Sports Illustrated*, 52 (May 19, 1980), 42.

numbers to 15,000 in basketball and 41,000 in football. The NFL drafted about 320 players each year; about 150 made the permanent rosters. Those who made it had an average playing career of about 4.2 seasons. The NBA annually drafted about 200 college players; about 50 made the teams. The average NBA career was 3.4 seasons. The odds against a youth making it to the pros were thus astronomical, something like 15,000 to 1.[20]

Moreover, of the few who made it to the pro ranks—at least in the instance of football—many faced the prospect of permanent, disabling injuries. Bob Stein, an attorney and former linebacker for the Kansas City Chiefs, asserted in 1981 that "You can't deny that [pro football is in the]...business of using up young men's bodies. Every guy comes out screwed up somehow."[21] Objective data seemed to confirm Stein's grim conclusion. Apart from injuries, the physical and psychological requirements of the game led an indeterminate number of players to use amphetamines and other more potent drugs. Although the team owners and Commissioner Rozelle claimed drug usage in the NFL was minimal, several former players and a psychiatrist, Arnold J. Mandell, a former consultant of the San Diego Chargers, charged that the number of players "gobbling down pills" before each game was "astronomical." Whatever the extent of drug usage, drugs could result in addiction and disguise injuries, leading to even more lasting physical disabilities.

In one sense the colleges shamelessly exploited the players. To build winning teams and thereby generate more revenues and publicity, recruitment and retention of the athletes for four years of varsity eligibility came before concern about the player's opportunities in pro sports or whether the athlete obtained an education, let alone a college degree. Athletic grants-in-aid at big-time schools "paid" less than would have been the case had a free market existed for the athlete's services.[22] Often the colleges recruited scholastically handicapped youths who had elementary level reading abilities. The student athletes then virtually majored in "eligibility" rather than an academic subject. To insure a student's eligibility, coaches often enrolled them in "snap," extension, or correspondence courses. Large time commitments to athletics also interfered with the students' chances of academic success. Moreover, many of the athletes themselves perceive the colleges as way stations or farm clubs preparing them for pro careers, not as educational institutions. While no accurate data existed for the number of athletes who obtained degrees, in the 1970s only one-third of the NFL players and even a smaller proportion of the NBA players earned degrees. The college authorities offered a weak defense of the system: namely that the athletes were better off within the system than they would be otherwise.

[20]See ibid., 60.

[21]Stein quoted in *Omaha World Herald*, Sept. 2, 1981. See also Arnold J. Mandell, *The Nightmare Season* (New York: Random House, 1976); and Douglas A. Noverr and Lawrence E. Ziewacz, "Violence in American Sports," in William J. Baker and John M. Carroll, eds. *Sports in Modern America* (St. Louis: River City, 1981), 129–45.

[22]See Allen L. Sack, "Big Time College Football: Whose Free Ride?" *Quest*, 27 (Winter 1977), 87–96; and Donald Spivey and Thomas E. Jones, "Intercollegiate Athletic Servitude: A Case Study of the Black Illini Student Athletes, 1931–1967," *Social Science Quarterly*, 55 (March 1975), 939–47.

18

The Triumph
of the Spectator:
An epilogue

Consoling a Little Chief baseball player. Courtesy
of the Journal Star Printing Company.

By 1980 the evolution of the informal folk games of colonial Americans into spectator-centered sports had been largely completed. Several folk games, such as boxing, wrestling, and pedestrianism, had long been commercial spectacles; essentially, they had never passed through a player-centered stage. Others, especially the ball games that became modern baseball and football, achieved their first organized forms at the initiative of the athletes. The players formed clubs, formulated written rules, scheduled matches, managed finances, and formed national associations. Presumably, they played for the fun of the game rather than for external rewards, but sport also served as a device to enhance their status or ethnic exclusiveness. In several instances the player-oriented stage quickly gave way to the spectator-centered phase; in others the transformation was gradual. For example, baseball quickly became a full-fledged spectator sport in the middle decades of the nineteenth century whereas tennis succumbed completely to a spectator-centered stage only in the 1970s.

The triumph of spectator-centeredness had significant implications for the history of American sports. First, it focused public attention upon professional sports. Professional sports served as models for nearly all levels of sport. Anxious to attract fans, both the colleges and high schools aped their professional counterparts. In some parts of the nation high schools openly recruited athletes and employed as many coaches as pro teams. The professional model reached down to the level of preadolescent youth sports. Little League Baseball had outfield fences, dugouts, grandstands, even a "draft" system, and Pop Warner football teams had nine-year-old cheerleaders. Even the struggle to win the America's Cup, presumably one of the last bastions of the player-centered era, took on many of the qualities of a pro sport. In 1980, Bob Banier, president of *Yachting* magazine, declared: "I just a little bit deplore that you've got to work for two years—every working day—to prepare for a sailboat race."[1]

Spectator-centeredness encouraged the growth of bureaucracies, specialization, and the placement of administrative concerns ahead of player concerns. The number of persons employed in sport bureaucracies grew much faster than the number of players. To succeed at the highest levels, especially in individual sports, youngsters had to begin to specialize at a tender age. Tennis players, for instance, often began to engage in systematic training by the age of five or six. Carefully designed programs to

---

[1]"Old Skippers Take New Stock," *Newsweek,* 96 (Sept. 22, 1980), 11. On youth sports see esp. Jonathan J. Brower, "The Professionalization of Youth Sports," *Annals of the American Academy of Political and Social Science,* 445 (Sept. 1979), 39–46.

select the most promising future athletes in early childhood became a reality. Modern technology assisted in this endeavor as well as in improving the performances of athletes. Fiberglass vaulting poles, new artificial running surfaces, domed stadiums, and dozens of other technological innovations assisted athletes in reaching new levels of performance. In the mid-1960s the Dallas Cowboys inaugurated the use of computers to select athletes for the draft and to scout opponents. In a few years, William O. Johnson of *Sports Illustrated* predicted, "every sideline bench will have one [a computer] to pop out sheets of probability tables to help call each play, each pitch, each infield shift."[2]

Whatever the faults of spectator-centeredness—and they were many—it did tend to assure peak athletic performances. Specialization, hours of hard training, expert coaching, and modern technology all contributed to a remarkable improvement in the achievements of the nation's athletes. The revolution in the records of track and field and swimming vividly revealed the superiority of modern athletes over their predecessors. Objective observers reluctantly conceded that, on the whole, the players in the team sports also outperformed past players. Consequently, sports, as art forms, achieved new, much higher plateaus of excellence.

Despite the pervasiveness of spectator-centeredness, it failed to erase totally the spirit of play in American sports. While the spectators might dictate the nature of professional, college, high school, and even most preadolescent children's programs, millions of Americans continued to engage in essentially player-oriented sports. They played in the intramural programs of high schools and colleges, in city recreation programs, and in sports on the nation's playgrounds.

In the 1950s and 1960s American presidents had urged the nation's citizens to engage in sports as a way of promoting physical fitness, but it was not until the 1970s that participation jumped markedly. In the 1970s tennis bubbles and racquet clubs sprouted up nearly everywhere and newspapers introduced special sections for those who played rather than watched sports. Manufacturers of sports equipment cited impressive statistics indicating the growth of squash, racquetball, handball, platform tennis, gymnastics, cycling, and even roller skating. By 1980 one could find racquetball courts—something nearly nonexistent in 1970—in cities ranging in size from New York (with over 200 courts for 7,895,000 people) to West Plains, Missouri (with two courts for a population of 7,785).

But all these physical activities paled beside the growth in running. *The New York Times* estimated that twenty million Americans took up running in the 1970s.[3] In 1970, 126 men entered the first New York marathon; in 1980, over 12,000 men and women ran in the event. In 1978 President Jimmy Carter began to jog between forty and fifty miles a week. On September 15, 1979, he nearly collapsed from heat exhaustion during a 6.2 mile race in Catoctin Mountains Park. When photographs of his haggard

---

[2]William O. Johnson, "From Here to 2000," *Sports Illustrated*, 41 (Dec. 23, 1974), 80.

[3]*New York Times*, Dec. 30, 1979, S6. See also Patricia A. Eisenman and C. Robert Barnett, "Physical Fitness in the 1950s and 1970s: Why Did One Fail and the Other Boom?" *Quest*, 31 (1979), 114–22.

face and detailed reports appeared in the newspapers the next morning, commentators were appalled that the President would endanger his life in such a fashion. But most joggers ran noncompetitively; many claimed that long-distance running not only reduced the likelihood of cardiovascular diseases but also gave them "highs," a sense of euphoria. For some, daily jogging apparently replaced weekly visits to the psychoanalysts.

The boom in sports participation appeared to be part of a far-reaching reaction against elite authority and such major institutions as corporations, universities, medicine, law, and governments. As these institutions seemed unable to solve problems or appeared to threaten the individual, growing numbers of Americans looked elsewhere for satisfaction. Interest in the occult, astrology, and charismatic religion thrived, and alternative routes to good health—from special diets to faith healing and jogging—competed with traditional medicine. Moreover, many Americans apparently found in participatory sports a way of giving meaning to their lives apart from the constraints of the modern hierarchical world of skills and careers. They sought to fashion lives that maximized personal pleasures while reducing formal ties to society.

That sport in the Age of Spectator had become a central feature of American culture was beyond debate. It could be documented in the many hours fans spent riveted to television screens, in the column inches in newspapers devoted to sports, and by samplings of cocktail conversations. Novelists, poets, and dramatists increasingly turned to sports for motifs. Scholars began to engage in minute investigations of the psychological, philosophical, and social significance of sports. In the twentieth century sports joined the electronic media, bureaucratic structures, and mass consumption as major pillars of a new social order. To some degree spectator sports replaced or supplemented the church, the family, the local community, subcommunities based upon status or ethnicity, and the older system of mutual class obligations as one of the sinews which held modern society together.

Index

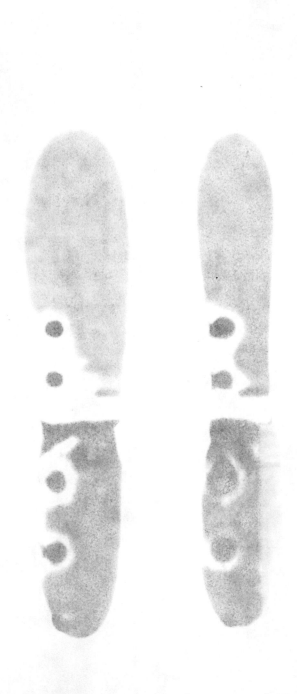